State and Local GOVERNMENT

FOURTH EDITION

Russell W. Maddox
Oregon State University

Robert F. Fuquay
Oregon State University

D. VAN NOSTRAND COMPANY

New York   Cincinnati   Toronto   London   Melbourne

Cover: The main hall of the Texas State Capitol Building, Austin, Texas. Stan Wakefield, photographer.

D. Van Nostrand Company Regional Offices:
New York   Cincinnati

D. Van Nostrand Company International Offices:
London   Toronto   Melbourne

Library of Congress Catalog Card Number: 80-53074
ISBN: 0-442-24454-1

Published by D. Van Nostrand Company
135 West 50th Street, New York, N.Y. 10020

10 9 8 7 6 5 4 3 2 1

Preface

When the first edition of *State and Local Government* was published nearly twenty years ago, it was designed to provide introductory students with a means of mastering the basics of the subject with a minimum of reliance upon formal classroom instruction. The principal goal was to enable students to achieve, through independent reading of textual material, a comprehensive appreciation of the fundamentals, thus permitting instructors to use class time more effectively. Reactions over the years from both students and instructors have supported this approach and, consequently, it remains the basis for the Fourth Edition.

While the orientation of this edition remains the same as in earlier versions, a number of changes have been made in response to the needs of instructors who teach this course. The text has been streamlined by using a more compact format, concise discussions, consolidation of several chapters, and careful reduction in the use of tabular material in an effort to provide a more manageable treatment of the subject for a one-semester or one-quarter course. These steps have made it possible to maintain comprehensiveness with a minimal loss in coverage. The most important changes, of course, relate to the inclusion of new materials reflecting the developments and innovations that have occurred in the area of state and local government over the past few years: the adoption of new constitutions, revisions in the public welfare system, alteration of intergovernmental fiscal patterns, complication of urban problems, reorganization in governmental administration, environmental concerns, new and changing demands for governmental services, tax reform campaigns, and refinements in legislative, executive, and judicial procedures. We have incorporated this new material into the familiar structural organization retained since the first edition.

Appendices have been added at the end of the text for reference: Appendix 1—Admission of the States; Appendix 2—The State Constitutions; Appendix 3—Model State Constitution; Appendix 4—Organization of Traditional State Government.

An Instructor's Manual, prepared by Larry Elowitz of Georgia College, is new to this edition and available from the publisher. The manual includes chapter summaries, outlines, key concepts, and test items.

Although only the names of the authors appear on the title page, a great many individuals have made valued and valuable contributions. The authors acknowledge the helpful reviews of Joseph E. Gibbs, Florida A. & M. University, and Jack Lippman, Dutchess Community College. For the advice, comments, consultation, and encouragement of friends, students, colleagues, public officers, government employees, and editors, the authors are deeply grateful.

R. W. M.
R. F. F.

Contents

From Colonies into States

1

Civil government in British North America had its beginnings at James-town, Virginia, the first permanent settlement planted by the English on the North American continent. In 1607 three ships of the London Company, a trading enterprise acting under a royal grant to develop the Virginia territory, landed 120 settlers near the mouth of the James River. Under the direction of a council of seven persons, a fort was built, a town laid out, and general preparations for community life were made.

The settlers were poorly equipped to meet the hardships of colonial living, and the necessity for strong leadership soon resulted in the concentration of all governmental authority in a governor selected by the Company. Still, progress was slow and profits few. Consequently, in the belief that self-government would contribute to prosperous development, a liberal group within the Company obtained the adoption of a plan of government giving to the colonists a measure of control over local affairs. Effective in 1619, an assembly was created to include representatives elected by the people. A council was provided to share the executive duties of the governor and to act with the governor as a high court of justice. This arrangement, continued after Virginia became a royal colony in 1624, set the basic governmental pattern for other English colonies.

Shortly after the Jamestown venture other settlements were undertaken. One after another, colonies were organized along the Atlantic Coast from the Carolinas to the northern areas of present-day Maine. The inland boundaries were indefinite, but for all practical purposes they extended to the chains of eastern mountains. By 1732, when the colony of Georgia was formed, the colonies destined to become the thirteen original states were in existence.

The prevailing governmental ideas and institutions throughout the colonial period were distinctly English in character. Writings by theorists such as Rousseau, Montesquieu, and Locke had their effect as did the colonial environment. In some areas where settlements were populated in large measure by colonists from countries other than England, deviations from English patterns existed. In general, however, English modes predominated.

THE COLONIAL GOVERNMENTS

Although governments in the colonies were by no means identical, they followed the same general outlines. Throughout the colonial period the governments underwent constant change. They may be classified, however, into three general categories according to the type of charter under which they existed.

Royal Colonies

As implied by the name, the royal colonies were those over which the British monarch exercised the highest degree of direct control. The pattern of government in royal colonies involved appointment by the King of a *royal governor* for each colony. The King also chose a council that served as adviser to the governor and as the "upper house" of the legislature. A "lower house" or assembly was composed of representatives elected by property owners qualified to vote. There were courts, but the council acted as the highest court of appeals. From time to time instructions for the government of the colonies were transmitted from London; and the governors, the most powerful figures in the royal colonies, were responsible for seeing that these were carried out.

At the time of the Revolution there were eight royal colonies: Georgia, Massachusetts, New Hampshire, New Jersey, New York, North Carolina, South Carolina, and Virginia. Of these, Virginia was the first, having been designated a royal colony in 1624. Massachusetts in 1691 and Georgia in 1732 were the last to join the list. It was in these colonies, frequently ruled by stern governors, that much of the agitation leading to the Revolution occurred.

Proprietary Colonies

On Independence Day in 1776 there were three proprietary colonies: Delaware, Maryland, and Pennsylvania. Their governmental system was much the same as that in the royal colonies, with the important difference that the authority to govern flowed directly from a *proprietor* instead of the King. The proprietor was an individual to whom the King had granted lands to be settled and developed. The monarch exercised general supervision, but the proprietor appointed the governor and provided for the other organs of government.

Charter Colonies

Only Connecticut and Rhode Island enjoyed the status of charter, or corporate, colonies at the time of the Revolution. The structure of government was much like that in the royal and proprietary colonies, but the character of government was radically different. A charter colony functioned much as a corporation under a charter granted by the King. According to these charters, property owners in each colony elected a governor and council as well as members of the assembly. The charters, however, were subject to revocation by the King. Massachusetts, long a charter colony but with a record of resistance to the Crown, had its charter revoked in 1684 and seven years later was made a royal colony. The Connecticut charter of 1662 and the Rhode Island charter of 1633 remained in force as constitutions, with only slight changes occasioned by the Revolution, until well into the nineteenth century.

PRELUDE TO REVOLUTION

British administration of the American colonies was poorly organized and without clearly determined goals. Parliament showed a great deal of interest in the regulation of colonial trade, but it was content to leave colonial administration to the King. In turn, the King permitted various governmental agencies to look after such colonial interests as he considered within their competence or jurisdiction. There was no central English colonial office in the colonies. As far as London was concerned, each of the thirteen American colonies was to be treated as a separate, individual entity.

This sort of supervision, without plan or preconceived goals, contributed to the development of a desire for self-government in the colonies. The lack of an over-all plan for colonial development, compounded by the isolation wrought by a 3,000-mile-wide ocean, literally forced the colonies to assume a large measure of self-government. When British colonial policies became more firm after George III ascended the throne in 1760, disagreements were inevitable. It was this basic conflict—the local desire for colonial autonomy versus increased control from the seat of British government—that eventually brought on the Revolution. The many incidents that followed were merely sparks that kindled the fire of rebellion.

During the 1760's Parliament enacted a series of tax and trade laws that stirred deep resentment among the colonials. Duties on imports from the West Indies were raised; the number of British troops garrisoned in the colonies was increased; and in 1765 the well-known Stamp Act was passed. The law required that tax stamps be affixed to all legal documents, newspapers, and recorded business agreements. Colonial reaction was immediate. Within months delegates from nine of the colonies assembled in New York as the Stamp Act Congress. A Declaration of Rights and Grievances was adopted in protest against the recent policies. The Stamp Act was repealed, but colonial resentment remained. Evasion of the laws, and boycotts, discontent, and open violence were common.

The events of the next few years led directly to open hostilities. In 1770, British soldiers stationed in Boston were goaded by a jeering mob into opening fire, resulting in the deaths of five colonials—an incident now known as the Boston Massacre. Three years later, local residents disguised as Indians boarded British ships anchored in Boston harbor and threw their cargoes of tea overboard. In retaliation the port was ordered closed. The Virginia Assembly proclaimed a day of mourning for the closing of the port and was summarily dissolved by the royal governor. In September, 1774, all of the colonies except Georgia sent delegates to Philadelphia to participate in the First Continental Congress. That assemblage sent formal protests to the King and openly encouraged the colonies to resist English trade policies. Before the Second Continental Congress could convene in May of the following year, hostilities between English troops and colonial revolutionists had occurred. On April 19, 1775, the battles of Lexington and Concord were fought.

Six weeks after Congress convened, this time with all the colonies represented, provision was made for a continental army. George Washington of Virginia was installed as Commander-in-Chief. Hostilities continued, but it was not until a year later, on June 7, 1776, that Richard Henry Lee of Virginia delegation proposed that Congress take the stand:

> *Resolved,* That these United States are, and of right ought to be, free and independent states, that they are absolved from all allegiance to the British Crown, and that all political connection between them and the State of Great Britain is, and ought to be, totally dissolved.

Delegates who felt that reconciliation might yet be accomplished succeeded only in delaying adoption of the resolution, and on July 2 it was unanimously passed. Two days later the Declaration of Independence was adopted and announced.

The break with England was, in the colonial view, complete. Not until the war was won, however, could anyone say that independence was actually accomplished. That day came in 1781 when the British were defeated on the fields of Yorktown, Virginia, and General Cornwallis surrendered. Peace was formalized by the treaty concluded in Paris in 1783.

THE NEW STATES

The changeover from colonial status to independent sovereign existence was not accompanied by a rash of governmental changes. There were some modifications, highly important in some cases; but the basic ideas and concepts of governmental form, processes, and relations with the citizenry underwent little alteration. The new state governments were, in effect, the old colonial governments operating in a different context.

Each of the states adopted a written constitution. Connecticut and Rhode Island simply deleted references to the English monarch from their charters, but the remainder of the states framed new instruments. In so doing, the states broke from their English heritage and departed from European custom. The concept of a written constitution setting forth the basic, organic law was reaffirmed and became a fixed part of the pattern of government in the American system.

The state constitutions were characterized by a number of concepts that reflected sentiments long held by the revolutionary element. *Popular sovereignty,* the recognition of the people as the source of all political power, was a premise upon which the new governments rested. *Limited government,* the idea that government may exercise only those powers granted by the people, was also apparent in each of the new state documents. As an added precaution each of the new constitutions contained guarantees of the fundamental civil rights of individuals, with separate Bills of Rights appearing in seven of the new instruments.

Fear of oppression and desire to prevent the recurrence of the strict governmental controls exercised by the former royal governors occasioned a substantial reduction in the powers of the governors of the new states. Much of the power formerly wielded by governors was placed in the hands of the legislatures, resulting in governments characterized by legislative supremacy. Still there was actual *separation of powers* with the executive, legislative, and judicial branches exercising *checks and balances* over each other. It was not until several decades after the Revolution, however, with the adoption of amendments and the framing of new constitutions, that the executive and judicial branches of state governments began to approach levels of authority comparable to that of the legislatures.

THE ARTICLES OF CONFEDERATION

Even though there was no constitutional basis for it, a central government composed solely of the Second Continental Congress came into existence in 1775. This Congress represented an informal union cemented by the need for collective action during the Revolutionary War. On that basis the Congress waged war, issued currency, loaned and borrowed money, sent and received ambassadors, and performed other acts ordinarily undertaken only by the governments of independent, sovereign states.

Congress was unable to agree upon a plan of union until 1777. In November of that year it adopted the Articles of Confederation, a document intended, in its own words, to establish a "perpetual Union between the

States" in the nature of "a firm league of friendship." Eleven states approved the Articles during the following year, but Delaware withheld assent until 1779, and ratification in Maryland was not obtained until 1781. The Articles of Confederation, in fact, were not legally in effect until six months before the British surrender at Yorktown.

In retrospect, it is not difficult to see that the union under the Articles was doomed to failure. As soon as the war was over, England was no longer an immediate threat to the security of the states. Only in matters of foreign affairs was the central government empowered to act, all other aspects of governmental activity being left to the discretion of the individual states. The return of peace with each state in virtually complete control of its own affairs saw the rise, or at least the emphasis, of interstate jealousies. Each state sought to protect its own interests, often at the expense of its neighbors. Relief through amendments to the Articles was thwarted in every instance due to the requirement that any change had to receive unanimous approval by the states.

The central government was powerless to help. Without authority to tax or to regulate commerce among the states, its credit exhausted, and its requisitions for funds ignored by the states, the Congress was little more than a debating forum. The situation worsened rapidly. In January, 1786, the Virginia Assembly called for a meeting to be held at Annapolis the following September. It was hoped that delegates from the various states would consider and possibly reach some agreement on "a federal plan for regulating commerce." Only five states—New York, New Jersey, Pennsylvania, Delaware, and Virginia—were represented at the Annapolis Convention. Although the lack of numbers defeated their original purpose, the delegates proposed that another meeting be held in Philadelphia in May, 1787, to devise provisions "necessary to render the constitution of the Federal Government adequate to the exigencies of the Union."

At its next session the Confederate Congress considered the possibilities of a convention as suggested at the Annapolis meeting. Spurred perhaps by the fact that seven states had already selected delegates, Congress, on February 17, 1787, called for a convention to be held in Philadelphia in May "for the sole purpose of revising the Articles of Confederation" in order that they be "adequate to the exigencies of Government and the preservation of the Union."

UNION UNDER THE CONSTITUTION

On Friday, May 25, 1787, the Constitutional Convention began its labors. Throughout the summer and until September 17, the delegates met in secret sessions during which an entirely new document was drafted in preference to a revised version of the Articles of Confederation. Of the seventy-four delegates originally named, fifty-five were present at one time or another. On the final day of the convention forty-two delegates were in attendance, and all but three affixed their signatures to the proposed new constitution.

The Constitution drafted by the Convention was much more than a revision of the Articles of Confederation. It provided for a true central government operating directly upon the people rather than upon the states. It called for a substantial surrender of power by the states and provided for a Union that in designated spheres of activity was superior to the states. Consequently, the course of ratification was stormy. Only after bitter argument and extended controversy in some states did the document win the favor of the popularly elected ratifying conventions. According to the terms of the Constitution itself, it was to take effect upon approval by nine states. The necessary number was achieved with ratification by the New Hampshire convention on June 21, 1788. But not until Virginia and New York, the tenth and eleventh states to approve the Constitution, formally entered the Union was the legal effect meaningful. In September, 1788, the Confederate Congress provided for the election of officials, and by the following spring the new government was in operation.

THE CONSTITUTION AND AFTER

Looking back over nearly two centuries of United States history, the Constitutional Convention of 1787 stands out as a monumental event. There is no doubt that the accomplishments of that assemblage ranks high, if not at the top, on the list of American political achievements. The wisdom exhibited by the leaders of the Convention in understanding the problems facing the states and providing adequate means for meeting and solving them is impressive.

Even so, careful note must be taken of a number of facts often ignored. The actions of the delegates were profoundly influenced, if not in fact dictated, by the circumstances of the prevailing situation. In order to relieve the economic ills of the day, real central authority had to be effected. At the same time, a transfer of total power from the states to a central government was out of the question. The solution, therefore, lay in an arrangement whereby the powers necessary for adequate national controls could be achieved without undue sacrifice of state authority. The genius of the delegates was demonstrated in their ability to recognize the range of action open to them and in their skill in providing for a workable government within such limitations.

An examination of the Constitution reveals that the basic principles of government which underlay the governments of the states were preserved. The principles of popular sovereignty, limited government, separation of powers, and checks and balances were as much a part of the national system as they were of the various state governments. Individual political and civil rights were not viewed in any different light with the birth of the new Union. In short, except for the idea of federalism established by the new document, the basic concepts upon which the Constitution rested were neither new nor untested.

The adoption of the Constitution and formation of the Union did not automatically solve the problems of the day. The means for solution were provided, but the cooperation of the states was still necessary. Acting alone, or against the efforts of the states, the infant national government would have been hard-pressed indeed to enforce its laws and decisions. The assistance of the states, or at least their acquiescence, was essential to any measure of national success during the early years of union.

Even the firm establishment of a federal union did not provide a solution of all governmental problems. While national regulation of commerce between the states brought chaotic trade conditions under control, there were still many other problems to be met. The states remained highly competitive and jealous of each other. The very existence of a true national government opened whole new areas of concern. Questions of states' rights versus national power began to unfold. Many phases of interstate relations remained as vexatious as before. Future development was bound to create new problems and in some cases to compound the old.

Government in the United States has undergone many changes since the days of the Jamestown settlement. Some alterations have been fundamental in nature, others superficial. Some have been accompanied by social, economic, and political upheavals; others have occurred almost unnoticed. Through all these changes certain concepts have remained constant, embedded in basic American political theory. It is to the description and analysis of these many areas of governmental concern and involvement that the chapters which follow are devoted.

Intergovernmental Relations: The Nation and the States

2

Within the American governmental system there are about 80,000 units of government, from the national government centered in Washington, D.C., to thousands of small, specialized local units. Each of them has a legally prescribed jurisdiction. Each of them has legally prescribed powers. Yet none of them can be considered islands in the sea of government. The affairs of each unit of government are to some degree related to those of many or all of the others.

The pattern of intergovernmental relations in the United States encompasses all levels and types of governments. Although all levels may be involved in some areas of concern, consideration of intergovernmental relations can be divided into four general categories: national-state relations; the relations among states; state-local relations; and national-local associations. It is with the first two categories that this chapter is concerned.

FEDERALISM

The governments of independent, sovereign countries in the world today can be regarded as either unitary or federal in form. The basic criterion for identification of both types is the manner of allocation of governmental authority. In unitary nations, which are by far in the majority, all power rests ultimately in the central government. The exercise of authority by local units of government is wholly determined by the central unit. Federal governments, on the other hand, are based upon a division of powers between the central government and the constituent units.

Allocation of Powers

By definition, a federal system is composed of two constitutionally recognized levels of government. In the United States the central level is known as the national or federal government; the local level is composed of a group of governmental units called states.[1] The powers of each level of government are determined by the Constitution in accordance with the Tenth Amendment which provides that "The powers not delegated to the United States by the Constitution, nor prohibited by it to the States, are reserved to the States respectively, or to the people."

Delegated Powers. With the exception of the inherent powers discussed below, the national government may exercise only those powers granted to it by the Constitution. Thus it may be said that the national government is a government of delegated powers. Throughout the seven articles and twenty-six amendments to the Constitution, specific enumerations of authority are made. Each of the three branches of the national government—legislative, executive, and judicial—is empowered to exercise designated powers.

Of great importance to the national government are those powers implied from specific grants of authority. The Constitution itself does not mention implied authority. Rather, the *doctrine of implied powers* was announced in 1819 by the United States Supreme Court in *McCulloch* v. *Maryland.*[2] Chief Justice John Marshall ruled that Congress had the implied authority to charter a national bank. Application of the doctrine to other delegated powers has broadened the scope of national power to an almost immeasurable extent.

Closely akin to implied authority are grants known as *resultant* powers. These powers cannot be implied from any single enumerated power but instead result from several of them. The power to punish violators of national laws, for example, logically results from the authority of Congress to exercise its enumerated powers. The power to issue paper money results from the expressed powers to borrow and to coin money.

Concurrent Powers. Not all powers delegated to the national government are exercised exclusively by that unit. Only those which are, by their nature, not susceptible to local exercise are the exclusive prerogatives of the central government. Thus the states as well as the national

---

1. A common misconception of American federalism is the notion that there are *three* levels of government—national, state, and local. Confusion in the matter can be dispelled when it is understood that in the legal sense local governments, such as counties, cities, towns, townships, and special districts, are in reality "creatures of the state." From the legal standpoint, such units are part of the state level of government. The confusion is due largely to the fact that in carrying out many administrative duties, local governments do in fact operate in a manner largely independent of the states.
2. 4 Wheaton 316.

government may tax, borrow money, charter corporations, and exercise the power of eminent domain. Also frequently included in this category is the authority of states to act in other fields not preempted or regulated completely by Congress. Consequently, states have at times been active with regard to bankruptcy laws, fixing standards of weights and measures, and some areas of interstate commerce.

Inherent Powers.   In the field of foreign relations many powers of the national government may be said to be inherent. They are powers that inhere in the sovereign state as a member of the family of nations. While such powers as the ability to declare war, make treaties, and maintain diplomatic relations are treated in the Constitution, they are powers which, even "if they had never been mentioned in the Constitution, would have vested in the Federal Government as necessary concomitants of nationality."[3]

Reserved Powers.   At the time the United States Constitution was drafted, virtually all governmental powers were vested in the states. The central government under the Articles of Confederation was limited primarily to the conduct of foreign affairs. Thus the creation of the national government under the Constitution involved the transfer, or delegation, to the national government of powers formerly wielded by the states. The powers not delegated were retained by, or reserved to, the states. Consequently, the reserved powers are not listed in the Constitution, nor, with few exceptions, are they set forth in state constitutions. In general, if a power may be exercised by government and is neither constitutionally granted to the national government nor denied to the states, it is a reserved power.

Growth and Expansion of Governmental Power

Today it is obvious to even the most casual observer that the powers of the federal government have been expanded at a more rapid pace than those of the states. The word "government" itself is, in the mind of the ordinary citizen, practically synonymous with "national government." Hardly an aspect of daily life is unaffected, either directly or indirectly, by policies and programs emanating from Washington, D.C. It is significant that, at the same time national powers have expanded so greatly, the powers and functions of state and local government have also increased. Yet, even though expansion at the state and local level has been notable, it has not kept abreast of the development and growth of federal authority.

The most important single factor contributing to enlargement of the federal sphere of action has been the doctrine of implied powers. By

3. *U.S. v. Curtiss Wright Export Corporation,* 229 U.S. 304 (1936).

means of liberal interpretation of the enumerated powers, the national government is now empowered to enter or regulate numerous areas of activity not apparent in the letter of the Constitution. Under the power to regulate interstate commerce, for example, the national government punishes kidnapers, white slavers, and those who transport stolen auto-mobiles across state lines. The same power permits federal regulation of railroads, trucking companies, air lines, labor standards, sales of stocks, agricultural commodities exchanges, radio, television, and many other activities. Other enumerated powers have been interpreted in much the same fashion.

Another important factor in the significant growth of national authority, especially since World War I, has been the use of the grant-in-aid. It has proved particularly useful, from the national viewpoint, in instances where constitutional authority to act is doubtful or direct federal action would be inadequate or politically inadvisable. In a few instances, minor expansion of federal power has been realized through reciprocal law enforcement and cooperative research programs.

ADMISSION OF STATES

The power to admit states is vested in Congress. Under the terms of the Constitution, "New States may be admitted by the Congress into this Union. . ."[4] The meaning of this brief phrase is clear: only Congress, in its discretion, is empowered to recognize the existence of a new state. Qualifications upon this power include the constitutional provisions that ". . . no new State shall be formed or erected within the jurisdiction of any other State; nor any State be formed by the junction of two or more States, or parts of States, without the consent of the legislatures of the States concerned as well as of the Congress." In addition, acts of admission are subject to presidential action in the same manner as other laws.

There is no fixed procedure that a prospective state must follow in order to gain admission to the Union. Usually an area achieves the status of a territory of the United States before taking steps to attain statehood. The first step involves sending a petition to Congress. Next, Congress passes an *enabling act* granting permission to the people of the prospective state to draft a constitution acceptable to them. This step is not absolutely necessary, for the people of a territory may already have drawn up such a document. The third major step in achieving statehood is congressional and presidential approval of the draft constitution. Should objectionable provisions be found, Congress may refuse to approve it until changes acceptable to Congress, the President, and the territorial residents have

---

4. Article IV, Section 3.

been made. When all differences are resolved, Congress enacts a resolution admitting the new state into the Union. It is possible for a statehood bill to require that further conditions be met. For example, statehood was conferred on both Alaska and Hawaii only after the residents of the territories approved the respective acts of admission at special elections.

Only slightly more than half of the states have actually gone through the phases noted above. The thirteen original states, of course, entered the Union merely by ratifying the Constitution. Five states were formed from the territories of other states. Texas was an independent, sovereign country at the time of admission. Altogether, eight states, excluding the original thirteen, have not passed through the state of territory before admission into the Union. (See Appendix 1.)

Equality of the States

Once admitted to the Union a state is upon a plane of equality with all other states. No state has more privileges or fewer obligations than any other. Nevertheless, questions have arisen with regard to the equality of newly admitted states in view of conditions placed upon admission. The rule governing such conditions is basically that states may be bound only if the conditions do not interfere with or attempt to control matters recognized as within the domain of state authority. In other words, if Congress or the President should require a prospective state to agree to certain terms before admission is granted, the agreement must be observed by the state only if conformity does not compromise the equality of the state with those already in the Union. For example, Oklahoma, admitted in 1907, was forced, by the terms of the enabling act of 1906, to agree to maintain its capital at Guthrie until 1913. The United States Supreme Court, however, upheld the right of Oklahoma to move the capital to Oklahoma City in 1910, declaring that the state had merely exercised powers that were "essentially and peculiarly state powers."[5] Similarly, Arizona was required to alter its draft constitution to eliminate a provision permitting the recall of judges, but once admitted as a state, Arizona promptly amended its organic law to restore the deleted clauses.

On the other hand, agreements that do not infringe upon essential state powers may be enforced as binding contracts. For example, Minnesota was compelled to refrain from taxing certain national lands in conformity with a condition accepted at the time of admission.[6] In the same way New Mexico was forbidden to use funds from the sale of lands granted by

5. *Coyle v. Smith*, 221 U.S. 559 (1911).
6. *Stearns v. Minnesota*, 179 U.S. 223 (1900).

the national government to the state for any purpose not listed in the act of admission.[7]

CONSTITUTIONAL RESTRICTIONS UPON THE STATES

Among the most important clauses in the Constitution are those that specifically restrict state authority. Through them two basic purposes are served. Areas of national power are more clearly discerned and individual rights and privileges are accorded the protection of constitutional provisions.

Restrictions in Support of National Authority

Article I, Section 10, of the Constitution is composed almost entirely of a list of limitations aimed at preventing state assumption of authority in various areas of national power. These prohibitions may be considered under four general categories—foreign affairs, military and war powers, taxation and commerce, and contracts.

Foreign Affairs. The Constitution unqualifiedly forbids the states to "enter into any treaty, alliance, or confederation." The utility of such a clause is obvious. If it were possible for a state to conclude pacts with foreign countries, not only would a unified national foreign policy be impossible, but the Union itself would be in constant danger of "international" strife and possible dissolution. The states are permitted to make compacts, however, subject to the approval of Congress.

Military and War Powers. The power of the national government to control the military affairs of the Union is effectively guaranteed by provisions in the Constitution that permit the states to maintain armed forces or to engage in war only with the consent of Congress.[8] Only if actually invaded or in imminent danger may a state do so without congressional permission. Under present legislation, states contribute to the maintenance of National Guard units that serve as state troops. These military units are subject to close national regulation, however, and may be incorporated into the national forces.

---

7. *Ervien v. United States,* 251 U.S. 41 (1919).
8. Article I, Section 10, also prohibits states from issuing "letters of marque and reprisal." Such letters were authorizations granted by warring states to private individuals permitting them to carry on hostile actions at sea. The clause is now virtually a dead letter of the Constitution.

Taxation and Commerce. In the interest of maintaining a uniform monetary system, the Constitution denies the states authority to coin money, emit bills of credit, or make anything but gold and silver legal tender. Despite these provisions state banks issued paper currency until the mid-nineteenth century. This practice was ended, however, by the simple expedient of a prohibitive national tax upon such notes in 1866.

State taxation of imports and exports is also constitutionally prohibited without specific congressional authorization. The only concession made by the Constitution in this regard is that states may exact fees in amounts sufficient to offset the costs of inspection of items being imported or exported. Tonnage taxes, or levies based upon the holding capacities of ships, are also forbidden except in pursuance of congressional permission.

Contracts. State authority to control the terms of contracts is severely restricted by the Obligation of Contracts Clause found in Article I, Section 10. Under its terms no state may enact any "law impairing the obligation of contracts." To be sure, a state may establish the conditions under which a contract may be made, but according to the literal provisions of the Constitution, a valid contract, once concluded, cannot be altered by subsequent legislation. The United States Supreme Court interpreted the clause strictly when it held, in 1819, that the state of New Hampshire could not, in violation of the school's charter, convert Dartmouth College into a public institution.[9] Later rulings have relaxed this interpretation, however, to the extent that charters are subject to legislation designed to protect the public health, safety, welfare, and morals. Further, the Supreme Court decision upholding the legality of moratoria, or suspensions for stated periods of time, on meeting mortgage payments during the depression of the 1930's indicates even greater relaxation of the apparent strictness of the Obligation of Contracts Clause.

Rights and Privileges

Individual rights and privileges are protected by a variety of constitutional provisions. The safeguards erected by the Constitution were designed to prevent arbitrary state action. Thus each provision is a denial of state authority.

Included in Article I, Section 10, are clauses prohibiting the states from granting titles of nobility and passing either bills of attainder or ex post facto laws.[10] The denial of power to establish a nobility of persons

9. *Dartmouth College v. Woodward,* 4 Wheaton 518.
10. Article I, Section 9, contains similar restrictions against the national government.

makes it impossible for a specially privileged class to be created on that basis. Legislatures may not, because of the attainder clause, enact legislation finding designated persons guilty of criminal acts and prescribing punishment. The Ex Post Facto Clause prevents state legislative bodies from passing criminal laws that operate retroactively to the disadvantage of any person who stands accused or has been convicted of a crime.

Freedom from slavery and involuntary servitude, not only against the states but the national government and private individuals as well, is affirmed by the Thirteenth Amendment. The only exception permitted by the letter of the Constitution is in regard to persons convicted of crimes. The Supreme Court has ruled that service in the armed forces as a result of being drafted and the obligation of fulfilling terms of service in the merchant marine are not forms of involuntary servitude.

State authority to fix voting qualifications is restricted by several constitutional provisions. Article I, Section 2, and the Seventeenth Amendment provide that representatives and senators shall be chosen by voters who "shall have the qualifications requisite for electors of the most numerous branch of the state legislature." The Fifteenth Amendment disallows qualifications based on "race, color, or previous condition of servitude." The Nineteenth Amendment bars restrictions based on sex, the Twenty-fourth Amendment prohibits poll taxes, and the Twenty-sixth Amendment fixes the minimum voting age at eighteen.

The most generally stated yet most extensive restrictions upon state action are found in the Fourteenth Amendment. Section 1 of that Amendment declares:

> No State shall make or enforce any law which shall abridge the privileges or immunities of citizens of the United States; nor shall any State deprive any person of life, liberty, or property, without due process of law; nor deny to any person within its jurisdiction the equal protection of the laws.[11]

The vagueness of these limitations has necessitated a great deal of definition and interpretation. The function of imparting specific meanings has been performed largely by the federal judiciary, especially the United States Supreme Court.

"Due process of law" has been defined by the Supreme Court in various decisions as relating primarily to procedure on the one hand and the substance of the law on the other. Hence the Court has developed dual concepts: procedural due process of law and substantive due process of law. Procedural due process obviously refers to the fairness of procedures involved in governmental contacts with individuals. Whether the re-

---

11. Discussion of the privileges and immunities of citizens is deferred to a later section of this chapter.

lationships involve proceedings in courts or before administrative agencies, the individual must be dealt with in such a way that all steps taken by the state are fair to the individual. Because there is no constitutional list of the procedures states must follow, the task of designating fair procedure within the framework of the due process clause is accomplished by federal courts.

The meaning of substantive due process of law depends upon the character of the right and the statute involved. In general, a statute denies due process of law on substantive grounds when its effect is such that a reasonable exercise of a right is thwarted. For example, a law that seeks to prevent the publication of newspapers or magazines that are openly critical of governmental officers and agencies by making them subject to court orders directing cessation of publication may be in violation of substantive due process. All procedures necessary to conform to the concept of procedural due process of law may be observed, yet the fact would remain that the statute itself might reduce freedom of the press to the point that it would consist of little more than freedom to praise. In other words, the *substance* of the right would be seriously reduced.

A literal application of the Equal Protection of the Laws Clause would mean that every person must be treated identically under all laws. Such a rigid interpretation would mean that minors and adults, natural persons and corporations, the insane and mentally sound would be required to conform to valid laws in exactly the same way. A less severe interpretation obviously is in order. Accordingly, states resort to classification in determining the application of various laws. Thus all bus companies, all banks, all professional boxers, or all motorists may be obliged to conform to statutes not applicable to the public as such. It is only when classifications are unreasonable, such as all blacks, or all Chinese laundries, that the Equal Protection Clause of the Fourteenth Amendment is violated.

INTERGOVERNMENTAL OBLIGATIONS

Just as the Constitution provides for a division of governmental powers and prohibits various types of governmental actions, it imposes a number of obligations upon the national and state governments. These duties, most of which are found in Article IV of the Constitution, include national obligations to the states, duties of the states for the benefit of the nation, and responsibilities of the states to each other.

National Obligations to the States

Republican Form of Government. Article IV, Section 4, of the Constitution provides that "The United States shall guarantee to every State in this Union a republican form of government. . . ." The exact meaning of this provision has never been determined. The United States Supreme Court has refused to impart precise meaning to the clause, ruling instead that the issue is a *political question* to be decided in nonjudicial fashion.

In a case growing out of Dorr's Rebellion in Rhode Island in 1841–1842 an attempt was made to draw from the Court a decision as to which of two factions was the legitimate government of the state. The Court declined to rule on the question, characterizing it as political in nature.[12] Again in 1912 the Supreme Court refused to rule on the meaning of the clause. In the case of *Pacific States Telephone and Telegraph Co.* v. *Oregon,* the company argued that a republican form of government was one which was representative, and on that basis a tax levied by means of the initiative was in violation of the Constitution.[13] The Supreme Court repeated its earlier view that a political question was involved.

The closest the Supreme Court came to defining the guarantee was simply to suggest that the question of whether Oregon had a republican form of government had been settled by the admission to membership by Congress of the state's senators and representatives. Today, in fact, about the only test applied by students of government is reference to the action of Congress in receiving new members. Even so, there is also the possibility that the President, through assigned military powers, may affect any decision respecting the republican character of a state government.

Territorial Integrity of the States. Although the power to admit states is vested in Congress, it is subject to various limitations. Article IV, Section 3, provides that "no new State shall be formed or erected within the jurisdiction of any other State; nor any State be formed by the juncture of two or more States, or parts of States, without the consent of the legislatures of the States concerned as well as of the Congress." From these phrases it is clear that Congress is obliged to respect the territorial integrity of all states—that is, it may not alter the geographical boundaries or area of a state unless the legislature of the state so affected gives specific approval.

Throughout the history of the Union very little difficulty has been encountered with respect to this obligation. Five states have been formed

---

12. *Luther* v. *Borden,* 7 Howard 1 (1849).
13. 223 U.S. 118.

from the territory of other states. In the cases of Vermont, Kentucky, Tennessee, and Maine, all constitutional prerequisites were complied with. Only the admission of West Virginia in 1863, during the Civil War, may be construed as possibly violative of constitutional restrictions. In that instance forty western counties of Virginia refused to comply with the declaration of secession adopted by the legislature and subsequently established a governmental organization of their own. Their successful petition for statehood was based, at least in part, upon congressional acceptance of the "consent" of that portion of the Virginia legislature that represented the western counties. It is interesting to note that in 1869 the Supreme Court, in a case not involving West Virginia, held that secession was constitutionally impossible.[14] If in fact none of the rebellious states had ever been out of the Union, the admission of West Virginia, it may be contended, was not in accord with the Constitution. Yet, after admission, West Virginia was entitled to equality with all other states. The incident is now merely of historical interest, but it is obvious that the spirit, if not the letter, of the Constitution was violated.

Protection and Assistance. Since control of the armed forces is vested primarily in the national government, the Constitution provides, in Article IV, Section 4, that the states are entitled to federal protection.[15] Inasmuch as the states are forbidden to maintain armed forces without congressional consent, and the territory of a state is also part of the nation, imposition of such a duty upon the national government is logical. There have been few instances when the obligation has been implemented for the purpose of combatting invaders, for with the exception of the War of 1812, the American states have not been invaded by the troops of a hostile power. Necessary protection has been extended, of course, during all wars in which the United States has been a belligerent.

Requests for national assistance in cases of domestic violence have not been uncommon. Ordinarily the governor has sought the aid, since state legislatures are in session for such short periods that they cannot usually be convened in special session rapidly enough in true emergency situations. In any event the President decides whether federal assistance will be granted.

Obligations of the States to the Nation

Election of Federal Officials. The national government does not hold elections. Members of the United States Senate and House of Representa-

---

14. *Texas* v. *White,* 7 Wallace 700.
15. "The United States . . . shall protect each of them against invasion; and on application of the legislature, or of the executive (when the legislature cannot be convened) against domestic violence."

tives and presidential electors are chosen by the people in elections conducted under state authority, administered by state and local officers, and paid for by state and local governments. Article I, Section 4, of the Constitution specifically empowers state legislatures to fix the "times, places, and manner" of election of senators and representatives. Congress has authority, under the same provision, to alter most state laws thus enacted, and it has prescribed the first Tuesday after the first Monday in November of even-numbered years as the day for such elections.

There is no constitutional clause under which a state may be forced to fulfill its obligations in respect to elections. None is necessary. Any state that fails to perform its electoral duties would lose its voice in the Congress and forego any part of the selection of the President and Vice President.

Consideration of Amendments. The Constitution contains no provision that compels the states to ratify or reject amendments. However, the manner prescribed for making changes in the basic document is such that the part played by the states is absolutely essential. The initiation of amendments takes place at the national level, but they must be approved by the states before becoming a part of the Constitution. The vital character of state participation implies a role that is obligatory in nature.

Interstate Obligations

Full Faith and Credit. Article IV, Section 1, provides that "Full faith and credit shall be given in each State to the public acts, records, and judicial proceedings of every other State." The need for such a provision in a federal system is obvious. Without it each state could regard all other states virtually as foreign countries. Moreover, each state would become a haven for anyone who wished to escape or avoid his duties and responsibilities under the laws of any other state.

The coverage of the Full Faith and Credit Clause is quite broad. "Public acts" refer to civil laws passed by state legislatures. "Records" include such things as mortgages, deeds, leases, birth certificates, or any other document that legally fixes, establishes, or determines an obligation, privilege, right, or fact. "Judicial proceedings" comprise decisions made by the courts of a state in all civil affairs *over which they have jurisdiction.* Matters of a criminal nature are not covered by the Full Faith and Credit Clause, for the United States Supreme Court has held that no state is obliged to enforce the criminal laws of another.

The effect of the Full Faith and Credit Clause is best understood by illustration. Assume, for example, that Smith and Jones enter into a valid contract in the state of Texas, and Jones later moves to Iowa where he attempts to escape fulfilling his obligations under the agreement. If Smith, or an agent of Smith, brings suit in an Iowa court to force Jones to honor the contract, the Iowa court will enforce the agreement according to Texas contract law. This would be true even if the contract failed to conform to the provisions of Iowa law relating to such documents.

One of the most confusing problems in regard to full faith and credit is the question of whether a state is compelled to recognize all divorces granted by another state. No question arises when a divorce involves persons who are bona fide residents of the state in which the decree was obtained. But what of the divorce action in which one or both principals have been in a state only long enough to establish residence for divorce purposes? In 1945 the United States Supreme Court ruled that North Carolina was not required to recognize a Nevada divorce decree awarded to a resident of North Carolina who had resided in Nevada six weeks—the period of residence required by that state before a person may enter a suit for divorce.[16] Even though the Nevada requirements had been met, it was held that no domicile, or true residence, had been established. Consequently, the validity of numerous similar divorces was placed in doubt. Three years later the Court stated that if both parties to a divorce action were represented and the question of whether the court had jurisdiction to grant the divorce was not raised during the proceedings, the question could not be raised at a later time.[17] While this ruling clarified the steps that could be taken to avoid difficulties raised by the question of valid domicile, the Williams decision was not overruled. The extent to which divorce decrees granted to individuals who have resided in a state barely long enough to meet minimum residence requirements are entitled to full faith and credit is uncertain.

Interstate Rendition. While no state has the responsibility of enforcing the criminal law of any other state, Article IV, Section 2, ostensibly obligates states to return fugitives to the states from which they flee. In the language of the Constitution,

> A person charged in any state with treason, felony, or other crime, who shall flee from justice, and be found in another State, shall on demand of the executive authority of the State from which he fled, be delivered up, to be removed to the State having jurisdiction of the crime.

The purpose of this provision—the "rendition clause"—is obvious. Since the states are essentially independent of each other, some means is necessary to prevent the frustration of criminal laws by the simple act of stepping over a state border.

The apparently mandatory character of the rendition clause is illusory. Its meaning has been softened considerably through Supreme Court interpretation. In the case of *Kentucky* v. *Dennison*[18] the Court was

---

16. *Williams* v. *North Carolina,* 325 U.S. 226.
17. *Sherrer* v. *Sherrer,* 334 U.S. 343 (1948).
18. 24 Howard 66 (1861).

asked to order the governor of Ohio to surrender a fugitive. There was reason to believe the Ohio executive would have refused to obey, so the Supreme Court, without power to coerce obedience, construed the clause as a statement of "moral duty." In other words, a governor who is requested to return a fugitive is morally obligated to do so, but there is no legal requirement that compels him to honor the request.

Although rendition, or "extradition" as it is more commonly called, is not compulsory, it is performed as a matter of course in the vast majority of cases. Once in a while a governor refuses to send a fugitive back to a state. Such instances involve a belief that the ends of justice would, in some way, not be served if the fugitive were extradited.

Privileges and Immunities. The framers of the Constitution were well aware of the fact that when citizens of one state traveled to another state they might encounter discriminatory treatment. A citizen of New York, for example, might find himself treated as an alien in Pennsylvania or New Jersey. Consequently, a clause was included in the organic law to provide that the "Citizens of each state shall be entitled to all the privileges and immunities of citizens of the several states."[19] Inclusive as the provision may appear, it does not protect corporations or aliens, as they are not citizens.

There is no complete list of the privileges and immunities protected by the Constitution. According to judicial interpretation, however, citizens are entitled to

> Protection by the government; the enjoyment of life and liberty, with the right to acquire and possess property of every kind, and to pursue and obtain happiness and safety; subject nevertheless to such restraints as the government may justly prescribe for the general good of the whole. The right of a citizen of one state to pass through, or to reside in any other state, for purposes of trade, agriculture, professional pursuits, or otherwise; to claim the benefit of the writ of habeas corpus; to institute and maintain actions of any kind in the courts of the state; to take, hold, and dispose of property, either real or personal; and an exemption from higher taxes or impositions than are paid by the other citizens of the state; . . .[20]

On the other hand, many of the privileges deriving from the use and enjoyment of the facilities, resources, and political processes of a state may be legally withheld from nonresidents. Most important of these is the privilege of voting. Others include the denial of permission to practice professions such as medicine or law, exclusion from institutions of higher education, and refusal of the privilege to hunt, fish, or trap within the state. Except for voting, however, states may extend privileges otherwise

19. Article IV, Section 2.
20. *Corfield* v. *Coryell,* 4 Wash. C.C. 371 (1825).

denied to nonresidents upon certain conditions, commonly the payment of fees higher than those charged its own citizens.

Some eighty years after the Constitution was drafted, a clause was added, as part of the Fourteenth Amendment, that prohibited states from abridging the rights and privileges that accrue as a result of national citizenship. Here again, no complete list of such privileges has been compiled. Nevertheless, the right of qualified persons to vote for members of Congress, as set forth in Article I, Section 2, and the Seventeenth Amendment, must be included. Traveling to and from the national capital, use of the navigable waters of the United States, and national protection while traveling abroad are further privileges of United States citizenship. The original intent of the clause—to protect the newly freed blacks—has never been fully realized.

CONFLICT AND COOPERATION AMONG THE STATES

Difficulties are almost certain to arise in any association of governments existing side by side upon a plane of equality. In the American federal system travel, trade, and transportation have become increasingly national in character. As a result, new problems and new complications must be added to the list of conflicts occurring between states.

Because each state is a separate entity, it is free to enact any valid law it chooses. With each state exercising its prerogatives in this respect, it is not unusual to find a great—and sometimes discouraging—diversity among state statutes dealing with the same subject. Trade barriers are erected in the form of quarantines, excessive license fees, and discriminatory taxes. Conflicts develop with respect to interstate problems such as use of the water of river systems, stream pollution, flood control, conservation, and construction of interstate bridges. Jurisdictional disputes and quarrels over the location of state boundaries have contributed to interstate troubles.

Voluntary Cooperation

Despite the fact that in past years there have been episodes involving discriminatory actions and reactions among the states, particularly in regard to trade barriers, the record of voluntary cooperation on an interstate basis is good. In many instances conflicts are kept under control by the informal cooperation of administrators. Private organizations devoted to the study and improvement of government have assisted in the solution of interstate problems. Also, conferences of both temporary and permanent character have contributed to greater cooperation among states.

Numerous organizations and agencies are dedicated to the improvement of state and local government. The National Municipal League, for example, has devoted years of research into the problems of government. Its *Model State Constitution* is generally regarded as particularly well adapted to the requirements of the American states. Since 1892 the National Conference of Commissioners on Uniform State Laws has devoted its efforts to the preparation of model statutes recommended for adoption or imitation by all states. Restatement of the common law in effect throughout the states has been the chosen task of the American Law Institute since 1923. The work of the Institute is accomplished through the cooperative efforts of judges, lawyers, and legal scholars from every state.

Probably the best known of the agencies concerned with problems of state government is the Council of State Governments. The Council is composed primarily of commissions on interstate cooperation from the various states and maintains a permanent headquarters and staff in Chicago. While it performs chiefly as a research agency and clearing house, publishing reports on special problems as well as the quarterly magazine *State Government* and the biennial reference *Book of the States,* the Council also serves as a secretariat for a number of organizations. Among them are such groups as the Governors' Conference, National Association of Secretaries of State, National Association of Attorneys General, Conference of Chief Justices, and the National Association of State Budget Officers.

Interstate Compacts

The principal formal device used in the settlement of interstate disputes is the interstate compact. Compacts are written agreements voluntarily entered into by two or more signatories. As the term "interstate compact" suggests, the signatories are usually states although the United States government or foreign countries may also become participating parties.

According to the Constitution, all compacts must be approved by Congress.[21] When such approval is formally given, Congress simply enacts the compact in the form of a national statute, an action that may be taken either before or after the compact is concluded. In some cases Congress may fail to take action, yet the compact in question may have full legal force and effect.[22] However, compacts that tend to increase state authority or encroach upon national power almost certainly would require formal congressional approval.

Compacts were not often used prior to the twentieth century. Before the year 1900 only nineteen compacts—all involving boundary disputes—had received congressional approval. Since the turn of the century, and especially during the past forty years, the number of compacts submitted

21. Article I, Section 10.
22. See *Virginia* v. *Tennessee,* 148 U.S. 503 (1893).

to Congress has soared, and in many instances the agreements have been multi-state in character.

Despite the recent popularity and successful application of the interstate compact, the device is not without shortcomings. It takes a great deal of time and negotiation to complete a multistate agreement. When haste is essential, the compact is not a satisfactory method of cooperation. The effectiveness of any compact is dependent upon the full, voluntary cooperation of member states. Thus any event that threatens the interests of a signatory state may well threaten the success of the compact.

Suits between States

Frequently, states find themselves unable to resolve their differences by any of the methods discussed above. When such a stalemate occurs, and one of the states feels that its legal rights are compromised, a lawsuit may result. Suits between states are heard in the United States Supreme Court, the only court in the country in which one state may sue another.

States have haled each other before the Supreme Court for a variety of reasons. Frequently the location of a boundary line has been the point of conflict. The use of water from rivers or river systems that involve the geographical area of several states has been the basis of many suits. Other litigation has arisen over disagreement as to the financial obligations of one state to another. Many similar illustrations could be cited, for the records of the Supreme Court contain numerous interstate suits.

The Basic Law— State Constitutions

3

Throughout United States history the basic law of each state, as well as that of the national government, has been set forth in a written constitution. While the constitutions in America today are highly similar, still each document is unique. The Constitution of the United States stands apart as the organic, supreme law of the country as a whole. The constitution of each state is distinguishable in that it reflects local ideas, conditions, and problems.

The position of a state constitution in the hierarchy of law in the United States is determined by the principle of supremacy of national law.[1] Thus state constitutions are subordinate to all national law. When conflicts occur between national law and a provision of a state organic document, or for that matter any type of state law, the national law takes precedence. At the same time, there is no higher state law than the constitution of a state.

In general terms a constitution is intended to accomplish two broad objectives. First, it defines and creates the principal organs of government. Second, it outlines the relations of these governmental organs with each other and with the people. Whether a constitution achieves these goals in a satisfactory, lasting manner depends upon many things. Foremost is the requirement that a stable system of government be established, but established in a way that permits necessary adaptation and change. There is no set pattern which must be followed to achieve these goals. All state constitutions, however, utilize the same basic approach even though there is wide variation as to detail.

---

1. Article VI, Section 2, of the United States Constitution provides that "This Constitution, and the laws of the United States which shall be made in pursuance thereof; and all treaties made, or which shall be made, under the authority of the United States, shall be the supreme law of the land; and the judges in every state shall be bound thereby, anything in the constitution of laws of any state to the contrary notwithstanding."

THE ORIGINAL STATE CONSTITUTIONS

New Hampshire led the colonies in the adoption of constitutions by framing a temporary document in January, 1776.[2] Within two months South Carolina followed suit. The Continental Congress adopted a resolution in May encouraging the colonies to adopt "such governments as shall, in the opinions of the representatives of the people, best conduce to the happiness and safety of their constituents in particular and America in general" and proclaimed the Declaration of Independence in July. During the remainder of the year fundamental documents were framed in Virginia, New Jersey, Delaware, Pennsylvania, Maryland, and North Carolina. In 1777 Georgia and New York were added to the list. The two charter colonies—Connecticut and Rhode Island—already enjoying established systems of self-government, merely deleted references to the King in their charters and did not adopt new constitutions until 1818 and 1843, respectively. Massachusetts' constitution was also a revised charter, but frankly recognized as a stop-gap instrument.

None of the constitutions adopted during 1776 and 1777 was submitted to the people for approval. While conventions were used, except in South Carolina, to draft the documents, they were merely the legislative bodies sitting as conventions. In all instances the constitutions depended, in one way or another, upon legislative approval before taking effect. A major role in selecting the membership of conventions and exercising the power to accept or reject constitutions was first exercised by the people of Massachusetts in 1780. The procedures used in Massachusetts, and soon thereafter in New Hampshire, set the general pattern subsequently followed in all states.

Characteristics

In comparison with state constitutions today, the early documents were notable examples of brevity. Covering only a few printed pages, they were for the most part confined to truly fundamental matters. Relatively few provisions of temporary application or significance were inserted in the early constitutions.

Popular sovereignty—the principle that recognizes the people as the source of all political power—characterized each of the first state constitutions. Reaction to the arbitrary controls exercised by England during the colonial days was thus expressed in the basic laws of the new states. Limited government, the companion principle of popular sovereignty, was

---

2. Copies of the Charters and Constitutions in effect in the various colonies and states to the turn of the present century have been collected in Francis N. Thorpe, *The Federal and State Constitutions,* 7 vols., 1909, printed as House of Representatives Document No. 357, 59th Congress, 2nd session.

made apparent in many provisions. The revolutionary view of government was principally one of distrust. Hence the freedom of action of public officials was severely restricted. In seven states a bill of rights was written into the Constitution, and in the remainder the civil rights of the people were protected through random clauses guaranteeing specific rights coupled with reliance upon the common law in effect at the time.

The distrust and suspicion of strong government that marked the revolutionary outlook was evidenced by the principles of separation of powers and checks and balances characteristic of the early constitutions. While fewer than half of the documents espoused the principles in so many words, each was careful to segregate legislative, executive, and judicial powers. Separate branches of government were established and their powers delineated. Each was vested, in theory at least, with powers that would tend to control the actions of the other branches.

In actual practice the theory of separation of powers was weakened in that the popularly elected legislatures were given far more authority than either the executive or judicial branches. Experience under royal colonial governors resulted in an organizational pattern in which the governor was reduced to a mere figurehead. He was generally limited to a one-year term, was chosen by the legislature in all states but New York and Massachusetts, and exercised the power of veto only in South Carolina and Massachusetts. State courts were also subordinate to the legislature since the early constitutions created a judicial framework, leaving the task of completing judicial organization and determining jurisdiction to legislative action. Thus the first years of government under the original state constitutions may correctly be described as a time of legislative supremacy.

STATE CONSTITUTIONS TODAY

As already noted, today's constitutions are similar, yet individual in character. Each establishes a framework of government very much like that in every other state. The principles upon which these documents rest are very nearly uniform, but each assumes unique characteristics because of problems peculiar to a state.

Age

American state constitutions vary widely in age. Within the last decade four states have adopted new constitutions, and about half of those currently in effect were adopted more than one hundred years ago, including three, those of Massachusetts, New Hampshire, and Vermont, which bear dates prior to the year 1800. While the age of a constitution must certainly be considered in assessing its character, age can be misleading. Many of the older constitutions have been subjected to frequent amendment, resulting in the inclusion of much recent material. Then, too, interpretation over the years by executive, legislative, and judicial branches can change the precise meanings of various provisions. Thus age is merely one criterion of the suitability of a constitution. (See Appendix 2.)

Length

Just as state constitutions vary widely in age, they also differ greatly in length. The Alabama constitution is about 125,000 words long while at the other extreme are Connecticut and Rhode Island with constitutions containing less than 8,000 words. Most state constitutions are somewhere between these two extremes with an average length of about 25,000 words.

Even though state constitutions may be considered excessively long, it is not always easy to decide which provisions are not of fundamental importance. What is and what is not fundamental may depend almost entirely upon the peculiarities of a particular state. For example, in states where water is in short supply, constitutions may properly contain provisions relating to the allocation of that resource. A state whose economy depends heavily upon tourism may be justified in devoting space in its fundamental document to a motor vehicles fuel tax. Or a state where forestry, mining, or other such activity is of major importance may consider constitutional references to such activities as fundamental.

Nature and Contents

State constitutions deal with a broad range of matters. Each document contains much that is unique, but all constitutions contain provisions that may be considered under several broad categories.

Principles of Government. In no respect are state constitutions more alike than in the governmental principles upon which they are based. It is necessary only to compare the basic structure and processes of a few states to realize that all have been cast from the same general mold. All state constitutions espouse the doctrine of *popular sovereignty,* recognizing the people as the source of political power and that government exists through popular consent. *Limited government,* the doctrine that government must operate within defined bounds, is implied if not actually stated in every state constitution. The fact that the powers of every state government are apportioned among legislative, executive, and judicial branches, each with certain powers over the others, illustrates the universal acceptance of the doctrines of *separation of powers* and *checks and balances.* As in the case of the national constitution, the fundamental instruments of the states assume the existence of *judicial review,* whereby courts are empowered to adjudge the constitutionality of statutes. Finally, all state constitutions exist within the framework of the American federal system. While none expresses the principle as such, the implicit acceptance of federalism is obvious.

Governmental Organization. Providing a framework of government is a basic task of a constitution, and while the same general technique is used in every state there is great variation in detail. All state constitutions contain individual articles establishing and describing the legislative, executive, and judicial branches. In addition, whole articles or scattered provisions outline, with varying degrees of detail, the organization of local governmental units.

The principal differences among state constitutions in regard to providing for the form of governments relate to the inclusion of detail. A few documents follow the national pattern in providing only broad outlines of organization. More often, however, not only is the general system of government described, but intricate details of administrative structure are set forth. Without exception, state constitutional provisions relating to the establishment of governmental framework go far beyond the essentials as set forth in the national Constitution.

The Processes of Government. After delineating the form of government, a constitution must prescribe the basic processes of government. The relations of government to citizens, intergovernmental relations, and the relative positions of component parts of the state organization must be described. In regard to these matters state constitutions are widely divergent.

Every constitution contains statements relating to the powers, limitations, duties, and obligations of the various elements of government. A Bill of Rights is found in each document; provisions for the initiative, referendum, and recall are contained in many; all provide for systems of taxation and finance; and public education, military affairs, corporate activity, and a variety of other governmental activities are dealt with. Some documents are extensively detailed, others are less so; some are highly restrictive, others liberal; and processes are regulated or described in some constitutions and not mentioned in others. Because of this wide variation, the question of whether a particular constitution is "good" or "bad" with respect to its treatment of governmental processes depends largely upon individual evaluation.

Protection of Civil Rights. Each constitution contains, usually in the first article, a list of individual rights. Called Bills of Rights or Declarations of Rights, they contain guarantees similar to those of the first ten amendments of the national Constitution. These lists are much longer than the national Bill of Rights. In addition to guarantees of freedom of speech, press, religion, assembly, petition, security from unreasonable searches and seizures, and the procedural rights of accused persons, state constitutions may list many others. In one constitution or another, for example, are found the rights to self-government, to alter or change the government, to be secure from imprisonment for debt, to emigrate from the state, to organize labor unions, to bargain collectively, to recover damages in suits at law, and even to fish in public waters!

Provision for Constitutional Change.   Since constitutions are written by people, none is perfect.   Sooner or later, for one reason or another, changes become necessary; and each document contains provisions setting forth the manner of formal change. These methods, termed "revisions" and "amendments," are discussed at length below.

Miscellaneous Provisions.   There are usually several portions of a state constitution that have little or no utility or application. Best known of these is the preamble which precedes the body of a constitution. A preamble has no legal effect whatever and is nothing more than a statement of goals and intentions. Constitutions also include "schedules," that is, articles that prescribe the conditions under which the document takes effect. Once the constitution is in force, the schedule serves no further purpose. Finally, all constitutions contain provisions of the "dead letter" variety, which for some reason have no current application. A section, for example, that determines the composition of the legislature until apportionment can be accomplished or one that relates to a specific bond issue soon becomes outdated. More frequently, however, ineffective provisions result from judicial decisions that render them unenforceable.

ADOPTING AND CHANGING CONSTITUTIONS

A constitution is not put together as the result of theoretical reflections by a group of framers. Rather, it is the formal recognition of an already existing and generally accepted collection of principles and concepts adhered to by the people. Those ideas are the accepted basic law and are given force and effect by governmental organization of some sort. In short, a written constitution is preceded by organized government.

Prior to its entry into the Union, each of the American states possessed an established government. The thirteen original states were first colonies, and after severing political ties with England they became independent. Some states were formed from lands that were part of, or were claimed by, other states, but in each instance a prospective new state was already governmentally organized. Texas was an independent nation, and California had been a province of Mexico. Slightly more than half of the states had organized territorial governments prior to admission.

Today the generally accepted method of writing and adopting a constitution is through a popularly elected convention followed by ratification by popular vote. A glance through the pages of history discloses that less democratic methods have been used. The constitutions of the original thirteen states were legislative products that were not submitted to the people. Massachusetts, Rhode Island, and Connecticut originally operated with basic laws consisting of legislatively revised colonial charters. In a few instances original constitutions were drafted and proclaimed by conventions without referral to the people.[3]

CONSTITUTIONAL GROWTH AND CHANGE

Constitutions are subject to change by informal and formal means. Informal change is manifested through growth by *custom and usage,*[4] or alteration by means of common acceptance of an established way of doing things; and by *interpretation,* or development through the construction and definition of constitutional provisions by public bodies and officials. Changes by these methods are likely to be gradual, often barely perceptible. Only when a constitutional clause is subjected to extensive redefinition, usually by a court, does general public awareness of the change result.

Formal changes are accomplished by means of *amendment* or *revision.* In the former, only a portion of the constitution, usually an article or a section, is altered. Revision, on the other hand, entails a general overhaul of the basic document. As indicated below, a new constitution usually results from the revision process.

Custom and Usage

A custom may be as strong as though it were set forth in the basic law. Since customs are not buttressed by written law, they do not, technically, have to be observed. However, a custom may become so fixed in the minds of the people and public officials, that to violate it would be tantamount to violating the constitution. Thus customs, while not actual parts of a state constitution, are very real parts of the *constitutional system.*

Interpretation

The courts of each state are often called upon in deciding cases to explain the meaning of constitutional provisions. In this way a clause or section may be construed as permitting actions previously thought to be forbidden, or conversely, as prohibiting others considered permissible. The legislative and executive branches are also extremely important instruments of constitutional interpretation. All laws enacted by the legislature

---

3. Alabama (1802), Arkansas (1836), Illinois (1818), Indiana (1816), Kentucky (1792), Missouri (1820), and Ohio (1802).
4. A *custom* is a general practice which by common consent has acquired the force of law. A *usage,* technically, is of local application and does not require a long period of application before it becomes established. Generally, however, the terms are used synonymously and no attempt is made here to distinguish them.

and all acts of the governor or his administrative officers must conform to constitutional requirements. Since this is true, it is obvious that their actions are the result of their interpretations of powers available to them under the constitution.

Interpretations of state constitutions have not resulted in appreciable expansion of state authority, reflecting a difference in character between the national Constitution and those of the states. Inasmuch as the national government is essentially a government of delegated powers, its every action must be authorized by the United States Constitution. Hence the doctrine of *implied powers,* according to which authority may be implied from expressed powers, has resulted in tremendous expansion of federal activity. On the other hand, the powers of the states, with few exceptions, are not listed in state constitutions. A power not delegated to the national government nor prohibited to the states is automatically a state power. Thus at the state level there is no doctrine of implied powers—a doctrine particularly adapted to delineation through interpretation of positive grants of authority. As a result, interpretation of state constitutional provisions is for the most part a matter of judging whether an action is within the broad area of the reserved powers of the states.

Amendment

Formal changes in state constitutions are accomplished most frequently through the process of amendment. Two steps are involved: *initiation* of the suggested change and *ratification,* or approval, of the initiated alteration. Initiation requires fulfillment of legal steps specified by the constitution, ordinarily approval by designated majorities in the legislative houses, or in the case of the initiative process, approval by a specified number of voters. Ratification in all states except Delaware is secured at elections, at which time the voters exercise their prerogative to approve or reject amendments.

Amendment by Legislative Action.   Only in Delaware can a constitutional amendment be adopted without formal action by the people at some stage. According to the Delaware Constitution, a favorable vote by two-thirds of all members elected to both houses of the legislature at two successive sessions is necessary for adoption of a constitutional amendment.[5] It would appear that this requirement of successive extraordinary majorities would tend to inhibit severely the number of alterations in the state's organic law. This is not the case, however, for the rate at which amendments have been adopted in Delaware exceeds that of two-thirds of the states.

Although participation in the formal steps of amendment is not avail-

5. Constitution of Delaware, Article XVI, Section 1.

able to the electors of Delaware, they are not altogether excluded. The entire membership of the House of Representatives and approximately half of the Senators are subject to election every two years. Aspirants to these legislative positions must be sensitive to the views of the people—including their attitudes on pending amendments. Obviously, opposition to a proposal by a large or important segment of voters will be reflected in the actions of the newly elected, or re-elected, legislators.

Initiation by Convention. The method least used for the initiation of constitutional amendments has been the convention. A slow and cumbersome procedure, its use has been limited to those situations where it was the only method available,[6] was considered to be the last resort, or was chosen as the most politically expedient method. For example, the Tennessee Constitution, adopted in 1870, proved so difficult to amend through the regular method that it went unchanged until 1953. In that year the people voted to call a convention for the initiation of amendments. Eight were initiated and subsequently approved by the people at a special election. The New York convention held in 1938 extensively revised that state's 1895 constitution and submitted proposals for change to the people as nine different amendments, of which only six were approved. Consequently, the document presently in effect contains many provisions unchanged from the earlier constitution. Therefore, the present New York Constitution, which took effect in 1939, is sometimes regarded as an amended version of the 1895 document.

The constitutions of many other states provide for conventions for the initiation of amendments. In Oregon, conventions have the power to "amend or propose amendments . . . or to propose a new Constitution."[7] Conventions in Ohio may "revise, amend, or change" the basic law.[8] In Oklahoma, constitutional "alterations, revisions, or amendments" may be accomplished by convention.[9] Nebraska conventions may "revise, amend, or change" the constitution of that state.[10] Even though available as an amending device, conventions are seldom used for that purpose. The great expense involved, the time necessarily consumed in the convention process, and the fact that regular amending procedures are easier to use, all militate against wide use of the convention for amending purposes.

Legislative Initiation. In each of the fifty states the legislature has authority to initiate constitutional amendments. In practically all states the

---

6. Prior to 1964 amendments to the New Hampshire Constitution could be initiated only by conventions which could be held no oftener than once every seven years. At the general election in November 1964 an amendment was adopted which provides that the legislature may initiate such alterations.
7. Article XVII, Section 1.
8. Article XVI, Section 2.
9. Article XXIV, Section 2.
10. Article XVI, Section 2.

power is shared equally by the two houses of the legislature. Nebraska, of course, is the most obvious exception since its legislature is unicameral. Two-thirds of the Vermont Senate makes original proposals which, if concurred in by a majority of the House, are held over for approval by a majority of both houses at the next biennial session. In Connecticut and New Jersey alternative methods of initiation are available to the legislature, and in Massachusetts amendments are proposed in joint sessions.

Other variations among the states are numerous. About one-fourth of the state constitutions stipulate that amendments may be initiated only after favorable action by two successive sessions of the legislature. Majorities required for approval also vary widely, ranging from simple majorities of those present and voting, to three-fourths of the members elected. In some instances, further barriers are placed in the path of amendment. The Kansas Constitution, for example, states that no more than three propositions to amend may be submitted to the voters at any one election. At one election Colorado legislators may offer amendments to no more than six articles of the constitution. In Illinois the maximum number of articles that may be amended at one time is three, and any given article may be subjected to amendment no oftener than once every four years. And in Vermont amendments may be submitted to the voters only once every ten years.

Initiation by Constitutional Initiative.   The constitutions of fourteen states now make it possible for the people to amend the constitution through the constitutional initiative.[11] This method consists of the circulation of petitions to collect a prescribed number of signatures. After the signatures have been gathered and verified, the amendment is considered initiated and subject to ratification at the next general election.

Ratification.   Not until an amendment has received final approval, that is, ratified in the manner prescribed by the constitution, does it take effect. The instrument of approval in all states except Delaware is the people. Ratification in Delaware is accomplished when two successive legislatures vote favorably on an amendment. Ratification of amendments proposed by constitutional initiative is accomplished by popular vote, with Nevada requiring that such measures win the approval of the electorate at two successive general elections.

Some states are more restrictive than others. In five states an amendment must receive favorable votes from a majority of the total number of voters participating in the election. The states of Illinois and New Hampshire require a majority of two-thirds of those voting on an amendment. Tennessee sets the figure at a majority of the vote cast for governor. South Carolina's constitution requires only a majority of those voting on an

11. See Chapter 12 for discussion of the various means of direct popular action, including the constitutional initiative.

amendment, but ratification is not complete unless the legislature concurs at its next session.

Constitutional Amendment—Easy or Difficult?   A principal point of controversy with respect to changing constitutions is the question of how difficult it should be to amend a state constitution. In a few states the process is little more than a minor hurdle, while in others amendment is extremely difficult to achieve. A short, well-written document that contains little more than truly fundamental law obviously would not need to be modified as often as a constitution overburdened with detailed, statute-like provisions. It may well be argued that fundamental law ought to be difficult to change, but at the same time a convincing case can be made for an easier amendatory process if a constitution contains many provisions likely to become outdated. The best solution, of course, is to keep unnecessary detail out of a constitution from the outset, but such reasoning does not meet the real problem.

Revision

When a constitution is badly in need of extensive change and it appears that the usual methods of amendment cannot adequately provide for the changes needed, resort is had to one or another of the revision procedures. Ordinarily, a document that needs alteration to the extent that revision is necessary should be replaced. With few exceptions, therefore, most successful efforts at revision have produced new constitutions rather than reworked versions of constitutions already in force.

Conventions.   The constitutional convention is by far the most commonly employed device for constitutional revision. With the exception of the Georgia Constitution of 1945, every state constitution now in effect is the product of such an assembly. While other means are available, the convention remains the generally accepted method for framing new basic documents.

Calling the Convention.   Normally, a convention results from cooperative efforts by the state legislature and the people. Even though one-fourth of the state constitutions make no provision for calling a convention, it is generally understood that the power may be exercised by a state legislative body.[12] Prior to the actual calling of a convention a legislature must

---

12. In the states of Arkansas, Louisiana, Massachusetts, Pennsylvania, Rhode Island, and Texas the constitutions are silent as to conventions, but statutes, court decisions, and opinions of attorney generals indicate that the respective legislatures are the proper agencies to call conventions. The constitutions of Indiana, New Jersey, North Dakota, and Vermont are also quiet on the topic of conventions, and the prerogative of the legislature to call them rests upon the effect of custom.

first submit to the people the question of whether a convention should be held.[13] If a "yes" vote results, the legislature may proceed to call the convention. In the absence of constitutional specifications, the act which formally calls the convention makes the necessary arrangements for the election of delegates, determines the time and place of the assemblage, provides for temporary organization, and appropriates funds to cover the costs of the meeting. The powers of the convention may also be outlined, at least in part. The details of procedure in arranging for a convention vary widely from state to state, and they may also vary in the same state with respect to successive conventions.

In recent years conventions have been prefaced by a considerable amount of research into problems to be dealt with by the delegates. While again there is wide variance as to organization and procedure among the states, a legislative reference bureau, consulting service, or special commission handles the task. Reports, pamphlets, manuals and the like are produced for the use of delegates once they set about the job of framing a constitution. The value of preliminary research is reflected in the fact that it has become practically an accepted part of the convention process over the past several decades.

Make-up and Organization.   State constitutions do not spell out the qualifications to be met by persons desiring to become delegates. In general, they are those of a qualified elector—the same qualifications ordinarily required for candidacy for most public offices. The calibre of conventions is, like that of state legislatures, dependent upon the chance results of elections. It is generally believed, however, that more competent people are attracted to convention membership because of the importance of a convention's work and the fact that conventions usually are of short duration.

In appearance a convention looks very much like a unicameral legislature. As part of organization, officers are chosen, rules are adopted, and committees are appointed. Usually, there is one committee for each article of the existing constitution, with special committees as necessary. The overall pattern of operation is similar to that of a legislative body.

Powers.   A constitutional convention is not free to do anything it chooses. In the first place, all constitutional limitations and restrictions must be observed, for until replaced or amended the existing constitution is still the supreme law within a state. The same condition applies in territories or other areas seeking statehood inasmuch as the prevailing organic law remains effective until replaced. Provisions of the legislative act calling

---

13. The constitutions of some states require that the question be submitted to the people at designated intervals. The periods are twenty years in Connecticut, Illinois, Maryland, Missouri, New York, Ohio, and Oklahoma; sixteen years in Michigan; and ten years in Alaska, Hawaii, Iowa, and New Hampshire.

the convention are viewed as mandatory in character, although conventions have on occasion successfully ignored legislative directions.

Within the framework of such limitations, a convention controls its own affairs. Once organized and ready for work, it is not subject to limitations by any other organ of government. It proceeds at its task in the manner it chooses and at the rate of speed it desires. However, the product of a convention may be challenged in the courts after the convention adjourns.

Ratification. Beginning with approval by the people of the Massachusetts Constitution of 1780, popular ratification has been a usual step in the adoption of new constitutions. Of the basic documents in effect today only those of Delaware (1897), Mississippi (1890), South Carolina (1895), and Vermont (1793) took effect without first being submitted to the people. Altogether the American states have framed about 140 constitutions since 1776. Excluding the original constitutions and the secession documents of the Confederate States, about ninety percent of them were ratified by the populace.

Throughout most of American history new constitutions have been presented as units to the voters. Accordingly, a new constitution was either accepted or rejected as a whole. The chief disadvantage of this method is that a few controversial provisions may, because of concentrated attacks by opponents, doom the entire document. To reduce the possibilities of complete failure, some new constitutions have been submitted in several parts. Thus the work of the New York Convention of 1938 was presented to the voters in nine sections. One, an omnibus proposal containing forty-nine general, noncontroversial changes, was approved. The other eight dealt with more debatable alterations, three of which were rejected.

The question of how large a majority is required for approval of a new constitution is not settled in all state documents. Half the constitutions are silent, thus leaving the matter for determination by the legislatures or conventions. A third provide that only a majority of those voting on the question of ratification is necessary for adoption. States in which extraordinary majorities are required include Minnesota, where a new document must be acceptable to three-fifths of those casting ballots, and New Hampshire and Rhode Island, where the majority is fixed at two-thirds. In practically all states a new constitution may be submitted at a special election, a desirable arrangement inasmuch as the proposed document is the only thing at issue and therefore more likely to be accepted or rejected on its merits.

Revision Commissions

From time to time over the past century about one-half of the states have used commissions in the pursuit of constitutional revision. A commission may be appointed by a governor on his own responsibility as in Kentucky in 1949, or as in the single instance of Florida in 1968 by a constitutional amendment, but such bodies are normally established by legislative action. As a result, the commission is responsible to the legislature, and the constitutional alterations decided upon by the commission take the form of recommendations to the legislature.

In some states a revision commission may not be practicable due to the effect of certain restrictive constitutional provisions. Since the proposals of a commission are put before the voters by the legislative body in the form of one or more amendments, an unduly restrictive amendatory procedure may severely curtail the extent of revision possible. In fact, true revision may not be possible at all. The Georgia Constitution of 1945, a revised document produced by a commission, was submitted to the voters in the form of a single amendment. The work of a revision commission in Florida was invalidated by a 1958 decision of that state's supreme court on the ground that no one amendment may alter more than one article of the existing constitution. Similar requirements in other states would limit the efficacy of revision commissions.

Make-up and Organization.   A revision commission may take any of a variety of forms. Agencies already in existence may function as commissions. The 1947 Oklahoma commission, for example, was in actuality the legislative council acting in a different capacity. The California commission which met in that same year was in reality a joint interim legislative committee. More commonly, however, revision commissions are made up of personnel appointed by the governor upon authorization by the legislature. Members may be drawn from private life as well as from the various branches of government. The size of a commission is determined by the creating authority, but in practice they have been small groups.

The Commission: Pro and Con.   Several convincing arguments may be advanced in support of the commission as a method of constitutional revision. Its small size indicates a saving in costs, and, since small groups operate more expeditiously than large ones, time is also saved. Freer debate is possible since there are fewer members to be heard. Perhaps the strongest argument is the fact that since a commission is not elective, persons with expert qualifications may be induced to accept membership—individuals who might be reluctant to campaign for election as delegates to a convention. Those who favor commissions also contend that pressure groups would be less likely to sway such persons.

Opponents of revision commissions are quick to point out that a constitution, the basic law of the state, should be democratically conceived. And the commission, removed from direct popular control and staffed without particular regard to the desires of the people, is contrary to democratic concepts. Further, it may be contended, the commission is not as free to act as its supporters insist, for being subordinate to the legislature it is conditioned by what it thinks the legislature will accept. It is also easy to "pack" a commission—that is, to appoint members who will suggest changes desired by leaders in the legislative and executive branches. Finally, in answer to the argument that commissions save time and money, opponents reply that such gains are immaterial unless the suggested revision is acceptable and finally adopted. On this point detractors recall that a majority of revision commissions have failed to see their work fully accepted.

Obviously, sound arguments can be posed both in support of and against the revision commission. To condemn all commissions because most have failed is as unrealistic as acclaiming the device because some have produced substantial revisions. The most sensible view judges each individual commission on its merits in the context of the legal structure within which it must operate.

Piecemeal Revision

In some states the constitutionally prescribed method of amending the fundamental law is so easy that frequent and numerous changes are made. Constitutions subjected to such alteration may be said, in effect, to undergo a sort of gradual, continuous revision. The undesirability of piecemeal revision is clearly indicated by its haphazard nature. There is no attempt to integrate changes, no pattern according to which a consistent development of constitutional content can be engineered. In the final analysis, extensive piecemeal change can create as much need for further change as it, by chance, remedies.

Revision by the Legislature

Oregon in 1960 and California in 1962 adopted constitutional amendments which provide an alternative method of constitutional revision. Under the terms of each of these provisions, the legislature itself may propose a revision of all or part of the state constitution by means of a two-thirds vote of all members in each house. Revisions proposed in this manner are subject to popular ratification with adoption dependent upon a favorable vote by a majority of those voting on the issue. Attempts at implementation have thus far proved unsuccessful.

THE MODEL STATE CONSTITUTION

In 1921 the Committee on State Government of the National Municipal League framed the Model State Constitution. That document, intended as a model of what a typical state constitution *ought* to be like has been periodically revised over the decades. It does not, of course, have any legal effect in any state, nor has it been adopted in its entirety by the voters of any state. Rather, its purpose is to serve as a guide to the delegates of constitutional conventions, members of revision commissions, persons and groups sponsoring amendments, and voters who ratify or reject constitutional alterations.

The Model State Constitution is not a radical document. The subjects dealt with are those usually covered by state constitutions. There is a bill of rights and provisions on suffrage, elections, the legislature, initiative and referendum, the executive, the judiciary, finance, local government, civil service, public schools, intergovernmental relations, general provisions, constitutional revision, and a schedule. Little is included that is not fundamental although questions may be raised on the basis of one's own convictions as to the necessity of some provisions. Still, the provisions included in the model document are generally conceded to comprise an appropriate list of fundamental provisions.

Not all the provisions of the model document have met with general acceptance. Only Nebraska, for example, uses a unicameral legislature as suggested in the Model Constitution. In fact, while some state constitutions contain provisions that are highly similar to corresponding sections of the model document, no state constitution embraces an article that is identical to any found in the Model Constitution. Even so, the Model State Constitution represents the thought of highly competent students of state government and fills well the role of guide to constitution makers across the nation. (See Appendix 3.)

State Executives

The responsibility of the executive branch is to take action necessary to accomplish the goals and purposes of a governmental unit. This chapter examines major component parts of this branch of government as found in the states. Attention is called not only to organizational aspects, but stress is also placed on the general nature of the executive function. Although each governor has major responsibilities relative to the executive function, the governor is often "first among equals." Consequently, it is important to gain some insight into the authority and responsibility of other executive officers such as the secretary of state, treasurer, and attorney general.

THE GOVERNOR

Historical Development of the Office

Following the American Revolution, power in the hands of government was considered dangerous. Serious doubt existed as to the effectiveness of popular control over a government with much authority. Distrust of power in the hands of the executive was especially strong as a result of experience with colonial governors who enjoyed extensive authority as representatives of the King of England or of individual proprietors.[1]

The prevailing tone reflected in the original state constitutions was "confidence in legislatures, mistrust of executives." Since all of these constitutions were the product of legislative action, supremacy of the legislative branch was to be expected. Most of the early state governors were chosen by the legislatures and possessed little authority.[2] In the

1. In Connecticut and Rhode Island, governors were chosen by the state legislatures and possessed few powers.
2. Even the popularly elected governors of Massachusetts and New York had little authority.

effort to guard against the dangers of a strong executive, most power was vested in the legislature, reflecting a failure to realize that the actual risk lay in a concentration of authority in *any* branch of the government.

Although some political leaders by the end of the eighteenth century were aware of problems inherent in a governmental system characterized by a weak executive, increases in authority came slowly.[3] According to Lipson, by 1830 there were signs that the governor "will one day develop into an officer existing in his own right, that he will cease to be a mere creature of the legislature."[4] Decreased legislative domination of the executive did not mean, however, that the governor had become chief executive in fact as well as name. Instead, the practice was to diffuse executive responsibility among individual officers, who as a result of the influence of "Jacksonian democracy" were popularly elected and hence were not subject to gubernatorial control.

Writing in the 1880's, James Bryce observed that "the governor remains in solitary glory the official head and representative of the majesty of the State. His powers are . . . more specious than solid. . . ."[5] Chief among the reasons why state governors were able to function at all satisfactorily with such diffusion of executive authority was the fact that their responsibilities were few. During the last quarter of the nineteenth century, changes came rapidly. The increased complexity of society resulting in large part from the rapid industrialization of the country made much greater demands upon government. Many new laws enacted by the state legislatures "threw an administrative burden upon an executive branch that was structurally unfitted to bear it."[6] Instead of attempting to develop a cohesive administrative organization, state legislatures chose to create new agencies that were largely independent of the governor.

In this chapter attention is directed to the efforts at reorganization that occurred in the states during the first quarter of the twentieth century. A foremost objective of these movements was "to make the governor chief executive in fact as well as name," and much effort was expended in this direction during the fifteen or so years following World War I. Although many proposals dear to the hearts of the advocates of thoroughgoing reorganization were not realized, the effectiveness of the executive had been greatly enhanced before World War II. Further efforts at strengthening the executive branch of our state governments followed upon the heels of the report of the first Hoover Commission, and in recent years major reorganizations have occurred in at least a dozen states and partial reorganization in twice that number.

3. This realization was clearly reflected in the powers granted to the President in the U.S. Constitution and to the governor in the Illinois Constitution of 1818.
4. Leslie Lipson, *The American Governor: From Figurehead to Leader,* University of Chicago Press, 1939, p. 19.
5. James Bryce, *The American Commonwealth,* Vol. I, The Commonwealth Publishing Co., New York, 1908, p. 533.
6. Lipson, *op. cit.,* p. 25.

Formal Qualifications for the Office

In every state constitution are found a few minimum qualifications that a person must possess in order to qualify as a gubernatorial candidate. All states require United States citizenship, and over one-third stipulate a minimum number of years of citizenship, ranging from two to twenty.[7] Periods of state residence, varying in length from one to ten years, are required in practically all states. As a rule, a candidate must have reached a specific age. Although the most common requirement is thirty years, a few states accept twenty-one or twenty-five. Even where no provisions are included in the state constitution pertaining to age, custom requires that a candidate for the governorship must be a mature person. Possession of formal qualifications obviously is insufficient to make a person a promising candidate.

Informal Qualifications—"Availability"

Much more significant than the formal qualifications are those arising from political necessity. The crucial question is, What qualifications will enhance the vote-getting capacity of the candidate? A party needs a candidate who will make the widest appeal and at the same time offend the smallest number of voters. A good candidate should not be too unlike the mass of voters in order to appeal to them. At the same time the candidate must be sufficiently different and be worthy of their trust. Consequently, the candidate must be persuasive; must possess a superior, practical knowledge of the problems of government; and must evince the ability to work with people. Perhaps above all, a good candidate needs to convince the voters that the program offered is designed to meet some of the state's most pressing problems.

In general, "availability" is measured in terms of such considerations as ability to work with party leaders, affiliation with various organizations, religion, nationality background, financial resources, gender, and experience in public office. Candidates who are acceptable to their party organization usually have a definite advantage over those opposed by the "regulars." Of course, the efforts of "independent" candidates are occasionally crowned with success, an eventuality that may result in part from popular reaction against the policies and practices associated with a particular party at a given time. A good candidate belongs to a number of "desirable" organizations, such as a church, one or more service clubs, professional or trade organizations, and civic action groups. Such a candidate should also be free from the taint of "undesirable" groups that espouse extremist or radical views or programs.

---

7. In the states with no explicit constitutional requirement as to citizenship, gubernatorial candidates must qualify as voters, who in turn must be citizens.

Although as a people we emphasize the value and importance of religious freedom, candidates to public office are not free, politically speaking, to belong to just any faith. In some areas a Catholic would not be "available," while in others the same would be true of a Protestant; members of the Mormon Church make especially attractive candidates in Utah, but their religion might be a political handicap in other parts of the country. Persons of obvious Irish, Polish, or Scandinavian ancestry, for example, have a definite advantage over persons of other nationalities in certain localities. In general, a candidate needs to have above average financial resources available. In the absence of personal financial resources, the candidate needs to know where to go to obtain assistance. This generalization should not be taken to mean that the well-to-do candidates do not need to seek help from persons interested in their candidacy, for the existence of individuals with "a stake" in their success is a definite asset to any person running for public office.[8]

With the advent of the women's liberation movement, the candidates' gender has become a less critical factor in determining success at the polls. Although many fewer women than men currently hold the office of mayor, governor,[9] or are members of the state legislature, recent trends in voter behavior indicate that the political climate is becoming more favorable toward female candidates. A 1972 poll shows increased acceptance among both sexes of female activity in politics and of the idea of a woman as president.[10] These changing attitudes should encourage more women to enter the political scene in the future and to gain the necessary political exposure and experience to be a successful candidate.

The importance of experience in public office has been documented in numerous studies, especially with relation to gubernatorial candidates, as a qualification desirable for those seeking election to positions in the public service. The candidate with a good record in positions of public trust has "proven" ability and thus has an advantage over the person who has had no such opportunity. Furthermore, the *type* of experience possessed by a candidate will affect availability. For example, one study indicates that prior membership in the state legislature is of particular value to gubernatorial aspirants, particularly in some states, while in others experience as law enforcement officers such as attorney general

8. One significant danger is inherent in this consideration, namely, that the voters may feel that the candidate has "sold out" to certain interests. Caution must be exercised with regard to the sources and amount of support accepted. Small contributions from a variety of sources are generally preferred and may be mandated by law.

9. Only five women have been elected to this office, and three of them followed their husbands— Miriam Ferguson of Texas, Nellie T. Ross of Wyoming, and Lurleen Wallace of Alabama. More recently, Ella Grasso was elected governor of Connecticut and Dixie Lee Ray was elected in Washington.

10. See Louis Harris and Associates, *The 1972 Virginia Slims American Women's Public Opinion Poll* (1972), p. 35. Also Hazel Erskine, "The Polls: Women's Role," *Public Opinion Quarterly,* XXXV (Summer, 1971), p. 277 ff.

or judge is very helpful.[11] In many states there is a typical career pattern followed by successful candidates for the office of governor.

Term of Office

As a consequence of popular distrust of the executive branch mentioned above, early state constitutions generally provided for annual election of governors. Beginning early in the nineteenth century, a lengthening of gubernatorial terms was noticeable. Today the constitutions of all states provide either two- or four-year terms for their governors.

At the same time that some states lengthened the term of office of their governors, restrictions were imposed upon the opportunity of a governor to succeed himself. In approximately half of the states no limitations exist. In the others, a variety of restrictions have been imposed, most often designed to prevent a governor from serving two terms in succession. In a handful of states a governor may serve *no more* than two terms, an arrangement that may prevent a person from ever serving more than two terms or may require an incumbent to retire from office for a specified number of years before seeking re-election.[12]

Although cogent arguments may be advanced in behalf of unlimited succession in terms of the "right" of the people to elect anyone they choose and in behalf of administrative efficiency and leadership, the fact remains that on several occasions the people have recently demonstrated their preference for restrictions. On a national scale this attitude was reflected in the adoption of the Twenty-second Amendment to the U.S. Constitution. In several of the state constitutions adopted in recent years—including Alaska, Florida, and New Jersey—limitations were placed on gubernatorial succession. After serving two terms, governors in these states may not serve again for at least one term.

Compensation

Traditionally, state governors have been inadequately compensated, although widespread improvements have taken place in recent years. As late as 1950 the average gubernatorial salary was only slightly in excess of $11,000; now it is about four times that amount. Tremendous differences exist, with New York paying its governor $85,000 and a number of states keeping the salary level at $35,000 or less. Of course, these figures do not reflect the total compensation associated with the office of governor in many states. Governors in forty-four states are provided with a residence

11. See Joseph A. Schlesinger, *How They Became Governor,* Michigan State University, East Lansing, Michigan, 1957.
12. In New Mexico, for example, a governor who has served two terms may not serve again until the expiration of two additional terms (four years). An Oregon governor may not serve more than eight years (two terms) in any twelve.

or "mansion." Most states also make allowances for expenses, commonly ranging upward from $5,000 per year. Too frequently, only persons with private means can afford to become governor.

Selection and Removal

Viewed superficially, procedures for the selection of governors are not especially complicated. State laws set forth the formal requirements providing that gubernatorial candidates shall be nominated by convention or direct primary and elected by vote of the people in a general election. However, complications arise in any effort to describe in detail the entire procedure involved in choosing governors because of "the variety of patterns . . . in the party processes which lie behind the legal pattern and which actually determine who is selected as the gubernatorial candidate of a given party."[13] Every student of government should recognize that the nominating process is a combination of the procedures required by law and the informal system developed by parties over a long period.

Although seldom used, means of removing governors from office are provided in all state constitutions. The governor of every state, with the exception of Oregon, may be removed upon conviction of impeachment charges. The normal procedure is for the lower house of the state legislature to bring the charges and for the upper house or senate to conduct a trial and determine guilt or innocence.[14] The only penalties usually authorized are removal from office and disqualification from holding office in the state government in the future. The governor who has committed a crime is liable to criminal action in the courts following his removal. In thirteen states, governors may be removed by the recall.[15] Recall procedure involves, first of all, the circulation of a petition setting forth charges against the officer. Such a petition must be signed by a specified percentage of qualified voters and then filed with the secretary of state. If all legal requirements have been met, a recall election is scheduled unless the governor chooses to resign. The only governor to be removed by this procedure was Lynn J. Frazier of North Dakota in 1921.

Succession and Disability

The constitutions of thirty-nine states provide that the lieutenant governor shall step into a vacancy in the office of governor. In the remaining

---

13. Coleman B. Ransone, Jr., *The Office of Governor in the United States,* University of Alabama Press, 1956, p. 4.
14. Alaska reverses these responsibilities. In Nebraska the supreme court tries impeachment cases. During this century, four governors have been impeached, convicted, and removed from office.
15. Oregon was the first state to provide for the recall in 1909. Since then it has been adopted in Alaska, Arizona, California, Colorado, Idaho, Kansas, Louisiana, Michigan, Nevada, North Dakota, Washington, and Wisconsin.

eleven states provision is made for some other state official, most often the president of the senate,[16] to take over the responsibilities of the governorship in case of a vacancy. Vacancies may be "permanent" in case of death, resignation, or removal; or they may be "temporary" because of illness or short periods of absence from the state. Although determination of when the governor is "temporarily absent" from the state within the meaning of a constitutional provision may cause some occasional inconvenience, the major difficulties relate to the matter of disability.[17] In no state is the term defined in detail by constitutional or statutory provisions. When is a governor sufficiently disabled to warrant the assumption of his duties by someone else? For how long should such disability continue before the governor's duties devolve upon some other officer? Who is to decide these questions of degree and time? The laws of most states neither answer these questions nor provide machinery to do so. Instead, reliance must be placed upon informal arrangements that are subject to abuse.

The constitutions of only a few states deal with the matter of deciding disability. In California the supreme court is empowered to make a determination. In Mississippi the Secretary of State may submit the question of gubernatorial disability to the state supreme court. In Michigan such action may be set in motion by request of the president pro tempore of the senate and the speaker of the house. In each state the court determines disability without assistance from criteria set forth by law. The New Jersey constitution is a bit more specific. It provides for the adoption of a concurrent resolution by two-thirds of the membership of each house of the legislature stating that a vacancy exists in the office of the governor on any of these grounds: (1) failure by governor-elect to qualify for office within six months of his election; (2) continuous absence from the state for six months; and (3) continuous inability to discharge the duties of office "by reason of mental or physical disability." After a hearing on such a resolution, the supreme court may declare the governor's office vacant. The Alabama Constitution provides that the question of "unsoundness of mind" of the governor may be presented to the state supreme court for determination. No guidance is provided, however, for determining disability on any other basis.[18]

16. Tennessee is unique. There the speaker of the senate, who is the governor's immediate successor, is designated by statute as lieutenant governor. In Alaska, the secretary of state functions as lieutenant governor.

17. Only the Alabama Constitution provides a definition for the term "temporary absence." It specifically states that the lieutenant governor may assume the powers and duties of the governor after the chief executive has been absent from the state for 20 days. The constitution of Alaska refers to "temporary absence" and further provides that whenever the governor has been absent for six months, the office shall be considered vacant.

18. In Oregon a board composed of the Chief Justice of the Supreme Court, the Superintendent of the State Hospital, and the Dean of the Medical School may examine the governor if there is reason to believe any incapacitation. Upon unanimous finding that the governor is unable to discharge assigned duties, the next in line becomes governor. In Nebraska similar authority is lodged with a committee consisting of the Chief Justice of the Supreme Court, the Director of the Nebraska Psychiatric Institute, and the Dean of the College of Medicine.

NATURE OF THE EXECUTIVE FUNCTION

Like the President of the United States, a governor's success or failure is measured more in terms of programmatic achievements rather than performance as an administrator. A governor is expected to have a "social conscience" and to provide solutions insofar as possible to the problems that plague the state. A governor is besieged by demands from many quarters to exert leadership potential—from the people, from the legislature, from the party, and from the bureaucracy. However, governors who attempt to meet the problems of their state as they see fit may be rewarded with defeat at the polls. Thus a governor who is convinced that the solution for the fiscal difficulties troubling the state lies in tax increases and uses all available resources in an effort to obtain them may alienate a sufficient number of voters to spell success for an opponent in the next election. In this way limits on gubernatorial tenure may increase the governor's ability to provide policy leadership without concern for re-election.

Even in the formal sense, the "executive function" encompasses a wide variety of duties and activities. Included are those tasks imposed upon the governor by law, such as "seeing that the laws are faithfully executed," presenting proposals to the legislature, signing or vetoing bills, and granting pardons. There are also many informal activities that are time-consuming and may be trivial, such as making speeches on many and varied occasions, making radio and television appearances, dedicating public works of all types, giving personal interviews to friends and constituents, and attending celebrations, festivals, rodeos, expositions, and so forth. Every governor spends long hours each week attempting to perform the many duties required and expected, although the amount of time varies, depending on the personality of the individual incumbent and the laws and customs of the state.

The formal responsibilities or powers of a governor are commonly divided for purposes of description into three major categories: executive, legislative, and judicial. Although such a combination of powers in the hands of one person is contrary to a strict application of the doctrine of separation of powers, practical considerations have made it necessary in the state governments as well as in the national government.

Execution of the Laws

The basic legal responsibility of the chief executive of any governmental unit is normally reflected in a phrase in the fundamental law to the effect that "the laws be faithfully executed." Although the division of responsibilities among various constitutional officers characteristic of our states makes it difficult for governors to perform this task, every incumbent has certain specific powers designed to assist in fulfilling this goal. For purposes of analysis it is possible to isolate and describe devices or techniques commonly used by governors in their efforts to *supervise* the administration of state affairs. At the same time it must be recognized that these techniques are not used in a vacuum. Personal and political considerations often determine when they are to be used, if at all, and in what manner they should be applied.

Appointment and Removal. Appointment and removal of principal subordinates are of major importance in guaranteeing that the affairs of a governmental unit are managed in accord with the wishes of the chief executive. Often a governor, honestly striving to improve the administration of a particular program, is frustrated because the head of a major department or agency has been chosen in some manner, perhaps by popular vote, that places that officer beyond gubernatorial control. Where the authority to make appointments is lodged with the governor, senatorial approval usually is required, an arrangement generally considered to be advisable.[19] Very rarely does a governor possess authority in this regard nearly comparable to that vested in the President of the United States. In many states the governor appoints a great variety of subordinate officers, often members of boards and commissions, as provided by statute. Such appointments, however, may not appreciably increase the supervisory authority of the governor.

Restricted as it is, the typical governor's power of appointment extends to appreciably more officers than does the power of removal. Few state constitutions grant the governor a general power of removal. Inclusive grants are found in Missouri, New Jersey, and Alaska, while in most states the governor may remove most officers only if there is "cause." In a few states removals as well as appointments are subject to senatorial approval. Rarely does a governor become sufficiently desperate to use methods like those employed by Governor Eugene Talmadge of Georgia in 1933. Unable to "remove" certain members of the Highway Board with whom he was in serious disagreement, Governor Talmadge invoked martial law and had the chairman and another member escorted from their offices by members of the National Guard. The governor then appointed two persons to take their places. Efforts by the ousted members to obtain redress through the courts proved unsuccessful.

The Budget. In the following chapter, emphasis will be placed on the importance of control over the budget as a means by which a governor may implement his executive responsibilities. However, brief attention should be directed to the budget at this point. Governmental agencies, like private enterprises, can accomplish very little without money. Personnel must be hired and matériel purchased. Consequently, the program

---

19. The requirement found in a few states that gubernatorial appointments must be approved by both houses of the legislature is unnecessarily cumbersome.

of an agency will be vitally affected by those persons whose hands are on the purse-strings. In most states today the governor is responsible for preparing an annual or biennial budget for submission to the legislature. Although the legislature usually has complete authority to make any changes it deems best with regard to appropriations made available to individual agencies, recommendations by the governor should and usually do carry great weight. The governor may be able to persuade the legislature that the program of one agency should be cut back while that of another is enlarged because of changing needs of the state or because of fiscal necessity. The conviction that a particular program is of special importance to the state may result in an increased allocation of funds. Although unable to appoint or remove the head of an agency, the governor may vitally affect its program in this way, and those wishes cannot safely be ignored.

Reports. The governor is empowered to require written reports to be submitted by officers in various administrative agencies either regularly or irregularly. Although such authority is normally considered to constitute a means by which a governor may implement responsibility to see that the laws are faithfully executed, it may be largely a matter of form. Usually, no means exists to guarantee that reports will be anything more than routine, perfunctory statements. Even if the governor is not satisfied with the contents of a report, it cannot be changed. In fact, the practice of sending to the chief executive reports that are too voluminous and too frequent may complicate problems of supervision.

Formulation of Policy

It has become fashionable to refer to governors as "chief legislators," an appellation that would have aroused much unfavorable reaction several generations ago. Indeed, the governor's major concern seems to be shaping the policies of the state government. In most states the people expect the governor to have "a program" and to use the necessary powers and influence to see that it is realized. The degree to which a governor is expected to influence the legislature to translate a program into law differs from state to state. The great importance of the chief executive in determining "public policy" in the sense of vitally affecting the law-making process should be appreciated by all students of state government. A governor's role in policy formulation or determination encompasses far more, however, than relations with the legislature. In this regard special emphasis should be given to relations between the governor and other groups—namely, the public, personnel in the executive branch, and political parties.

Relations with the Legislature. The laws of each state provide for certain specific, formal procedures through which a governor is empowered to affect the deliberations and actions of the legislature. These formal or "constitutional" procedures are usually classified into three major categories: presentation of messages, calling special sessions, and use of the veto.[20] In many of the early state constitutions framed in the eighteenth century provisions were included authorizing governors to recommend programs to legislatures. The general feeling at the time seems to have been that such authority was merely permissive and imposed upon governors no obligation to prepare a program for presentation. In recent times the trend has been to look upon this task as an obligation, a development caused in part by the popular election of many able individuals as governors.

Today governors customarily present a message to their legislatures at the beginning of each regular session. Such a message is designed to "orient" the legislators with regard to the condition of the state, major problems, and executive proposals designed to meet the needs of the state. These messages may also point with pride to recent accomplishments of the administration, particularly if the administration and a majority of the members of the legislature are of the same party. In most states the general messages are soon followed by a budget message, which is usually much more significant in its effect on governmental policy. Special messages may be sent at intervals and on various topics at the governor's discretion.

Each state constitution empowers the governor to call special or extraordinary sessions of the legislature. This power usually rests exclusively with the governor, but in a few states, particularly in recent years, members of the legislature have been empowered to call special sessions. In a few states the governor is required to call a special session when requested to do so by a certain proportion of the membership of the legislature. The legislature in special session may be limited to consideration of items specified by the governor or the range of permissible topics may be unrestricted entirely or limited by the constitution to such matters as impeachment and examination of state accounts. Recently, governors have called special legislative sessions most often to consider financial matters.

The governors of all states except North Carolina are granted the veto power by their respective constitutions. Although this power is viewed by some students of state government as the most significant legislative power possessed by governors, it is most often used only after other methods, formal and informal, have proved to be unavailing. Where the veto power exists, a governor has three courses of action available: sign the bill, veto it, or do nothing. If the bill is signed, it becomes law im-

20. Although in nineteen states the governor may adjourn the legislature upon failure by the two houses to agree on a time for adjournment, this power has been of no consequence in affecting executive-legislative relations.

mediately or at some future date specified in the act. If the veto is applied, the governor must return the bill to the house of its origin along with the objections to it. In all states the legislature may override the veto, a course of action requiring some extraordinary majority in most states— usually two-thirds of the members of each house. The consequences of no gubernatorial action vary among the states. All governors are allowed a specified period of time in which to decide what they wish to do. In all instances absence of gubernatorial action within the designated time results in a bill's becoming law *if* the legislature remains in session. Adjournment of the legislature before expiration of the alloted time may result in the death of the bill because of gubernatorial inaction, in which case it is said that the "pocket veto" has been applied. On the other hand, in some states the bill still becomes law unless it is formally vetoed.

The governors of forty-four states possess the "item veto," empowering them to veto portions of bills and approve the remainder. This power is often restricted to appropriation bills and is generally favored as a means of allowing the governor to delete excessive or otherwise undesirable appropriations. Its existence may encourage legislators to approve for political reasons items of appropriation which they know the governor will veto, thereby diverting from themselves and to the governor the displeasure of persons who would have benefited from the appropriations. In a few states governors may reduce items according to their discretion.

In an effort to measure the strength of governors with relation to their respective legislatures, studies have been made of the degree of success experienced by governors in the use of the veto power. It appears that on the whole governors have been quite successful, increasingly so in recent years. The low percentage of vetoes overridden in recent times (averaging about two percent) testifies to gubernatorial restraint in the use of the device and to legislative reluctance to override executive disapproval. Of course, the usefulness of the veto power cannot be measured in this manner with complete accuracy, because such figures cannot reflect possible effects produced on legislation by a *threat* of veto. Legislators are often informed that the passage of a particular bill in a certain form will result in its veto. Although no information is available to measure the effectiveness of this practice, it is an important aspect of the veto power.

Relations with the Public. Although the proportion varies from state to state, every governor must spend a great deal of time in activities that may be characterized as "public relations." Public appearances, press conferences, interviews, and correspondence with private citizens play an important role in the lives of governors. Basically, such activities are designed to build public support, and they constitute an important aspect of gubernatorial efforts in regard to the formulation as well as the execution of public policy.

Studies of the routine activities of governors indicate that the typical governor devotes about half of each day to conferences and interviews, exclusive of press conferences. Most persons conferring with the governor may be placed in one of three categories: administrative personnel, legislators, or the public. When a state legislature is in session, the governor normally meets with a number of legislators each day. Often the chief purpose of these conferences is to enable the governor to explain his or her viewpoint and wishes concerning matters before the legislature. Governors may solicit the support of a particular legislator for their program, or they may talk "strategy" with legislative leaders. On the other hand, a legislator may seek clarification of the chief executive's position on a certain matter or attempt to enlist support in behalf of some program or project.

Viewed generally, governors of the smaller or less populous states maintain more of an "open-door" policy toward the public than those of the larger states. Although in accord with democratic traditions, such a policy seriously diminishes the time the governor has left to attend to the state's business. The more time that must be spent with department heads and other administrators, the less remains for other activities. Citizens are often unreasonable in the demands they make. They feel that they have a "right" to an audience with the governor, who in turn has an obligation to acknowledge their social call or to help them with their personal problems. Great care must be exercised lest the belief become widespread that a citizen is likely to receive a "brush-off" in the governor's office. When it is not necessary or feasible to permit an audience with the chief executive, some member of his staff must be prepared to care for the visitor. Failure to make such arrangements will impair efforts to obtain public support for policies and programs advanced by the governor.

An important aspect of public relations concerns gubernatorial efforts to develop public opinion favorable to certain programs and practices. The governor who is convinced of the need to improve educational facilities in the state or to emphasize rigid enforcement of traffic laws will need public support. Particularly if the legislature has indicated opposition to appropriating more funds for the support of education, for example, effective development of public favor for an improved program will be essential. Governors who are able to persuade the people to bring pressure on the legislature in behalf of their proposals possess a very powerful weapon in dealing with that body. Because this approach to obtaining cooperation is resented by some legislators, it is often used as a last resort. Appeal to public sentiment may be made *in advance* of legislative consideration and thus pave the way for favorable action without creating the impression of attempting to "bludgeon" the legislature.

A favorable climate of public opinion may be created as a by-product of routine activities not specifically designed for that purpose, such as press conferences, correspondence, speeches, and appearances at functions of all types. A governor's conduct at press conferences may be quite significant. A governor who is pleasant and forthright in providing answers to questions from reporters will probably receive a "good press," a consideration of no small significance in view of the importance of the media in affecting public opinion. Some governors hold as many as two press conferences a day, while others hold as few as one or two a week. Governors generally recognize the importance of speeches and appearances throughout their states and spend a considerable portion of their time meeting demands of this kind.

Relations with Personnel in the Executive Branch.   Although governors commonly do not possess legal authority adequate to control the activities of many persons generally considered as their subordinates, they must engage in a certain amount of *supervisory* activity over a large number of state functions. Often the difficulties and handicaps involved are very discouraging, and the governor must resort to "coordination by persuasions." Although the governor may be unable to control them, department heads should keep in close contact with the chief executive, a goal achieved in some states by regular "cabinet" meetings. Such meetings may be attended by all department heads and perhaps certain other important persons designated by the governor. Sometimes, however, they are composed of only selected individuals in whom the governor has special confidence. Such a practice is not conducive to cooperation on the part of those of comparable rank and responsibilities who are excluded. Some type of cabinet arrangement exists in about three-fourths of the states.

A governor's position in the party affects in many ways relations with persons in the executive branch. In most circumstances where cooperation is being sought from executive and administrative personnel, it is important for the chief executive to refrain from emphasizing partisanship. A nonpartisan approach is more likely to secure the desired results by stressing the importance of getting the work effectively done for the benefit of all of the people of the state. Such an approach seems particularly important in those states with strong civil service or merit system programs and high-level administrators chosen on the basis of competence in specific fields. In the remaining states emphasis on partisanship is no longer as strong as it once was, even in those often designated as "one-party" states. More and more persons in the public service are adhering to the view that partisanship has little or no place in *carrying out* or *administering* public policy. It is perfectly legitimate for the governor to seek the advice of other party members on policy matters that are or are likely to become partisan issues. Indeed, failure to do so will result in the accusation that the governor is trying to run the state's business in a "dictatorial" manner.

Relations with Political Parties. Although very difficult to describe or assess, the role of a governor in relation to political parties is highly important. Often a governor is referred to as "leader" or "head" of his or her party. Such a title may or may not be accurate, depending on local circumstances. In the "one-party" states, where the governor may represent only the dominant faction within a party, the governor's efforts must be directed toward building support inside the party with an eye to fending off opposition from within rather than from another party. Even in those states characterized as "normally" Democratic or Republican, governors often represent a dominant intraparty faction. Due to the existence of actually or potentially effective opposition in these states, governors must seek support both inside and outside their parties. Whenever the governor is of one party and the majority in the legislature of another, the need for biparty support is particularly acute. In "two-party" states when the governor and the legislative majority are of the same party, the chief executive becomes the leader of the party in the effective sense.

Even in this last set of circumstances, gubernatorial leadership may be more apparent than real. An individual seldom becomes governor without incurring extensive political obligations. Sometimes governors are "put into office" by powerful groups or cliques, which then seek to advance their ideas and purposes through the chief executive. Even where no such relation exists, governors may be committed to foster the wishes of those who contributed effectively to their election. Nevertheless, the honor and prestige associated with the *office* itself will inevitably gain for the incumbent respectful attention from many persons.

Military Powers

In every state the governor is commander-in-chief of the militia or National Guard unless it has been "nationalized" to enforce national law and prevent violence.[21] When the President "calls up" a state unit of the National Guard, it ceases to be under state jurisdiction and becomes an integral part of the military forces of the United States. In times of unusual occurrences like riots and natural disasters, a governor may call out the state Guard to maintain law and order and generally to assist in restoring normalcy. In such circumstances the Guard usually functions to assist civil agencies, but the governor may see fit to declare martial law and supplant civil authority with military. On rare occasions a governor has resorted to use of military powers to accomplish purposes apparently not contemplated by provisions of either the state constitu-

---

21. Although legally responsible, the governor does not normally assume direct command, a task performed by an adjutant-general who reports to the governor.

tion or statutes.[22] The United States Supreme Court has indicated that the national Constitution imposes certain restrictions on the free exercise of military power by a state governor.[23]

Judicial Powers

Governors exercise a variety of powers of a judicial nature, including the granting of pardons, commutations, reprieves, paroles, and authorizing rendition (extradition). With the exceptions of parole and rendition, these actions are usually referred to as "executive clemency." A *pardon* is a release from the legal consequences of a crime. Sometimes conditions are attached to a pardon; if the recipient violates them, the pardon is void. Although legal responsibility for granting pardons is vested solely in the governor in over half of the states, an advisory board empowered to hold hearings and make recommendations to the chief executive is frequently provided. In some dozen states executive pardons may be granted only with the concurrence of some agency like a pardon board. In an equal number of states the pardoning power is vested in a board of which the governor is a member. In a few states, authority to grant pardons has been removed entirely from the governor's hands. The power to grant pardons, wherever located, is usually unrestricted except that in most states it may not be applied until after conviction, and in some it may not extend to cases involving treason and impeachment.

A *commutation* is a reduction in sentence. Through the exercise of this power a governor may, for example, change a sentence from death to life imprisonment. The power to commute sentences is less widely vested in governors than other acts of executive clemency. A *reprieve* is a postponement in the execution of a sentence, usually for a period of a few hours or as much as thirty days. Such a delay is normally granted to allow time for an additional appeal to the courts because of the discovery of some new evidence or grounds for appeal not previously ruled upon by the judiciary.

A *parole* is a conditional release of a person who has served part of the term for which he or she was sentenced to prison. Paroles constitute a regular, integral part of the law enforcement process, and they are often not considered as acts of executive clemency. Where governors do not share the legal responsibility for granting paroles with some sort of board, they usually accept the recommendations of some such agency. Investigation of the records of persons eligible for parole is a difficult and time-consuming task, one in which no governor should be required to parti-

---

22. See especially Robert S. Rankin, *When Civil Law Fails*, Duke University Press, Durham, N.C., 1939. For example, in 1934 Governor Long of Louisiana ordered the militia to seize the voting lists in New Orleans in order to assure the triumph of his political machine in an election.
23. *Sterling* v. *Constantin*, 287 U.S. 378 (1932).

cipate in any way. *Rendition* or *extradition* involves the return of fugitives from justice to the state where they have been accused of a crime by order of the governor of the state to which they have fled. Although governors seldom refuse to "deliver up" such a person as provided by the U.S. Constitution, it is their responsibility under federal law to review each such request and decide on the course of action to be taken.[24] A governor may spend long hours hearing arguments on both sides before a decision is made, an action that is definitely judicial in nature.

OTHER EXECUTIVE OFFICERS

Responsibility for administration of the affairs of the states is scattered among a number of officers who are commonly independent of the governor as a result of popular election or appointment by a board. They bear a large share of the responsibility for carrying on the day-to-day work required by law and expected by the people. No examination of the executive function can afford to overlook them. Included in this group are the lieutenant governor, secretary of state, treasurer, attorney general, superintendent of public instruction and auditor.

Lieutenant Governor

The office of lieutenant governor, which exists in forty states,[25] is sometimes referred to as a "fifth wheel." To some it seems rather difficult to justify the office in view of the relatively unimportant duties traditionally assigned to it. In about two-thirds of the states, the lieutenant governor presides over sessions of the state senate. Otherwise, the lieutenant governor "stands by" in case the governor should die, resign, be disabled, be removed, or be temporarily absent from the state. Occasionally, they are assigned minor duties like *ex officio* membership on certain boards, but such duties could easily be performed by someone else.

In a few states (especially Colorado, Illinois, and New Mexico), lieutenant governors have informally assumed the duties of an *ombudsman.* In recent years in the United States, increasing attention has been given to this Swedish innovation, an office that exists to promote fair and efficient administration in the public service. When an aggrieved citizen contacts the governor's office with a complaint, the usual practice is to refer the matter to the agency in question for investigation and reply. For obvious reasons, this procedure is not always satisfactory. Where an

---

24. In *Kentucky* v. *Dennison,* 24 How. 66 (1861), the U.S. Supreme Court ruled that the obligation to render a fugitive is a moral one that a governor cannot be compelled to perform.
25. In Tennessee the speaker of the Senate is *ex officio* lieutenant governor. Alaska's secretary of state functions as lieutenant governor.

ombudsman exists, the person holding this position functions as an intermediary between the citizen and bureaucracy to facilitate the handling of complaints. In light of the critical view of bureaucracy widespread in this country, it is remarkable that the office of ombudsman has not been more widely established.

The major argument in behalf of a lieutenant governor is that by electing one the people directly choose the person first in line to succeed the governor. (Nearly half of the states now provide for "team election" of the governor and lieutenant governor.) The same goal may be achieved by designating a specific state officer chosen by popular vote, like the secretary of state, as first in line for the position of chief executive. Such an arrangement exists in Alaska, Arizona, Oregon, Utah, and Wyoming, five of the states having no lieutenant governor. In the other five states without a lieutenant governor—Maine, Maryland, New Hampshire, New Jersey, and West Virginia—the president of the senate serves as the governor's successor. Since in these states each senate chooses its own president, that body determines the individual who may have to assume the responsibilities of chief executive.

Secretary of State

The office of secretary of state is found in every state, and incumbents are popularly elected in all but ten.[26] The typical secretary of state's office performs a great variety of functions, most of them ministerial and routine in nature. The nature of the functions must not be allowed to obscure their importance, however. A brief examination of some responsibilities of secretaries of state reveals their day-to-day value to state government.

Secretaries of state are, first of all, keepers of the archives, custodians of public documents like acts of the legislature and proclamations of the governor, which must be filed and maintained in a manner to make them accessible to persons wishing to use them. They also keep the state seal used to authenticate many public documents. They record descriptions of land owned by the state. An important task commonly lodged with the secretary of state involves the supervision of elections to see that legal requirements are met. Many persons, when they go to the polls on election day, fail to realize the great amount of preparation that has been required. State election laws may impose upon the secretary of state responsibility to see that nominating as well as initiative, referendum, and recall petitions have been properly filed and the required number of valid signatures obtained. Commissions of election and appointment to various state offices also emanate from the secretary of state.

26. The ten states in which choice is made by appointment are Delaware, Maine, Maryland, New Hampshire, New Jersey, New York, Pennsylvania, Tennessee, Texas, and Virginia. In Hawaii the lieutenant governor functions as secretary of state in relation to certain activities.

In many states certificates of incorporation as well as automobile and drivers' licenses are issued by the secretary of state's office. Regularly, the collection and publication of a variety of data and statistics on state government in the form of a manual or "Blue Book" is another responsibility of the office. The secretary of state is also commonly custodian of certain state buildings and may serve on various boards and commissions—some important and others insignificant. In a few states the secretary of state has certain audit functions.

State Treasurer

Treasurers, who are popularly elected in most states, have the important responsibility to act as custodian of state funds and to pay them out on proper authority. Usually they possess discretion with regard to the selection of banks that will act as depositories of state funds. Treasurers are sometimes required to collect certain taxes, but the responsibility for custodianship extends to practically all state revenue. As in the case of the secretary of state, the importance of treasurers in most states cannot be measured solely in terms of the duties they are required by law to perform. Treasurers are usually well-known figures in the state and have considerable political influence. They are often re-elected for several terms, and as a consequence their opinions, especially with regard to financial matters, are sought and respected. Furthermore, the office may be a steppingstone to the governership.

Attorney General

The attorney general, a state's chief legal officer, is popularly elected in most states. It is usually the duty of this office to prosecute and defend cases to which the state is a party. The attorney general is also supposed to serve as the legal adviser to the governor, various state agencies, and to the legislature. In a few states, attorneys general provide bill-drafting services for members of the legislature. In many states they also exercise supervisory responsibilities over local prosecuting attorneys. These and similar tasks require a large staff, particularly in the more populous states.

Providing legal advice for officers and agencies of a state is an important duty, although it may sound somewhat casual. In order for laws to be administered, they must be interpreted. Although a few agencies have their own legal staffs because they must constantly construe the law in order to perform their duties, the great majority of state officers rely on the attorney general to inform them as to what they may and may not do within the framework of the law. In order to facilitate this responsibility, each attorney general regularly issues a series of volumes of "Opinions of the Attorney General" to which personnel in state government and private citizens may refer in order to determine the meaning of various constitutional and statutory provisions, particularly when specific issues have not been adjudicated by the courts. The importance of these opinions is emphasized by the fact that most of the issues "decided" by them are never reviewed by the courts.

An opinion of the attorney general is seriously weakened when a contrary decision is rendered by any court of record in the state and is voided by such a decision from the state supreme court. Until a specific question has been decided by the courts, any public officials who take action contrary to opinions rendered by the state's chief legal officer are following a perilous course of action, possibly subjecting themselves to civil suit or even criminal prosecution. On the other hand, since these opinions do not actually have the force of law, administrators may find themselves in difficulty as a consequence of following them. If the issue is a serious one, the best course of action is to seek judicial construction of the law.

Another important responsibility of the typical attorney general's office is the conduct of investigations. Either upon their own motion or as a result of a request by the governor or some other high state official, attorneys general may investigate the manner in which a state agency is doing its job to determine whether the law is being observed. If they find that it is not, legal action may be instituted against responsible persons. If an investigation does not uncover derelictions that may serve as a basis for prosecution, it may bring to light certain "shady practices" that are contrary to ethical conduct. The consequences for those involved may be serious, administratively and politically if not legally. Also, the attorney general may decide to look into crime conditions, either state-wide or in certain localities. Energetic action on the part of the attorney general with regard to the suppression of crime will greatly hamper the activities of lawless elements, and it will sometimes serve to embarrass other law-enforcement agencies because of the light shed upon their laxity.

Superintendent of Public Instruction

Although public education has been traditionally viewed in this country as primarily a responsibility of local government, the states have played an increasingly important role in supervising and financing this important activity. Today all states have a superintendent of public instruction or comparable official, and in about half of them the individual is popularly elected. Contrary to the practice with regard to other officials discussed, it is common for the superintendent to be elected without reference to party affiliation. Responsibilities of this officer include apportioning state school support funds, certifying teachers, accrediting schools, developing curriculum requirements for primary and secondary schools, preparing lists of approved textbooks, and supervising programs of special education such as vocational training and education for exceptional children. Also, superintendents of public instruction often render opinions to local school districts interpreting state laws governing the administration of education. Since these laws are voluminous and highly technical, such action greatly reduces the amount of formal litigation required to settle points of law.

Auditor

Auditors perform a variety of functions in state governments. Traditionally a major responsibility of auditors has been to authorize the payment of obligations—the task of preaudit that belongs, more properly, with a comptroller who determines the legality of proposed expenditures and the availability of funds prior to incurring obligations. About three-fourths of the states now provide for comptrollers, and in those states the auditor is primarily concerned with the postaudit.[27] The chief purpose of the postaudit is to determine the fidelity and legality of expenditures after they have been made. This is a large and important task in every state today, and many experts in fiscal administration agree that it should be performed by someone responsible to the legislature, although auditors are elected in some thirty states.

Other State Officers

A number of other top-level state officers are occasionally elected, including tax commissioners, directors of agriculture, labor commissioners, and public utilities commissioners. However, the more common practice is to have these and similar officers appointed by some authority, most often the governor. The duties usually delegated to these officers are discussed in the following chapters dealing with their respective areas of responsibility.

27. In a few states a limited preaudit is also conducted by the auditor.

Executive Direction and Administration

5

When used to designate one of the three major branches of government in the United States—whether on the national, state, or local level—the term "executive" encompasses a great deal. In fact, virtually all functions not obviously a responsibility of the legislature or the courts are normally considered to be the responsibility of the executive branch. In order for these functions to be carried out, the efforts of many people are required; collectively, they constitute the executive branch. Public school teachers, highway engineers, traffic officers, and technicians who administer civil service examinations illustrate the variety of personnel involved. All such persons are carrying out, or administering, policies that have been determined by responsible authorities. In the words of the state constitutions, they are faithfully executing the laws. Their concerted activities are often referred to simply as "administration."

POLITICS AND ADMINISTRATION

It should not be assumed that the executive function involves only responsibility for carrying out policies that have been determined by some outside authority. Efforts have been made by some American scholars to distinguish administration from other elements of governmental activity. Many persons have accepted the idea that all government responsibilities, perhaps with the exception of the judicial, could be neatly divided between administration on the one hand and "politics" on the other. With some modifications, this concept of an essential dichotomy or separation between politics—the formation of public policy—and administration—its execution—has continued to affect the analyses of government and the beliefs of people in general. In this frame of reference, politics is conceived to encompass those activities involved in the expression of the people's will, while administration is concerned with translating that will into action.

In recent years there has been a noticeable trend away from a separation of the responsibilities of policy-making and those of policy-execution. Indeed, many persons take the position that "administration is a branch of politics." Most critical observers of our governmental system today agree that all its processes are necessarily interrelated, and the executive function encompasses both policy-making and policy-execution.

ORGANIZATION—THE LEGAL FRAMEWORK

In order to achieve any goal or accomplish any purpose, a governmental unit must have organization. As one astute student has observed, organization "is the relating of efforts and capacities of individuals and groups engaged upon a common task in such a way as to secure the desired objective with the least friction and the most satisfaction to those for whom the task is done and those engaged in the enterprise."[1] The task of providing the many services required of state governments has grown tremendously in recent years. As a result, administrative organization in each state has become more complex. A brief examination of the major organizational patterns is in order.

Basic Types of Organization

Some forty years ago A. E. Buck identified three types of state administrative organization that are still useful: (1) the integrated type in which department heads are subject to appointment and removal by the governor; (2) partially integrated states with a number of top-level elective administrators and certain agencies, especially of the regulatory variety, largely independent of the governor; and (3) the fiscal control type where reliance is placed on the ability of the governor to control administration of state affairs to a large extent through supervision of budgetary matters.[2] Any attempt to allocate each of the fifty states to one or the other of these categories would be extremely difficult because many states might reasonably be placed in two or more.

The Integrated Type. A prime example of integrated state governmental structure is found in New Jersey, where the present organization stems from the constitution adopted in 1947. The governor of New Jersey is a chief executive in fact as well as in name. The governor's appointive authority extends directly to the officials who head each of the fourteen departments into which all executive and administrative agencies of the

---

1. John M. Gaus, *Frontiers in Public Administration,* University of Chicago Press, Chicago, 1936.
2. Buck identified a fourth type designated as the commission or plural executive form, which is now of historical interest only.

state have been placed. This arrangement is far different from that found in most states, and the constitutional revision that made it possible was accomplished only after years of effort.

The Partially Integrated Type. Even though organizational details vary appreciably, most states, from the structural viewpoint, are of the second type. In contrast to the New Jersey arrangement, the voters of the "traditional state" elect the heads of a half dozen or more major departments. Consequently, it is impossible for the governor to exercise effective control over their activities. Such officers as the attorney general, the secretary of state, and the treasurer owe their primary allegiance to the voters, and it is entirely possible for them to feel that they have a "mandate" to run their respective offices in a manner contrary to the wishes of the governor. It is true, as noted in the previous chapter, that governors may influence in various ways the policies of departments headed by elective executives, but they cannot be responsible under such circumstances for their actions in any real sense. In partially integrated states, the appointive power of the governor encompasses a great number of officers, boards, commissions, and agencies, most of which are of a subordinate, unifunctional character. These agencies are in a sense responsible to the governor, but their work often is of such a technical or specialized nature and extends to such a variety of subjects that the governor cannot and should not be expected to supervise or coordinate their activities. Each agency possesses extensive autonomy to carry out its responsibilities in a highly independent manner. (See Appendix 4.)

The Fiscal Control Type. The fiscal control type of state administrative organization, unlike those above, is based on considerations not primarily structural in character. The crucial element is the influence exercised by the governor in relation to raising and spending money for state programs. Accordingly, a state may belong in this category and at the same time be wholly or partially integrated.

Who, in the *executive branch* of a state government, has responsibility for determining how much money will be spent during a fiscal period and the manner in which it will be allocated to various agencies and programs? If this responsibility lies primarily in the hands of the governor, the state may be classified as belonging to the fiscal control type. In no state does this task rest entirely with the governor. Without question, the chief legal responsibility for determining expenditures in any state lies with the legislature. In some instances, the voters may partially determine fiscal policy through the initiative or referendum.

The budget is the most important fiscal device through which authority of chief executives on all levels of government has been augmented. Not all states place the duty of preparing the budget in the hands of the governor, although most of them have done so. Once a budget has been formulated, it must go to the legislature for approval. An important reason for the consideration normally accorded an executive budget is the realization by individual legislators that it represents a large amount of work over a considerable period of time by people having intimate knowledge and understanding of state affairs the like of which a legislator can seldom possess. Too much emphasis can hardly be placed on the fact, however, that legislators, as representatives of the people, have the primary responsibility to determine what services shall be provided for the people and how much money shall be spent for them. The existence of a plan already worked out by public officials—a budget—is of inestimable value in accomplishing this task.

REORGANIZATION

Principles of Administrative Organization and Management

In an effort to provide a systematic basis for attempts at structural reorganization, many persons have sought to develop "principles" of administrative organization. Advocates of what may be termed the orthodox view believe that a true *science* of public administration can be developed and applied to problem situations with little concern for the beliefs, attitudes and values of persons closely involved. This viewpoint has prevailed, at least until recently, in the literature of public administration. Such an attitude reflects a conviction that there are certain fundamental principles of general application that must be observed if efficient administration is to be obtained.[3] What are these principles on which so much emphasis has been placed by advocates of structural reorganization? No one has developed a universally accepted list. However, the following series incorporates some of the more widely accepted ideas as they apply to state governments:

1. There should be a hierarchy arranged so as to fix the lines of responsibility and authority for the administration of the various functions and activities of the executive branch. The lines of authority should run from the governor through the department heads and subordinate officers to individual employees.
2. The principal administrative units immediately under the governor, usually known as departments, should be composed of activities

3. See W. F. Willoughby, *Principles of Public Administration,* Johns Hopkins Press, 1927, for one of the earliest significant efforts to develop this idea. For a later statement see Luther Gulick and L. Urwick (eds.), *Papers on the Science of Administration,* Institute of Public Administration, New York, 1937. Skeptical analyses are found in F. W. Coker, "Dogmas of Administrative Reform," *American Political Science Review,* August, 1922; and Harvey Walker, "Theory and Practice in State Administrative Reorganization," *National Municipal Review,* April, 1930.

grouped on the basis of function or general purpose. In this way coordination of activities may be facilitated, and overlapping and duplication may be reduced to a minimum.

3. The number of such departments should be sufficiently small to enable the chief executive to exercise an effective "span of control."
4. The governor should possess executive authority commensurate with his or her responsibilities to the people.
5. There should be staff services adequate to facilitate the exercise of legal authority residing in the hands of responsible officials.[4]

These "principles" are in no sense immutable or applicable to all situations without modification. A principle may be defined as a rule of action; it may also be defined as a fundamental belief. According to one authority:

> Traditional concepts of administrative organization have been characterized as proverbs and myths. They have been called proverbs in order to emphasize that they are not immutable principles. They have been termed myths because they have some value in rationalizing how people should be treated in organization. . . . But whatever name one may give them, there are certain principles, dogmas, tribal beliefs, or rules of action concerning administrative structure and behavior which warrant the respectful attention of students of administration.[5]

The important point is that these principles are little more than "guides" or "signposts" to assist students and practitioners in the field of administration.[6] They are helpful, but they are not sacred.

Hierarchy. Essentially, a hierarchy is a system of persons or things based on rank. Thus the chain of command in a military organization is an excellent example of a rigid hierarchical arrangement. To a considerable degree, hierarchy is conceived in terms of legal relations. The arrangement in traditional state government shows disregard for hierarchy because the governor does not have direct control over those department heads elected by the people. The chain of command is broken.

Those who stress the importance of hierarchy assume that the definite location of more or less complete legal power is a good thing. Many who do not adhere to this assumption are concerned about the old adage that power corrupts. No known method of selecting chief executives guarantees that men and women of great ability, good faith, or even honesty will always be chosen. People of superior ability and quality have commonly

4. This list is an adaptation of the compilation in John M. Pfiffner, *Public Administration,* Ronald Press Co., New York, 1946, p. 65.
5. John M. Pfiffner and R. V. Presthus, *Public Administration,* Ronald Press Co., New York, 1953, p. 170.
6. See Dwight Waldo, *The Administrative State,* Ronald Press Co., New York, 1948, especially Chapter 9.

been elected as governors of the states, but there have been a few notable exceptions. No thoroughly satisfactory answer exists for those who fear serious consequences that would result if an individual motivated chiefly by desire for personal power were chosen chief executive in a state where the governor had nearly complete control over all top-level executives responsible for the administration of the affairs of the state.

Functional Grouping. The second principle reflects what has been termed the "dominant dogma of the professional group in public administration," known as *functional integration*. Over the years, there has been a tendency in the states to create new units to administer newly added programs and activities. These units often have been largely autonomous, partly as a result of the efforts of pressure groups. One consequence of this practice has been duplication and overlapping of functions. Efforts aimed at integration are designed to bring together related activities into a single department or agency, and most students of public administration agree that such reorganization should be based primarily on *purpose*. To illustrate, all those persons concerned with police and public safety would be located in a Department of Public Safety. Examples of persons included in such a department would be criminal investigators, traffic control personnel, crime laboratory technicians and the staff of a police school, as well as clerks, stenographers, messengers, accountants and others required to run the organization.

Span of Control. According to the third principle, consideration must be given to the number of persons directly supervised by a single official. No one possesses unlimited capacity to supervise others. Studies of administration on all levels of government have noted that executives and administrators often have too many people reporting to them. "The psychological conception of 'the span of attention' places strict limits on the number of separate factors which the human mind can grasp simultaneously."[7] Although efforts have been made to determine precisely the limits to which an individual's span of attention or control may extend, no satisfactory formula has been developed. Failure in this undertaking has resulted largely from the fact that many factors involved are not subject to exact measurement. Individual capacity is one variable; the nature of the work is another; characteristics of reporting individuals constitute a third. Professionally trained persons provide more self-direction than those not so trained. If personalities harmonize and work well together, less supervision is required than under circumstances characterized by discord and bickering. If frequent, complex decisions have to be made, supervision is usually more difficult than when tasks are of a simple, routine nature.

7. L. Urwick, "Organization As a Technical Problem," in Gulick and Urwick, *op. cit.,* p. 54.

Authority Equal to Responsibility. In the preceding chapter stress was laid upon the constitutional duty of the governor to see that the laws of the state are faithfully executed. Attention was called also to widespread failure to endow the chief executive with sufficient legal power over other executive officers to implement that responsibility in an effective manner. In order to provide governors with authority commensurate with their responsibility as suggested in principle number four, all the powers discussed in the foregoing chapter must be extended to them plus powers comparable with those of the President of the United States with regard to appointment and removal of subordinates. Chief among the obstacles to the accomplishment of this objective is popular election of subordinate executive officials such as secretaries of state, attorney generals, and treasurers. Election of such officers must be abandoned if this principle is to be observed.

Staff Assistance. In order that the governors may effectively perform their duties, help must be provided. Concern for this need is reflected in principle number five. Few persons question the importance to a chief executive of adequate tools for overall management. The first Hoover Commission maintained that "wise exercise of authority is impossible without the aid which staff institutions can provide to assemble facts and recommendations upon which judgment may be made and to supervise and report upon the execution of decisions."[8] Many efforts have been made to describe the role of staff agencies, and still no complete agreement exists as to their proper responsibilities. There may be many varieties of staff agencies, but as one student of state government has pointed out, "The purpose of the staff agency is to help the governor in effectuating control by giving him information and advice and rendering service."[9] This statement is pertinent whether the particular unit happens to be a budget bureau, a civil service department, a central purchasing agency, a planning commission or a research agency. Sometimes such agencies are referred to as "auxiliary" or "overhead" units, terms which emphasize the idea that staff agencies are supposed to provide *assistance* of one kind or another to officials responsible for carrying out governmental programs.

Use of Boards and Commissions. Some students of public administration would add a sixth principle to the list. Boards and commissions, it is frequently contended, are not suitable for "purely administrative" work and such tasks should not be given to them. A statement by Leonard D. White goes to the heart of the matter: "The 'direct performance of

---

8. The Hoover Commission, *General Management of the Executive Branch,* Government Printing Office, Washington, D.C., 1949, p. 1.
9. W. B. Graves, *American State Government,* D. C. Heath and Co., New York, 1953, p. 359.

work' in a field where major policy and objectives are generally accepted, where standards are well developed, and where the public interest is well defined and broadly recognized, normally calls for agencies managed by a single administrator, especially those concerned with the vital interests of personal and community protection."[10] Assuming the validity of White's analysis, it is difficult to justify a hard and fast rule concerning the "proper" role of boards and commissions. There is general agreement that such agencies may perform a valuable service in areas where inquiries need to be conducted, rules must be made, and disputes resolved concerning the application of law to controversial areas such as public transportation, public utilities, banking, and insurance. In performing such functions boards and commissions are required to make decisions in much the same manner as a court and to issue rules and regulations that have the effect of law. Consequently, they are sometimes termed *quasi*-legislative and *quasi*-judicial agencies. It seems entirely possible, however, for such duties to be performed satisfactorily by an agency headed by a single executive.

The Criterion of Efficiency

In the eyes of many persons, the chief purpose of governmental reorganization is the achievement of a higher degree of "efficiency," although the precise meaning of the term is by no means always clear. Actually, few words in the language of reorganization have such a variety of meanings and implications. It may mean nothing more than a reduction in expenditures, especially when used in conjunction with "economy."[11] Some people are so enamored of the term that they consider efficiency a *goal* of governmental action. This viewpoint is mistaken, for it must be kept in mind that efficiency is not properly viewed as an end in itself; it indicates how well a task is done, not whether it is worth doing.

Probably the most defensible view of efficiency regards the term as descriptive of arrangements and procedures whereby an optimum of "output" is achieved for each unit of "input." Thus an efficient Department of Public Safety would provide the greatest amount of protection possible *for each tax dollar spent*, and an efficient Department of Education would provide the best educational program possible for the

---

10. Leonard D. White, *Introduction to Study of Public Administration*, The Macmillan Co., N.Y., 1955, p. 189.
11. John A. Perkins has made an excellent comment pertinent to this point: "The late Lent D. Upson, veteran of many reorganization efforts on the state and local levels of government, liked to point out, to the consternation of his tax-conscious friends, that better government seldom meant cheaper government. Good government, like good food, good clothes or any other quality article, is likely to cost more money. Because it is efficient, such government is apt to inspire added services. Well-organized administration often begets professional public servants who are not satisfied with either a low standard or a minimum level of public services." "Reflections on State Reorganizations," *American Political Science Review*, June 1951, p. 509.

amount of money invested. Obviously, the efficiency of these services will improve as knowledge of police science and techniques of education advance. Accordingly, efficiency involves the achievement of the optimum results with the minimum expenditures necessary to achieve those results. Stated another way, a method is efficient if it achieves the best possible results with given costs, or if it achieves a given level of results with the lowest possible costs.

Officials responsible for the conduct of public affairs cannot always be guided by a criterion of efficiency equated in terms of costs. A particular practice or course of action may be inefficient according to such a standard, but it may be advisable because it reflects the desires of the people—and a democratic government must be responsive to the public will. If more elaborate school buildings are desired, it is the responsibility of school officials to provide them even though the input may be disproportionate to the output. If the people want twice as many acres of public parks as information in the hands of recreation specialists indicates will be used effectively, the desired acreage should be provided. It is, of course, legitimate for the "experts" to seek to inform the public and in this way modify popular wishes; indeed, such is their responsibility. But once the information has been provided and the arguments heard, popular wishes must prevail.

RESULTS OF REORGANIZATION EFFORTS

Although principles for the guidance of reorganization efforts have been known for some fifty years, very few states have conformed to them. In its outstanding study of reorganization of state governments published in 1950, the Council of State Governments early noted that among states that had undergone partial or "complete" reorganization the great majority still had over twenty major departments and about half of those were under the supervision of boards or commissions.[12] Difficult as it may be to prove that more efficient and economical government has resulted for any appreciable time from efforts at state reorganization, scholars have called attention to certain achievements that should be credited at least in part to the reorganization movement. In those states that have reorganized fairly extensively, the ballot has been shortened as a result of a decrease in the number of elected officials, providing greater opportunity for intelligent voting. Associated with reorganization has been an increasing use of desirable administrative techniques such as modern accounting methods, the merit system, and executive budgets.

In general, an examination of the results of reorganization on the state level should cause neither great satisfaction nor great despair. Ambitious

12. Council of State Governments, *Reorganizing State Government,* Chicago, 1950.

and productive reorganization efforts have been made, for example, in Arkansas, California, Florida, Illinois, Massachusetts, Michigan, Missouri, New Jersey, New York, and North Carolina. Major reorganizations have occurred in nearly half of the states in the last fifteen years. Interest in reorganization appears to have been spurred by the realization that poor structure inhibits the efforts of the state governments to meet the demands imposed upon them.

REORGANIZATION PRACTICE AND POLITICS

Reorganization in practice is a far more delicate matter than reorganization in principle. With reference to the principles of centralization and integration, Clyde Snider observed that they "appear to be basically sound." "But," he adds, "that is not to say that complete reorganization on those principles is the wisest course of action in every state and under all circumstances."[13] His observation is applicable to other principles as well. Experience seems to demonstrate clearly that reorganization for reorganization's sake should not be undertaken. When a particular agency is operating effectively, it probably is best to leave it alone, "even though its organization violates theoretical principles dear to the hearts of 'efficiency experts.'"[14] Such considerations raise the question of how far advocates of reorganization should seek to push their programs. There is no entirely satisfactory answer to this query, and any meaningful answer must emphasize judgment. Compromise usually must play as large a part in a reorganization program as in other proposals involving major changes in public policy. Wisdom may dictate acceptance of "half a loaf," because the alternative may be to achieve little or nothing.

Emphasis on compromise certainly does not mean that all phases of governmental organization and management should not be thoroughly explored. Nor does it mean that those responsible for needed studies and investigations should hesitate to make proposals that they believe will result in more effective government. Once studies have been completed and proposals have reached the political arena, advocates of reorganization must take care. At that point they need to develop as much support and as little opposition as possible. In other words, reformers must be cautious lest their goals be "unrealistic in not meeting the demands of practical necessity, and . . . tend to overemphasize rational objectives at the expense of value and political considerations."[15]

Plans for administrative reorganization often have come to grief because of failure to give due consideration to three basic factors. First among these is the normal suspicion and conflict characteristic of legislative-

13. Clyde F. Snider, *American State and Local Government,* Appleton-Century-Crofts, New York, 1965, p. 293.
14. *Loc. cit.*
15. Pfiffner and Presthus, *op. cit.,* p. 236.

executive relations. Legislators often look upon the executive branch as a convenient place to lay responsibility for all kinds of difficulties and failures, and they may evidence hostility toward proposals designed in any way to strengthen the position of the chief executive. This attitude is motivated in part by a concern that a strengthened executive might in some way reduce the importance of the legislature. A second factor is the usual resistance of groups who fear a possible reduction of their influence over activities of agencies with whose programs they are vitally concerned. Interestingly, reorganization proposals are sometimes opposed on the ground that their implementation would result in an increase of "political" control. Thus a proposal to remove a fish and game division from the control of an independent board and integrate it into a department of conservation may cause sportsmen to cry "politics," because the head of the department would be responsible to the governor. A third significant source of opposition lies inside the administrative organization itself. Those officials and employees whose agencies are affected are likely to oppose new proposals. They fear adverse results, real or imagined, to themselves or to their programs, and they may enlist the assistance of their clientele. Opposition on the part of such people is thoroughly understandable. "Their security is threatened by proposed change—not only job security but the psychological security of familiar ways of doing things."[16]

The Task of Salesmanship

The success of reorganization proposals depends in large measure upon the source from which they come. No matter how wise a suggestion may be, it must be "sold." It should be based upon sound reorganization theory; it must not arouse the suspicions and fears of entrenched, key political figures; but above all, it must emanate from or be supported by individuals who are influential in the determination of public policy.

The "little Hoover Commissions," which have been responsible for many reorganization proposals on the state level, are cases in point. These bodies generally have been composed of able, successful citizens with a strong desire to improve the quality of government in their states; but that fact alone has not been sufficient for success. In addition, political influence has been required. In order to accomplish needed improvements, legislators must be persuaded, and support must be developed among the voters. Accordingly, groups proposing governmental reorganization should not be perceived as having selfish motivations behind their recommendations. If the members of such groups are carefully chosen, the task of salesmanship is immeasurably lightened, and the likelihood of success greatly increased.

Building support for a reorganization effort is both important and

16. *Ibid.*, p. 240.

difficult. Generally, evidence indicates that the greatest degree of success is achieved where reorganization has the active support of the governor. Gubernatorial support alone, however, is not sufficient to guarantee success. Legislative support is vital, and it is wise to have members of the legislature, and perhaps some ex-members, on the reorganization commission. Care must be taken in the choice of these persons, all of whom should have demonstrated an interest in reorganization, although this consideration does *not* mean that they should all be ardent advocates of reorganization. Indeed, wisdom dictates appointment of some individuals who have evidenced skepticism as to the desirability of reorganization. Their doubts facilitate close scrutiny of proposed changes and foreshadow the criticisms that inevitably arise once proposals are made public. One danger inherent in this consideration, however, is that if the opponents of reorganization are members of the legislature who cannot be won over, proposals of the commission may suffer from "built-in" opposition when its recommendations go before the legislature.

An aspect of building support for governmental reorganization concerns the wisdom of organizing groups of citizens to work in behalf of the proposals. This course of action was followed with notable success on the national level in regard to the first Hoover Commission; similar efforts with respect to the second Hoover Commission, however, were not so productive. Perhaps some of the difficulties encountered in implementing its proposals stemmed from recommendations made in the area of governmental *policy*. Placing authority to make policy suggestions in the hands of a reorganization group is of doubtful wisdom.

Responsiveness to Public Opinion

"The administrative state demands results; its god is efficiency. Its efficiency becomes impersonal and knowledge renders it contemptuous of public opinion."[17] This observation is significant; it poses a serious problem that demands consideration by all who are interested in government. Administrators exert great influence on public policy, and the vast majority of them are convinced that their efforts should be exerted in behalf of the public interest. However, administrators often are in a poor position to determine the courses of action best designed to promote the public interest. Their training and experience give them confidence in their own judgment and make them suspicious of persons who do not have knowledge in a particular area of governmental activity. Yet those without such knowledge constitute the mass of citizens who, in the final analysis, must determine what should and should not be done to further the public interest in a democratic society. Many public administrators are unable to act as formal representatives of anyone, particularly if they

17. Francis G. Wilson, *Elements of Modern Politics*, McGraw-Hill Book Co., New York, 1936, p. 393.

are not popularly elected. Those who are so elected must be somewhat responsive to public opinion—at least if they plan to run again for public office in the immediate future. This situation may pose serious problems from the standpoint of effective internal control and direction of administration. Accordingly, Professor Wilson is correct in his assertion that "Up to the present time, a solution of the conflict between democracy and the science of public administration has not been found."[18]

Structural arrangements are important for the administration of public policy in a manner that is efficient and in accord with the will of the people. If these goals are to be realized, *direction* must be given to administrative activities in order that disagreements and conflicts may be held to a minimum. Under circumstances where each popularly elected official is free to choose his or her own courses of action, citizens are often at a loss to determine where praise or censure should be placed. The basic direction of administrative activities must reside in the hands of persons popularly elected, and care must be exercised to locate responsibility in a sufficiently definite manner that the people can know exactly where it rests.

SUNSET LAWS

Since their inception in Colorado in 1977, about three-fourths of the states have adopted "sunset laws" that control the growth of government agencies. These laws, brought into being largely as consequence of the lobbying efforts of Common Cause, have been designed to force legislatures to fulfill their responsibility of overseeing administrative agencies and possibly terminating those that no longer perform a needed function. Sunset laws may require legislative review of most or all state agencies, or they may apply only to relatively minor ones such as licensing boards and regulatory commissions. Usually, the requirement is to review a number of agencies at each legislative session or to examine individual agencies at specific intervals.

Sunset laws not only encourage termination of unneeded agencies, they also may cause agencies to modify their activities in such a way as to enhance their usefulness. Also, legislatures may choose to increase the scope of responsibilities of an agency in order to make it more effective. In any event, legislative review is required.

Thus far the consequences of sunset laws have not been as significant as anticipated by their advocates. Few agencies have been terminated, and they have been mostly small ones that do not have large budgets or powerful clienteles. The amount of time required to undertake thorough reviews imposes excessive demands upon already crowded legislative schedules.

18. *Loc. cit.*

The State Legislature: Organization and Powers

It is a fundamental principle of the American governmental system that all political authority flows from the people. In many New England towns the people still gather to determine the nature and course of local public policy. In some states the public decides on policy items by initiative and referendum. Throughout the country the people make decisions in regard to the nomination and election of public officials. Except for such examples of direct popular action, however, the authority of the American people is exercised through elected representatives.

THE OFFICIAL DESIGNATION

The term *state legislature* is used generally to refer to the legislative bodies in the various states, but it is the official title in only twenty-six of them. Nineteen others designate the legislative body as the *general assembly.* In Massachusetts and New Hampshire the legal name is the *general court;* Oregon, Montana, and North Dakota use the title of *legislative assembly.* The upper house of the legislative branch in each state is known as the *senate,* a term used also to designate the one-house legislature of Nebraska.[1] A variety of titles are used to identify the lower houses although *house of representatives* is most often used. Maryland, Virginia, and West Virginia employ the term *house of delegates,* in California, Nevada, New York, and Wisconsin the title of *assembly* has been adopted. In New Jersey alone the lower house is officially referred to as the *general assembly.*

---

1. Article III, the legislative article of the Nebraska Constitution, does not refer directly to the single house of that state as the Senate. Similarly, the members of the legislature are not specifically designated as Senators. The titles derive from a resolution passed at the first meeting of the legislature in which the members officially adopted the name of "Senate."

BICAMERALISM AND UNICAMERALISM

In 1934 the voters of Nebraska approved a constitutional amendment abolishing their bicameral legislature and replacing it with a body composed of a single house. The first session of the new unicameral legislature, held three years later, marked the first time in over one-hundred years that a state legislature had consisted of a single chamber. Georgia, Pennsylvania, and Vermont had unicameral legislatures upon their entry into the Union, but in 1789 Georgia adopted the bicameral plan, and Pennsylvania followed suit a year later. Only in Vermont, where it persisted until 1836, had unicameralism been in effect for an extended period of time.

The traditional bicameralism of American state legislatures has been defended on various grounds over a long period of years. The merits usually claimed are that bicameral legislatures are less likely to produce hasty, ill-considered laws, that they are less easily controlled by lobbies, that they are less subject to the impact of popular passions and impulses, and that they are in harmony with established institutions and practices. Proponents of unicameralism stress that, aside from the obvious factors of simpler procedures and lower costs, a single legislative chamber attracts more qualified members because of the greater prestige associated with a unicameral body, that responsibility is more easily fixed, that it is easier for the public to follow legislative developments, that better executive-legislative relationships are fostered due to the concentration of leadership, and finally that because of these advantages, lobbies are not likely to influence or control legislative decisions. There is no mass of data on the operation of unicameral legislatures against which to test these claims and counterclaims. The Nebraska experience serves as the best available yardstick, and it is generally conceded that unicameralism has been a success there—but a single example does not provide an adequate basis of evidence for meaningful conclusions.

Support for unicameralism continues to come largely from individuals and groups with a professional interest in the improvement of governmental organization. Political scientists generally favor single-chambered legislatures. The Model State Constitution prepared by the National Municipal League provides for a unicameral body. On the other hand, most persons who serve in, or have formerly served in, state legislatures are opposed to departure from the bicameral system. Perhaps the most important factor to be considered in assessing the desirability of either type of structure is the quality of personnel involved in each, for in the final analysis "no mere institutional device can be substituted for character and intelligence on the part of the body of citizens and of those they elect to public office."[2]

2. Roger V. Shumate, "The Nebraska Unicameral Legislature," *Western Political Quarterly,* September 1952, p. 512.

DESCRIPTIVE FEATURES OF STATE LEGISLATURES

Size

The range in size of state legislatures is impressive. While none of them is equal in size to the United States Congress, a few contain several hundred members. In most states apparently little if any attention is paid to the question of the optimum number of members, if indeed such a number can be determined, for getting the work of a legislature done. The question is probably of slight importance inasmuch as the significant consideration is the ability of the legislature to enact sound policy.

The greatest variations in size occur in the lower houses, ranging from forty members in Alaska to 400[3] in New Hampshire. In general, the largest houses are found in the New England states where the numerous towns serve as election districts. The smallest lower houses generally are found in the western states where approximately sixty to seventy members are not uncommon. In other areas of the country the lower houses of state legislatures contain from 100 to 200 members.

Upper houses, known as senates in all states, do not present startlingly wide variations, although only twenty members sit in the upper houses of Alaska and Nevada, and sixty-seven members compose that body in Minnesota. In one-fifth of the states senate membership numbers thirty or less; in another fifth the figure is fifty or more; in the remaining states the number of members falls somewhere between the two figures. No geographical pattern such as that relating to lower houses is apparent.

Terms

The length of terms served by members of state legislatures does not vary greatly. In every state they are of either two or four years' duration. Senators serve for four years in three-fourths of the states and for half that time in the remainder. Only in the New England area, where senate terms are uniformly fixed at two years, can any regional pattern be noted. Members of lower houses usually are elected to two years of service; only four states—Alabama, Louisiana, Maryland, and Mississippi—set both senate and house terms at four years. In Nebraska's unicameral legislature there is, of course, no lower chamber.

Compensation

Despite the fact that in recent years a few states have provided substantial salaries for their legislators, no public servant in relation to his or her responsibilities is more underpaid. About one-fifth of the states pay salaries in

---

3. This number may vary from 375 to 400 depending upon the number and size of towns eligible to elect representatives.

excess of $15,000 per year. At the other end of the scale, legislators in Rhode Island receive only five dollars per day and in New Hampshire, regardless of the length of the session, legislative labors are rewarded by the sum of $200 per session.

In most of the states, legislators also receive expense allowances that range from a few dollars per day to considerable sums. The states also allow "mileage" costs, that is, reimbursement of expenses incurred in travelling to and from the place of meeting; but a limit may be placed upon the number of trips per member.

Public service is an honor, but in the case of the state legislature it is an honor that many people cannot afford. Consequently, qualified persons who could render distinguished service commonly find it impracticable to seek state legislative offices. Salaries sufficient to prevent personal financial sacrifices have often been suggested, but usually with disappointing results. Although constitutional provisions fixing levels of compensation present obstacles in some states, legislatures usually have authority to raise their own salaries, but on many occasions have been reluctant to do so because of concern for hostile public reaction. To avoid this difficulty the compensation commission is now employed in half the states. These commissions, the first of which was created in Wisconsin in 1965, range in size from five to fifteen members who are appointed to terms as brief as two years or for an indefinite period. In most instances the recommendations made by the commissions are advisory, but in a few states their decisions are final unless overruled by legislative action. Experience seems to indicate that legislative salary increases are more readily achieved with the participation of a compensation commission, but the problem remains one of the most sensitive in state government.

Sessions

Among the perennial problems concerning state legislatures are the questions of how often regular sessions should be held and how long they should last. Well into the twentieth century, most states provided for a single regular session every two years, but the trend in recent decades has decidedly been toward annual sessions. Today, regular sessions of the legislature are held annually in three-fourths of the states. Positive limitations on the length of sessions are found in about half of the states, and in several others legislative salaries stop after a designated period—provisions which have the practical effect of prescribed limits. The range is from comparatively brief periods of thirty days in Alabama and forty days in Wyoming to the approximate six-months maximum permitted in Delaware. However, the most commonly prescribed limitation is sixty days.

Special, or extraordinary, sessions may be held in every state. They are, as the name implies, called for the purpose of considering matters that require immediate treatment. In all states the governor is empowered to call special sessions, and the legislators of about one-third of the states can call themselves together for such meetings. In recent years special sessions have been called frequently, especially in states where regular sessions are held biennially, to deal with a variety of problems, particularly those dealing with taxes and legislative apportionment.

ELECTION OF STATE LEGISLATORS

In a democratic society the people choose many of their public officials. In conformity with this principle, legislators in every state are chosen by popular vote. With some exceptions, the nomination of candidates is also left to the voters in a direct primary.

Every state uses the district system in the selection of members of its legislature. Under such a system the entire territory of the state is subdivided, usually along county boundary lines, into a number of districts. The voters in each district cast ballots for one or more candidates, depending upon the number of positions assigned to the area. Ordinarily, two separate district plans are employed—one for use in the election of members to the lower house, and the other for the selection of senators. Since there are, in every state, fewer senatorial positions than lower house seats, a senatorial district normally encompasses several house districts.

Fixing the boundaries of election districts is a legislative prerogative, a situation that makes gerrymandering possible. Gerrymandering is the process by which the political party with a majority in a legislature prescribes the boundaries of election districts in such a way that as many districts as possible contain a majority of that party's voters. This practice has become increasingly difficult to carry out in recent years, however, because of the constraints placed upon legislatures by judicial decisions in apportionment cases. In some instances population shifts across district lines favor one party over another, and if redistricting is prevented or delayed, the party favored is said to benefit from a "silent gerrymander."

THE STATE LEGISLATOR: QUALIFICATIONS AND CHARACTERISTICS

The men and women who comprise the membership of state legislative bodies are not a class apart from the rest of society. Rather they are representative of most elements of the social structure, even though they are not an accurate cross section of the public they serve. If any one trait distinguishes them from their fellow citizens it is, upon whatever reason based, their interest in government and their desire to serve in public office.

Qualifications

Constitutionally, the conditions placed upon legislative candidates are not restrictive. Legal qualifications set forth in the state constitutions are based on age, citizenship, and residence. In all states a candidate for membership in the lower house must be at least twenty-one years old, and in some states a senatorial aspirant must be several years older. United States citizenship is a universal requirement, as is a prescribed period of state residence. The candidate for legislative office is also required, either by law or by custom to live in the district from which elected. By and large, anyone who qualifies as a legal voter is constitutionally eligible to become a candidate.

While it is a fairly simple matter to meet the constitutional requirements for candidacy, the extralegal qualifications may cause more difficulty. Factors which determine the *political availability* of a person vary from state to state and even among areas within a state. They relate to an individual's vote-getting ability and may be determined by religion, occupation, education, race, personality traits, vindictiveness of political enemies, or any number of other matters. Any one factor, or a number of them in combination, may make it unlikely that a candidate can be elected even though all legal qualifications are met.

Occupational Background

Unlike their counterparts in Washington, D.C., the vast majority of the 7,600 state legislators are not professional politicians. Only a few states pay salaries high enough to enable their legislators to devote most of their efforts to legislative matters. Therefore, when the legislatures are not in session the typical member, like other citizens, is at work earning a living at a chosen profession or trade.

Traditionally, state legislatures have been dominated by lawyers, followed closely by farmers and business people. In recent years, however, business people have sought legislative offices in increasing numbers and now lead all other occupational fields. It is true, of course, that scores of occupational pursuits are represented in state legislative chambers. In addition to the three largest groups, doctors, teachers, laborers, retired individuals, and many others are found. Business people, lawyers, and farmers, however, still occupy most of the seats in the typical state legislative assembly.

Turnover

The percentage of new members at each regular session of a state legislature is extremely high. Usually a lower house will have more new faces, proportionally, than a senate, but of the total membership of all state legislatures combined approximately half are serving their first term. The reasons that state legislators in general do not serve for long periods seem to be the discouragement of low salaries, the insecurity of the positions, and their political instability. Longer periods of service are more frequent in states which offer substantial salaries and in which one party is dominant.

Level of Performance

Probably no public servant is more consistently criticized and castigated than the state legislator. Surely some criticism is deserved, for often a young lawyer or business person seeks the office for the sole purpose of establishing contacts. Or an aspiring politician uses the office as a steppingstone to a higher position. Undoubtedly, some opportunists look upon legislative membership as a means of promoting or protecting selfish interests. At other times poorly qualified persons are elected because the opposition provides such poor competition. Commentators from time to time have lamented the "decay" and incompetence of state legislatures.

Despite admitted shortcomings and obstacles, state legislators do a commendable job. Theirs is a task that requires decisions on matters of tax policy, commerce, industry, agriculture, public health, welfare, criminology, civil rights, conservation, education, law enforcement, public works and a host of other equally vexatious topics. At the same time the handicaps of the short term, niggardly salaries, constant pressure of lobbyists, and threat of executive veto and popular referral limit their freedom of action. Yet, with exceptionally few instances of outright dishonesty and collusion, state legislators generally have lived up to the responsibilities of their offices.

PARTY CONTROL OF LEGISLATURES

American state legislatures are organized on the basis of the party affiliations of their members. Before a legislature begins its session there is little if any doubt as to who will be chosen to fill the Speaker's chair, or who will serve as President of the upper house. Usually, appointees for less important positions also have been informally determined. Party leaders and members, meeting in caucus, reach agreement on such matters before a session convenes, and though party control of members may be lacking with regard to individual bills and even general programs, a legislator does not often desert his party on an organizational vote.

Party control of legislatures generally is not as pronounced in the states as it is in the United States Congress. Whereas the major parties in Washington, D.C., are frequently able to command loyalty to party positions, state parties are less able to do so. In fact, only those states where the two major parties are approximately equal in strength can it be said that parties exert strong controls. The weakest party organizations are found in one-party states, although factions within the dominant party may exercise influence over members.

LEGISLATIVE OFFICERS AND EMPLOYEES

The Speaker

The presiding officer of the lower house of every bicameral state legislature is known as the speaker. The speaker is regularly chosen by the full membership of the house on a partisan basis. Among the powers of the speaker is the authority to appoint members of standing committees. Seniority, party status, and consultation with party leaders figure prominently in the actual selection of committee members, but since speakers must ultimately make the decisions in regard to committee membership, they wield great power. The speaker also has full authority to refer bills to committees. In many instances custom or house rule requires that certain types of bills must be sent to designated committees. Where alternative committees may be chosen, however, the speaker is free to determine whether a bill goes to a favorable or to an antagonistic group. The power of recognition is another important instrument of authority available to the presiding officer of the house. Potentially, at least, the speaker can control debate and thereby increase or diminish the effectiveness of various members. The speaker also interprets and applies rules of procedure. Even though their rulings are usually subject to appeal to the whole membership, astute speakers can, through clever application and manipulation of the rules, profoundly influence the course of legislative action.

The Lieutenant Governor

In forty-two states lieutenant governors are elected by the people, and although they are executive officers they may exercise important legislative functions. In fact, lieutenant governors are constitutionally assigned the function of presiding over the senate in three-fifths of the states. When presiding they exercise the power of recognition, apply and interpret the rules, and have authority to refer bills to committees. The powers and effectiveness of lieutenant governors are diminished, however, by the fact that they may vote only when necessary to break ties.

The President of the Senate

The senate in each of the fifty states except Tennessee and North Carolina selects from its membership an officer known as the president or president *pro tem.*[4] In states where there is no lieutenant governor or that official is not designated as the presiding officer, the president presides over senate deliberations. The authority of senate presidents varies widely across the nation. Where they are second in command, they obviously must share power with the lieutenant governor. The powers of referral, recognition, and rules interpretation are exercised by the officer actually presiding at a particular time, but the authority to appoint committees is variously assigned.

Other Officers and Employees

Each chamber, whether a senate or lower house, also chooses officers to discharge necessary routine functions. Included are a clerk, chaplain, and sergeant-at-arms, whose responsibilities have little, if any, effect upon the course or content of legislation. In addition, numbers of employees are hired to handle clerical, stenographic, and custodial tasks.

THE COMMITTEE SYSTEM

The problems confronting legislatures today are exceedingly numerous and difficult. Few, if any, legislators are competent to decide all questions of public policy. Even if competency were not involved, it is doubtful that a legislative body, operating under parliamentary rules in open debate, would have time to consider more than a minor fraction of all bills that are introduced. It is absolutely necessary, therefore, for a legislature to organize in such a way that it at least has an *opportunity* to perform its job. The organizational pattern employed in all states to realize that opportunity is the committee system.

The standing committees, which are organized on a partisan basis, have long been regarded as the "workhorses" of state legislatures. To them all the bills are referred, and measures receive their closest scrutiny in the committee rooms. Bills may be overhauled completely, amended to various degrees, or as is commonly the case, ignored altogether. Whether a bill is considered by the full membership of a legislative chamber usually depends upon the decision made by the committee to which it was referred.

It is also important to observe that committees are often large and unwieldy and thus subject to control by dominant members. As a conse-

---

4. The term *pro tempore,* usually shortened to *pro tem,* means "temporary." Commonly, the lieutenant governor is termed the president of the senate, and the member elected to preside in his absence is called the president *pro tem.* In states where there is no lieutenant governor, the member chosen to preside is entitled president of the senate. In Tennessee and North Carolina the title "speaker" is used.

quence, a small number of persons, perhaps a subcommittee or a clique led by the chair, might for all practical purposes make decisions for the committee. Because of the obviously unfortunate effects of such a development upon the content of public policy, it is important that citizens have an understanding of the organization, procedures, and problems of the committee system.

Number and Size of Committees

Practically all state legislatures are subject to the criticism that they maintain too many standing committees. While no particular number is best for all legislative chambers, it is generally agreed that a small number of committees with well-defined areas of jurisdiction is best adapted to legislative needs. The value of this arrangement is especially notable in light of the fact that most of the bills introduced during a legislative session are referred to a handful of the most important committees.

In most instances the number of standing committees maintained by a house bears little or no relation to the total number of members. The New Hampshire legislature is about three times larger than that of North Carolina, yet the latter has more standing committees. The lower houses of Florida and Rhode Island are comparable in size, but the former has three times as many committees. Senates, as a general rule, maintain fewer committees than do lower houses.

Use of Joint Committees

With occasional exceptions the gears of legislative machinery turn slowly, and in a great many instances, inefficiently. A prominent factor causing delay is the necessity for independent action by each house of a bicameral legislature. Procedures followed in each house are substantially the same, yet conflicts arise that prevent the effective meshing of house and senate efforts.

Among devices used to save time, effort, money, and tempers is the joint standing committee, a permanent working group composed of members of both houses. Such a committee can greatly reduce the total labors necessary in the consideration of a bill. Today nearly a third of the states maintain one or more joint committees, but only in New England are they fully utilized. In Connecticut, for example, about twenty joint committees function in the place of conventional standing committees in each house. In Maine and Massachusetts the individual houses have retained a few committees, but the great bulk of work is done in cooperative groups. Vermont has kept the usual standing committees, but ordinarily corresponding house and senate groups meet jointly for the consideration of bills.

Selection of Chair

The choice of a committee chair is usually the prerogative of the presiding officer, although they may be selected by a designated committee or by the whole membership of a house. More important than identification of the appointing authority are the factors that influence the actual choice. Admittedly, logic demands that ability should be a prime requisite. In most cases, however, selection is based largely upon party affiliation, seniority, and personal influence. Frequently, capable individuals who qualify on such bases are chosen, but unfortunately current practices do not guarantee able leadership of committees.

Rules of Procedure

Procedure followed by committees vary widely not only from state to state, but often among committees in the same house. Such variations are justifiable in many instances, for not all standing committees have the same tasks and problems. Differences in jurisdiction and workload of committees make uniformity of procedural requirements impractical and undesirable. Committees that consider large numbers of bills obviously need a more clearly defined system of procedures than do those that rarely function. Nevertheless, an obvious need exists widely for some changes.

Foremost among problem areas are a lack of definitely scheduled meetings, failure to publicize public hearings, poorly kept or incomplete records of committee action, and the practice of keeping in committee bills that should be reported out. When committees indulge in such actions and practices, there is danger that the course and content of public policy will be determined less by the legislative membership and more by a faction exercising committee control. A few states have sought to correct abuses stemming from these practices by a reduction in number and size of committees, the use of joint committees, prohibition of closed sessions, and more workable procedures to force bills out of committees.

Research Assistance

The great variety and complexity of matters dealt with in the legislative process make necessary the provision of research and technical assistance. No matter how experienced or competent legislators may be, they cannot, with limited resources, achieve their maximum potential. Most states have set up legislative reference services; legislative councils operate in most states; and interim committees are now widely used. These aids, however, are intended to serve legislative bodies as a whole without specific reference to individual committees.

PRIVILEGES AND IMMUNITIES OF LEGISLATORS

Special privileges enjoyed by members of state legislatures are very limited, those that are granted applying only to conditions of debate and attendance at legislative sessions. Derived from British and American colonial usage, state constitutions provide typically that

> The Senators and Representatives shall, in all cases, except treason, felony or breach of the peace, be privileged from arrest during their attendance at the session of their respective Houses, and in going to and returning from the same; and for any speech or debate in either House they shall not be questioned in any other place.[5]

Obviously, the phrase "except treason, felony or breach of the peace" is sufficiently inclusive of all possible offenses to reduce immunity from arrest to little more than freedom from detention for trivial matters. On the other hand, immunity from prosecution for utterances in debate is broad. Under it legislators can, on the floors of the legislature and in committee sessions, say anything they please, restrained only by legislative rules of procedure governing their conduct and deportment. While there have been instances of abuse, the immunity is easily defensible, for without protection from suits for slander, it is doubtful that free and open debate could be maintained.

THE PROBLEM OF APPORTIONMENT

On March 26, 1962, Justice Brennan delivered an opinion of the United States Supreme Court that was to have a profound effect upon every state legislature in the country. As a direct result of that decision the validity of the apportionment of seats in most legislatures has been challenged in both state and federal courts. In the comparatively few states in which law suits have not resulted, reexamination of apportionment criteria has been occasioned. The decision which brought on this turmoil was *Baker* v. *Carr*,[6] in which the Supreme Court ruled that federal courts have jurisdiction to decide whether a state legislature is apportioned in accordance with constitutional provisions.

The Baker Case

The controversy in the Baker case grew out of the failure of the Tennessee legislature to apportion for sixty years. During that period the

---

5. Constitution of Delaware, Article III, Section 13. Note the similarity, typical of most state constitutions, to the corresponding provision found in Article I, Section 6, of the United States Constitution.
6. 369 U.S. 186 (1962).

population of the state increased about forty-five percent, with most of the gains concentrated in urban areas. The changing character of the population resulted in such inequities under the 1901 apportionments still in effect that in 1960 one-third of the voters elected two-thirds of the legislators. Consequently, a suit was brought by a group of urban voters.

Historically, both state and federal courts have been reluctant to consider questions involving the composition of legislative bodies. The usual judicial response in pre-Baker cases was to follow a self-imposed rule of nonintervention in deference to the political character of reapportionment issues. In other words, the composition of a legislative body was regarded as a political question to be resolved by the legislatures or the voters. The district court in Tennessee which heard the arguments in the Baker case followed this reasoning and dismissed the complaint, although in doing so it expressed doubt as to whether any definite precedent existed in support of a policy of judicial nonintervention.[7]

The decision was appealed to the United States Supreme Court which heard arguments and rearguments for a year and a half before announcing its decision. When it did so, it reversed the lower court, holding that courts have jurisdiction to decide questions involving the validity of apportionments and that previous cases had not established a rule of judicial nonintervention.[8] Within a matter of days, suits were instituted in a number of other states, and many others were in preparation.

The Apportionment Background

State constitutions typically provide for reapportionment every ten years and often contain complicated provisions fixing minimum or maximum allotments per district. Prior to the Baker case, the most serious difficulties in reapportionment arose out of the frequent neglect or refusal of legislatures to fulfill the constitutional obligation to apportion. This problem was relieved in some states by divesting the legislature of responsibility through providing for "automatic" apportionment by a board,

---

7. 175 F. Supp. 649; 179 F. Supp. 824 (1960).
8. In its arguments before the Supreme Court, Tennessee relied heavily upon the case of *Colegrove* v. *Green*, 328 U.S. 549 (1946), in which the court had refused, by a 4-3 vote, to consider whether congressional districts in Illinois were validly drawn. In the majority opinion Justice Frankfurter characterized the issue as one which "must be resolved by considerations on the basis of which this Court, from time to time, has refused to intervene in controversies. It has refused to do so because due regard for the effective working of our government revealed this issue to be of a peculiarly political nature and therefore not meet for judicial determination." It is interesting to note that despite the Colegrove ruling, on two occasions prior to the decision in *Baker* v. *Carr*, federal district courts exercised jurisdiction in apportionment disputes. In fact, *Dyer* v. *Kazuhisa*, 138 F. Supp. 220 (1956), held the Hawaiian territorial legislature invalidly constituted; and in *Magraw* v. *Donovan*, 163 F. Supp. 184 (1958), a federal district court took jurisdiction of an attack on the composition of the Minnesota legislature. Both cases ended inconsequentially, however, because of subsequent reapportionments of the legislatures involved.

court, or executive officer. In one state, Oregon, the initiative was used to achieve a valid reapportionment. Until the Baker decision, however, courts declined to assist in effecting reapportionment.

Underlying the widespread controversy over reapportionment is the clash of rural and urban interests. Allotting seats on the basis of population usually results in shifting control of state legislatures from rural to urban majorities, a move strongly resisted by legislators chosen from rural districts. It is ironic to note that prior to 1920, when the federal census revealed a majority of urban dwellers in the United States, rural primacy in state legislatures was generally consistent with population distribution.

The Population Factor in Apportionment

The Baker decision did not answer the extremely important question of what criteria may be used in reapportionment. The answer to this question was provided in several cases decided the same day in 1964, the principal one of which was *Reynolds* v. *Sims*.[9] In declaring the Alabama apportionment of 1901 invalid, Chief Justice Warren observed that legislators "represent people, not trees or acres," and went on to assert that "as a basic constitutional standard, the Equal Protection Clause requires that the seats in both houses of a bicameral state legislature must be apportioned on a population basis." All other factors were rejected as possible bases of apportionment. Thus, the only valid apportionment is one which accords as nearly as possible with population distribution.

Reactions and Implications

The effects of the Baker and Sims cases were obvious and predictable. Reapportionment of state legislatures on the basis of population alone meant that majorities would be controlled by legislators elected from urban areas. In turn, the character of state political systems was bound to undergo fundamental change, with public policy oriented more toward urban needs. Inasmuch as congressional districts are determined by state legislatures, and must also be laid out in accordance with population distribution, Congress itself would be profoundly affected. Today these important changes have been largely realized. Only in those states having predominantly rural populations, and those in which the economic mainstays are primarily agricultural, have the effects of the Baker and Sims decisions been minimal.

9. 377 U.S. 533, (1964). Several months earlier, in *Wesberry* v. *Sanders*, 376 U.S. 1 (1964), the Court invalidated the statute establishing congressional districts in Georgia. In that decision Justice Black stated that "construed in its historical context, the command of Art. I, § 2, that Representatives be chosen 'by the People in the several States' means that as nearly as is practicable one man's vote in a congressional election is to be worth as much as another's."

POWERS OF THE LEGISLATURE

In the American federal system governmental power is divided between the nation and the states. Under the United States Constitution the national government has such powers as are *delegated* to it, with the remaining powers *reserved* to the states. As stated in the Tenth Amendment, "The powers not delegated to the United States by the Constitution, nor prohibited by it to the States, are reserved to the States respectively, or to the people." The powers reserved to the states are vested largely in the state legislatures, but they do not exercise their powers free from restraint.

Limitation by National Law

Article VI, Section 2, of the national Constitution provides that the Constitution itself, and all laws and treaties made under it, are the "supreme law of the land." Consequently, no state legislative enactment can be contrary to national law and still be valid. Whenever conflicts occur, the national law prevails.

Many specific limitations upon the exercise of state authority are contained in the Constitution. Article I, Section 10, sets forth a detailed list of prohibitions forbidding the states, among other things, to conclude treaties, join alliances, coin or print money, grant titles of nobility, tax imports or exports, or keep troops in time of peace.[10] In other portions of the document additional limitations are imposed. In effect a delegation of power to the national government is, or can be, a limitation, for it may totally pre-empt an area of authority that would otherwise belong exclusively to the states.

State Constitutional Limitations

The fundamental law of a state, the constitution, is the source of numerous restrictions upon, or denials of, legislative authority. Designed to protect certain rights and powers from legislative encroachment and to prevent abuse of legislative authority, the limitations fall into a number of categories. First, all state constitutions contain Bills of Rights—lists of guarantees against infringement of individual rights. Second, constitutions in a third of the states contain initiative and referendum clauses that preserve the right of the people directly to enact or repeal legislation. Third, most state legislatures are forbidden to enact special or local legislation of certain designated types. Usually, a state constitution con-

---

10. The states may maintain troops provided Congress approves. The National Guard serves both as the military organization of the various states and as a component of the armed forces of the United States.

tains a list of prohibitions denying the legislature authority to pass laws that apply to single individuals, groups, or local governments with respect to such matters as granting divorces, changing names, granting franchises, altering the rate of interest, and impaneling juries. The object is to eliminate partisanship and discrimination in individual instances. Fourth, restrictive provisions relating to finance are commonly found in the organic law of a state. Legislatures must levy taxes uniformly, are not permitted to grant tax exemptions except in specified instances, may not borrow money beyond a prescribed limit, cannot appropriate money for the use of religious groups, and may not loan the credit of the state to private corporations. Since every state constitution adheres either by express statement or by implication to the doctrine of separation of powers, legislatures may not, except in designated areas, exercise powers assigned other branches of government.

Extent of Legislative Power

In performing its essential function of policymaking, a wide range of powers is available to a state legislature. It is not possible, however, to develop a comprehensive list of legislative powers. Since any power not delegated to the national government nor prohibited to the states by the national Constitution is a reserved power, it is not feasible to catalog state legislative authority. Stated in general terms, the authority of a state legislature is bounded, in theory at least, only by the negative effect of national law and by the restrictions imposed by the state constitution.

While legislative powers are not detailed in state constitutions, the major areas of authority are set forth or are generally identifiable. The powers to tax, appropriate and borrow money, impose regulations upon commercial ventures within a state, establish courts and fix their jurisdictions, and to define crimes and prescribe punishments are among powers usually mentioned in state constitutions. Not listed is the broad, loosely defined power to legislate in behalf of the public health, safety, welfare, and morals—the well-known "police power."

It is not possible to subject the police power to precise definition. Under it legislatures are empowered to enact legislation imposing quarantines, requiring vaccinations, compelling food inspection, forbidding gambling, prohibiting the manufacture or sale of fireworks, banning ownership of dangerous weapons, fixing automobile speed limits, barring immoral or indecent entertainment, prescribing safety requirements for industrial plants, and a host of other limitations on freedom of action. Often the police power overlaps other areas of legislative authority, or it may be conceived as a part of other powers. For example, a statutory requirement that dangerous machinery be enclosed by wire guards is in the interest of the public safety and therefore an exercise of the police power; at the same time it may be an expression of legislative authority to regulate intrastate commerce. In reality the extent of the police power is so vague that only through the process of examining judicial decisions involving the question of whether it has been exceeded can its limits be approximately determined. Even then judicial interpretations provide only temporary understandings, since future decisions may reinterpret the police power to meet the exigencies of changing conditions.

Nonlegislative Powers

When a legislature exercises authority that is similar to the powers of a court it is said to have *judicial powers*. The most common prerogative of legislatures in this category is impeachment. All state legislatures except that of Oregon are empowered to bring charges against executive and judicial officers and upon conviction to remove them from office.[11] Impeachment itself is merely accusation; thus when a lower house votes to accuse an officer, that individual is impeached. The role of the senate is to sit as jury, hear arguments on the charges, and ultimately to decide the guilt or innocence of the person impeached.[12] Conviction on impeachment charges results in removal from office, and later prosecution in the regular courts is not prevented by the outcome of the impeachment trial.

Legislatures also exercise authority of a judicial nature over their members. Since legislators are not subject to impeachment, legislative bodies may subject them to censure, a form of reprimand for improper conduct, or in extreme cases to expulsion. If questions arise as to whether a member was validly elected, or if two or more persons claim the same legislative seat, the house involved is empowered to decide who shall be seated.

Every state legislature shares in the process of amending the state constitution and the creation of constitutional conventions. These prerogatives are known as *constituent powers* and are of fundamental importance. As indicated in an earlier chapter, the role of the legislature in making changes in state constitutions varies widely across the nation.

Among the broad grants of authority vested in state legislatures are those regarded as *executive* in nature. For example, gubernatorial appointments to high state offices ordinarily are subject to approval by the upper house of a legislature. In some half-dozen states judges of some courts are chosen by the legislature, and in a similar number high-ranking officials such as the secretary of state, attorney general, and treasurer are legisla-

---

11. In Oregon public officials accused of improper conduct in office may be removed by action brought in the regular courts. In such proceedings conventional criminal procedure is followed. (Constitution of Oregon, Article VII, Section 6). The recall may also be used against elective officers in Oregon.

12. Typically, the lower house of a legislature is vested with the sole power to impeach, and the trial is held before the senate. In Missouri, impeachment cases are tried before the supreme court. The unicameral legislature of Nebraska impeaches, and the trial is conducted before the supreme court. In Alaska the usual roles of the two houses in the impeachment process are reversed; the senate impeaches, and the trial is held before the house of representatives.

tively selected. Conversely, the legislatures of some states may, by extraordinary majority vote, remove judges from office without resorting to the impeachment process. Frequently, legislatures are empowered to approve or reject actions of a governor in the removal of local officials. In all states interstate compacts to which a state becomes a signatory are subject to approval by the legislature.

Usually not specified in constitutional or statutory provisions, but certainly among the important powers of a legislature, are those that may be designated as *administrative*. It is primarily through these powers that oversight of administration is accomplished. Best known among such devices is the investigation, a process by which a legislative group, most often a standing or interim committee, inquires into some aspect of governmental activity. Conducted ostensibly for the purpose of gaining information upon which to base legislation, an investigation provides a method of supervising the performance of executive officers. Further control is exercised through the device of requiring designated administrative units to submit reports. In conducting hearings preparatory to the consideration of appropriation bills legislatures may probe deeply into administrative affairs. In a few states, legislative bodies require administrative agencies to open their accounts to a complete inspection by a legislatively chosen auditor.

The State Legislature: The Making of Laws

7

Determination of public policy through the passage of laws is the most important function of a legislative body. There are times, of course, when other functions such as initiating constitutional amendments or bringing and hearing impeachment charges may seem more vital. Such instances are usually accompanied by headlines and a high degree of public interest. However, the deliberations that result in decisions as to what government will or will not do—the formulations of policies and programs—is the very *raison d' être* of the state legislature.

THE LEGISLATIVE PROCESS

In the performance of its basic function, a state legislature follows certain predetermined steps. From the moment a bill is introduced until it clears the legislative halls and is sent to the governor for consideration, its progress can be noted by reference to those steps. These phases through which all measures must go are termed simply *legislative procedure*—the procedure by means of which laws are enacted.

The *legislative process* entails far more than what takes place within the legislature. Obviously, the governor participates in the legislative process. A governor's veto power, messages to the legislature, recommendations, threats, appeals to the people, or other such expressions certainly have their effect upon the minds and actions of legislators. Viewed broadly, the legislative and gubernatorial phases are only the culmination of the legislative process. The origin and basic development of legislation takes place *before* it is formally introduced in a legislature.

It is not always possible to tell just where the idea for a new law originates. A social worker may feel that existing welfare legislation contains inequities, a businessman may be dissatisfied with prevailing methods of taxing inventories, a teacher may resent restrictions upon the freedom to engage in political affairs, or a housewife may object to the fixing of prices of certain commodities. In each instance someone, or some group, is dissatisfied with existing laws or the lack of them, and desires a change in policy.

Isolated studies indicate public officials and agencies are responsible for approximately one-third of all bills introduced at a legislative session. Other sources of draft legislation include: interim committees, legislative councils, special investigating commissions, pressure or special interest groups, and private individuals. Technically, however, only members of the state legislature may introduce bills. Thus of all the bills that pass through legislative halls, very few are actually written by the senators or representatives who sign them.

THE LEGISLATIVE PROGRAM—OR LACK OF IT

Among the worst features of American state legislatures is the lack of a comprehensive legislative program. While legislative councils have brought about some improvement, a typical legislature convenes with little more than a general idea of how it will proceed. The essential pattern of a legislative session, within the context of its organization and rules of procedure, is determined by the vicissitudes of circumstance. Bills that are ready for consideration on the floor are discussed and debated without particular regard to logical subject matter sequence. It is not inaccurate to observe that the effects of pressures, circumstances, and advantages of the moment are more important in determining the course of legislative action than are other factors.

The inadvisability of an unplanned approach is emphasized by the dangers involved. The most obvious peril is that legislation that should be considered may not come to the attention of the legislature at all. This danger is especially present in the many state legislative bodies whose sessions are constitutionally limited to a fixed number of days. In much the same vein, a legislative session that is operated without some preplanning is in danger of acting on bills without the benefit of crucial information. Although this may happen at any time, it is most likely to occur during the latter stages of the session when the members are facing a deadline for adjournment or are eager to return to their regular livelihoods. A third major peril is that without planning, the final days of a session witness a congested backlog of bills, many of which are "must" legislation. As a result, measures which deserve consideration are simply allowed to die, while others are enacted with little or no debate. When such conditions prevail, the incidence of poorly written legislation is likely to be high, and the danger of conflicting bills enacted at the same session is increased. The availability of expert bill drafting services may reduce the number of poorly drafted bills, but amendments and alterations of bills as they proceed to enactment may result in flaws and inconsistencies.

More subtle but no less important is the threat that the absence of preplanning may be fostered or turned to advantage by selfish interests. Lobbies, organizations geared for continuing, year-round activity, are ordinarily careful to capitalize on any turn of events that may produce a result favorable to them. While lobbies and lobbyists are frequently invaluable to legislators in terms of disclosing information necessary to intelligent action, their desire to achieve policy decisions favorable to their interests is paramount. Similarly, administrative agencies, local governments, political party factions, or even individual members of the legislature may be able to exact advantages.

Clearly, the misuse of time and opportunity that permits such shortcomings is not conducive to sound, comprehensive legislation in areas of vital public concern. The problem has not gone unnoticed in state governmental circles, and efforts of a sort have been made to correct it. While no state has come up with a solution regarded as the best that can be obtained, impressive steps have been taken in the form of prelegislative investigation and reports through the use of interim committees and legislative councils.

LEGISLATIVE COUNCILS

Without doubt the most important strides toward achievement of legislative planning have been realized through legislative councils. These bodies are composed of members of the legislature who meet between legislative sessions to consider matters of probable interest to the succeeding session of the legislature. Since 1933, the year the first council was established in Kansas, similar organizations have been created in most states. Various titles are used to identify them, but the most common is simply "Legislative Council."

The legislative council has been characterized as "essentially a super interim committee with an area of action as wide as that of the legislature."[1] It must be remembered, however, that a council is an *advisory* body, possessing no authority to enact legislation or to compel the legislature to act on matters it has considered. In reality it is a permanent joint committee, aided by a permanent research staff, to provide assistance to the legislature on major problems of policy. While no two councils exercise identical powers, all function to provide factual information on important problems, insure continuing legislative study of major problems

1. Bell Zeller (ed.), *American State Legislatures*, Report of the Committee on American Legislatures, American Political Science Association, Thomas Y. Crowell Co., New York, 1954, p. 128.

between sessions, and issue reports for legislators and the public, usually before a legislative session begins.

INTERIM COMMITTEES

Interim committees resemble legislative councils in many ways, but they are significantly different in two important respects: the interim committee is a temporary legislative agency established to inquire into a specific topic, and it does not have a permanent research staff. Although dating from the earliest days of state legislatures, the interim committee was not widely used until the present century. They were common during the early 1900's, used even more widely in the 1920's, and by 1950 were employed in three-fourths of the states. Since their function is similar to that of a legislative council, interim committees are least common in those states with active councils.

The record of accomplishment of interim committees has not been impressive. Some, of course, have been of great value, contributing much to the intelligent consideration by legislatures of the committees' subjects of inquiry. Because an interim committee can devote its entire effort to a single topic in which its members may have an intense interest, the potential contribution of such a committee is considerable. However, time lost in organization, the difficulty of assembling a competent staff for a relatively short period, the fact that the committee itself is temporary, and the lack of integration with other committees are weaknesses difficult to overcome.

LEGISLATIVE SERVICE AGENCIES

In addition to legislative councils and interim committees, various other aids are available to state legislators. Advice, information, and assistance are rendered in different states by reference services, bill drafting agencies, legislative counsels, legal revision and codification bodies, and staff agencies responsible for fiscal management. Without help from such aids, the tasks of individual legislators would be overwhelming.

Legislative Reference Services

The basic purpose of a legislative reference service is, as the name implies, to provide information and other assistance to legislators in the performance of their legislative duties. If a member of a state legislature needs information in the preparation or revision of a bill about to be introduced, the reference service can be of help. Most such agencies perform a variety of services including bill drafting, law summaries, statutory revision, research reports, spot research for legislators, or any other services requested which they are equipped to render.

Legislative research services were among the first aids legislatures created. At the turn of the present century Wisconsin and New York established research agencies and within a decade or so, about a dozen states had followed suit. By 1940, legislative research arms were functioning in half the states, and today each state maintains some type of agency to furnish research assistance to its legislators.

Several state legislative reference agencies function independently of other organizations, but in most instances the reference function is handled by the legislative council, a division of the state library, or a department within the executive branch. In some states the research assistance that ordinarily would be provided by a single reference bureau is rendered by several agencies which serve the legislature.

Bill Drafting

There is a world of difference between the exercise of intelligent discretion in determining what public policy ought to be and the ability to master the technique of expressing policy in the form of legislative bills. The vast majority of state legislators might be described as amateurs, or at best semipros, in drafting legislation. Classic examples of legislative *faux pas* of the past include the Massachusetts law which required all hotel rooms to have plastered walls and floors and an Ohio statute which provided that the state coat of arms was to be engraved on state officials. A prohibition enacted by the Tennessee legislature forbade owners of livestock to run at large, but the most quoted legislative misstep of all is the Kansas measure which required that trains meeting on a single track should each proceed to a siding from which neither should move until the other had passed. Such measures obviously are the result of careless, inept draftsmanship.

In all states it is now possible for legislators to secure help in bill drafting from at least one governmental officer or agency. The legislative councils, law revisors, legislative reference bureaus, and attorney generals are the usual sources of assistance. In previous years a great deal of reliance was placed upon the attorney generals in the belief that bill drafting could best be performed by individuals with substantial legal training. Today, primary reliance is upon research agencies under direct control of the legislatures, particularly the legislative councils.

Legislative Counsels

The office of legislative *counsel,* which should not be confused with the legislative *council,* is found in several states. The word *counsel* refers to a person trained in the law, and a legislative counsel, therefore, is an attorney retained by a legislative body. However, in the few states where the office exists as a separate agency, the duties and functions performed are hardly distinguishable from those of other legislative service agencies.

In California the Legislative Counsel Bureau functions as a reference service, bill drafting agency, and legal revision department. In Georgia and Nevada the office provides general staff services to the legislative council. Oregon's Legislative Counsel Committee performs the tasks of research, bill drafting, and legal revision as well as advising legislators on legal matters.

Legal Revisions

At each regular session of every state legislature at least several hundred new laws are enacted. Some of the laws are completely new; others change specified parts of laws already on the books; still others may complement, conflict with, or compromise already existing law. If some means did not exist to relate the new laws to those already in existence, a state's legal system would soon become seriously entangled.

A legal revisor does not actually enact law. Rather, the function of the revisor is to consolidate overlapping provisions; correct inaccurate, prolix, or redundant expressions; eliminate obscurities and conflicts; and collect the whole into a logical, compact arrangement without change in effect. Within the last few years several states have authorized revisors to make recommendations as to the substantive content of laws. However, only the legislative body has power to enact laws, and the validity of a compilation, revision, or codification depends upon approval by the state legislature.

LOBBIES AND LOBBYISTS

At each session of every state legislature, decisions are made that alter the content and effect of existing public policy. Since the policy decisions made by the legislators are of fundamental importance to various economic, social, or political groups, it is not surprising that those groups should seek to maintain and extend public policy favorable to them. The agents who perform this function are referred to as *lobbyists*.

Lobby and *pressure group* are terms that are often used interchangeably, but it is helpful to recognize that differences between the two may exist. Both are organized groups that seek, by various means, to bring about or maintain what they consider favorable public policy. To be sure, a pressure group may operate as a lobby, but in a manner of speaking the lobby is best characterized as the legislative arm of the pressure group. Thus, railroad companies, labor unions, and veterans' organizations may function as pressure groups and at the same time maintain offices or organizations which operate as lobbies. In any event it is possible to say that all lobbies either represent or are themselves pressure groups, but that not all pressure groups are to be regarded as lobbies.

In a general sense all organizations which actively attempt to influence public policy can be considered pressure groups. However, some organizations such as fraternal lodges, hobbyists' clubs, and civic groups may be only temporarily or casually interested in some aspect of public policy. Ordinarily, issues such as the tax status of club property or the feasibility of public assistance in the purchase of playground equipment for a park represent the pressure activities of these groups. Inasmuch as they do not attempt continuously to influence policy, it is somewhat misleading to regard them either as lobbies or as pressure groups.

In the minds of many, lobbying consists only of the act of contacting legislators and attempting to convince them of a certain point of view. Such actions are certainly included, but are only one of many tactics employed in lobbying. Direct contacts include not only the "buttonholing" of legislators, but also appearances as witnesses at committee hearings, dissemination of information in the form of pamphlets, tracts and reports directly to legislators, and sponsorship of social functions at which attendance of legislators is sought. More effective are the lobbying activities of an indirect nature. Propaganda designed to win support of the general public, pressures exerted on administrators, maintenance of speakers bureaus, mass letterwriting, advertising and sponsorship of radio and television programs are suggestive of the variety of means used to influence opinion and mold attitudes that are bound to have an effect upon legislators.

It should be noted that lobbying, as such, is not an undesirable practice. In fact, lobbyists frequently perform valuable services in the provision of information, particularly where legislative reference services do not exist or do not function well. There have been, of course, examples of bribery and corruption, and occasional actions of questionable ethical character lend an aura of suspicion to lobbying. Consequently, most state legislatures have made some attempts to regulate the practice by enacting laws which require lobbyists to register and to file periodic reports of expenditures. Although these statutes ostensibly impose fines and imprisonment for violations, few prosecutions have been attempted, except in Wisconsin, where enforcement appears to have been most successful. In most states there have been no prosecutions at all.

Various suggestions have been made in the interest of better methods of controlling lobbies and lobbyists, the most promising of which involve wider publicity of pressure activities coupled with closer surveillance. As a burglar prefers darkness, so unethical lobbyists prefer secrecy, or at least a minimum of attention. By requiring lobbyists *and* their employers not only to register but also to report itemized accounts of all sums spent in their attempts to influence public policy, the public as well as legislators can be more fully informed. It has been suggested that special agencies be established for the enforcement of lobby regulations, thus securing supervision superior to the part-time efforts of attorney generals, secretaries of state, or legislative officers. Valuable as these proposals are, it is doubtful that greatly improved controls will be achieved until the value of the lobbyist to the legislator has been diminished. By providing adequate staff assistance and research and information facilities, legislators—even those in their first terms—can function more effectively without assistance from lobbyists. It is probable that all lobbying activities can never be fully controlled, especially those that are indirect in character, but suggested improvements offer the promise of curbing most abuses.

LAWMAKING PROCEDURE

Steps involved in the course of a bill through a legislature are much the same from state to state. The unicameral system of Nebraska, of course, represents the greatest departure from the "norm," but even there procedures are much like those of a chamber within a bicameral system. Despite much similarity, there are numerous variations in detail in the passage of bills by state legislatures. These differences can best be noted by an examination of the principal procedural steps.

Rules of Procedure

In each state constitution there are a few provisions that affect the procedures by which bills are passed, but each house of every state legislature is free to adopt the great bulk of its own rules of procedure. Technically, rules are adopted at the beginning of each regular session, a step which usually amounts to nothing more than adoption of the rules in effect during the previous regular session. Of course, changes in the rules may be made, but practically all alterations in the rules come slowly through interpretations during the course of legislative sessions.

Introduction of Bills

One of the simplest steps in legislative procedure is the introduction of a bill. The process consists of depositing a copy of the bill with the clerk of either house. In three-fourths of the states, bills are printed upon introduction. Procedure in the other states calls for printing at a later stage, ordinarily after standing committee approval or second reading.

Since many legislative sessions are limited in length and there is a tendency to delay consideration of many bills, three-fourths of the state legislatures have limited the period during which measures may be introduced in order to reduce congestion at the end of each session. A unique arrangement is found in Massachusetts, where all bills *must* be introduced a full month before the legislature convenes, with exceptions permitted only by a four-fifths majority or request of the governor! To allow for emergency situations, most state legislatures that have limited the period during which measures may be introduced provide for exceptions by gubernatorial request, an extraordinary majority, or by exempting appropriations and revenue bills. One method of circumventing limitations on introduction is by means of parliamentary technicalities such as amending a bill under discussion in such a way that it embodies provisions that would otherwise have been the subject of separate legislation.

First Reading

All state legislative chambers operate under rules which provide that bills be read to the members—usually three times—before votes are taken. Ordinarily, each of the readings must take place on different days, and at least one must be of the entire contents of the bill. The object of different readings, of course, is to prevent hasty passage of legislation, the extreme forms of which are known as *railroading*. At times, dispatch may be necessary or desirable. Consequently, the rules of most houses permit, usually after an extraordinary majority vote, some readings to be dispensed with or all readings heard on a single day. A reading requirement may often be satisfied merely by reading the title. Indeed, the first reading usually consists of nothing more than a recitation of the title by a clerk. At first glance such a practice may seem ill-advised, but in view of the fact that a newly introduced bill must be referred for committee action a first reading in full would serve only to delay later, important procedural steps.

Referral

In each house of every state legislature provision is made for standing committees to which all bills are referred for consideration. Referral of bills—the assignment of bills to various committees—is usually performed by the speaker of the house or the president of the senate. In about forty lower houses the referral power is lodged with the speaker, while a third of the upper houses either restrict the president of the senate or place the authority in other hands. In the great majority of instances, referral involves no discretion and could be handled adequately by a clerk. Sometimes a bill could reasonably be referred to any of several committees, a decision that properly should be made by a designated officer or committee. The power of referral may determine the fate of a bill, depending upon whether the committee to which it is referred is favorably disposed toward its provisions.

Committee Action

Standing committees of legislative bodies are, for all practical purposes, miniature legislatures. A committee may alter a bill in virtually any way it chooses, ranging from reporting the bill to the floor unchanged with a recommendation that it be passed, to other extremes of changing the content completely or simply failing to consider it at all. Committees in about one-third of the states are required to report all bills back to the floor, but a bill that has received no attention from a committee has little chance of passage. On occasion a committee may refuse to report an important bill for consideration by the whole house. The rules of procedure usually provide that a committee can be forced to *discharge* a bill upon a majority vote of the house. Discharge rules, however, are seldom invoked.

Committee Reports

Practically all important bills that committees send to the floor are accompanied by recommendations as to their disposition. Frequently, reports are printed setting forth reasons for the committee's actions, and in many cases both the majority and minority of the committee prepare reports. Decision on the merits of a bill does not take place at this stage. The only decision made is whether to send the bill back to the committee or to place it on a calendar.

The Calendar Stage

After a bill has been reported out by a committee the measure is placed on a *calendar*. A calendar is nothing more than a list of bills, in chronological order, that have been acted upon by standing committees and are ready for debate by the full house. In some chambers there is only one calendar; others have several for bills of different types. In all instances, consideration of bills is required, technically at least, in the order in which they are reported from committees.

Frequently an important bill, or one a majority wants to consider immediately, may be at the bottom or far down on a calendar. Since the rules provide that bills must be taken up in order, special action is necessary before any bill other than the first one on the calendar may be discussed. Inasmuch as rules of procedure are determined by the legislative body itself, the rules can be suspended, and the desired bill then considered. Because suspension ordinarily requires an extraordinary majority vote, an easier process is usually employed. A common procedure is the adoption of a special rule permitting a specific bill to be considered out of order. A simple majority plus favorable action of a rules committee is required before such a rule can be brought into play. The role of the rules committee furnishes a possible obstacle to the process, but since the majority party in the house also has a majority on the committee, special rules are seldom refused.

Floor Action

When a bill is ready for floor action, it receives a second reading. In all states except those with constitutional provisions requiring a third reading in full, it is at this stage that a bill is debated and amendments offered. Usual procedure is for a clerk to read the bill aloud, with the presiding officer inquiring as to the agreement of the house as each section is concluded. At any such interval full, extended debate may occur and amendments may be adopted. Unimportant or noncontroversial bills may be read in a rapid, unintelligible drone, or as has happened in a few instances, several such bills may be read simultaneously!

In some states full reading often occurs in *committee of the whole.* Consisting of the full membership of the house, although fewer members may constitute a quorum, a committee of the whole is not bound by the rules of the house as such and is not presided over by the regular presiding officer of the chamber. Debate and discussion are much freer and more informal. Decisions reached in the committee are "reported" to the house which formalizes them under the regular rules of procedure.

Technically, the decision made by a legislative chamber on second reading is whether to restore a bill to the calendar to await third reading, but technicalities aside, the second reading usually results, for all practical purposes, in a decision by the house. Again, except where a full third reading is constitutionally mandatory, it is common practice that after debate is ended a bill is *engrossed*—printed again to incorporate all changes approved during debate—a perfunctory third reading by title is given, and a formal vote taken.

Voting

The most important single act in the course of a bill through a legislative chamber is the vote of the members to approve or reject it. There are several methods of voting, the most formal of which is the *roll call.* When such a vote is cast, a clerk calls the names of members who verbally announce their decisions. The votes are recorded as announced and become a permanent part of the recorded proceedings. Roll calls commonly are required on the final passage of bills, but when they are not compulsory, other methods may be used either to save time or to escape publicity on what might later prove to be an unpopular vote. The *viva voce,* or voice vote, is the most frequently used method of determining the consensus of a legislative body, but when more accurate assessment is necessary, the *show of hands* or *teller* votes are used. In the former, as the term indicates, members merely raise their hands to be counted. A teller vote requires members to file by a clerk who tallies votes as announced by each legislator.

Much time is spent, even wasted, in the vote-taking process in state legislatures, especially when large numbers of roll calls are involved. During the latter portion of the session when time is at a premium its loss can be costly. Consequently, many states have installed electrical voting devices to speed up the process. Such devices have proved their worth, accurately recording in a few seconds roll calls that formerly took ten to twenty minutes.

Conference Committees

Valid enactment of a law by a bicameral legislature requires that the bill be passed in identical form by each house. There can be no variation whatever; every comma, semicolon, and apostrophe must appear in identical locations. As frequently occurs, however, especially with important or controversial bills, committee action and amendment on the floor result in differences. The usual formal method for resolving differences is through use of conference committees.

Appointed by the presiding officers of the respective houses, conference committees usually are composed of two or three members from each chamber. A separate committee is appointed for each bill, and the conferees, meeting in closed sessions, normally are limited to discussion of points of difference between the bills in conflict. Some states permit such committees to consider any desirable change, and on occasion, despite limitations in the rules, conference committees substantially rewrite measures. When reported to the legislative chambers, recommendations of the conference may be debated, but only rarely are they amendable. Recommendations normally must be accepted as a whole or rejected altogether. Ordinarily, rejection has the effect of killing a bill, although once in a while a new conference committee is appointed for further efforts to reconcile differences.

Enrollment

The final step in legislative procedure before a bill is sent to the governor is *enrollment*. After it has been passed in identical form by both houses, a bill is then printed in final form, and the signatures of the presiding officers of the respective houses are affixed. At this point, only the governor stands between the bill and its inclusion as a part of the law of a state.

To the Governor

The governor of every state except North Carolina is constitutionally vested with the power of veto. As the chief executive of the state a governor has the authority, in fact the duty, to examine closely all bills passed by the legislature and to veto, or negate, those which are not expressions of sound public policy. In the case of a veto, the governor is obliged to return the bill to the legislative house where it was introduced with a message setting forth reasons for the veto. Since a veto represents a difference of opinion between two equal, coordinate branches of government, a method of resolving the conflict is necessary. In all instances the disagreement may be resolved by the vote of an extraordinary legislative majority to *override* the veto. Usually a two-thirds majority of each house is required to cancel the effect of an executive veto, a number that is in most cases extremely difficult to muster.

If a governor does not veto a bill, there are several alternatives open: the measure may be signed, as happens in the vast majority of cases, or the governor may also permit the bill to become law without a signature. Governors have from three to fifteen days, with the limit in most states set at five or ten, to act on bills while the legislature is in session. Should a governor fail to act on a bill, it automatically becomes law at the end of the prescribed period. In about twenty states, bills sent to the governor *after* the legislative session is over, or which are on his desk at the time of adjournment, do not become law if left unsigned. Instead, such bills die, and are said to be subject to the *pocket veto.* Forty-three governors can also exercise the *item veto,* by means of which parts of bills may be disapproved. This particular veto power is ordinarily limited to appropriations bills, although the governor of Washington may apply it to any provision in any bill containing more than one item or section.

After clearing the governor's desk, a bill does not necessarily take immediate legal effect. Usually there is a fixed date upon which bills passed at a session are legally enforceable. The date may be fixed by the constitution, as in Texas, at ninety days days after adjournment. Indiana laws must be distributed to the counties and proclaimed by the governor, and in Kansas legal force is effective upon publication. Laws enacted in Maryland are considered effective on the first day of June following the legislative sessions unless otherwise declared. If the constitution is silent on the matter, the effective date is determined by the legislature.

A new law may take effect earlier through a provision known as an *emergency clause.* In the event a legislature desires an earlier effective date for a particular law than is usual, and there is no constitutional restriction on doing so, the law may be written to include a provision declaring the bill an emergency measure. As a result, when the procedural steps of lawmaking are concluded, the law takes immediate effect.

IMPROVEMENT OF STATE LEGISLATURES

Legislative powers, organization, and procedure are human creations, and like their creators have many weaknesses and shortcomings. For purposes of textual examination the various aspects of state legislatures can be separately considered, but in reality, powers, organization and procedure are so thoroughly enmeshed and integrated that true understanding of the legislative process requires that they be considered as a whole. Powers hamstrung by unrealistic constitutional limitations can result in poor organization and cumbersome procedures; poor organization can negate power and complicate procedure; and a confused procedural maze nullifies adequate power and lessens the effectiveness of good organization. Consequently, improvements in legislative procedure necessitate concern with organization and allocation of authority.

The most thorough contemporary analysis of state legislatures as a group is contained in the work of the Citizens Conference on State Legislatures, a non-profit research organization formed in 1965 for the study of legislative institutions. After an intensive two-year effort the Conference issued its findings and recommendations in a 1971 report that included a catalog of general suggestions and a list of specific recommendations for each of the states.[2] Since publication of its study, the Conference has devoted its resources to follow-up studies and reports on developments in the legislative field.

The recommendations of the Conference covered all aspects of organization and procedure, offering remedies for the full range of problems and shortcomings associated with legislatures. In general, the list of proposals was not unlike the suggestions contained in the foregoing pages of this volume. It is also interesting to note that the recommendations are remarkably similar to the suggestions offered by earlier study groups. In fact, with some exceptions, much the same conclusions were reached in a study directed by Professor Belle Zeller nearly three decades ago,[3] and by a study group of the Council of State Governments in the late 1940's.[4]

As each new study group drafts lists of recommendations which are substantially the same as those of earlier groups, it would appear that little or no progress has been made. This is not the case, however, for in some states impressive strides have been taken, and national trends towards improvement can be noted in some areas, as observed in earlier pages. Admittedly, many states have done nothing of consequence to improve their legislatures, and in terms of professional criteria and expectations, none has done enough. Experience shows that change comes slowly in the transformation of traditional institutions and practices, and that what change does occur takes place in piecemeal fashion. Yet society changes constantly, the demands and requirements of the people fluctuate, and public policy is being continuously adjusted.

---

2. Citizens Conference on State Legislatures, *The Sometime Governments: A Critical Study of the 50 American Legislatures,* Bantam Books, Inc., New York, 1971.
3. Belle Zeller (ed.), *American State Legislatures,* Report of the Committee on American Legislatures, American Political Science Association, Thomas Y. Crowell Co., New York, 1954.
4. Council of State Governments, Committee on Legislative Processes and Procedures, *Our State Legislatures,* revised edition, Chicago, 1948.

The State Judiciary

Courts and the people who staff them—known as the judiciary—are maintained by governments to perform the basic function of hearing and deciding legal controversies. It makes no difference how simple or how complex a case may be, the same basic process is employed in all courts: the facts must be determined, the law must be ascertained, and the law must be applied to the facts. The differences among courts and cases are due to such factors as complexity of the law, character of the facts, scope of court jurisdiction, and status of litigants.

A distinctive characteristic of courts is their lack of power to initiate judicial action. The judicial power is basically a passive thing that can be brought into play only when it is invoked by a litigant who complains to a court that his legal rights have been violated. Variations occur, for example, when an advisory opinion is sought, or a lower court certifies a question to a higher court. But the principle remains undisturbed—judicial power is at rest until it is set in motion by an individual, group, or government outside the judiciary.

Despite the importance of the judicial function, courts have no power to enforce their decisions. Introductory students are often surprised to learn that courts must depend entirely upon outside assistance for enforcement of their orders and decrees. Basically, the effectiveness of judicial decisions ultimately rests upon the degree of public confidence courts can command. In other words, the strength of the judiciary depends upon its prestige. From a more practical, realistic viewpoint, the effectiveness of judicial decisions is dependent upon the willingness of the executive branch to carry them out.

The proper role of the judiciary as it relates to the content of public policy expressed in law traditionally has been that courts interpret and apply policy, but do not make it; that is, the legislature, and to some extent the executive, perform the function of policymaking and the courts merely clarify and apply that policy in controversies that come before them. If all law were absolutely clear and all issues in every contro-versy equally unclouded, perhaps such a concept would be completely acceptable. Unfortunately, laws are often indefinite, uncertain, even conflicting, and courts must of necessity determine *what the law is.* In one view the court merely ascertains the meaning of the law as *intended* by the legislature; thus judicial interpretation is not an origination of policy. A more realistic view is that an ambiguous law has no certain meaning and that by interpretation courts give meaning to it, a form of policy-making which produces what is often characterized as "judicial legislation."

INDEPENDENCE OF THE JUDICIARY

The vast majority of public offices and institutions in America are operated on the basis of political partisanship. With few exceptions, mostly local, legislative bodies at all levels of government are expected to act, at least to some extent, on the basis of the party affiliations of their members. Public officers in most instances are chosen with a view to their party preferences, and no one is surprised when their actions take on partisan characteristics. In some states even judges are elected on partisan ballots. But whatever the method of choice, judges and the courts they preside over are expected to forego partisanship. The judiciary thus stands apart from the remainder of government in this important respect.

Objectivity in proceedings is another requirement that Americans impose upon the judiciary. Any judge, regardless of the court, who favors one party to a controversy over another damages the prestige and integrity of the court. Isolated instances of such favoritism may lead to reversal of decisions, and repeated, habitual partiality normally leads to a judge's removal or failure of reelection or reappointment. A conviction that the courts should not be, nor should ever become, the tool of any public or private interest is firmly entrenched in the American system. Judges, for example, may not be sued for making allegedly "wrong" decisions. Any person who attempts to interfere with the conduct of proper judicial proceedings may be liable to criminal prosecution. The salaries of indi-vidual judges may not be reduced, or raised, during their terms of office. In short, the concept of an independent judiciary is implemented by measures designed to preserve every opportunity for objective, impartial application of the law.

STATE AND FEDERAL COURT SYSTEMS

The system of courts in the United States is compartmentalized in line with the requirements of federalism. Just as it is possible to say that there is a national system of law and a legal system in each of the states, reference may also be made to the national judiciary and the fifty state court systems. The state judiciaries are on an equal plane in relation to the national, or federal, system, and each is a separate, distinct system of courts. However, since federal and state courts operate in the same geographical areas, and in some cases apply the same laws, points of contact and possibilities of conflict are numerous.

Although details are left largely to legislative determination, the basic division of judicial authority is provided by the Constitution of the United States. Article VI, Section 2, for example, provides that the Constitution, federal statutes, and treaties are the "supreme law of the land" which state as well as federal judges are bound to uphold. In the event state law conflicts with national law, the national law takes precedence. Article III provides that the judicial power of the United States extends to all cases arising under *national law* and to certain designated classes of cases.[1] Inasmuch as the national government, including the national courts, have only such powers as are delegated by the Constitution, all other power, judicial as well as legislative and executive, remains in the states.

It should be stressed that the placement of subjects within the jurisdiction of federal courts does not mean that those subjects must of necessity, be dealt with *only* by federal courts. In fact, only when Congress, by law, gives the federal courts *exclusive* jurisdiction are the state courts without power to act. Examples of cases which can be heard only by federal courts include prosecutions for violations of federal criminal laws, controversies between states, patent and copyright cases, charges against ambassadors or consuls, and proceedings in bankruptcy. In other proceedings state courts *may* hear cases involving federal law that litigants choose to bring before them.

In diversity of citizenship cases—that is, when a citizen of one state brings a civil action against a citizen of another state—the case may be brought in a state court. If the suit involves more than $10,000, the plaintiff may choose to bring action in a federal court regardless of whether any point of federal law is involved.[2] If the case is started in a state court, the defendant has the privilege of having it removed to a federal district court for trial. Removal privileges also exist in other cases, particularly in instances where violations of state criminal laws are charged against federal officers in the course of performing their official duties.

Frequently a single act may violate both a state and a federal criminal

---

1. As listed in Article III, Section 2, federal jurisdiction includes cases involving ambassadors, public ministers, and consuls; admiralty and maritime cases, controversies to which the United States is a party; controversies between states; cases between citizens of different states; and certain cases involving land grants.
2. If less than $10,000 is at stake, the federal courts have no jurisdiction in the absence of an issue of federal law. Until 1958, when the amount was fixed at the current sum, the amount in controversy was set at a minimum of $3,000.

law. For example, a culprit who steals an automobile and takes it across a state boundary may be subject to two separate prosecutions—by the state for auto theft, and by the national government for transporting a stolen car in interstate commerce. In reality there is no conflict of jurisdiction; only a question of which government will prosecute first. National and state laws dealing with narcotics, prostitution, kidnaping, bootlegging, robbery of federally insured banks and the like, multiply the number of such dual offense cases. The order of prosecution is usually determined by informal agreement among law enforcement officials.

Review by the United States Supreme Court of state court decisions is restricted to those cases involving a *federal question*. This requirement means that a case must include an issue of federal law. Review is often sought on the grounds that state action has resulted in a denial of due process of law as guaranteed by the Fourteenth Amendment to the U.S. Constitution. The Supreme Court must then decide whether the federal question is "substantial," or important enough to warrant a review of the case.

It is interesting to note that *comity*, or judicial courtesy, has resulted in the understanding that federal courts will accept and apply the interpretations of state law made by a state supreme court. Thus if a state case is being reviewed by the United States Supreme Court and a question of the meaning of a provision of the state constitution or a state statute must be decided, and if there is no question of conflict with federal law, the meanings imparted by the state court are applied. Only if the state courts have not spoken do the federal courts interpret state law in such cases.

ORGANIZATION AND JURISDICTION OF STATE COURTS

To the casual observer the typical state court system is a bewildering maze. The array of courts, from the lowest to the highest, and including every tribunal within a state, may number several hundred, and in a few of the more populous states even several thousand. The average citizen is even less familiar with the judiciary than with elective executive officers and members of the legislature.

An erroneous impression held by many individuals is that a state judiciary is divided into two broad classifications, "state" and "local" courts. Since some courts have broad, general jurisdiction and others are associated with localities, the derivation of the notion is understandable. However, in the American federal system all powers not exclusively delegated to the national government are *state* powers. As a result, all power exercised by any local government, or any branch of any local unit, is *state* power. Obviously then, every court in the state system exercises state power and consequently must be regarded formally as a state court.

The Justice of the Peace

The office of justice of the peace is the lowest station in the judicial pattern of organization. Formerly an appointive office it has, since the days of Andrew Jackson, usually been filled by election. With few exceptions legal training is not required, compensation is often in the form of fees collected from litigants,[3] and the term of office is short, usually two years. While the office was at one time found in virtually all localities, it is fast disappearing in urban areas and is now looked upon primarily as a method of *rural* judicial administration.

The jurisdiction of justices of the peace varies among the states, but in all instances it is very limited. The justice of the peace ordinarily has authority to settle civil disputes involving sums of no more than a few hundred dollars. Criminal jurisdiction is restricted to misdemeanor cases. Juries are rarely used in either type of proceeding. Other duties include such things as holding preliminary hearings, issuing various kinds of warrants, and performing marriage ceremonies. Decisions of the justice are commonly appealable to higher courts where the cases may be tried *de novo*—that is, complete, new proceedings may be had.

Decades ago when travel was difficult and communications were slow, justices of the peace served a useful purpose. They could settle petty cases without the expense and loss of time involved in carrying grievances to higher courts. Today, however, the need for the office has diminished, and it is beginning to take leave of the judicial scene. Critics of the system point out that the characteristic lack of required legal training results in the election of many persons totally unfit to administer the law. In fact, illiterates have been chosen on occasion, and the office is commonly filled by small-time politicians more interested in the political opportunities of the office than in its legal responsibilities. The justice also operates without a courtroom, with the result that proceedings may be, and usually are, conducted in any kind of surroundings. No clerical assistance is provided, thus forcing justices to keep their own records. In the absence of statutory requirements, which is the usual case, this means that no permanent records are kept. Again, the justice is ordinarily without supervision by any central judicial agency or court.

Magistrates' Courts

The urban counterpart of the rural justice of the peace is the magistrate. The courts over which magistrates preside, sometimes termed "police

---

3. When income depends entirely upon fees, the more cases a justice handles, the higher the income—an arrangement that invites activities calculated to produce more cases. Probably the best known abuse of this type is the "speed trap." Another lucrative method of increasing cases is the practice of "fee splitting," in which competing justices offer to split their fees with arresting officers who agree to bring cases to them.

courts," have about the same jurisdiction as the justice of the peace. The most significant contrasts are the urban setting of the magistrate and the resulting differences in character of the cases handled. Depending upon whether a city maintains special courts for traffic violations, juvenile cases, small claims, and the like, the types of cases heard by a magistrate vary from place to place.

Magistrates' courts are subject to the same criticisms that have been directed at justices of the peace. In addition, it may be said that pressures and influences exerted upon magistrates by unethical politicians and other interested persons have been apparent from time to time. Such conditions have contributed to a general feeling among some students of government that the magistrates' courts are even more in need of reform than the system of justice courts.

Municipal Courts

In larger cities across the nation the volume of cases to be tried has warranted the establishment of municipal courts. The jurisdiction of these courts is sufficiently broad to include many cases that might be heard by magistrates or the general trial courts of the state. In general the jurisdiction of a municipal court enables it to hear civil cases involving amounts up to several thousand dollars, misdemeanor cases, and appeals from magistrates' courts if such courts are retained after the establishment of the municipal tribunals. The first municipal court in the United States was established in the city of Chicago in 1906. Today many of the heavily populated cities have followed the Chicago example by creating similar municipal courts.

The judicial climate of the municipal court is much more conducive to proper judicial administration than is the case with magistrates and justices of the peace. Elected to longer terms, the judges, who must be trained in the law, receive adequate salaries and are provided with courtrooms and clerical assistance. Consequently, more capable individuals are attracted to service as municipal judges.

Other Local Courts

In those cities having municipal courts organized on a functional basis certain divisions hear only cases of a given type. All small claims, for example, would be heard before a single tribunal. Whether a unified municipal court system exists or not, other cities frequently have similar specialized courts. Thus a city or a county, regardless of size, may create special courts for small claims, probation of wills, juvenile delinquency, or disputes between married persons. No pattern of uniformity for the creation of such courts exists from state to state. In fact, unless a constitutional provision or statutory enactment prescribes the method by which localities must set up these bodies, each local government is largely free to create them as it chooses.

The General Trial Courts

Every state in the Union is divided into judicial districts, each district usually composed of one or more counties.[4] In each district is a court in which most of the legal action brought under state law is begun. Known by a variety of titles,[5] these general trial courts are presided over by a single judge who is elected in almost three-fourths of the states to terms usually of four or six years. The judge, who must be a member of the bar, presides over scheduled sessions held in courtrooms located in the county courthouses.

Persons accused of major crimes are prosecuted in the general trial courts. The attorney who prosecutes in the name of the state is the locally elected prosecutor known variously as the district attorney, county attorney, or county prosecutor. Trials are held only after formal accusation, whether by indictment or information, and except when such procedure may be waived by the defendant, they are conducted before juries. As a rule, unless trial in some other court is specifically directed, violations of state criminal laws are tried in general trial courts.

There is no limit on the amount in controversy in civil suits heard by general trial courts. Suits at law involving millions of dollars in property, claims, or damages are heard as well as minor suits that might have been brought in lower courts. Suits in equity, or chancery, are also heard although four states, Arkansas, Delaware, Mississippi, and Tennessee maintain separate tribunals for such actions.

Decisions made by general trial judges are final—that is, all facts are determined as required by law, the law is applied to the facts thus found, and a decision is reached. Any further action must be in the form of some type of review by an appellate court higher in the judicial hierarchy.

Intermediate Appellate Courts

In order to reduce the number of cases that must be reviewed by the state supreme court, about half the states maintain intermediate courts of appeals. These courts are composed of three or more judges who serve terms which, with few exceptions, are the same as those of justices of the state supreme courts. In a few states there is technically only one inter-

---

4. In Louisiana the *parish,* which corresponds to the county in other states, is used as the basic unit in drawing district lines. Connecticut abolished its counties in 1959 and now uses *towns* for judicial purposes, while in Alaska the *borough* is employed.
5. Depending upon the state they are called County, Circuit, District, and Superior Courts, or Courts of Common Pleas.

mediate appellate court, which is divided into divisions or departments, each of which serves a prescribed geographical district.

The work of intermediate appellate courts is almost completely a matter of reviewing cases heard originally in lower courts. As appellate tribunals, these courts do not hold trials. In both civil and criminal appeals the usual procedure is to hear oral arguments by attorneys, study the briefs submitted, and examine the record of the case in the lower court. After consultation, a decision is reached by means of a majority vote. Exceptions exist, of course, but ordinarily an appeals court does not concern itself with the facts of a case, basing most decisions upon whether the law was correctly interpreted and applied. Review may be had of decisions by intermediate appellate courts, but in practice the decisions of such courts represent the final step in the judicial ladder for most cases.

The Supreme Court

Topping the hierarchy of every state court system is an appellate court of last resort usually called the state supreme court.[6] Staffed by *justices,*[7] they range in size from three to nine, with five or seven the usual number. In about three-fourths of the states justices are elected, with those of the remaining states selected by the governor or the legislature. The terms vary from six years to life tenure.

One member of a supreme court serves as *chief justice,* presiding over the court and supervising court business, but having no more voting power than the *associate justices.* Chief justices are chosen in a variety of ways, with no particular method predominant. A fifth are popularly elected to the position, and an equal number are appointed by governors. In Rhode Island and South Carolina, they are legislatively chosen, and the remainder are so designated by reason of seniority, having the shortest term to serve, rotation of the position, choice by the court, or a combination of these. Tenure as chief justice depends largely on how the position is filled and ranges from the length of a term remaining, which can be very short, up to life in Rhode Island.

All state courts of last resort have jurisdiction to review any civil case that may be brought before them. Full jurisdiction to hear criminal appeals is vested in each of the supreme courts except in Oklahoma and Texas where separate courts of criminal appeals exercise that authority. The original jurisdiction of supreme courts is severely restricted, about two-thirds of them being empowered to issue original writs in special

6. Confusion may arise with respect to the court system of New York for in that state the term Supreme Court is used to designate a trial court. An intermediate appellate court is termed a Supreme Court, Appellate Division and the highest court is called simply the Court of Appeals.

7. The use of the term "justice" as contrasted with "judge" implies nothing more than rank and prestige of office. The work done by a justice and a judge is virtually the same, the only differences stemming from the jurisdiction of the courts on which they sit.

types of cases. A supreme court may also have a few advisory and administrative functions, but the great bulk of its time and effort is devoted to the consideration of cases before it for review.

For most cases, decision by a state supreme court marks the end of litigation. If a case does not involve some point of federal law, the "federal question" discussed earlier, creating the possibility of review by the United States Supreme Court, the only chance for alteration of a decision is for the court to reverse itself. The court might, for example, grant what is known as a *rehearing*. On the basis of new or further argument at a rehearing the Court may change all or part of a previous decision, but this occurs only on extremely rare occasions.

JUDGES

The individuals who sit on the bench during sessions of courts—the judges and justices—perform a highly specialized, vital function. It is their job to know the law and to apply it. When presiding they have full charge of their courtrooms. They determine, within the context of the rules of procedure, the course of proceedings. It is both their function and their responsibility to maintain a dignified court where the law is fairly and impartially applied.

Qualifications

No greater range in the qualifications required of public officers is found among the states than in those demanded of appellate and general trial court judges. In Massachusetts and New Hampshire there are no legal qualifications whatever. All other states impose qualifications based variously upon such factors as citizenship, residence, age, legal training, and legal experience. In general, the imposition of qualifications is intended to limit judicial selection to citizens of mature years who are experienced in legal matters. In any event, the imposition of legal qualifications, or lack of them, at the general trial court level and above has not been of great concern. The nature of the work of judges at these levels is such that only competent persons could perform it successfully.

Lack of qualifications for judges of minor, local courts—in contrast to the higher officers—produces glaring weaknesses in the judicial system of virtually every state. In fact, the great majority of minor judges have had no legal training at all except the experience gained sitting as judges! The typical citizen would not think of calling in a neighbor to repair a television set, but apparently is willing to accept such judgment in frequently important legal controversies. Such a system leads to numerous examples of gross incompetency among justices of the peace, magistrates, and other local judicial officers.

Selection of Judges

Several methods are employed in the states for the selection of judges. Most are popularly elected, some are appointed by governors, some are selected by legislatures, and others are originally appointed with continuation in office dependent upon later election. As is the case with most other types of public officials, there are wide variations among the states as well as striking differences in methods used within a single state.

The most widely used method in the choice of judges is popular election. Justices of most of the state supreme courts as well as those who fill the lowest ranking positions of a state judiciary are chosen in this manner. The doctrine of separation of powers and the democratic nature of elections are fundamental propositions which support the elective mode of choice. However, since judgeships are not representative in character and involve a highly specialized function, students of government generally feel that the selection of judges should not be entrusted to the vagaries of public election. Instead, to insure competence on the bench, judges ought to be appointed on the basis of demonstrated ability in the field of law.

A half dozen states—Delaware, Hawaii, Maine, Massachusetts, New Hampshire, and New Jersey—empower the governor to choose all higher court judges. In Connecticut, Rhode Island, South Carolina, and Virginia these positions are filled by legislative selection. Approximately half the states rely exclusively upon election as the means of judicial selection, with a scant majority of them on a nonpartisan basis. About a dozen states use plans of selection that involve gubernatorial appointment followed by popular election after a period in office.

The California Plan. Under a 1934 constitutional amendment, judges of the California supreme court and district courts of appeals may not be opposed for re-election. Instead, a judge declares candidacy and runs on the basis of performance in office. If the voters approve the judge's record and vote to retain, the judge is re-elected to another term. In the event a judge is not re-elected, or should retire, resign, or be removed from office, the vacancy is filled by gubernatorial appointment subject to approval by a commission composed of the chief justice of the supreme court, the attorney general, and a judge of the court on which the appointee will serve. After taking office a new appointee serves until the next general election, then must go before the voters on the basis of record in office. Approval by the voters means that a newly appointed justice of the supreme court or of a district court may complete a twelve-year term. The plan does not apply to the superior courts, the general trial courts found in each county, unless by local option it is adopted by the voters.

The Missouri Plan. In 1940 the voters of Missouri approved a constitutional amendment, carried over in the Constitution of 1945, for a plan of judicial selection almost identical to that used in California. The principal differences are that the governor must make each appointment from a list of three nominees submitted by a commission composed of the chief justice, three attorneys chosen by the organized bar, and three laypersons selected by the governor; the plan is made applicable to the two most populous counties; and election to determine retention in office may not come earlier than one year after appointment.

Variations in Other States. The system devised in Missouri, known simply as the Missouri Plan, has served as the model for similar selection procedures adopted in other states since the late 1950's. The principal features of the Missouri Plan were adopted by Kansas in 1958, and within four years the list included Alaska, Iowa, and Nebraska. Since that date all or some of the provisions of the Missouri Plan have been adopted in a dozen additional states.

Terms

The longest terms of office served by any state public officials as a group are those of judges of courts of last resort. Supreme court justices of Rhode Island are appointed for life; those in New Jersey may be re-appointed to age seventy after serving a seven-year term; and in New Hampshire judges of the high court serve until they reach the age of seventy. The shortest terms—six years—occur in one-third of the states. Terms of intermediate appellate judges range from four years in Kansas to twelve in California and Missouri. From the general trial level down, variations in tenure are broad. Justices of the peace and magistrates are everywhere limited to terms of two to six years. Judges of lower courts in Massachusetts, New Hampshire, and with some exceptions in Rhode Island, enjoy the same tenure as their brethren on the state supreme court. In general, however, such judges serve for terms of four or six years.

Removal of Judges

Occasionally incompetence, disability, or even dishonesty leads to demands that judges be removed from their positions. Death, resignation, retirement, or failure of a judge to win re-election or reappointment may solve the problem, but should such a judge insist upon remaining in office one or more methods for removal are now available in each state. In almost all states judges are subject to *impeachment,* but since the process is clumsy, time-consuming, and tends to be political in nature, it is rarely used. Another method of removing judges, also infrequently used, is *legislative address.* This process requires that a resolution directing the removal of a judge be passed by an extraordinary majority of both legislative houses. No trial is involved; the governor simply declares the office vacant following the legislative action. The *recall,* available in eight states, is regarded by many as unsuited to the removal of judges in that it makes possible a means of recrimination for unpopular legal decisions. The point is largely academic, however, since the procedure has never been successfully used against a higher court judge. Following the lead of California in 1960, practically all states now utilize *judicial qualification commissions* in dealing with the sensitive question of removal. Known by various titles, these bodies receive and investigate complaints and, usually, make recommendations to the supreme court. In some instances the commission may impose discipline itself or may transmit its recommendations to the governor for implementation.

The problems associated with the removal of judges are among the most sensitive in government—and the most difficult to resolve. Until recently impeachment, legislative address, and recall were the only methods relied upon, which frequently meant that no practicable solution was available. Experience over the past two decades seems to indicate, however, that the qualification commission is a reasonably effective means of dealing with removals.

THE JURY SYSTEM

Two basis types of juries are used today, the *grand jury* and the *petit jury.* The function of a grand jury is to determine whether there is sufficient probability of guilt to bring a person to trial. Obviously it is used only in criminal proceedings. The petit jury, used in both civil and criminal proceedings, is the body which hears and determines the facts at the time a case is tried.

Grand Jury

Composed of six to twenty-three persons, grand juries are chosen by lot to serve for a prescribed period of time. New juries may be chosen every few weeks or months, but it is common in sparsely settled, peaceful areas for a single, annual jury to suffice. The members of a grand jury deliberate in secret, usually considering only the evidence presented to them by the prosecuting attorney. Decisions of a grand jury are reached by majority vote and are reported by the foreman to the judge in whose court the accused persons will be tried. Grand juries accuse by means of a *true bill of indictment,* or by *presentment* if accusation rests on evidence turned up by initiative of the jury. After its decisions are reported, a grand jury is dismissed.

Experience has shown the grand jury to be cumbersome. It adds to the already excessive delay and expense of enforcing criminal laws. Consequently, some states have virtually replaced the grand jury with a much simpler process by which the prosecuting attorney files a formal accusation known as an *information* with the clerk of the court in which trial is to be held. Indictment by grand jury is still generally used in connection with major offenses, but in the majority of states the information is used for all lesser crimes.

Petit Jury

The function of the petit or trial jury is to hear and determine the facts in civil and criminal trials. In a few instances they may have some authority to apply the law, as in capital criminal cases when the failure of a jury to recommend mercy means imposition of the death penalty. Juries in some states have power to reduce a charge as when a person tried for *first*-degree murder is convicted of *second*-degree murder.

Under the common law, petit juries consisted of twelve persons who were required to reach unanimous agreement before a verdict could be returned. Today the character of the jury is somewhat altered. Unanimous decisions by twelve-member juries are still required in the trial of major crimes, but for lesser offenses and in civil suits smaller juries reaching decisions by majority vote are common. Misdemeanor cases and civil proceedings involving trifling sums ordinarily are heard before juries only on demand of the parties. Many states permit even major crimes to be tried solely by a judge if the accused, being fully informed of all rights, waives the right to trial by jury.

Selection and Qualifications of Jurors

Juries are always chosen by lot. There are as many different methods of choice as there are states, but there is enough similarity from state to state to permit generalization. At least once a year, and usually oftener, a jury list is prepared by a legally designated local officer or agency—the sheriff, judge, clerk of a court, county governing board, special jury commissioners, or in New England, officers of the towns. The lists are of considerable length and, depending upon the state, may be prepared from voter registration books or tax assessor's rolls. From these lists names are chosen at random whenever jurors are needed. Persons thus selected for jury duty are summoned; some of those called are excused if good reason is given; and the names of the remainder are retained. The list of persons thus determined as eligible for jury service is called the *panel of veniremen.*

In each state the qualifications of jurors are set forth in statutes. Minors and persons over sixty or seventy are excluded. Literacy, residence, education, prior jury service, health, citizenship, eligibility to vote, and ability to speak and understand English are qualifications found in all or part of the states. Also, certain groups of individuals are by law rendered ineligible for jury service. In many states those engaged in professions or businesses vital to the public interest, such as physicians, lawyers, teachers, and druggists, are excused. Many governmental officials are similarly excluded, as are individuals to whom jury duty would entail extreme hardship.

Improving the System

Numerous suggestions have been advanced for improving the jury system, many of which have been generally adopted and fully implemented. Outright abolition of jury trials, for example, has been accomplished in certain technical fields by empowering expert administrative boards and commissioners to resolve legal controversies. Public utilities commissions, civil service boards, licensing bodies, and similar agencies are able to handle many situations which, if litigated in the regular courts, would require juries. Ordinarily, a petit jury consists of twelve persons, but many states now have statutes, and in some cases constitutional provisions, which permit use of a smaller number, particularly in civil proceedings. Over half the states have abandoned the idea that juries must agree unanimously in civil cases, requiring instead an extraordinary majority such as three-fourths or five-sixths. In all states the right to jury trial can be waived in minor cases, and in a third of the states even in trials on felony charges. A promising development within the jury system is the "blue ribbon" jury used in New York. When a judge in that state feels that a case is particularly complex or otherwise requires a jury of superior quality, he may direct that the jury be drawn from a special panel consisting of persons of education and ability, a process that has been approved by the United States Supreme Court.[8]

JUDICIAL REVIEW

One of the most potent weapons in the arsenal of the judiciary is judicial review, the power to declare null and void laws that are contrary to constitutional provisions. Since 1803, when John Marshall, Chief Justice of the United States, handed down the opinion of *Marbury* v. *Madison*,[9] the power has been a mainstay of federal courts. Many persons credit Marshall with origination of the doctrine, and indeed he is responsible for its introduction at the national level, but more than a dozen precedents in decisions of colonial and state courts predated his historic opinion.

8. *Fay* v. *New York*, 332 U.S. 261 (1947).
9. 1 Cranch 137.

Colonial cases involving judicial review date from the early eighteenth century, and the doctrine was applied or discussed in state court opinions prior to Marshall's enunciation.

No mention is made of the doctrine of judicial review in the United States Constitution, although provision for its use is made in some state constitutions. But whether specifically provided for or not, the courts of all states are empowered to invoke the doctrine in cases brought before them. Frequently, laws that are challenged on constitutional grounds cause almost even splits among justices, leading to the criticism that, in effect, the opinions of one or two justices can spell the difference between validity and unconstitutionality. It is strongly felt in some quarters that before a law is rendered null and void, it should be clearly and unmistakably beyond the pale of legality. Consequently in three states—Nebraska, North Dakota, and Ohio—findings of unconstitutionality must be supported by extraordinary majorities. [10]

Considered in terms of the many thousands of statutes, both state and federal, that have been enacted since the beginning of the Union, relatively few have been stricken down by means of judicial review. About one hundred and fifteen provisions of federal law and more than a thousand state laws have been voided by the United States Supreme Court. No count has been made of the state statutes voided by state courts. Laws thus invalidated are not expunged from the statute books. They remain in print until repealed or deleted by codifiers or revisors, but after being found contrary to higher law they lose their legal force, and courts will not hear future cases based upon them.

ADVISORY OPINIONS

Ordinarily, courts do not act upon issues unless they arise in a case or controversy. Contrary to usual practice, the supreme courts in eleven states are authorized to render advisory opinions. The constitutions of Colorado, Maine, Massachusetts, Michigan, New Hampshire, and Rhode Island provide that the governor or either house of the legislature may obtain advice. In Florida and South Dakota only the governor enjoys this constitutional privilege. Except in Michigan the court in each of these states is obligated to respond. The governor of Delaware, and in Alabama both the governor and legislature, may request advisory opinions as a result of statutory authorization. In compliance with long-standing custom the supreme court of North Carolina renders opinions when asked to do so by the governor or either house of the legislature.

There are several advantages in the use of advisory opinions. When

10. The Nebraska Constitution, Article V, Section 2, requires a majority of five of the seven supreme court justices; the North Dakota Constitution, Article IV, Section 89, sets the majority at four of five; and the Ohio Constitution, Article IV, Section 2, requires that six of the seven justices concur in findings of unconstitutionality.

obtained by the legislature, they may serve to deter the enactment of statutes of questionable constitutionality. The governor of a state also has at hand a useful guide to aid in deciding whether to sign or veto legislation about which there is constitutional doubts, or whether certain laws already enacted are in fact enforceable. Advisory opinions, as the name indicates, are *advisory* only except in Colorado where they have the legal force of a supreme court decision. Even though a supreme court advisory opinion may serve a utilitarian purpose, it is generally disapproved because the function is properly one which should be performed by an attorney general.

DECLARATORY JUDGMENTS

Today legislation has been enacted in practically all the states authorizing courts to render declaratory judgments. Unlike an ordinary suit at law or in equity, the declaratory judgment does not require a party to allege an actual or impending legal wrong. Instead, all that is required is that there be a controversy between parties as to their respective rights under a legal instrument such as a statute, ordinance, will, deed, or contract. The judgments, which are legally binding upon the parties involved, are available *before* any actual wrong is committed. They serve, therefore, to prevent injury and the needless costs and delay that might be occasioned by a lawsuit.

Declaratory judgments and advisory opinions are often confused since both are designed to forestall subsequent legal difficulties. As indicated earlier, however, the advisory opinion is generally not binding and is available only to governors and legislative bodies. The declaratory judgment, on the other hand, resembles a lawsuit in that *any* party to a controversy can petition for it and the resulting declaration is binding. The usefulness and desirability of the declaratory judgment is readily attested by its nearly universal use among the states and adoption by the federal government in 1934.

JUDICIAL COUNCILS

Few of today's state court systems are the result of consciously drafted plans for efficient organization. When New Jersey's Constitution of 1948 was being drafted, the court system was designed to achieve functional and organizational unity. But in most states courts have been added and altered as required, with the result that integration is largely lacking. Consequently, excessive delay and cost, overlapping jurisdictions, and crowded dockets are common. It is to the solution of problems arising out of such shortcomings that the attention of a *judicial council* is focused.

Judicial councils, now found in all states, are composed of judges, lawyers, legislators, attorney generals, and laypersons. They vary in size from a half-dozen members to more than fifty, but in most instances there are about a dozen members. Wisconsin in 1913 and Massachusetts in 1919 created agencies similar to today's judicial councils, but the first modern council was probably that of Ohio in 1923. They usually are created by statute, but in a few states establishment is based upon constitutional provisions.

The functions of a judicial council are primarily investigatory and advisory. They inquire into the organizational and administrative problems of the judiciary and on the basis of their findings recommend desirable changes to the legislature or governor. In a few states the council has power to prepare judicial rules of procedure, but usually this power is exercised by the supreme court, the legislature, or both. Since the judicial council movement is of comparatively recent origin, and since their authority is advisory, the accomplishments of the councils have not been as impressive as their supporters have hoped. The fact, however, that all states now have permanent councils designed to consider judicial problems on a continuing basis bodes well for future improvements.

ADMINISTRATIVE OFFICERS

The principal function of courts is to hear and determine cases, but they also have a great many internal administrative chores. Preparation of payrolls, accounting of funds, budget preparation, purchasing supplies, and many other essential tasks must be performed if the courts are to operate smoothly. Experience at the federal level indicates that centralization of these administrative activities can be highly beneficial. Since 1939 the Administrative Office of the United States Courts, headed by a director, collects judicial statistics, administers all financial matters respecting the courts, and supervises all administrative personnel of the national judiciary. Federal judges have thus been relieved of most administrative tasks and have more time to devote to their judicial responsibilities.

Use of administrative officers by state supreme courts is a phenomenon of recent origin. The state high tribunals employ these valuable aides, who twenty years ago were scarcely in evidence at all. In most instances administrators are chosen by the full court, but in some cases are appointed by the chief justice, judicial council, or administrative board. Their titles are varied, including the rather terse Director as well as the more impressive appellations Executive Secretary of the Supreme Court, and Administrative Director of the Courts. In no two states are their duties identical, but in general they perform in much the same manner as their federal counterpart. Now organized in a National Conference of Court Administrators, annual meetings are held at which suggested improvements in judicial administration are discussed and explored.

Nature and Functions of the Electorate

9

The successful operation and continued existence of democratic institutions is dependent upon an informed, politically active citizenry willing and able to control governmental policy and personnel. That control can be effected in a number of ways. The principal mechanism through which the people in a democratic society, acting in a peaceful, orderly manner, exercise and implement their will is the *suffrage*—the process of voting.

Understanding the suffrage necessitates an appreciation of the role of the electorate in a democratic society. After all, the voting process is merely a mechanism operating within the context of a pattern of citizen-society-government relationships. Important as the suffrage is, its real significance derives from the vital role of the people, or that part of them called the electorate, as related to the tasks of government. What is the "electorate"? Who are "the people"? What are their duties, privileges, and responsibilities? What is the role of the individual in the voting process?

In a democratic society the people—the sum total of the citizenry—are the source of all political power. What government is and what government does ultimately are determined by the people. That tremendous power carries with it the responsibility, indeed the duty, to make decisions intelligently. Usually, those decisions are made indirectly through the election of representatives who implement the people's will. Through their representatives the people make decisions as to the basic form and powers of the national government by means of amending the national constitution. At the state level those same decisions are, in part at least, made directly by means of balloting to accept or reject constitutional amendments and revisions. In some states the people participate directly in the making of public policy through the initiative and referendum.

Although the term "people" includes *everyone*—men, women, and children—it is obvious that many of the people are unable or unfit to participate in making basic decisions. Infants, the mentally incapacitated, and certain groups such as aliens, vagrants, persons convicted of felonies, and others are excluded from sharing in legally recognized decision making.[1] In short, certain standards are prescribed, and those who qualify are entitled, but not forced, to take part. That portion of the people is termed the *electorate,* and it is they who, directly or indirectly, make decisions that determine the nature and character of government.

VOTING—RIGHT OR PRIVILEGE?

Confusion exists in the minds of many persons as to whether there is, in fact, a *right* vested in Americans to cast ballots, or whether voting is a privilege extended by government. In partial answer to the question, it is certain that there is no constitutional right to vote. Nowhere in the national Constitution nor in the constitutions of any of the states is anyone guaranteed the right to cast a ballot in the same way that the rights to free speech, press, or religion are protected. Wherever the phrase "right to vote" is used in those documents the context clearly indicates that voting is conditional upon the satisfaction of legal qualifications. At the same time, voting is not a privilege in the sense that the entitlement of a single individual to cast a ballot can be withdrawn by the government whenever it pleases. If voting is to be termed a privilege, then it must be added that it is a privilege made available to all persons on the basis of meeting certain prescribed conditions.

Voting may be compared to a legally regulated activity such as operating an automobile. Before people may legally drive cars on public roads they must be as physically fit as the law requires them to be, pass a written examination on traffic regulations, and demonstrate their ability behind the wheel. After meeting these standards individuals are entitled to a driver's license. Since laws respecting the operation of motor vehicles apply to all persons alike, a person passing the various tests might be said to have the same "right" to drive as all others who do so. Similarly, qualifications for voting are established by laws, and a person who meets the qualifications has the same "right" to cast a ballot as all others who meet them.

SUFFRAGE AND THE CONSTITUTION

The Constitution of the United States does not delegate to the national government power to fix voting requirements. Setting suffrage qualifica-

---

1. Note the use of the word "legally" here, for these usually excluded groups could share in decision-making through such extralegal processes as revolutions, riots, and public demonstrations. They have, in fact, done so in the past.

tions is, therefore, among the reserved powers of the states. Since each state is independent of all other states in suffrage matters, there is no legal connection between the requirements imposed in one state and those established in others. With respect to the federal government, a state need only avoid conflict with the limitations found in the national Constitution and federal statutes.

As written by the framers, the Constitution contained only one provision restricting the power of the states to regulate suffrage. Article I, Section 2 provides that persons eligible to participate in the election of members of the House of Representatives shall be those who "have the qualifications requisite for electors of the most numerous branch of the State legislature." In other words, a person who qualifies to vote for candidates for the lower house of a state legislature, or in Nebraska for members of that state's unicameral legislature, may also vote for representatives in Congress. An identical clause applicable to the election of United States senators was added to the Constitution when, in 1913, the Seventeenth Amendment made senators subject to popular election. These clauses prevent the states from restricting the choice of members of Congress to a privileged portion of the electorate.

Shortly after the Civil War, Congress initiated the Fifteenth Amendment, intended to prevent discrimination against the black voter. It should be noted that the Amendment does not guarantee suffrage to blacks. Instead, it provides that states may not discriminate against *any* person because of "race, color, or previous condition of servitude." The obvious intent, however, at the time of adoption was to buttress the status of the newly freed black.

The Nineteenth Amendment became part of the Constitution in 1920 and specifically forbade the states to deny or abridge the franchise "on account of sex." The Amendment is not a specific guarantee of female suffrage. Rather, it is cast in terms of *sex,* a wording that technically includes men as well as women. However, the practical effect was to enfranchise women in those states where they did not enjoy full voting privileges. At the time, women voted on a plane of equality with men in a fourth of the states and could cast ballots in some elections in a few others.

The Twenty-fourth Amendment, added in 1964, provides that "failure to pay any poll tax or other tax" may not be made the reason for denying otherwise qualified persons the right to participate in the nomination and election of federal officials. Several states, however, continued to impose poll taxes as a qualification on voting for candidates for state offices until 1966, when the national Supreme Court ruled that poll taxes were unconstitutional.[2]

2. In *Harper* v. *Virginia Board of Elections,* 383 U.S. 663 (1966), poll taxes were ruled in violation of the Equal Protection of the Laws Clause.

In 1971 the Twenty-sixth Amendment became a part of the Constitution, providing that the suffrage rights of United States citizens "who are eighteen years of age or older" may not be abridged by the states "on account of age." The immediate, practical effect of the Amendment was to extend voting privileges to persons aged eighteen to twenty. It should be noted, however, that the legal effect is to forbid states to treat *any* age group or individual over eighteen differently, if such treatment can be construed as an abridgment of suffrage rights. Also, the Amendment does not *fix* a minimum voting age at eighteen. It merely says that the minimum shall be no higher than eighteen, leaving the states free, at their option, to extend suffrage rights to persons under that age.

Another clause of the Constitution that limits the power of the states to control suffrage is the Equal Protection of the Laws Clause of the Fourteenth Amendment. This provision of the Constitution applies to all state law, not just to statutes or state constitutional provisions relating to suffrage. Nevertheless, any action by a state that has the effect of abridging the legal right of a qualified person to vote, even though consistent with other provisions of the United States Constitution, might be challenged as denying equal treatment before the law.

GROWTH OF THE SUFFRAGE

Prevailing democratic ideas in the early years of state government in the United States did not include the concept of universal suffrage. Despite the glowing language of the Declaration of Independence and the tendency of modern writers to eulogize early American figures, opinions concerning the common people held by most founders of the Union reflected suspicion and distrust. Those in a position to influence the nature of the suffrage, generally the aristocratic, educated, landowning, well-to-do element, acted to protect the upper classes. As a result the suffrage was so highly restricted at the time the Constitution of the United States was written that fewer than five per cent of the total population could vote.

Since fear for the safety of property ownership was a principal motivating factor in restricting the suffrage during those early years, it is natural that property ownership should have been a common voting qualification. After the separation from England, each new state fixed qualifications based either upon owning real estate or the payment of taxes. In either case the emphasis was upon the economic worth of the individual. Such qualifications, in one form or another and with varying degrees of severity, persisted in the states until well after the Union was formed. Property ownership as a general suffrage qualification slowly began to disappear, was found in only a half-dozen states by 1821, and vanished altogether when North Carolina discontinued its property requirement in 1856.

The first few decades of independence saw the states limit the suffrage not only by property restrictions, but by religious qualifications as well. It was a common practice to exclude from the franchise those who did not believe in a supreme being, or in a few instances, did not adhere to the principles of the New Testament. The rationalization was that only the best people were entitled to vote, and the best people obviously were the responsible citizens with a property stake and religious scruples. Pressures based on the absence of a national church and the right of free exercise of religion soon prevailed, however, and religious qualifications were rapidly dropped after the adoption of the national Constitution. By 1810 the imposition of religious tests as a suffrage qualification had disappeared in every state in the Union, and none has been required by any state subsequently admitted.

With the turn of the nineteenth century the suffrage began to broaden. The open frontier, the formation of more unified political parties, improving communications, the beginnings of urbanization, and especially the Jacksonian concept of popular democracy brought on a liberalization of suffrage qualifications. By the time of the Civil War, universal white male suffrage was virtually achieved. The Fifteenth Amendment resulted in legally enfranchising black males, and in 1920 women were made eligible.

PRESENT-DAY VOTING QUALIFICATIONS

Restrictions placed on exercise of the suffrage by the states can be classified into two categories. In the first group are the *universal* qualifications, or those found in all the states. Included in this group are the requirements of United States citizenship, a minimum age, and a minimum period of residence within the state. The second category includes all those qualifications imposed in some, but not all, states. This group includes restrictions based on literacy, registration, and miscellaneous requirements such as those relating to moral character and the taking of oaths.

In addition to the usual array of voting qualifications each state excludes from the polls certain classes of people. The great majority withhold the franchise, for example, from the insane and retarded. Persons convicted of major crimes may not vote in virtually all states, and in some instances the privilege may never be restored. Persons dishonorably discharged from the armed forces of the United States, those convicted of subversive activities, and those who engage in dueling are disfranchised in one or more states.

The National Role

The authority to fix suffrage qualifications is essentially a state prerogative and may be exercised by a state free from interference by the national government as long as the state does not infringe or abridge any rights secured to individuals by the Constitution of the United States or valid national statutes. Whenever state action runs afoul of any such national provision, whether it be the Equal Protection of the Laws Clause, the Privileges and Immunities Clause, one of the more specific clauses relating to the suffrage, or a statute, federal authority becomes a factor. Until recent years the invocation of federal power was most frequently accomplished through individual lawsuits in which an aggrieved party sought a court-imposed remedy which might include a ruling that a particular suffrage regulation was invalid. However, until the last thirty years or so, the judiciary, and especially the United States Supreme Court, in most instances construed rights legislation rather narrowly. From the end of the Reconstruction period until the late 1950's Congress was almost totally ineffective in matters of rights legislation. Any bill could be defeated by a filibustering minority in the Senate, no matter what its prospects in the House of Representatives. Thus for more than three-quarters of a century a timid Supreme Court and a hamstrung Congress did little or nothing while the states were free to enact, if they chose, discriminatory suffrage laws.

Congress responded to new and insistent pressures in the 1950's and began to enact rights legislation, including stronger enforcement laws regarding suffrage. The most sweeping enactments were the Voting Rights Act of 1965 and the Voting Rights Act Amendments of 1970. In the 1965 legislation Congress authorized the appointment, by the United States Civil Service Commission, of federal voting registrars with full authority to register voters in states or subdivisions of states found by a federal district court to be guilty of discriminatory practices. Also, upon certification by the Attorney General of the United States that discrimination existed in a state, that a literacy test or equivalent device was in effect on November 1, 1964, and that less than half the persons old enough to vote were registered by that date, the literacy test of a state could be suspended. In the 1970 enactment Congress extended the effective life of the earlier law to 1975, when still another extension, to August 6, 1982, was approved.

United States Citizenship

For more than fifty years the states have been unanimous in the requirement that voters must be citizens of the United States. At one time about a fourth of the states permitted aliens who had applied for naturalization to cast ballots. Most of them were western states desirous of attracting residents, while in the east, where large numbers of the foreign born were concentrated, the opposite attitude prevailed. The practice of alien voting was gradually dropped, however, Arkansas being the last state to abandon it in 1926. The theoretical basis of the requirement is that only those persons who are legally part of the people should share in making decisions that affect the people.

Age

In the legal systems of the American states the age of twenty-one has generally been taken as the age of majority—the time at which a person is entitled to full management of personal affairs. It is quite understandable then that twenty-one became the age at which voting eligibility began. Until 1943, when Georgia lowered its minimum age qualification to eighteen, twenty-one was the minimum voting age in all states. In 1955 Kentucky reduced it to eighteen; and upon entry into the union in 1959, Alaska set the minimum age at nineteen and Hawaii at twenty. During the following decade, in response to the considerable pressure that was generated by various groups seeking extension of the franchise to younger voters, Massachusetts and Montana lowered the minimum age to nineteen, and in Maine and Nebraska it was reduced to twenty. In 1970 Congress enacted the Voting Rights Act Amendments, which provided that the minimum voting age should be eighteen in all elections, but the United States Supreme Court ruled that while the congressional action was valid as applied to elections in which federal officers were chosen, it could not lower the voting age for state elections.[3] Consequently, Congress proposed the Twenty-sixth Amendment which, when it went into effect in 1971, had the effect of preventing all states from setting the minimum age of suffrage eligibility any higher than eighteen.

Residence

Until the 1970's all states imposed durational residency requirements, usually of six months or a year. In 1972, however, the United States Supreme Court severely restricted the use of such requirements in *Dunn* v. *Blumstein*.[4] In that case a law school professor in Tennessee was not permitted to register as a voter, even though he was a state resident, because he had not met the one-year residence requirement. He conceded that the state could require him to be a resident, but contended that the length of the period was so unreasonable as to discriminate against him, thus depriving him of his constitutional right to equal protection of the laws. The Court agreed with him, and pointed out that while a state may impose a durational residence requirement it must have a "substantial and compelling reason" for doing so. One of the principal reasons asserted by Tennessee in this case was the prevention of election fraud, such as dual registration and multiple voting, reasons which were not questioned by the Court. However, in arriving at its decision the Court noted that for such purposes thirty days was an adequate period of time. The opinion did *not* prescribe any particular time spans which could be considered reasonable for given state purposes.

3. *Oregon* v. *Mitchell*, 400 U.S. 112 (1970).
4. 92 S. Ct. 995.

Nevertheless, in the three-fifths of the states that impose durational residency requirements, all but a few fix the period at thirty days.

Registration

In order to prevent abuse of the suffrage by persons ineligible to vote, some means must be used to identify those who have legally qualified to cast ballots. The method now used in most states is a process by which all persons who can qualify are required to enter their names on official lists— in other words, to register. Registration as a means of preventing voting frauds was begun in Massachusetts in 1800 and was adopted in most states from the end of the Civil War to 1910. Today all states except North Dakota require or permit registration, although some registration laws apply only to the larger cities and voting districts.

Technically, registration is not a qualification on the suffrage. Instead, it is a part of the election process whereby voters who have *already qualified* register their names for future identification at the polls. From the practical viewpoint, compulsory registration has the same effect as an age, citizenship, or residence requirement. If a person is otherwise qualified, but is not registered, that person is not permitted to cast a ballot. Hence, registration may well be regarded as a suffrage qualification.

Basically, there are two types of registration systems: the *permanent* and the *periodic.* In a permanent system voters need not reregister at any time unless they should move from the locale where they are registered or by virtue of some infraction of the law become ineligible to vote. Under a periodic system all voters must at some prescribed time reregister or forfeit their voting privileges. In theory, periodic registration is superior, for by requiring reregistration at stated intervals the lists of voters can be kept accurate and up to date. On the other hand, the process is expensive and voters find it inconvenient. Consequently, practically all states now use permanent systems. In any event, most states with permanent systems approximate some of the advantages of periodic registration by providing that the registration of a person becomes void unless that person actually votes in state elections.

Literacy

The only suffrage qualification imposed by the states that is related to the *quality* of the electorate is the requirement that voters be literate. Connecticut in 1855 and Massachusetts two years later were the first states to require that voters demonstrate their literacy. By 1965, twenty states in all sections of the country had adopted literacy qualifications which, in most cases, required no more than that a person be able to read and write.

The status of literacy qualifications today is widely misunderstood because of the effects of the Voting Rights Act of 1965 and the Voting Rights Act Amendments of 1970. Contrary to popular belief, these federal laws did not outlaw literacy tests. The 1965 statute made possible the suspension of literacy qualifications; the 1970 enactment suspended them until 1975—when they were again suspended for an additional seven years. In 1982 Congress will again have the option of continuing the suspension or permitting the affected states to impose literacy qualifications.

Poll Taxes

The first poll tax imposed as a suffrage qualification was levied by Florida in 1889. In combination with literacy and long residence requirements, the poll tax proved an effective method of discriminating against blacks, and by the beginning of the twentieth century it had been adopted by most southern states. The tax was attacked as undemocratic and, after repeal was achieved in North Carolina in 1920, it began slowly to lose favor. At the time that poll taxes were held unconstitutional in 1966, they were in effect in only four states—Alabama, Mississippi, Texas, and Virginia.

As applied to the nomination and election of federal office holders poll taxes were outlawed in 1964 when the Twenty-fourth Amendment was ratified as a part of the United States Constitution. Contrary to the impression held by many people, the Amendment did not forbid the imposition of poll taxes as such. The states could still require that such taxes be paid before one could participate in the nomination and election of candidates for state offices. In fact, almost simultaneously with the ratification of the Twenty-fourth Amendment the legislature of Virginia enacted a statute making a poll tax applicable in the selection of non-federal elective officials. However, it was this statute that the United States Supreme Court invalidated in 1966, declaring that voting qualifications "have no relation to wealth nor to paying or not paying this or any other tax."[5]

THE BLACK SUFFRAGE PROBLEM

Because of the unfortunate antipathies and prejudices toward blacks, particularly in the southeastern United States, a serious problem exists with respect to the voting equality of the black minority. The causes of these intense feelings go back over a century to the days when slavery was an accepted American institution. The bitterness of the Civil War and the events that followed nurtured attitudes still strongly in evidence over a century later.

5. *Harper* v. *Virginia Board of Elections,* 383 U.S. 663 (1966).

The Reconstruction Period

During the years following the war, the white southerners were literally divested of any substantial control of state government. Under the Reconstruction Acts the southern states were organized into military districts commanded by Union army officers. The military commanders had authority to remove civil officers and to control virtually all aspects of civil government. During this period unscrupulous individuals—northerners contemptuously called "carpet baggers" and southerners referred to as "scalawags"—through graft, corruption, and collusion made a mockery of civil government. The newly freed black male became the scapegoat. Uneducated and propertyless, blacks became the foils manipulated by those who could exploit them. In short, blacks were made to appear responsible for many of the excesses of the Reconstruction Period. When President Hayes ordered an end to military occupation of the South in 1877 and the white southerners once again regained control of the governmental reins, resentment toward blacks was displayed.

The Mississippi Plan

By the 1880's the whites were firmly in control of the political processes in the southern states and set about seeking methods to bar blacks legally from the polls. In 1890 Mississippi amended its constitution to tighten suffrage qualifications in such a way that most blacks would not be able to qualify. Included in the plan were a two-dollar poll tax, a two-year residence restriction, and a literacy qualification that required prospective voters to be able to read, write, and understand any part of the state constitution. Obviously, the great bulk of blacks would be eliminated for they were still largely illiterate, propertyless, and rarely able to afford two dollars for poll taxes. Upheld by the United States Supreme Court[6] as being legal on its face, the Mississippi plan was rapidly adopted by other southern states. While effective in keeping blacks from the polls, the Mississippi Plan had an unintended effect that rankled many whites: great numbers of poor white voters were also disfranchised.

The Grandfather Clauses

To restore suffrage rights to the large numbers of disfranchised whites, "grandfather clauses" were devised. They provided that persons who were citizens before 1866, or 1867, or descendants of such citizens, were excused from literacy qualifications. Since blacks were not citizens in that year, they were not privileged under the clauses, as were most whites. To avoid conflict with the Fifteenth Amendment, grandfather clauses,

6. *Williams* v. *Mississippi*, 170 U.S. 213 (1898).

though usually in the form of constitutional provisions, were made temporary. By the time a case could be carried to the United States Supreme Court a challenged clause would expire. However, the grandfather clause added to the Oklahoma constitution in 1910 was successfully attacked five years later and found by the highest federal court to be contrary to the provisions of the Fifteenth Amendment forbidding abridgment of the suffrage on the basis of race.[7]

The Democractic White Primary

With the passage of time the effectiveness of Mississippi Plans began to wane, and further refinements of methods of discrimination were sought. The answer to the southerners' search was suggested by a United States Supreme Court decision holding that primary elections were beyond the regulation of Congress.[8] Since the vast majority of southerners were Democrats, whoever won nomination in the Democratic Party primary was virtually certain to be elected. Hence, if the Democratic primary was limited to white voters only, the black would, for all practical purposes, be excluded from the polls. After a series of cases in which it was declared finally that states as such could not close the primaries to blacks, the Democratic Party in Texas, acting on its own volition in convention, adopted a resolution restricting party membership to white persons. In *Grovey* v. *Townsend*, decided in 1935, the United States Supreme Court upheld the action of the convention.[9] Thus the Democratic White Primary, from which blacks were totally excluded, was sanctioned by the highest court in the land.

For several years after the *Townsend* ruling the outlook for black suffrage in the South was bleak. Then, in a 1941 case that did not involve blacks in any way, the Supreme Court handed down an opinion that seemed to offer grounds for a new attack on the white primary.[10] An election commissioner had been caught falsely counting and certifying ballots in a Louisiana primary and had been convicted under *federal* law. In upholding the conviction the Court ruled that primaries were an integral part of the election process and thus subject to federal control. Soon another Texas case involving the white primary was brought and in 1944, in *Smith* v. *Allwright,* the Supreme Court reversed the *Townsend* decision and struck down the white primary.[11] South Carolina later attempted to retain its white primary by repealing all state laws relating to the subject of primary elections. The idea behind the action was that if the primary did not exist in state law, it would be beyond

7. *Guinn* v. *United States,* 238 U.S. 347 (1915).
8. *Newberry* v. *United States,* 256 U.S. 232 (1921).
9. 295 U.S. 45.
10. *United States* v. *Classic,* 313 U.S. 299.
11. 321 U.S. 649.

the reach of the courts. However, a lower court decision which the Supreme Court refused to review condemned the action as merely a stratagem to avoid federal law and therefore invalid.[12] Throughout the following decade attempts were made in several southern states to deny the legal right of blacks to participate in primary elections, but these efforts were also struck down by the Supreme Court.

The Situation Today

The passing of the white primary did not result in substantially increased black participation in elections. Having a legal right to do something and actually exercising that right are two radically different things. Discrimination against blacks seeking to exercise the suffrage has continued, although considerable progress toward equality has been realized during the last decade.

Improvements were made under federal civil rights legislation enacted in 1957, 1960, and 1964, especially when a pattern of discrimination in suffrage matters was involved. The legislation which offers most promise of achieving equality in the exercise of suffrage rights is the federal Voting Rights Act of 1965. By the terms of this legislation, various state-imposed qualifications can be suspended in any state or county in which less than half of the voting age population was registered for or actually voted in the general election of 1964. Federal examiners may then step in and register persons who comply with such state requirements as age and residency. Since 1960 the number of blacks registered to vote has, in fact, increased dramatically, but such gains are not solutions to the basic problem of race prejudice.

NONVOTING

In the United States a turnout on election day of sixty to sixty-five per cent of the total possible number of voters is considered good. This level of performance contrasts sharply with voting behavior in many European countries where it is common for upwards of eighty-five or ninety per cent of the eligible voters to cast ballots.

A variety of reasons can be cited to explain why so many Americans fail to vote. At the head of the list is the plain fact that many individuals are simply indifferent to political matters. They take no interest in the affairs of government and, presumably as long as their personal situations are not drastically affected by political activity, they cannot be expected to become interested. Perhaps as many as half of those who fail to vote are included in this group. Swelling the ranks of the nonvoters are the

---

12. *Elmore* v. *Rice,* 72 F. Supp. 516 (1947); *Rice* v. *Elmore* 165 F. 2d 382 (1947).

millions of blacks and members of other minorities who, because of intimidation or discrimination by election officials, are unable to qualify. Also counted in the millions are those persons who, at the time of elections, are ill or otherwise physically handicapped and either cannot or do not take advantage of absentee voting privileges. Work or study away from home accounts for a large number of nonvoters, and a few do not cast ballots for religious reasons. Still others do not participate for such superficial reasons as inconvenience, distance from the polls, or refusal to take time from other activities.

Frequently, campaigns are conducted by politically interested groups to encourage people to register and vote. The motives behind such activities are praiseworthy, but the result may be a mixed blessing. Everything possible should be done to remind the citizenry that an election is approaching and to encourage people to qualify themselves to cast ballots. At the same time it should be remembered that little is gained when uninformed, ordinarily disinterested people are encouraged to vote simply for the sake of voting. It may reasonably be said that an uninformed vote is as bad, if not worse, than no vote at all. Since nonvoting appears to be most prevalent among those least informed, efforts by civic-minded individuals and groups to get out the vote would be more meritorious if directed at *informing* nonvoters on issues and candidates and then prompting them to vote.

COMPULSORY VOTING

Compelling people to vote has been proposed at times on the ground that democracy operates best when there is wide citizen participation. Today compulsory voting exists, or has been used, in only a few countries scattered around the world. Its longest and perhaps most successful application has been in Belgium, where it was adopted in 1892. Compulsory voting has never been looked upon with favor in the United States. It was rejected by the voters of Oregon in 1920 by a margin of two to one. The constitutions of Massachusetts and North Dakota authorize compulsory voting, but the legislatures of those states have not enacted legislation on the subject.[13] What appears to be the only example of a form of compulsory voting in the United States since colonial days occurred in the 1890's in Kansas City, Missouri. The city charter imposed a poll tax but exempted all voters who cast ballots in municipal elections. The charter provision was set aside by the Missouri supreme court which held that a right to vote could not be made a legal obligation.[14]

---

13. Massachusetts Constitution, Article of Amendment 61; North Dakota Constitution, Article II, Section 127.
14. *Kansas City* v. *Whipple,* 136 Mo. 475 (1896).

Whatever fate a compulsory voting law might meet if contested in the courts today, it is certain that the idea is contrary to American tradition. There is little likelihood that a system of compulsion would be seriously considered in any state. It is probably just as well that the idea of compulsory voting has not been well received, for the system has an inherent flaw that makes it of questionable value. It is possible to force most people to the polls, but to do so invites millions of uninformed, unintelligent votes. In such an event the cure for nonvoting would undoubtedly be worse than the ill of abstention! Considering the possible consequences of compulsory voting and the traditions of American democracy, it appears that the best antidote for nonvoting lies in improving the suffrage and electoral systems rather than in herding reluctant voters into the polls.

ABSENTEE VOTING

On election day there are many voters who, for one reason or another, cannot be present to cast ballots in their local precincts. Members of the armed forces, for example, cannot leave their posts and return home to vote. Other voters may be ill, physically disabled, away from home on business, or, as migrant laborers, forced to go where employment can be found. Since any or all such persons may earnestly desire to cast ballots and are qualified to do so, all states now make it possible for them to participate in elections by means of the absentee ballot.

The use of absentee ballots dates back to the Civil War when they were used, without much success, to enable soldiers and sailors to vote. It was not until 1896, in Vermont, that the first statute extending the privilege of absentee balloting to both civilians and military personnel was enacted. Most of the impetus for absentee voting legislation has come during wartime when large numbers of voters are in the armed forces. During World War II Congress created a War Ballot Commission to facilitate voting by military personnel for candidates for national offices in the 1944 general election. Twenty states recognized the validity of the ballots distributed by the Commission, and the remaining states permitted military personnel to vote on state ballots. Since World War II several states have liberalized their absentee laws, and in a few others provisions have become more stringent.

Casting an absentee ballot is a tedious process. The details vary from state to state, but basic procedures are much the same everywhere. First a voter must apply to the proper official, usually the clerk of the county in which one's home precinct is located, for a ballot. The application must be accompanied by a notarized affidavit attesting to the eligibility of the voter and must be received by the appropriate official before a designated date. After the voter receives a ballot, it must be filled out secretly but *in the presence of* an officer authorized to administer oaths. The ballot is then returned in an official, sealed envelope accompanied by a notarized affidavit declaring that the voter marked the ballot in secret. The ballot must be received by a designated deadline if it is to be counted. Since the time during which all these steps must be performed may be less than a month, although usually longer, action by a voter in executing an absentee ballot is convincing evidence of appreciation of the suffrage.

SUFFRAGE IN THE DISTRICT OF COLUMBIA

When the Twenty-third Amendment became a part of the Constitution in 1961, residents of the District of Columbia acquired the right to participate in the choice of presidential electors for the first time in the history of the Union. Under the Amendment the federal district "shall appoint in such manner as the Congress may direct" presidential electors, "but in no event more than the least populous state." Since presidential electors are chosen by popular vote, qualified residents of the district cast ballots choosing three members of the electoral college.

Although district residents may now vote in presidential elections, they have no voice in the selection of local governmental officials. Beginning in 1802 mayors were appointed by the President, with council members chosen by popular vote. In 1874, Congress revised the system of district government, withdrawing all voting privileges enjoyed by the residents. The only other occasions on which the population of the District of Columbia has participated in the electoral process have been presidential primaries, the first of which was held in 1956.

The fact that district residents were denied suffrage rights prior to adoption of the Twenty-third Amendment can be easily explained. The power to set suffrage qualifications is a reserved power vested in the states—and the District of Columbia is not a state. Congress could restore local elections, but it could not, by legislative act, authorize residents to cast ballots for national officers. Thus it was necessary to amend the Constitution to confer upon residents of the District of Columbia suffrage rights similar to those enjoyed by residents of the states.

Political Parties and Pressure Groups

10

Writing in 1770 the English statesman Edmund Burke defined a political party as "a body of men united, for promoting by their joint endeavours the national interest, upon some particular principle in which they are all agreed." This definition does not accurately describe the major political parties in the United States. In both major American parties—the Democratic and Republican—membership includes persons of widely varying interests. The conservative "Dixiecrats" of the southeastern part of the country are counted as Democrats, but they have little in common with liberal members of the party. Within the Republican Party the "old Guard" conservatives contrast sharply with the liberal "progressive" wing. Numerous examples of individual party members who cannot agree with their associates upon "some particular principle" could be cited. Consequently, a more accurate definition must be framed.

Casting a definition in terms of the principles that bring people together in parties invites inaccuracy because of the different ways in which individuals perceive and understand those concepts. More meaningful understanding can be attained by emphasizing the *basic purpose* of political parties and the *methods* they employ. Viewed in terms of these criteria, it is possible to say that a political party is a voluntary association of persons joined together for the purpose of achieving power through winning elections and running the government.

LEGAL STATUS

Parties exist as legal entities only if they can qualify according to specifications set forth in state law. These criteria vary widely among the states. In Colorado, for example, a political group is recognized as a party if its candidate for governor received at least ten per cent of the votes cast for that office at the last preceding general election. Nevada parties must attract five per cent of the votes cast for candidates for the state's one seat in the United States House of Representatives. A political party in New Hampshire enjoys legal recognition if its gubernatorial candidate wins three per cent of the votes. In New York a party must poll only 50,000 votes for its candidate for governor—a figure that represents a fraction of one per cent of the votes cast in that state's general elections. Most severe in their qualifications are Alabama, Kentucky, Oregon, and Virginia. In the first three a party must attract twenty per cent of the total vote cast for presidential electors, and in Virginia the figure is twenty-five per cent. Since a party must be in existence before it can offer candidates, some means must be provided for them to get started. Illustrative of this process is the Oregon procedure by which a "minor" party gains legal status by circulating petitions to gather signatures of registered voters equal in number to five per cent of the total votes cast in the last general election for candidates for membership in the lower house of Congress.

Since the legal existence of parties derives from state authority, a question naturally arises as to the legal status of *national* parties. On this point confusion may arise. However, if the state political party is viewed primarily as an organization for the nomination of candidates for public office, the confusion is quickly dispelled. Since the holding of elections is a state function, and parties operate as nominating agents in those elections, it follows that the parties may be subjected to regulation by the state. Since a state may exercise legal authority only over matters within its jurisdiction, it may determine the qualifications for a political party within state boundaries, but it can do no more than recognize the existence of a national organization and, as all states have done, regulate to some extent the ways in which persons within the state participate in the national organization. Obviously then, there are fifty different state parties in the loose association of groups known as the Republican Party and an equal number in the Democratic Party.

At the national level, political parties must be regarded as extralegal. Congress does not undertake to establish a legal definition of them although it does of course recognize the fact that political parties exist. Indeed, the organization of Congress itself is based on the party affiliation of the senators and representatives. In many statutes dealing with a wide variety of topics, party action and affiliation is recognized. Contributions to parties, for example, are regulated by statute. A civil servant cannot be discharged for reasons of party preference. The membership of certain governmental commissions must be divided as evenly as possible between members of the major parties. Scores of other statutes involve the same type of recognition.

THE AMERICAN PARTY SYSTEM

Viewed nationally, party activity in the United States has taken the form of a "two-party" system, meaning that two *major* parties are dominant, and to them are attracted the great bulk of voters. Other parties known as *third* parties exist, but usually they are shortlived or do not seriously threaten the supremacy of the major parties.

Many explanations have been offered as to why a two-party system exists in this country when all over the world, except in the English-speaking countries, "multiple" party systems with several parties possessing considerable strength are found. While no authoritative, documented list of reasons may be cited, it appears that the best rationale rests upon a complex of factors. First, the effects of *initial form* must be taken into account. When Americans were confronted with the major political decision of adopting or rejecting the Constitution, only two courses of action were open to them. Political alignments had to be made on that basis, and later when parties began to take form the pattern of alignment tended to persist. Second, *institutional factors* certainly have exerted a profound influence. Most elective offices in the United States are filled by means of the *plurality* system, meaning simply that the candidate who gets the most votes is elected. Since most elective public officials are chosen from single-member districts, only one person can be elected regardless of the number of candidates in a district. The fewer candidates who run for an office, the greater are the mathematical chances of election for each aspirant. Accordingly there is a tendency for political groups to align themselves into as few parties as possible in order to increase their possibilities of success. Under such a system the minor party is at a distinct disadvantage. The use of electors in choosing the President of the United States is in reality a method of combining the results of fifty election districts, the states; and, in view of the plurality rule, this procedure all but eliminates the possibility of a third party electing a President. A third factor that tends to strengthen and perpetuate the two-party system is the general approval accorded to it by the American people. Relatively few groups in the United States are so dogmatically attached to a single idea or principle that they cannot merge with other groups in one or the other of the two major parties.

State and Local Patterns

Despite the fact that nationally the two-party system prevails, a variety of systems, or "subsystems," are found at the state and local levels. In some areas the party system is like the national pattern. In others only one party is of any consequence. The party system in a few areas is characterized by third parties that have been able to contend seriously with the Democrats and Republicans. As a matter of fact, third parties have for limited periods become dominant, relegating the traditional major parties to virtual minor party status. In still other areas, formal party designations have been abandoned, resulting in nonpartisan elections, at least in form.

In most states, large cities, and counties there are two principal parties, the Democrats and Republicans, offering candidates for practically all offices. There are areas, however, where deviation from the two-party pattern has persisted. Best known of these exceptional areas is the Democratically dominated southeastern United States, often called the "Solid South."

In view of the prospects of almost certain Democratic victories, Republican candidacies usually have been limited to only the most important offices. Throughout the South there are a few areas where Republicans have been able to establish themselves as a contending party. In New England the pattern of party domination is reversed. Traditionally, the Republican Party has been strong in those states, and particularly in Maine and Vermont Republican supremacy has been characterized as one-party domination.

Nonpartisan Systems

Except for the election without party labels of members of the Nebraska legislatures, many judges, and a few executive officers such as superintendents of public instruction, nonpartisanship is confined to municipalities and special districts. A principal argument in support of nonpartisanship on the local level is that parties are closely identified with national and state issues and when national, state, and local elections are held simultaneously, questions of local importance tend to be obscured. As a result, the local citizenry is not as likely to give as much thought and attention to local matters as they should. Other reasons for the greater incidence of nonpartisanship at the local level derive primarily from the technical or business nature of the functions involved. In choosing the personnel of a governing board for a drainage district, for example, it would be rather difficult to maintain that there is a Republican as opposed to a Democratic method of draining a swamp. The same reasoning applies to other types of governmental programs involving technical problems. Governing a municipality is sometimes said to be similar in many ways to the management of a business, as suggested by the term municipal *corporation.* Operating water systems, power plants, and sewage-disposal facilities, paving streets, maintaining libraries, and providing parks and other such municipal functions are similar to business ventures, and in the judgment of many persons they are hampered more than helped when subjected to partisan control. In short, the theory of nonpartisanship holds that by minimizing the influence of political parties more effective and efficient government can be achieved.

Running a government, no matter how large or how small it may be, always involves making policy—and policymaking is a process that is potentially controversial and contentious. The example of draining a swamp cited above admittedly involves questions of a technical nature that have little or no connection with partisan activity. But what of the question as to whether the swamp *ought* to be drained? Should bonds be issued or new taxes levied to finance the project? These are questions of policy that invite disagreement and partisanship. It is thus almost impossible to conceive of a governmental activity that does not, at one stage or another, take on a partisan character.

Viewed strictly from the standpoint of theory, there is little doubt that a nonpartisan system is highly desirable. In practice, however, the theory often does not hold up. Removing party labels from candidates does not transform them into nonpartisans. A Democrat who is elected to a city council on a nonpartisan ballot remains a Democrat. Republicans similarly chosen to serve on a school board do not drop their party preference after taking office. Although the actions of nonpartisan officials and boards may not be *formally* associated with the programs of political parties, identification is often unmistakable.

Another weakness in the nonpartisan rationale lies in the fact that when political parties as such are dispensed with, other political action groups of a partisan nature assume greater prominence and in a sense replace them. In a given locality, for instance, labor unions, chambers of commerce, farm groups, veterans' organizations, civic improvement clubs, churches, newspapers and the like may campaign for certain policies or endorse some "nonpartisan" candidates in preference to others. When this occurs, as it often does, it is obvious that the theoretical advantages of nonpartisanship are lost. The partisan pattern is merely altered.

It is not to be denied that nonpartisanship can work. When citizens in a community are overwhelmingly like-minded, partisan activity is at a minimum. A lack of controversial issues deadens partisan spirit. Such conditions are not common, however, and when they do prevail they are usually of temporary duration.

Third Parties

In addition to the two major parties in the United States there traditionally has been a varying number of third parties. Some have persisted for long periods of time while others have lasted for only a few years. National prominence and importance have been achieved by some while others have flourished in only a limited number of states. In some instances a third party has been active within only one state or even a single community. Only once in American history has a third party replaced one of the major parties. That event occurred when the Republican Party of today rose to fill the void created by the disintegration of the Whigs.

Third parties generally have been of two types: those dedicated to the fulfillment of an easily identifiable general principle or goal, and those composed of the devoted followers of an outstanding personality. The Prohibitionists, Socialists, and Populists are examples of groups that are, or have been, "idea" parties. Probably the best example of a "personality" party is the "Bull Moose" Progressive Party which split from the Republicans in 1912 under the leadership of Theodore Roosevelt. Failing to win the presidency in that year, Roosevelt was never again a presidential candidate, and the party disappeared.

At the state and local levels particularly, it must not be assumed that a third party is necessarily "minor" in character. A third party may be able to contend on equal terms with the Democrats and Republicans. In fact, a third party may, for a short period at least, become dominant. In 1948 the States' Rights Party, known as the Dixiecrats, was dominant in several southern states, as the American Independent Party, led by Governor George C. Wallace, was in 1968. The Liberal Party of New York has been highly influential in that state, and in North Dakota the Nonpartisan League, operating as a faction within the two major parties, has been the controlling factor in the outcome of many elections. Though now merged with the Democrats, the Farmer-Labor Party has been a vital force in Minnesota politics. Sometimes third parties are unable to exert appreciable statewide influence but are important in certain localities. The Socialist Party, for example, has realized success in Milwaukee, Wisconsin, Bridgeport, Connecticut, and Reading, Pennsylvania, although its influence throughout those states has been negligible. It is important to bear in mind that the national pattern of two-partyism does not, at any one time, necessarily prevail in a particular state or locality.

Third parties never have been able to win a great many public offices or to exercise sustained control over public policy. They have, nevertheless, contributed significantly to the American political system. Their chief effect has been to introduce new ideas which, at the time of inception, were shunned by the major parties as politically risky. Antitrust legislation, income taxes, popular election of United States senators, and female suffrage were matters championed by third parties. After it became obvious that substantial numbers of voters were favorably disposed, those proposals were absorbed into the programs of one or both major parties. Their programs thus taken over, third parties usually declined in importance or disappeared altogether. A significant result of activities by third parties has been to stimulate realignment of groups, factions, and individuals within the major parties. For example, the Republican Party was seriously rent in 1912 when literally millions of voters were wooed away by Theodore Roosevelt. The Progressive and States' Rights movements in 1948 weakened the Democratic Party to a dangerous extent, though not enough to bring about defeat of the party's presidential candidate.

Functions of Political Parties

The principal function of a political party is to choose candidates and secure their election to public office. Parties perform other functions too, but virtually every action of a party can be rationalized in terms of its contribution toward winning votes. This situation should not be surprising, for a party that is unable to attract enough votes to elect at least a reasonable number of its candidates can hardly be regarded as an effective vehicle of political action.

In its drive to win popular following and establish itself in a position of dominance, a political party must discharge certain functions and bear definite responsibilities. First, voters tend generally to hold a party accountable for its candidates who are elected to office. Just as a party profits from outstanding performance by its members in office, its status is likewise damaged by dishonest, incompetent, or even politically unpopular actions on the part of party members in public service. In this respect the party is frequently termed a "bonding agent" to insure satisfactory performance of its electees.

A party also acts as informant to the electorate by presenting a program and taking stands on issues. It is true that each party slants information to favor its own views, but since both major parties and third parties act in their own interests, the voters get a variety of views on issues of interest to political parties. Next, a party serves as "watchdog" or "critic" of governmental affairs. While all parties are active in this capacity, the major party out of power fills the role best. Hoping to capitalize on mistakes made by the party in power, the "out" party stands ready to inform the voters about the mistakes of the opposition. Finally, parties are a means by which cohesion is achieved both within and between the legislative and executive branches at all levels. Party affiliations of officials in various positions in government, especially those that involve the making of policy decisions, provide a basis for cooperation. Legislatures, for example, are organized on the basis of party. An administration controlled by the party possessing a majority in the legislature is more likely to enjoy amicable relations with the lawmakers. Appointments usually are made on the basis of party. Indeed, political parties are the inter-connecting tissue in the fabric of government.

PARTY ORGANIZATION

A political party, like any other group, must be well organized to operate effectively. Without organization a party would be little more than a vaguely definable association of individuals sharing similar viewpoints on a number of issues. With effective organization it is a collection of individuals and groups which, potentially, can control the policies and personnel of government.

Since there is no legal connection between state and national party organizations, each American political party is separately organized on the national and state levels. In other words, a major party is made up of fifty different state organizations and a single national organization which is not empowered to exercise full legal controls over the state components. Third parties vary from the pattern in that they do not legally exist in many states and may be treated in a manner different from that applicable to the major parties.

National Organization

At the apex of each of the major American political parties is its *national committee.* These committees usually meet in January of presidential election years to fix the time and place of the national convention. Other meetings of the full membership are infrequent, ordinarily including only organizational meetings, an assembly at the time of the national convention, and a strategy meeting held prior to the general election conducted between presidential election years. At other times committee work is actually performed by the national chairman or divisions of the committee dealing with such matters as finance, research, women's affairs, and publicity. Entirely separate from the national committees are the senatorial and congressional campaign committees found in both major parties. These committees are accountable only to the respective legislative groups, but because of common interests they frequently cooperate with the national committee.

The general director of party affairs is the national chairman. Although, not a member of the national committee, the national chairman presides over its meetings. Officially, the chairman is chosen by the national committee, but in practice the committee usually does no more than approve the choice of the party's presidential nominee. In case of a vacancy in the chairmanship of the party in power, the President of the United States dictates the choice of the person who fills the post. Should a vacancy occur in the defeated party's chairmanship, the national committee, perhaps influenced by party leaders, selects the new chairman. The principal function of a national chairman is to manage the presidential campaign, but after the election the chairman continues to act as organizer, fund-raiser, trouble-shooter, general publicity manager, and outspoken critic of the opposition.

Every four years national conventions are held by American parties. Composed of delegates chosen in accordance with state statutes and the regulations of the parties, the principal function of a national convention is to nominate candidates for the offices of President and Vice President. As the supreme policymaking organ of a party, the convention draws up a *platform* or statement of party position on issues of political interest. Usually a boisterous affair at which much dealing and compromising occurs, the convention has prevailed as the presidential nominating device of all major and most third parties since 1831.[1]

State and Local Organization

Within each state political party, organization corresponds generally to the boundaries of election districts. That is, a committee exists at the state level, and others are organized in counties, cities, wards, towns, congressional districts, and the like. In no two states are parties organized in identical fashion, but all systems are similar enough to permit generalization.

At the head of a party's state organization is the state *central committee.* In describing these committees the late Professor V. O. Key commented that

> Variety characterizes their composition, method of selection, duties, and even formal titles. They range in size from a handful to a group that can meet only in a convention hall. Their authority at one extreme amounts to that of a constituent body for the party in a state; at the other it amounts to little more than the ministerial performance of duties minutely prescribed by statute.[2]

Generally, in states where statutory controls are not extensive or excessively detailed, notably in the southeastern area of the country, the discretion of a state central committee is broadest. Even there, however, the one-party nature of state politics with all major candidates in the same party results in pressure for impartiality on the part of the committee.

Chosen by, but ordinarily not a member of, the state central committee is the titular head of the party, the state chairperson. Resembling the national chairman in that promotion of party candidates in general elections and fostering party harmony are principal functions, the state chairperson is not the real leader of the party. Often the governor, a United States Senator, a national committee member, or some other person or group is much more influential than the state chairperson. Moreover, state chairpersons commonly have found it difficult, if not impossible, to exercise control over local political "bosses."

Between the state central committee and the local units of organization are found various district committees set up on the basis of congressional, state legislative, or state judicial districts. In most states such committees are relatively unimportant. Their only function usually is to assist in the

---

1. One of the most vivid reactions to national conventions in this country was that of the Russian observer, M. Ostrogorski, who declared after watching a convention in action "you cannot help repeating the American saying: 'God takes care of drunkards, of little children, and of the United States,'" M. Ostrogorski, *Democracy and the Organization of Political Parties,* trans. by Frederick Clarke, The Macmillan Co., New York, 1902, vol. II, pp. 278-279.
2. V. O. Key, Jr., *Politics, Parties, and Pressure Groups,* 4th ed., Thomas Y. Crowell Co., New York, 1958, p. 357.

election of the party's candidate in the district, a task often performed by county personnel or the candidate's personal committee. In some instances these committees have authority to nominate candidates in the event of death or withdrawal of the regularly chosen nominees, and they often influence appointment of party followers to governmental jobs.

Precincts are the "building blocks" of local party machinery. These election districts are plotted geographically to contain a certain number of voters, 300 to 500 being common. Party organization within a precinct sometimes consists of a committee, but usually there is a precinct *committeeman* or *captain.* Elected in most instances in the party primary, the precinct captain's function is to win over the precinct voters. The fact that no party, especially in two-party areas, can expect to win consistently without effective precinct personnel attests to the importance of this local office.

At the local level the *county committee,* headed by the *county chairman* or *chairwoman,* is the most significant unit of party organization. Members of this committee are selected in various ways. Some are chosen by conventions, a few are picked by candidates, but most are elected in the precincts at party primaries. Election as a precinct committeeman frequently carries with it membership on the county committee. Operating in practical independence from the state committee and with little control over other local committees, the typical county committee performs such functions as managing conventions, carrying on campaigns, and supervising party affairs throughout the county. The county committee ordinarily is an important and vigorous unit in party machinery.

Party organization in urban areas presents a broad range of patterns. In some states the county organization is all that exists apart from citizens' or candidates' committees. Very often, however, parties in urban areas have a multilevel organizational hierarchy, with large cities tending to have more complex systems. While details of composition, selection, and functions vary, the *ward* is commonly the level next above the precinct, and above the ward is the city-wide organization. Titles differ widely, but usually they are derived from the designation of the election districts involved, such as precinct, ward, city, and town. At each level one person functions as chairperson or leader. The duties of all these organizations are similar and are much like those of their counterparts at higher levels.

PARTY MEMBERSHIP

Membership in an American political party is purely voluntary. A prospective member does not have to fill out an application to join, pay dues, or work for the party. A party member cannot be expelled, is not required to take an oath of loyalty, is not compelled to assume party responsibilities, and cannot be forced to support the party's candidates or accept its whole program. Even when a voter designates a party at the time of registration, as is required in most states, such designation is not necessarily conclusive. A person regarded as a Republican may register as a Democrat in order to vote in a particular primary, or a registered Democrat may change party preference without reregistering. Party membership is more a *state of mind* than a legal affiliation.

Party membership often is estimated in terms of the votes cast for a party's candidates or the number of voters registered as party members. Such criteria are merely approximations, however accurate they may at times be. How, for example, is the person who votes evenly between two parties to be classified? What is the status of the underage partisan? How are the criteria to be adjusted when registration favors one party, but the opposition elects more candidates? The only logical conclusion is that party membership is, indeed, a vaguely defined thing that is subject to change at any time by individual will.

PARTY FINANCE

Running for office in the United States is an expensive undertaking. There are times when sizable expenditures are not necessary, as when a candidate is unopposed or when some minor local officers are involved, but ordinarily candidates and their backers must have a considerable sum of money at their disposal if they expect to win. Election costs have risen steadily over the years. Today there are more voters to be reached, a wider variety of publicity media available to campaigners, and more refined techniques of research and analysis that precede campaigns. A candidate who earnestly desires election can ill afford to neglect any process that may win votes. Consequently, even after discounting the effects of inflation upon the present-day dollar, electioneering costs are much higher today than formerly.

Campaign expenditures vary greatly in proportion to the importance of the office to be filled. The largest sums are spent in behalf of presidential candidates with decreasingly smaller amounts paid out in efforts to secure election to the positions of United States senator, representative to Congress, governor, and lower offices. It must be remembered, however, that at a given time an office may take on importance that it does not normally have. For example, an otherwise comparatively unimportant seat in a state legislature may be the one that determines which party will control a legislative house, or an incumbent running in an unpredictable district may be a key figure in party organization. Greater efforts, financial and otherwise, must be exerted under such circumstances than under other conditions. In any event, money has become an extremely important factor in the conduct of elections, necessitating governmental regulation.

Raising enough money to carry on effective campaigns takes time, organization, and a great deal of energy. Since American parties, except for some third parties, do not collect dues from their members, they must turn to other sources. These sources include individuals and families; persons in office and those seeking office; private organizations such as pressure groups; committees organized to support certain candidates; and party functions such as dinners, dances, and rallies. Despite the variety of sources and the emphasis both major parties place on small contributions from many individuals, the great bulk of funds contributed to parties comes from a relatively small number of donors. This observation is applicable to both the national and state levels and has caused concern over the possibility that parties or candidates may incur "liabilities" or be effectively "controlled" by heavy contributors. As a result, Congress and each state legislature has enacted legislation to regulate party finance and "corrupt practices" in general.

National Regulation

Numerous federal statutes attempt to regulate financial and other affairs of political parties. Since the national government has no authority to control purely state affairs, these laws are limited in application to party activities at the national level and to state activities assisted by or directly involving the national government. The principal federal legislation in this regard is the Federal Election Campaign Act which was enacted in 1971 and amended extensively in 1977. This Act provides for reporting of contributions and expenditures, imposes limitations on spending in most federal elections, and provides a voluntary system of public financing for presidential candidates. Importantly, the Act also creates a Federal Election Commission, vests it with rule-making authority, and charges it with the responsibility of administering the statute. As is usually the case with new and essentially experimental legislation, the effectiveness of this approach must await a trial period of reasonable duration.

Other federal controls of political parties include corrupt practices legislation which prohibits candidates for federal offices from offering governmental jobs, or threatening dismissal of government workers, in order to secure political support. Civil service workers are not permitted to participate actively in political campaigns. Persons or firms entering into contracts with the national government may not contribute to campaign funds. Measures such as these are intended to guard against illegal, unethical practices by government groups. They have been largely effective in preventing illegal actions, but evasions within the letter of the law indicate that unethical conduct has not been eliminated.

State Regulation

Following the lead of New York in 1890, every state has enacted legislation designed to keep political party activities honest. These laws vary greatly in form and coverage, but everywhere certain acts are defined as criminal and therefore prohibited. For example, bribery, which includes giving gifts to influence political activity, is a criminal act. Criminal laws also prohibit embezzlement, libel, slander, extortion, and many other acts contrary to public dignity and order. Any candidate or party member who perpetrates any such act would be liable to prosecution.

In some states corrupt practices legislation goes no further than to impose criminal sanctions similar to those mentioned above. By way of contrast other states have fashioned rather comprehensive statutes with detailed provisions pertaining to party finances. Regulating party finance aims generally at four major activities: "(1) publicity of sources of income and expenditures, (2) limitation on sources of income, (3) limitation on expenditures, and (4) prevention of bribery and pernicious political activity."[3] Laws on these matters are difficult to enforce, not so much because of brazen defiance by candidates, but because it is easy to evade them. The evasion techniques mentioned above in connection with national regulation are practiced at the state level with equal or more success.

Within the past few years nearly a third of the states have enacted laws providing for some form of public funding of gubernatorial campaigns. These statutes are much like the federal law and are designed to achieve the same goals. Not all of them have been fully tried, and some hardly at all. And as with the federal law, it is much too early to assess their value.

PRESSURE GROUPS

Making public policy is a process that necessarily involves compromise of interests. Every cause, movement, and organization has its supporters who would like to see public policy framed in such a way that their interests are favorably treated. But policymakers, chiefly legislators and executive officials, cannot be all things to all individuals and all groups. To satisfy all the requests of one or a few groups would place others at extreme disadvantage. The demands of all groups cannot be met, yet all cannot be ignored. Interests must somehow be compromised so that resulting policy is not determined without regard for the interests of most segments of society.

Viewed in this manner, the formulation of public policy is clearly a process that is susceptible to pressures by interested individuals and groups. Legislators, administrators, and the general public are exposed

3. Hugh A. Bone, *American Politics and the Party System,* 3rd edition, McGraw-Hill, Inc., New York, 1965, p. 419.

constantly to the exertions of those seeking changes in policy. In the struggle for favorable treatment groups are formed to promote special interests. The character and purpose of these organizations are revealed in the observation that

> When divisions within a society become so conscious of their desires that they perfect a definite organization, draw up a platform of objectives, and actively seek to bring about the realization of their aspirations by influencing elected and appointive officials, they have attained the status of a pressure group.[4]

Pressure groups are found everywhere in the United States. They appear in many forms and may be interested in a single phase of policy or in many. Some are tightly organized, while others are loosely knit. Some are affluent, and others are virtually penniless. Whatever their individual composition may be, all pressure groups have one thing in common: the promotion of a particular interest.

Pressure groups, like political parties, serve as means of political expression for millions of people. However, even though political expression is the underlying basis of both parties and pressure groups, there are fundamental differences between them. First, pressure groups do not nominate candidates for office, but they are interested in who is elected and often endorse candidates and give them financial aid. Even so, pressure groups are more interested in what is done by successful candidates *after* they assume office. A second major difference lies in the fact that political parties are, indeed must be, concerned with all phases of public affairs, whereas pressure groups are primarily interested in matters that involve the particular interests they seek to promote. Implicit in these distinctions is a third: the broad representation of interests characteristic of a major political party as contrasted with the comparatively narrow interests of the pressure group.

Pressure groups may be classified in several ways. Categories may be based on the level or branch of government to which their attentions are directed. Since many pressure groups exert pressures at all levels and upon numerous governmental agencies and try to popularize their points of view with the general public, they are best classified according to the general subject matter in which they are interested. Accordingly, the most significant pressure groups are dedicated to promoting the interests of business and industry, labor, agriculture, professions, veterans, religion, consumers, better government, ethnic groups, and government workers. Some groups are not readily classifiable or may fit into more than one of these classifications. This list, as others like it, is not exhaustive. Nevertheless, it serves to convey an impression of the wide range of interests that stimulate pressure groups and to stress the fact that scarcely a facet of public policy escapes their attention.

4. Harold Zink, Howard R. Penniman, and Guy B. Hathorn, *American Government and Politics,* D. Van Nostrand Co., Inc., Princeton, 1958, p. 98.

The strategy and tactics of pressure groups are such that virtually every avenue of legal—and sometimes illegal—activity is utilized. When engaged in lobbying activities, pressure groups direct their most intensified efforts upon governmental personnel, especially members of legislatures. Pressure groups and lobbies do not, however, cease activity after a legislative session ends. Instead, pressure activities continue, being aimed at governmental officers and employees as well as the general public. Pressuring administrators can be as productive as efforts directed toward legislators, for the meaning and significance of many statutes and rules depend upon interpretations by administrators and the vigor with which they are enforced. Since public acceptance of their ideas is of inestimable value to pressure groups, they constantly strive to achieve that goal. Pressure groups of one type or another work year-round to create public sympathy that may lead to desired alterations in public policy. All communication media are employed to get a point of view across, with the intensity of a group's efforts varying in accord with the resources available to it.

Occasional acts of an illegal or selfish nature have fostered suspicion of pressure organizations as a whole, but regardless of such unfortunate incidents, pressure groups serve a useful purpose. Congress and state legislatures alike use and sometimes depend heavily upon information supplied by these groups. Their representation of functional interests in American society has inspired the observation that pressure groups constitute "the third house of the legislature." It is not to be denied that pressure organizations may stimulate improvement of government. Some pressure groups seek improvement of governmental organization and administration, while others have prodded government into paying more attention to various areas of social concern. Pressure organizations provide channels of political expression for individuals dedicated to the fulfillment of ideas that political parties may or may not endorse. Inasmuch as parties cannot accommodate all persons and all groups, pressure groups play a significant role in politics.

INFLUENCE OF PUBLIC OPINION

Holding a public office, regardless of how high or low it happens to be, is usually not easy. Every public official has some connection with public policy: making it, carrying it out, and in some instances both. As a result, public officers are constantly, at least potentially, under public scrutiny. They are subject to pressures for changes in policy or in the manner in which it is administered. Their very jobs often depend directly or indirectly upon the action of the public at the ballot box. It is not surprising that public officers are sensitive to the changing attitudes of the public. They are, in short, responsive to public opinion.

The term "public opinion" has been subjected to much analysis by various writers over the years. Interpretations vary, but there seems to be agreement on the point that "public" does not necessarily include everyone. In fact, a public may consist of any group of two or more persons. "Opinion" can be any attitude held by such a group, but the attitude does not constitute real opinion until it is *expressed.* In other words, public opinion consists of expressed group attitudes. Viewed in this way it is clear that public opinion is not necessarily a single, easily recognizable viewpoint held by the entire population. Instead, it consists of many attitudes that conflict as well as those that harmonize. In responding to public opinion, the task of public officers actually becomes one of trying to decide which public opinions are sufficiently important or influential for them to give their serious consideration.

Because of their connection with public policy and the effect of citizen opinion upon the nature and content of that policy, it is essential that public officers be as aware as possible of popular sentiments. All such officers and supporters have their own ideas as to the tenor of public opinion at a given moment, but that is not enough. Public opinion is so complex and so productive of differing viewpoints that it is dangerous to rely upon personal estimates. Something as seemingly noncontroversial as the street paving program of a small community, for example, can stimulate reactions that might easily bewilder a well-meaning, civic-minded councilmember. Motorists may welcome the program; affected property owners may object because of anticipated assessments; real estate promoters may push only for that phase of the program that benefits certain areas; civic clubs may voice concern over total costs; other groups conceivably may object to priorities with relation to street lighting, park development, or library expansion. From such a maze of attitudes and reactions who can say, without risk of error, exactly what "public opinion" is with respect to the paving program?

Despite the difficulties of doing so, efforts to assess public opinion must be made. Every interested individual as well as pressure groups, political parties, civic clubs, professional associations, and other organizations try both to mold opinion and to measure it. In an effort to determine the character of public opinion resort may be had to such procedures as assessing the nature and intensity of pressure group activity, making direct contacts with citizens, and evaluating the results of polls and surveys. These methods involve pitfalls, however, for in practically every case it is not possible to contact every person or group involved, and in any event no method exists to register intensity of feeling or to predict changes in opinion. In the last analysis probably the most reliable index of public opinion, particularly in the view of the public officer, is the election. Such knowledge may come too late, however, to benefit the anxious public official.

Nominations
and Elections

11

In a democratic society the people are the source of political power. Ultimately they are responsible for everything that government is or does. For practical reasons, however, the people cannot, as an assembled unit, make all the decisions required of them. Instead, representative forms and processes must be used. The methods employed in selecting the representatives of the people—nomination and public election—are fundamental procedures in the operation of democratic society.

The processes of nomination and election are separate and distinct, yet intimately related. Most simply defined, nomination is a general term designating a number of methods by means of which individuals are selected as candidates for office. An election is a method whereby the people, by casting ballots, choose from among the nominees those persons who will fill public offices. Except for those public office holders who are selected by means of appointment, all governmental officials, whether legislative, executive, or judicial in character, are subject to some type of nomination and election. These processes operate in much the same manner throughout the United States, but each is found in various forms with wide variations in detail.

NATIONAL AND STATE POWERS

Authority to control the processes of nomination and election is lodged chiefly in the states. Since the national government may exercise only those powers delegated to it by the Constitution of the United States, and since that document does not convey to the central government general power in the matter of selecting public officers, regulation of nominations and elections is largely within the area of reserved state authority. Subject to limitations imposed by the Constitution, the fifty states provide for methods of nomination and stage the elections in which the great bulk of the more than one-half million public, elective offices in the United States are filled.[1]

Even though state power is paramount regarding nominations and elections, the states are limited by some provisions of federal law. In the first place there are a number of provisions in the national Constitution that affect state authority. Qualifications for the offices of President and Vice President of the United States, United States senator, and representative in Congress are set forth in the Constitution, thereby eliminating any possibility of state-imposed qualifications. The Twelfth and Twentieth Amendments prescribe steps to be followed in the selection of the President and Vice President. Popular election is designated as the method of choosing representatives by Article I, Section 2, and the Seventeenth Amendment applies the same procedure to the choice of United States senators. Section 4 of Article I attests that the states have power to prescribe the "times, places, and manner of holding elections for Senators and Representatives," but goes on to add that "Congress may at any time by law make or alter such regulations."[2]

Pursuant to authority derived from the Constitution, Congress has enacted statutes that profoundly affect the process of selecting public officers. Under an act of 1842, for example, members of the House of Representatives must be chosen from single-member districts, a requirement that goes far in determining the nomenclature of state nomination and election procedures.[3] As indicated in the previous chapter, federal corrupt practices legislation extends to nomination and election processes in the states which involve federal elective offices. Congress has, for all practical purposes, fixed the date upon which most elections are held. In 1872 a national statute fixed the first Tuesday after the first Monday in November of even-numbered years as the day for election of members

---

1. The only places where the national government may exercise full power over these important processes are the territorial possessions and, subject to the Twenty-third Amendment, the District of Columbia.

2. This clause also denies Congress authority to regulate "the places of choosing Senators." This provision had real meaning when senators were chosen by state legislatures, but became rather insignificant with the addition of the Seventeenth Amendment which provided for popular election of senators.

3. In 1872 Congress enacted the requirements that representative districts be "compact and contiguous" and of as nearly equal populations "as practicable," but failed to include these provisions in the Reapportionment Act of 1929. Subsequently, the United States Supreme Court ruled in *Wood* v. *Broom,* 287 U.S. 1 (1932), that the states were no longer bound by these restrictions. However, restoration of the equal populations feature may have been accomplished by judicial decision in *Wesberry* v. *Sanders,* 376 U.S. 1 (1964), in which the Supreme Court held invalid the state statute establishing congressional districts in Georgia. The Court stated that Article I, Section 2, requires that "one man's vote in a congressional election is to be worth as much as another's."

of the House of Representatives.[4] Following ratification of the Seventeenth Amendment, the same day was designated for election of United States senators. Today some state and local officers are elected at different times, but for the most part the day chosen by Congress has been designated by the states as the day for electing public officials.

The power of the national government to police elections in which national officers are chosen is clearly reflected in decisions of the United States Supreme Court. In the Maryland congressional election of 1878 several persons were arrested for stuffing ballot boxes contrary to state laws. They were brought to trial and convicted in a federal court under a federal statute of 1870 that made it a crime for anyone to interfere with federal supervisors attempting to see that state election laws were fairly administered. This extensive national authority was upheld by the Court.[5] That further supervisory authority may be exercised by the national government was evidenced by the decision in *United States* v. *Classic,* upholding federal conviction of persons found guilty of fraudulent acts in a Louisiana primary election.[6] Thus national power of regulation and supervision includes not only the elections themselves, but also the primaries in which candidates are nominated.

METHODS OF NOMINATION

Before a person can be elected to a public office he or she must be nominated as a candidate. This process can be rather simple with a minimum of red tape, or it can be quite complicated. Today most nominees are selected in primary elections, but other methods also are used. No two states employ precisely the same combination of methods. Some states permit procedures that others forbid, and alternative methods are available in some states. However, even though the details of nomination vary among the states, basic methods are much the same throughout the country.

Self-Announcement

The oldest form of nomination is self-announcement which consists of nothing more than a public declaration of candidacy. People who aspire

---

4. Congress provided, however, that a state might hold elections at other times if its constitution specified a different date. Consequently, congressional elections in Maine were conducted in September until 1960 when, pursuant to a 1957 amendment, the November date became effective. As adopted, the Constitution of Alaska directed that general elections be held in October, but also provided that the date might be altered by the legislature. As of the first session of the legislature in 1959 the date was changed to conform to the day established by Congress.
5. *Ex parte Siebold,* 100 U.S. 371 (1880).
6. 313 U.S. 299 (1941).

to a public office indicate their intentions simply by letting people know that they are candidates. The announcement may be accomplished by means of public speech, a published statement, word of mouth, or any other method available to the candidate. Self-announcement was in use in colonial times and is still used today.

Use of self-announcement as a method of nomination is largely confined to candidacies for minor local offices. However, public offices of higher station are also subject to this method, with election dependent upon whether the candidate can marshal sufficient write-in votes to outpoll the opposition. An impressive example of these procedures at work occurred in 1954 when Strom Thurmond announced his candidacy for the position of United States senator from South Carolina and, by means of write-in votes, won the office by a substantial margin.

The Caucus

Until the early decades of the nineteenth century, candidates were commonly chosen at meetings—or caucuses—of political leaders. The procedure was simple: acknowledged leaders met and discussed potential candidates, eventually deciding upon whom the group would support for each office to be filled. Since there were no political parties as they are known today and elections were local, the caucus worked satisfactorily as a nominating device. Competing political factions, acting in separate caucuses, produced opposing candidates.

Independence and subsequent union, along with the rise of the party system, occasioned difficulties in use of the caucus. Nominations for state and national offices could not be made practically in local meetings. To meet this difficulty the *legislative caucus* and the *congressional caucus* were developed. A legislative caucus consisted of all the members of a party or political faction within a state legislature, and its function was to select party nominees for state offices. Presidential and Vice Presidential candidates were nominated by party members in Congress who served collectively as the congressional caucus.

As the political party system became firmly established and demand for more democratic methods of nomination mounted, the nominating caucus fell into disuse. The controls exerted by small groups led to dissatisfaction with "King Caucus." Telling blows were struck by Andrew Jackson and his supporters, and by the 1840's the caucus had been abandoned at the national and state levels. Today only a few local offices, primarily in New England, are subject to the nominating caucus.

The Convention

Several decades before the nominating caucus passed from the national and state scenes, the method that was to replace it—the delegate convention—was already in use. Throughout the states in the middle Atlantic area county conventions were in common use by 1804. A state convention was called in New York in 1824, and by 1830 state conventions were used widely in the northeast. The Anti-Masonic Party nominated its candidate for President by convention in 1831 for the next year's election. The major parties followed suit, and within a few years the convention was in general use.

The convention clearly is, in theory at least, a much more democratic device than the caucus. While a caucus is a "closed corporation," a convention is composed of delegates representing party members throughout the election district involved. At the same time, it is equally clear that conventions can be controlled. Any political process is only as effective and reliable as the people who conduct it. While many, probably most, conventions worked as well as reason could demand throughout the period of their widest use, the last half of the nineteenth century, there were numerous examples of rigged, dishonest conventions.[7] Public reaction to controlled conventions was such that by the early twentieth century the states began to turn to the direct primary.

Although the direct primary is now used or is available in some form in all fifty states, the convention is still used, or may be used, in about a fourth of them. It exists as an alternative to the primary election in several southern states, and conventions are held in Iowa and South Dakota *after* the primary election to choose candidates for any office for which no one was able to get a plurality of at least thirty-five per cent of the votes cast. Also, several states have nomination systems in which conventions are held *before* the primary elections, for the purpose either of choosing candidates for the primary or of endorsing a candidate who has already qualified.

Nomination by Petition

Aspirants for public office who have no major party affiliation and are thereby unable to secure nominations in conventions or primary elections may in many states formalize their candidacies by means of a *nominating petition.* Included in this group are the independents who spurn party membership, candidates in nonpartisan elections, and the members of minor parties which, in some states, are not permitted to select candidates in primary elections. In some states where the nominating petition is not available such candidates may get their names on the ballot by making a deposit of money, the "filing fee," with a designated official. In some

7. A good example of the extent to which conventions may be controlled is the Cook County, Illinois (includes Chicago), convention of 1896. That body was composed of 723 delegates of whom 265 were saloon keepers, 148 were public office holders, and 128 were ex-convicts! Only under the oddest of circumstances could such an assemblage nominate a slate of uncompromised candidates.

instances fees are required of all candidates in primary as well as general elections.

Care must be taken not to confuse the nominating petition which results in placement of a candidate's name on the general election ballot with filing petitions which authorize candidacies in primary elections. A nominating petition has the effect of making a person a candidate for an office. The primary petition does nothing more than make it possible for individuals to present themselves in a primary election which, in turn, may result in their nomination.

The Direct Primary

The only method of nomination that is used in each of the fifty states, the direct primary, made its initial appearance at about the time the convention method was achieving general acceptance. In 1842 members of the Democratic Party in Crawford County, Pennsylvania, cast ballots in what is generally considered the first primary election held in the United States. Throughout the next half-century the primary spread slowly but steadily. Party leaders fought hard against it, and in many instances lack of governmental regulation resulted in manipulation and fraud, but gradually the primary took hold. Wisconsin set the pattern for other states by enacting, in 1904, the first state-wide mandatory system of nomination by primary. The convention is still used in some states for some nominations, but nominations for the vast majority of offices today, whether national, state, or local, are made by means of primaries.

As applied to public offices the term "primary election" is a misnomer, for although the process outwardly resembles an actual election, it is simply a method of choosing candidates who, at a later date, will run for office in an election. Except for nonpartisan and open primaries, the primary is a *party* affair in which members select from among themselves the party's candidates.[8] The only sense in which a primary is truly an election is when it is used as a means of electing people to *party* offices.

Running in a primary election is not a privilege free from all legal conditions and available to anyone for the mere asking. A prospective candidate must, first of all, be affiliated with a legally recognized political party.[9] Thus independents and members of so-called minor parties must resort to other nominating methods. State laws may provide that some

---

8. This does not, of course, mean that the primary is not related to the electoral process or not subject to governmental control. Indeed each of the fifty states regulates primaries in minute detail, and the United States Supreme Court has declared them to be an "integral part" of the electoral process.
9. Until 1959 candidates in California were permitted to "cross-file," a means by which a person might run in the primary elections of both Republican and Democratic parties. Former Governor Earl Warren won both party nominations in 1946 as did ex-Senator William F. Knowland in 1952.

offices are not subject to primary elections, give parties the choice of whether to nominate in primaries, or limit candidacies by requiring aspirants first to make creditable showings in party conventions. For example, primaries in Connecticut, where they have been available since 1955, are held only on demand of candidates who have won at least twenty per cent of the votes cast in party nominating conventions. State laws also require persons desiring to run in the primaries to post filing fees or present petitions bearing a designated number of signatures.

Open versus Closed Primaries. Partisan direct primaries used in the United States can be classified as *open* or *closed*. As the terms imply, an open primary, the form in which the direct primary originated, is a nominating election in which *any* qualified voter may take part, while participation in a closed primary is restricted to party members only. Today most states have closed primary elections, the open form being used in one-fifth of the states.[10]

The closed primary, which is favored by party leaders and officials, is closed to all voters who are not party members. In most states having such primaries this requirement is met by means of registration or *enrollment*. At the time of registration the voter is listed as member of a party, but if the party does not or cannot stage a primary election, the voter is restricted to nonpartisan candidacies. A second method of determining party attachment is the challenge system. Under this procedure a voter whose ballot is challenged must assert, under oath, support of the party and its candidates.

Party membership is not required for participation in an open primary, but a voter may take part in the primary election of only one party. In other words, any qualified voter may cast a primary ballot, but must make a choice of parties. Party preferences are kept secret either by printing identical but separate ballots for each party and permitting the voter to discard all but one of them, or by listing candidates by party columns on the same ballot with the voter confined to a single party column. In a *wide-open* primary, commonly called a *blanket* primary, candidates are listed by office and the voter may ignore party designations so long as only one vote is cast for each office.

The fact that the closed form of the direct primary is used in four times as many states as the open type is largely attributable to a practice known as *raiding*. During the early years of the direct primary, the open form was used, making it possible for a party organization to instruct members to vote for the weakest candidate in the opposing party's primary. By securing the nomination of a weak opposition candidate, the

---

10. Alaska, Idaho, Louisiana, Michigan, Minnesota, Montana, North Dakota, Utah, Vermont, Washington, and Wisconsin.

raiding party's chances of success at the ensuing general election were strengthened. Closing primaries to all but party members made raiding much more difficult.

A comparison of open and closed primaries reveals several strong points in favor of each. As already indicated, the closed primary greatly reduces the probability of party raiding. It tends to make candidates more responsible to their parties and to increase the political awareness of the electorate since voters must choose between parties. On the other hand, it can be argued that unlike the closed form, an open primary protects the secrecy of the ballot, makes it possible for *all* qualified persons to vote, and tends to emphasize the quality of individual candidates rather than parties. The arguments in favor of one form indicate weaknesses of the other, and the choice between them is a policy determination to be decided by the people and their representatives in each state.

Run-off Primaries. In the primary elections of most states, whether open or closed, the person who gets the most votes in a particular contest is nominated. If only two candidates are vying for a nomination, one of them is practically certain to get a majority of the votes. However, should three or more persons contend for a nomination and none receive a majority, then the one receiving the highest number of votes would win by a *plurality*.

The plurality rule is followed in the great majority of the states, but in a fifth of the states, mostly in the southeast, primary laws require that nominations be based upon a majority. In justification of these provisions is the fact that in these states nomination in a primary election held by the Democratic Party means almost certain success in the subsequent general election. In some southern states about ninety per cent of the electorate is affiliated with the Democratic Party, a situation wherein opposition parties voting full strength in a general election are unable, except on extremely rare occasions, to defeat a small turnout of Democrats. Consequently, to make sure that a person who fills a public office has been chosen by a majority of the voters, a majority in the Democratic primary is required. When necessary, runoff primaries are held about a month after the regular primary to assure that each nominee has obtained a majority vote.

Nonpartisan Primaries. Many local and some state offices are filled by candidates bearing no official party label. Nebraska elects state legislators on a nonpartisan basis, but nonpartisan selection generally is confined to judges and certain administrative officers, such as school officials. Nonpartisan primary elections are ordinarily little more than a "sifting and eliminating" process, because in most instances the results are merely to reduce the number of candidates for a particular office to the two highest.

Then, at the general election these two candidates contest for the office at stake. A candidate who receives a majority of votes in the primary is declared elected and is not required to run in the general election.

The Place of the Primary.   The direct primary is not without faults, but regardless of its shortcomings it promises to remain the principal method of nomination in the United States. It represents a full swing away from the early days of control by party leaders in caucuses over slates of nominees. Despite the fact that primaries have been and to some extent still can be controlled, their democratic character is favored by American voters.

Attractive as it is in comparison with other methods of nomination, the direct primary is open to criticism on a number of logical grounds. First, it is expensive: the process entails mobilization of all, or most, of the election machinery in a state. At the same time, each candidate must finance a campaign for nomination and a second if obliged to enter a runoff primary, as well as a general election effort. Second, the relative ease with which persons may become primary candidates and the tendency to make more and more offices subject to primary elections have resulted in lengthening ballots that are already too long. Third, the plurality rule may result in nomination by a minority of party members. While it is probable that most of the candidates chosen by pluralities would be nominated in any event, some would not. This fact strengthens arguments that candidacies should be limited, majorities required, or that party committees or conventions should be given more control over nominations. Fourth, primaries may be held eight or nine months in advance of the general election although most of them occur in the late spring or summer. Such extended intervals contribute to a loss of voter interest and unnecessarily long campaigns. Finally, primaries weaken political parties in that intra-party fights are encouraged and candidates must seek favor from the voters rather than approval by the party organization.

Some improvements in the direct primary might be accomplished by legislative action, but some features that have evoked criticism could not be altered without changing the character of the primary. The direct primary is necessarily more costly than other nominating methods since it involves use of all or most election machinery in a jurisdiction. The complaint that parties do not have adequate control of primary candidates probably cannot be completely satisfied, but party control can be strengthened by permitting parties to endorse one candidate over all others, by limiting the number of candidates, by permitting preprimary conventions, or by a combination of these. As indicated earlier, a few states have such provisions already in effect. The long ballot so often found in primaries can be moderated by reducing the number of offices filled by election. The plurality rule can be replaced, where it is felt desirable, by a majority requirement, or as in Iowa and South Dakota, supplemented by a post-primary convention. Proper timing of the primary in relation to the general election is probably the easiest improvement to realize, for only a change in dates is necessary.

Presidential Primaries. Although the great majority of nominations are made through direct primaries, the most prominent officers of them all, the President and Vice President of the United States, are subject to nomination by delegate convention. Sentiment has long existed in many quarters for replacing the convention with a national direct primary. President Woodrow Wilson, the only professional political scientist ever to serve in that office, recommended such a primary in his first message to Congress, and public attention frequently has been directed to the issue. However, the only progress of note toward an actual national primary has been in the form of the *presidential primary* and the *presidential preference primary.*

The presidential primary, despite the implications of the title, is *not* a method of nominating presidential candidates. First used in Oregon in 1910 and enjoying its greatest development in the following ten years, the presidential primary is merely a means of choosing, in a party primary, delegates to the national convention of a political party. The popularly elected delegates then participate, in the convention, in the nomination of their party's presidential and vice presidential candidates.

In some states where the presidential primary is used the voters not only cast ballots for convention delegates, but also indicate their preferences as to the person they would like to see the convention nominate. This variation has become known as the presidential preference primary. No uniformity exists among the states with respect to the effect of the voters' preferences. The extent to which delegates are bound to support the presidential aspirant receiving the greatest voter support differs from state to state, ranging from no formal requirement at all to compulsory support until released by the candidate.

Whether preference primaries serve a genuinely useful purpose is open to question. Supporters contend that they provide a means of countering abuses and excesses of the convention system and provide a basis for wider popular participation. Perhaps if all states used preference primaries, and if all delegates were directed to honor their results, an approximation of a national direct primary could be achieved. Some of the states ignore the process altogether, and those with primaries have made no collective attempt to standardize requirements. One of the glaring weaknesses is that candidates cannot be compelled to enter primaries and are thus able to avoid contests they are not sure of winning. "Favorite son" candidates often divert votes from serious contenders, and little or no attention is given to vice-presidential aspirants.

THE ELECTION PROCESS

After candidates are nominated their battles are only half won. Except in one-party states where nomination by the dominant party virtually assures election, each candidate faces the usually difficult task of winning in the general election. After nomination, whether by means of direct primary, convention, a combination of both, or otherwise, candidates begin to plot their courses of action in preparation for the general election usually held on the first Tuesday after the first Monday in November of even-numbered years. [11]

Campaigns

During the period between nomination and the day upon which the voters go to the polls campaigns are conducted. In one sense, campaigns can be said to have begun during the period when candidates are seeking nomination. Political campaigns vary in nature according to numerous factors, including the personality and status of the candidate, the nature and importance of the office, the character of the times, the size and temper of the electorate, and the disposition of pressure groups. Every campaign is intended to influence voters, but obviously not all campaigns are carried on the same way. A presidential candidate, a person running for a seat in a state senate, and an aspirant for a position on a city council face different problems.

There is no reliable way to determine how many votes are won by campaigning. In all but the rarest instances a candidate who does no campaigning is at a disadvantage if the opponent makes any effort at all. *Some* voters can be influenced, and general voter interest can be stimulated. Political observers felt for many years that campaigns actually won few votes because most voters had decided how they were going to cast their ballots by the time candidates took to the campaign trail. Then in 1948, after most observers and commentators had conceded the presidential election to Governor Thomas E Dewey of New York, incumbent Harry Truman was returned to office. Undoubtedly the arduous, effective campaign conducted by Mr. Truman had won votes. How many, it would be difficult to say. Attitudes toward the value of campaigns have been changed, however, and until more precise assessments can be made, candidates—national, state, and local—will be heartened in their campaign efforts by the Truman experience in 1948.

---

11. This is the date fixed by Congress for general elections in which presidential electors and members of Congress are chosen. Elections in which only state and/or local officials are chosen can be held at other times.

Holding the Election

Elections are not simple affairs that can be organized overnight and carried off with little effort. Instead, they are highly complex, well-organized activities that demand impressive expenditures of time, energy, and money. As in virtually all areas of government activity, each of the fifty states has its own individual election system. Wide variation in detail exists from state to state; local elections within a single state differ; and a state system may be, and frequently is, altered at each legislative session. Nevertheless, the basic procedures involved in the conduct of elections in the states are the same, making it possible to characterize a "typical" mode of election.

Administration

Although there is election machinery at the state level—at least a board to canvass and certify results of designated elections and an official, usually the secretary of state, to see that state laws are observed—most election functions are performed by local personnel. In each local voting district, generally called a *precinct,* an election board staffs the polling place and counts the votes. There are usually three or four members, entitled *judges* or *inspectors,* on an election board with clerks to assist them. These officials are chosen by a city or county board of elections, by the governing bodies of counties or cities, by the clerks of these governments, or by popular election. In nearly all states, appointments to precinct election boards are divided equally, or as nearly so as possible, between the major political parties. Consequently, service on such a board has become largely a matter of patronage controlled by local party organizations.

Election laws in each of the states provide in detail for virtually every aspect of elections. Preparing an election is largely a matter of following statutory directions. Laying out precincts, choosing polling places, printing ballots, obtaining booths and ballot boxes, procuring voting machines, choosing precinct officials, and other tasks are carried out as provided by law. Paying the costs of holding an election, as dictated by statute, is generally the obligation of local governments, particularly counties and cities.

Time, Place, and Hours

Except for the elections in which national officers are chosen, fixing election dates is a prerogative of the state legislature. For purposes of convenience, particularly to avoid the costs of a second election, most state officials are elected at the time national offices are filled. However, Kentucky, Louisiana, New Jersey, and Virginia hold their state elections in odd-numbered years. Many local governments avoid coincidence with state and national elections by conducting their elections at other times, usually in the spring.

In each precinct a poll, or location at which votes are cast, must be designated. To reduce costs, public buildings are utilized where possible. When public buildings are not available, space is rented, often on a patronage basis, in private structures such as churches, business establishments, or private dwellings. The hours during which balloting may take place are determined by state statute, and in virtually all instances it is a continuous twelve-hour period beginning at seven or eight o'clock in the morning.

Casting ballots

When a voter enters a polling place to vote, identification is required. In states where all voters must be registered this step is relatively simple. By requiring each voter to sign in, the signatures can be compared with those on the registration forms. In North Dakota, which has no registration system, voter identification depends largely upon successful operation of the challenge system. The problem is not as serious as it might be elsewhere for the state has less than a million population with only about thirty per cent of them residing in a dozen or so cities.

After recognition a voter is ready to cast a ballot, an act undertaken in the privacy of a voting booth. The marked ballot is then deposited by the voter in a locked ballot box. When mechanical voting devices are used, adaptation of procedures or physical modification of booths may be necessary to preserve secrecy of the ballot. The voter is not limited in terms of time, and a second ballot may be requested should the first be spoiled. Instructions on the use of a voting machine may also be requested. Where illiterate persons are permitted to vote, they may be accompanied by a literate assistant. The physically handicapped likewise may, on request, be aided in the execution of their ballots.

Counting the Votes

The votes are usually counted by a separate board of judges and the process begins soon after the polls are open. Where voting machines are used counting is not done until after the polls close. Counting devices built into the machines keep cumulative totals on all candidates so that it is necessary only to copy the totals. After the figures have been recorded the machines are locked with the counters undisturbed in the event a later recount is ordered. The greatest expenditure of effort occurs where paper ballots are used, for each ballot must be carefully examined and the votes recorded on work sheets. With precinct tallies completed, canvassing boards at city, county, and state levels then assemble totals. The entire process normally lasts many hours and may run into several days.

Whether machines or paper ballots are used, measures are taken to reduce temptations to cheat faced by election board members and clerks. It would be strange indeed, for example, to find an election board composed solely of members of a single political party. In some states, courts are empowered to appoint overseers, and in nearly all states *watchers* may be chosen by the political parties offering candidates. These watchdogs are present throughout election day, checking their lists of voters and observing the conduct of the election judges.

THE BALLOT

During the colonial period and early years of statehood, balloting was not regarded as a secret, personal act. Rather, those qualified to cast ballots did so simply by appearing at the polls and publicly telling the elections clerk the names of the candidates they wished to support. Tellers or vote-counters were used when necessary and sometimes, when the situation permitted, a show of hands was adequate. Paper ballots, when used, were furnished by candidates or parties. They were slight improvement over oral voting, for they were usually distinctively colored, bore only the names of one party's candidates, and were already marked when given to the voter!

The Australian Ballot

As suggested by its title, the Australian ballot derives its name from the country where it was introduced in 1856. It spread from there to several Anglo-Saxon and continental European countries during the next thirty years, at the same time winning advocates in the United States. In 1885, and again two years later, abortive attempts were made to bring about its adoption in Michigan. The Kentucky legislature, in 1888, enacted the first law providing for the Australian ballot but limited its use to municipal elections in Louisville. The first statute requiring statewide employment of the ballot was passed later that year by the Massachusetts General Court. During the following three years—that is, by the end of the general legislative sessions of 1891—over three-fourths of the states had followed suit, and within a decade only a few states had failed to adopt some form of the Australian ballot. For about twenty-five years South Carolina remained the sole holdout, finally capitulating in 1950. Today some form of the Australian ballot is used in all fifty states.

Tersely defined, the Australian ballot is an official ballot which is printed at public expense, contains the names of all duly nominated candidates, is distributed by public officials, and is executed in secret at the polls. These features, in combination, made it possible to reduce ballot irregularities impressively. Parties no longer could favor themselves in the provision of printed ballots, and checking on the way an individual voted was rendered extremely difficult if not impossible. The two essential features of the Australian ballot—secrecy and official status—have made it the capstone of integrity in American elections.

There are two basic types of the Australian ballot: the Massachusetts *office-block* and the Indiana *party column.* The original form of the Australian ballot carried no party designation, resembling the nonpartisan ballot of today, and when adopted in Massachusetts candidates were grouped according to the office they sought. Thus a "block" of candidates was listed by office rather than by parties. Since such grouping tends to minimize the influence of party and makes straight-party voting cumbersome, party leaders have been strongly opposed to office-block ballots. Indiana adopted a statewide Australian ballot law a year after Massachusetts had done so, but party leaders achieved an important modification in the Hoosier version. All candidates of the same party were placed in a single column headed by the name of the party—hence the name party column. On such ballots it was possible to vote for all candidates of a party simply by placing a mark by the name of the party, a method termed "straight party" or "straight ticket" voting. Today party column ballots are used in half the states.

Voting Machines

Voting machines were first used in an American election in 1892 in the city of Lockport, New York. Thereafter mechanical voting devices of one type or another were increasingly approved until today they are employed in every state. Less than a fifth of the states require that all balloting be done on mechanical devices, but in half the states a majority of voting districts are equipped with them.

Students of government are virtually unanimous in the opinion that the use of voting machines is a substantial improvement in voting procedures. They eliminate the need for a manual court of votes, reduce the number of persons required to administer elections, speed up voting, make ballot spoilage impossible, and reduce the possibility of cheating. Why, then, are machines not more widely used? The principal difficulty appears to be the initial cost. Machines cost several thousand dollars each, and even the simpler punch-card devices, while much less expensive, represent a substantial investment. A second reason is the fact that many voters, especially in rural areas, resist giving up the traditional paper ballot. Finally, machines would be impractical in some instances, particularly in sparsely settled areas where few votes are cast and election costs are low.

Consideration of Minor Political Groups

American elections, with their plurality or majority requirements and the single member election district, are a formidable hurdle for minor political groups. In fact, minority parties normally have been unable to elect candidates and almost never in proportion to their voter strength. While no concessions have been made to improve the chances of minor groups in the election of their candidates to national offices, some special balloting methods have been used in regard to various state and local positions.

Since 1870 members of the Illinois House of Representatives have been elected from three-member districts on the basis of *cumulative voting*. Each voter has three votes and all three may be cast for one candidate, two for one candidate and one for another, one and a half for each of two aspirants, or one vote for each of three candidates. Under this system a well-organized minor party may succeed in capturing one or more seats in the legislature, if its members "plunk" all their votes within a district on the party candidate.[12]

Another balloting method devised to increase minority chances of success is *limited voting*. Used in a few states in the selection of some county commissioners and city council members, limited voting gives the voter fewer votes than there are offices to be filled. The idea behind limited voting is that since major party voters cannot elect all the members of a board, minority supporters have a better chance to elect the remainder. Like cumulative balloting, limited voting is subject to criticism in that it can be used only when several offices are to be filled and does not result in representation in proportion to voting strength.

Voting systems designed to reflect the voting strength of political groups are known as *proportional representation,* or more simply as "PR." National and state offices have never been made subject to PR, but a few municipalities have employed it in the selection of council members. Probably the best known type is the Hare System.[13] Invented in 1857 by an Englishman, Thomas Hare, and popularized by the political philosopher, John Stuart Mill, the system utilizes what is termed the "single transferable vote." The voters indicate not only their first choice, but also their second, third, fourth, and so on. When the votes are counted, each candidate receiving enough first place votes according to the Hare formula is declared elected.[14] Second place votes are then added to first choices

---

12. Cumulative voting procedures were not used in the selection of Illinois representatives in 1964. Apportionment of the legislature was judicially invalidated, leading to special legislation providing for at-large election of members of the lower house.

13. In some western European countries the List System of PR is used. Under this plan a list of candidates is offered by each political party. Votes are cast for the list rather than individuals, and seats are filled, from the top of the list, in proportion to the percentage of votes cast for the list.

14. A successful candidate must receive votes equal to the "quota," determined by dividing the number of seats plus one into the number of votes cast and adding one to the quotient. Thus, if nine seats are to be filled and 100,000 votes are cast the quota would be $\frac{100,000}{9+1} + 1$ or 10,001.

to select additional winners; then third-, fourth-, and fifth-place votes—and on down the line as necessary until all positions are filled. In actual use the Hare plan has been subjected to various modifications, but the basic principle of the transferable vote has been preserved in each instance.

Advocates of proportional representation stress that it guarantees representation of minorities, eliminates "wasted" ballots in that each vote helps elect one or more candidates, and helps to minimize the effects of political machines. On the other hand, there is the fear that many parties or factions in a legislative body, a possible result of PR, may introduce an element of instability in government. Whether this development occurs or not, there is no doubt that the Hare System involves a highly complicated vote count—enough so to discourage its adoption or hasten its abandonment. It has virtually disappeared in the United States, although it has been used in places as widely separated as West Hartford, Connecticut, and Coos Bay, Oregon. Among the larger cities that have given PR a trial are Cincinnati, Ohio, from 1924 to 1957, and New York City, where between 1937 and 1947 a form of the Hare System was used.

Election Frauds

If elections are not conducted honestly, the spirit and significance of democracy are destroyed. When a few unscrupulous individuals are able to capture public offices by illegal tactics, then the means by which the will of the people is expressed is seriously impaired. It is not surprising, therefore, that both the nation and the states have enacted a great many laws to prevent and punish election frauds.

Before the Australian ballot came into general use and states began to police elections more rigorously, many elections were in fact little more than circuses. Today frauds are not nearly so common as in earlier years, but cheating at the polls has not been eliminated. To list and describe all the ways to cheat in elections would fill several volumes, but a few examples serve to indicate their general nature. Bribery, intimidation, coercion, and violence still occur here and there. Stuffing ballot boxes with stolen or counterfeit ballots is a familiar type of fraud. Casting ballots for voters who have died, moved away, or even for imaginary persons, is still a problem where registration is lacking or poorly administered. The "Tasmanian Dodge" or "endless chain," whereby bribed voters turn in a marked ballot and collect their money when they return their own unmarked ballot to be used by the next bribed voter, still occurs, but it has virtually disappeared due to the use of numbered ballot stubs. Most effective are the fraudulent activities of election judges, especially when they act in collusion. Their opportunities to cheat while assisting illiterate voters are obvious. When counting ballots it is possible to mark them, or perhaps spoil them, with a fragment of graphite attached to the finger—a practice known as "short pencilling." Tearing ballots, and thus spoiling them, is an old trick. Substituting tally sheets after the count has altered the results of elections. Transposing figures can work wonders for candidates, as when a vote total of 361 is "inadvertently" recorded as 631.

There are many laws designed to prevent and punish chicanery at the polls. Federal laws apply to primary and general elections in which federal officers are chosen, and the statute books in each state bulge with provisions intended to protect the integrity of the ballot. Although laws providing punishment for dishonest acts are necessary, preventing such actions is more important. Consequently, better results are obtainable through improved registration systems, stricter policing of the balloting process, and improvement of that process to eliminate opportunities for fraud, as by use of voting machines, punch card ballots, electronic vote counters, and similar devices. Laws and voting machines cannot, in and of themselves, produce completely honest elections. If the people who conduct elections are corrupt, there is little reason to believe they will perform honestly. Today little effort is made to insure that election officials are well qualified to do their jobs. In fact, except for literacy, party affiliation and loyalty are the qualifications most commonly required. Unless and until higher qualifications are demanded, instances of fraud will continue, since the honesty of any election depends ultimately upon the honesty of those who administer it.

The Short Ballot

Frequently when marking ballots voters are confronted with a mass of names and proposals. In some election jurisdictions the voter must grope through the names of more than one hundred candidates plus the text of constitutional amendments and perhaps a number of initiated or referred measures. Casting an intelligent ballot under such circumstances is difficult for a well-informed voter and practically impossible for most. Many voters, either in desperation or fear of doing the wrong thing, simply ignore many offices and questions.

The *short ballot,* which ideally contains only the names of candidates for the most important offices, has been championed actively since the turn of the century as a remedy for the cluttered, confusing, and excessively long ballot. Advocates of the short ballot formed the National Short Ballot Organization in 1909, merging twelve years later with the National Municipal League. The goal of the short ballot movement can probably best be stated as one of persuading state and local governments to pattern their ballots as much as possible after the example of the national government. Except when vacancies must be filled by election or at-large candidacies occur, voters never find it necessary to consider more than four national offices—the presidency, vice-presidency, and one seat each in the United States Senate and House of Representatives.

Progress in achieving the short ballot has been slow. Most states still have ballots that are much too long, but a few states have shortened their ballots considerably by making all but the most important state offices subject to appointment or by staggering elections so that the voters choose officers for only one level of government at a time. Only a half-dozen states use short ballots, but at the municipal level encouraging gains have been made. Most major cities and literally hundreds of smaller ones have adopted the short ballot.

Contested Elections

After the votes have been counted and canvassed, the results are certified and proclaimed official. In the vast majority of instances the election process is then over, and the winners sit back and wait for their terms of office to begin. Occasionally, however, an apparent loser refuses to accept the result, claiming it is based upon error, fraud, or other impropriety.

If the public office in a contested election is a legislative seat, the argument is usually settled by the legislative house involved, since such bodies generally are the sole judges of members' qualifications. In some states courts are given jurisdiction to hear complaints and to determine the victor in contested elections. Also, contests may result in a *recount* of the votes, a process that is easily accomplished in some states, while in others some proof of fraud or error must be advanced. Some states require that the costs involved in a recount must be borne by the person demanding it. Such restrictions create a risk of putting fraudulent election results beyond correction, but at the same time they also discourage frivolous, petty demands for recounts.

Except when fraud or other illegal acts are alleged, recounts are rarely demanded unless the results clearly show that slight errors could have changed the outcome. For example, when a winning candidate's margin of victory is less than one per cent of the total votes cast, a request for a recount is reasonable. In the Minnesota gubernatorial election of 1962 the official count showed that Governor Elmer L. Andersen had won re-election by a margin of 142 votes. However, after a recount, his opponent, Karl Rolvaag, was declared the winner by 91 votes out of 1,239,593 cast—a majority by only .000073 per cent!

Direct Popular Action: Initiative, Referendum, and Recall

12

Voters in many states are faced not only with large numbers of candidates during elections, they must also decide questions of public policy. Since the end of the nineteenth century nearly half of the states and many cities have provided for direct popular participation in the governmental process through the initiative, referendum, and recall. These devices were conceived as a means of making government more responsive to the people, who may approve or veto acts of legislatures through the referendum or enact laws by means of the initiative when unresponsive legislatures refuse to act. Through the recall, voters can remove from office public officials against whom there is strong public sentiment.

Toward the end of the 1800's many persons felt that the orthodox channels of representative government did not provide adequately for expression of popular desires. The conviction was widespread that many legislators had "sold out" to powerful interest groups and were no longer sensitive to the wishes of their constituents. Consequently, reformers urged that the traditional lawmaking processes should be supplemented by devices for direct popular participation. In governmental jurisdictions where the initiative and referendum have been adopted, recognition has been given, in effect, to *two* legislative authorities: the legislature and the people.

The recall, on the other hand, is not directly concerned with the determination of public policy. Instead, it is intended to influence the manner in which public officials, particularly those who have been popularly elected, administer the affairs of government. As a "potential club to wield over recalcitrant officials," the recall seeks to require a minimum of honesty and efficiency. The rationale behind this device for popular control was well stated by W. B. Munro:

> Just when the people have elected a man burning with patriotic zeal, he suffers some sort of intracerebral accident. He is no longer able to interpret *vox populi.*

175

His memory fails him. His formerly clear-cut views upon public questions become confused and incoherent . . . . The ayes and nayes in the legislative journal, when read in the glow of his former zest for public service, appear unintelligible, sometimes villainous. The recall proposes to aid the office-holder in retaining a candidate's state of mind.[1]

Although not as frequently used as the initiative and referendum, the recall on occasion has proved to be a useful weapon in the arsenal of direct democracy—the "shotgun behind the door."

LAWMAKING BY POPULAR VOTE

While under control of the Populists, South Dakota in 1898 became the first state to provide for the initiative and referendum for state legislation. That same year San Francisco and Vallejo, California, adopted these devices. In the next twenty years the direct legislation movement spread very rapidly to nearly all of the twenty-three states that now provide for the initiative and referendum; two other states use the referendum only.[2] The initiative and referendum have been much more widely used on the local than on the state level. In some cities in almost all states the voters are able to use one or both of these devices.

The Initiative. The initiative is a "device by which any person or group of persons may draft a proposed ordinance, law or constitutional amendment and by securing in its behalf a designated number of signatures may require that such proposal be submitted to the voters for their acceptance or rejection."[3] This short definition requires explanation. It is possible in fifteen states[4] to amend the state constitution by means of the initiative, a practice commonly referred to as the "constitutional initiative." Procedural details are similar to those required for the enactment of statutes. The major difference is the usual requirement that a larger number of signatures be obtained on a petition for a constitutional amendment than for a statutory provision.

The number of signatures demanded on an initiative petition usually is

---

1. W. B. Munro, *The Initiative, Referendum, and Recall,* D. Appleton and Co., New York, 1912, pp. 299-300.
2. The initiative and referendum are actually available for use in only twenty-two states: Alaska, Arizona, Arkansas, California, Colorado, Florida, Illinois, Maine, Massachusetts, Michigan, Missouri, Montana, Nebraska, Nevada, North Dakota, Ohio, Oklahoma, Oregon, South Dakota, Utah, Washington, and Wyoming. The Idaho legislature has never enacted the necessary enabling legislation to make them operative. The two states that use the referendum only are Maryland and New Mexico.
3. W. B. Munro, "Initiative and Referendum," *Encyclopedia of the Social Sciences,* Vol. VIII, p. 50.
4. Arizona, Arkansas, California, Colorado, Florida, Illinois, Massachusetts, Michigan, Missouri, Nebraska, North Dakota, Ohio, Oklahoma, and Oregon.

expressed in terms of a percentage of the votes cast for some state officer elected in a preceding general election. The range is between eight and fifteen per cent. In two states a specific number of signatures is required by law. Occasionally, a state requires that signatures be gathered from various geographical areas of the state. Once the necessary signatures have been obtained and verified, the proposed amendment is ready to be placed on the ballot, usually at the next general election.

In contrast to the "constitutional initiative," the procedure whereby the voters enact or amend statutes is termed the "statutory initiative." In turn, this type of initiative is subdivided into the "direct" and "indirect" forms. Most states provide for the direct initiative only, meaning that a measure must be submitted directly to the voters once the required number of valid signatures has been obtained. In the states with the indirect initiative, a measure must be referred to the legislature before it is submitted to the voters. In a few states either procedure may be followed, depending upon the number of signatures obtained. In each of these states a larger percentage is required for the direct initiative. Whenever the indirect procedure is followed, approval by the legislature ends the process, but a measure is submitted to popular vote if the legislature fails to enact it or some acceptable compromise.

When the direct initiative is used, six significant steps are involved in carrying a measure to a successful conclusion: (1) drafting the proposal; (2) preliminary filing; (3) circulation of petitions to obtain signatures; (4) verification of signatures and final filing; (5) education of the public; and (6) the election. Submission to the legislature is a substitute for steps five and six in the indirect method. Any individual or group may draft an initiative measure. Adequate legal counsel should be obtained at this point to avoid future complications resulting from poor drafting.

After a draft has been prepared, it must be submitted to some officer designated by law—usually the secretary of state when a state statute or constitutional amendment is involved. This officer then specifies the exact form and procedure that must be observed in preparing the petition and obtaining signatures. Next, the proponents must make arrangements for circulation. Abuses sometimes arise because of "petition-hawking," a practice whereby organizations are hired to get persons to sign a petition at a rate of so much per signature. To curtail this commercialization a few states, like Oregon, have enacted laws forbidding persons to receive money for the circulation of petitions.

After signatures have been obtained, they must be verified in order to eliminate names of those who are unqualified. Since "shrinkage" always occurs, it is desirable to have an excess of signers. Some states permit the acquisition of supplementary signatures within a specified time if the original number proves to be inadequate. Once this task has been accomplished, the petition is officially filed so the proposed measure will appear on the ballot. In some states informing the voters concerning arguments for and against initiative proposals is not a governmental responsibility. Instead, interested parties perform this task. A few states issue to registered voters an official "voters' pamphlet," containing information on candidates and proposed direct legislation. Persons wishing to present arguments in such pamphlets, either for or against proposals, may be afforded an opportunity to do so at moderate cost. In most states a simple majority of those voting on a measure is sufficient for enactment.

The Referendum. The referendum is "an arrangement whereby any measure which has been passed by a city council or state legislature may under certain circumstances be withheld from going into force until the voters have had an opportunity to render their decision upon it."[5] Like the initiative, the referendum is not new. It was known as early as the seventeenth century in Massachusetts, and the constitution of that state was the first to be ratified by popular vote in 1780. For purposes of study and description, three types of referenda are generally recognized: mandatory or compulsory; optional; and protest or "petition." As explained in an earlier chapter, amendments to state constitutions are regularly submitted to popular vote in all states except Delaware. Often bond issues and certain tax measures must also be submitted to such a vote. Required by law, this type of referendum is termed *mandatory*.

Under the *optional* referendum a legislative body may refer a measure to the voters for their approval or disapproval. Some confusion of terminology exists with regard to optional referenda, depending upon the *consequences* of the popular vote. Earlier practice was to consider the people's vote as advisory only—hence the term "advisory" referendum often associated with it. The common practice today is to regard the voters' reaction on each issue submitted to them as a final decision. As used here, the term "optional referendum" refers to the latter process.

The third variety of referendum, the *protest* or *petition* type, enables the voters to vote on measures already passed by a legislative body. In order that the people may have an opportunity to vote on such measures, referendum laws provide that statutes shall not take effect for a specified period following passage or for a designated time after the legislature adjourns—usually sixty or ninety days. "Emergency" measures, which become effective immediately, are not subject to the referendum but may be repudiated by popular vote only through the initiative. During the period of suspension any interested group may inaugurate action leading to a popular vote.

Steps in the referendum process are very similar to those involved in the initiative. A petition must be prepared; the necessary signatures must be obtained, usually a smaller number than for the initiative; the petition must be filed; the public informed; and an election held. Most

5. W. B. Munro, *loc. cit.*

often a majority of those voting on a measure is sufficient to determine the fate of a measure.

A Constitutional Question

Every young person is aware of the "representative system" of government in the United States. At all levels, national, state, and local, the voters elect a small number of persons to represent the people in the process of translating public will into law. In governmental jurisdictions where the initiative and referendum are available, recognition is given to two legislative powers: the legislature and the people. Shortly after its adoption in Oregon in 1903, direct legislation was challenged in the courts on the ground of unconstitutionality. Specifically, the claim was advanced that the initiative and referendum destroyed the "republican" nature of Oregon's government in violation of the U.S. Constitution[6] This viewpoint reflected the contention that in a republican government the legislative function must be performed exclusively by a representative assembly.

In a noteworthy opinion, the Oregon Supreme Court observed:

> No particular style of government is designated in the Constitution as republican, nor is its exact form in any way prescribed. A republican form of government is a government administered by representatives chosen or appointed by the people or by their authority. . . . Now the initiative and referendum does not destroy the republican form of government and substitute another in its place. The representative character of the government still remains. The people have simply reserved to themselves a larger share of the legislative process.[7]

Although it presented a cogent statement of the compatibility of the processes of direct legislation with representative government, the opinion did not satisfy opponents of the initiative and referendum. Consequently, the constitutional question was raised again in 1909, but the opinion of the Oregon courts did not change.[8] Three years later the United States Supreme Court ruled that the question of whether a state has a republican form of government is a political one, beyond the competence of a court to determine.[9] Instead the issue is a matter to be settled by Congress—and so long as the Senate and House of Representatives seat members-elect from a state, they thereby indicate acceptance of its system of government.

---

6. Article IV, Section 4 provides, "The United States shall guarantee to every State in this Union a republican form of government . . ."
7. *Kadderly* v. *Portland,* 44 Ore. 145 (1903).
8. *Oregon* v. *Pacific States Telephone and Telegraph Company,* 53 Ore. 162 (1909).
9. *Pacific States Telephone and Telegraph Company* v. *Oregon,* 233 U.S. 118 (1912).

Use of the Initiative and Referendum

Unfortunately, studies on the use of the initiative and referendum are not available for most states. However, especially helpful investigations have been conducted in California, Michigan, and Oregon.[10] Although admittedly not an adequate sample, the information pertaining to three states provides some insight into the operation of these devices of direct democracy. In addition, they make possible some tentative observations concerning the use of the initiative and referendum that are more "scientific" than the general statements often made without adequate investigation of the manner in which these devices actually work.

Even though it is fashionable in some circles to comment critically that the ballot is made excessively long by direct legislation, few serious students of the subject deny that solid accomplishments have been realized through the initiative and referendum. Most proposals voted on by the people have not been of the "ham and eggs" variety. Viewed in general terms, matters voted on by the electorate may be classified into three major groups: modifications in the structure of government, finances, and public policy.[11] Examples of measures passed by Californians include an executive budget law, a civil service system, improved procedures for the selection of judges, and the well-known "Proposition 13." Oregonians have provided for the reorganization of school districts, revised procedures for reapportioning the state legislature, authorized the practice of denture technology, and empowered the legislature to call itself into special session.

Voters in Oregon have been especially active with regard to financial matters. Of several hundred measures voted on in the last half-century approximately one-third were directly concerned with finances of the state and local units of government. A number of these measures, such as salaries of legislators, the general sales tax, and the cigarette tax, were submitted to the voters more than once. Although some persons have claimed that the people regularly vote "No" on revenue measures, an analysis of the votes in Oregon as well as California and Michigan does not support this assertion. It is true that the people have voted against some major sources of revenue, but they have acted favorably on others. It seems more accurate to conclude that the voters have exercised discrimination.

The initiative and referendum have been more widely utilized at the local level, especially in cities, than at the state level. In many states where these devices of direct democracy are unavailable statewide, they have been au-

10. W. W. Crouch, *The Initiative and Referendum in California*, The Haynes Foundation, Los Angeles, 1950; J. K. Pollock, *The Initiative and Referendum in Michigan*, University of Michigan Press, Ann Arbor, 1940; J. G. La Palombara, *The Initiative and Referendum in Oregon: 1938-1948*, Oregon State College Press, Corvallis, 1950.
11. Classification suggested by La Palombara, *op. cit.*, p. 83.

thorized locally by statutory and charter provisions. Local voters regularly express their views on both important and trivial matters, including taxes, bond issues, local option, legalized gambling, annexations, and street routes. On the whole, it seems that the people have been "conservative" and have voted their opposition to measures representing a significant departure from the status quo.

The Case for Direct Legislation

With the exception of Alaska, where they were a part of the original constitution, no state has adopted the initiative and referendum for some fifty years. Nevertheless, a strong case may be developed in their behalf. Of course, direct legislation is subject to abuses, and numerous arguments have been advanced against its use. First the claims of the proponents of direct legislation will be examined briefly.

Strengthening Popular Sovereignty. It is a fundamental axiom of the American system of government that political power flows from the people. Direct legislation was conceived as a means of strengthening the people's control over their government at a time when a feeling was widespread that legislative bodies often were not motivated by concern for the public welfare. It has never been viewed, except by a few extremists, as a substitute for legislative action; it has been designed to function as a complement. Through it the voters may translate their desires into law regardless of the attitudes of their representatives, who conceivably may *mis*represent the people. Direct legislation strengthens the people's opportunity for accurate political expression.

Control of Special Interests. The influence of special interests, or pressure groups, is a major concern of all persons interested in the legislative process. Advocates of direct legislation argue that it "controls" these groups in the sense that influencing public policy is more difficult when the mass of the voters must be persuaded rather than individual legislators. Hence the effectiveness of pressure organizations may be impaired. In relation to this issue, W. B. Munro asserted that "no individual will ever vote for or willingly assent to a change, unless satisfied that the change will directly benefit him individually, or that the action will bring improved general welfare to the community. . . ."[12]

Hardly anyone denies that the people are susceptible to the propaganda of special interests. Two facts must be noted, however. First, more often than not, there are *competing* interest groups seeking to persuade the voters. If the arguments of one appear more persuasive than those of another, the popular vote may be influenced accordingly, and it is very

12. W. B. Munro, *The Initiative, Referendum, and Recall,* D. Appleton and Company, New York, 1912, p. 197.

difficult to argue that it should not be. Second, a basic criticism levied against legislatures when they follow the wishes of pressure groups is that when they do so they are acting contrary to the people's welfare. If the two are in accord, the basis for criticism vanishes.

Influence on the Legislature. It is asserted that direct legislation influences legislative bodies in at least two important ways. First, it serves as a stimulus to action. Where the voters may enact legislation, legislators may be motivated to take action on matters that otherwise would be neglected because of inertia or selfish interests. The people's representatives might also feel, perhaps with some justification, that they could prepare a law which would accomplish desired purposes more effectively than one drawn up by interested citizens.

A second argument is that the initiative and referendum, particularly the latter, function to "check" the legislature by preventing enactment of legislation that does not meet popular approval. Opportunities for overriding the legislature may be somewhat limited, however, by the use of "emergency" clauses. When such a clause is attached to a bill, it becomes effective immediately and is not subject to the usual waiting period of sixty or ninety days. Since legislatures usually exhibit discretion in this matter, the people have the opportunity to vote on the great bulk of significant legislation if they so desire. One careful student has concluded that "this feature of direct legislation appears the most important and effective argument in its favor."[13]

Voter Education. Even though voters may sometimes act on the basis of emotion rather than intelligence and reason, direct legislation stimulates interest in public issues. However, the degree to which voters have become more educated and interested in public affairs is difficult, if not impossible, to determine. Still, it cannot be assumed that efforts in this direction at election time produce no results. Some states publish an official voters' pamphlet in which arguments are presented for and against measures. Even if a voter does not comprehend *all* the material presented, perhaps the level of interest and basic knowledge will be increased.

Education of the voter is not limited to official efforts. At least three other sources of information are generally significant: groups interested in specific measures, newspapers, and civic organizations of various kinds. Although much of the material might more accurately be termed propaganda, the voter is presented with an opportunity to weigh the claims of all sides. In most communities of any size, newspapers run factual and editorial articles on initiative and referendum measures, again presenting the voters with an opportunity to separate the wheat from the chaff. Organizations like the League of Women Voters and businesspeople's

13. La Palombara, *op. cit.*, p. 118.

"city clubs" study proposals carefully and prepare balanced presentations of arguments pro and con. The influence of such groups is not limited to their membership, since they commonly make concerted efforts to disseminate the information that they have prepared.

Effect on Constitutions and Charters. Proponents of direct legislation sometimes maintain that state constitutions and local charters need not be encumbered with so many restrictions on legislative action when the people may directly determine public policy. A comparison of constitutions in those states using direct legislation with the constitutions of other states does not seem to support this generalization. The average of constitutions in the two groups of states is about the same, and restrictions on legislative discretion are numerous in both.

The Case Against Direct Legislation

Numerous criticisms have been directed against the initiative and referendum. Both the theory and practice of direct legislation have been targets of concentrated attack. The fact remains, however, that no state has abandoned these processes, a compelling indication that they have won approval from the people.

Impairment of Representative Government. Attention has been called to court decisions repudiating the idea that, legally speaking, the initiative and referendum destroy the representative nature of government. The existence of devices for direct popular participation in the governmental process means that a *redistribution* of functions has taken place in order to give the people more control. If sovereignty resides with the people, "then it must follow that they enjoy the right to expand or limit the functions of a governmental agency which owes its very existence to the will of the people."[14]

Few persons will deny that the system of representative government found in the states has exhibited some defects. Direct legislation reflects only *one method* of seeking to remedy these defects. The conclusion of one early student of direct legislation with regard to its constituting a threat to representative governments has been justified by experience:

> But whatever the amount of competition with the legislative assembly, from the ever-increasing amount of legislation enacted by the assembly . . . it is clear that there is no danger that the representative legislature will be superseded by the direct action of the people.[15]

14. *Ibid.,* p. 102.
15. J. D. Barnett, *The Operation of the Initiative, Referendum, and Recall in Oregon,* The Macmillan Co., New York, 1915, p. 166. A similar view was expressed by C. A. Beard and B. E. Shultz, *Documents on the State-Wide Initiative, Referendum and Recall,* The Macmillan Co., New York, 1912, p. 23.

Impairment of Legislative Responsibility. Closely related to the foregoing criticism is the claim that direct legislation impairs the sense of responsibility of a legislative body. Such a development may stem from two closely related factors. A sense of "timidity" may develop on the part of individual legislators, resulting in the referral of "hot" issues to the voters. In this way the legislators may avoid the necessity of having to take a stand on controversial issues in order to maintain their popularity with constituents. Early in American experience with direct legislation, J. D. Barnett observed:

> The constitutional provision which permits the legislative assembly to submit statutes to the people of the state for approval or rejection is vicious in that it may tempt the assembly to shift the responsibility for the enactment of legislation, for which it has been chosen, back upon the electors . . .[16]

One writer has aptly noted that this argument "begs the question" because the optional referendum was instituted "for the purpose of allowing the legislature to refer to the people those measures about which it entertained genuine doubts."[17] It could be as logically argued that *failure* by the legislature to use the referendum under such circumstances would reflect a disregard for its responsibilities.

Nevertheless, it is true that the optional referendum *may* be used as a means of abdicating legislative responsibility. If legislators use this device "to refer what they fear to enact," the people are called upon to make decisions that should be made by their representatives. When genuine doubt exists as to the wisdom of a particular course of action with regard to a matter of real public concern, reference to the voters is entirely justifiable.

Lengthening of the Ballot. No one can deny that the initiative and referendum operate to increase the length of ballots, and the assertion is often made that long ballots are undesirable. The impact on ballots, however, has differed from state to state and from time to time within states. Moderate use has been made of the initiative and referendum in some states like Michigan, while in others like California the voters have regularly decided a variety of issues. Indeed, voters have on occasion been faced with as many as three or four dozen measures at a single election! Not only do many voters find it difficult to make intelligent decisions on so many controversial matters, they may even be discouraged from going to the polls at all.

It is a truism that any virtue may become a vice when carried to an excess. This old saw is applicable to the initiative and referendum. Used discriminatingly, they serve a very useful purpose; employed without

16. Barnett, *op. cit.,* pp. 169-170.
17. La Palombara, *op. cit.,* p. 105.

discrimination, they impose an intolerable burden upon the voters. However, advocates of the short ballot should not become so ardent as to overlook the value of obtaining an expression of public opinion on certain issues. Occasional abuses do occur, sometimes as a result of repeated referrals of the same question within a short period of time.

Lawmaking by Minorities.   Many voters do not go to the polls on election day, and among those who vote on candidates there are many who fail to vote on propositions. As a result, critics of direct legislation argue that it often produces laws enacted by a minority. This claim is undoubtedly true, but its impact is appreciably lessened by recognition of the fact that all lawmaking bodies are subject to the same vice. Thus in many legislative houses a majority constitutes a quorum, and a majority of the quorum is sufficient to pass a law.

Another consideration is that it is not necessarily desirable that all persons who go to the polls should vote on all measures. There is little if any value in an uninformed, ignorant vote. Furthermore, some voters actually do not care whether a particular measure is accepted or rejected. They are willing to abide by whatever decision is made by those who are interested and informed. Such an attitude may, in fact, be praiseworthy. Of course, there is the risk that selfish minorities may determine public policy. The fact is that within the framework of democratic government no arrangement has been devised to prevent this from happening, regardless of who makes the laws.

Control of Government by Special Interests.   Closely related to the foregoing criticism is the claim that direct legislation facilitates control of government by special interests. Some believe pressure groups are evil and should be curbed, an attitude that ignores the right of people to associate and to seek to influence their government. One writer has observed with much insight that "it can be reasonably assumed that public policy will always be synonymous with the ideas of those groups which have found successful political expression."[18] Special interests are going to influence the formulation of public policy, whether action is taken by legislative bodies or by the people directly.

The ability of pressure groups to get their pet projects on the ballot or to engineer support for them is not nearly so great a threat to public welfare as the opportunity to affect governmental policy secretly. It is true that voters may not always be able to identify the major groups supporting a measure, but the difficulties of hiding such identity when conducting a mass campaign are probably greater than when seeking to influence the votes of a few legislators. Logical analysis does not support

18. La Palombara, *op. cit.*, p. 109.

the assertion that the people are more susceptible to control by special interests than are their representatives.

Poorly Drafted Legislation. Provisions submitted to the voters through the initiative may be poorly drafted, but so may bills prepared by legislative bodies. Indeed, it is very questionable to assume that legislatures have generally done a superior job preparing legislation than have the people. It is reasonable to assume that those groups sponsoring a measure probably exercise care in phraseology so that the desired goals will be obtained should the measure pass. Legal talent is available to such groups so that a creditable job of drafting may be accomplished.

Weakening the Constitution. Basic to American government, national and state, is the idea that constitutions are "fundamental law." Granting the wisdom of the distinction between constitutional and other types of law, it is argued that the initiative is undesirable because it tends to obscure this difference. As early as 1914 one writer advanced the thesis that the initiative "tends to incorporate into the constitution matters that have no proper place there. . ."[19] Experience in states where the initiative has been most frequently used seems to support this assertion.[20]

High Cost. The claim is sometimes made that direct legislation is costly in comparison with the enactment of laws by legislative bodies. Expenses are involved in drafting measures, obtaining signatures on petitions, verifying signatures, educating the public and counting votes. However, no studies have been made of these costs as compared with those required in order to get a bill through a legislature. Consequently, any conclusions on this point must be based on guesswork.

Evaluation

As indicated by the arguments pro and con, direct legislation has both strengths and weaknesses. It is certainly not a panacea for political ills as some of its early advocates believed it to be. Nor does it constitute the great threat to our basic governmental institutions that many of its opponents have decried. Undoubtedly, the initiative and referendum place a burden upon the voters, but democracy by its nature imposes heavy burdens on them. If government operates more effectively to

19. A. L. Lowell, *Public Opinion and Popular Government,* Longmans, Green and Company, New York, 1914, p. 218.
20. See J. G. La Palombara, *op. cit.,* p. 115; and W. W. Crouch, *op. cit.,* p. 42, Table II. According to Crouch's table, 348 of the 450 measures submitted to popular vote between 1912 and 1949 were constitutional amendments.

implement the wishes of the people, the additional burden imposed by direct legislation is hardly a significant argument against it. If as a result of the initiative and referendum many voters take a more active interest in governmental affairs, the effort is worth the price.

Used with moderation, direct legislation can make truly significant contributions to state and local government. Legislatures continue to decide the bulk of public policy questions and to set the tone of government as long as they *choose* to do so. Occasionally, they are overruled by popular vote, sometimes as a result of repeatedly seeking to do things that have already been disapproved by the public. It is also true that the people sometimes make strange and apparently illogical decisions, but such is the price of democracy.

THE RECALL

By means of the recall voters may remove an official from public office prior to the expiration of his term. Although similar to the initiative and referendum in certain respects, the recall is less widely used. It was first adopted in this country by the city of Los Angeles in 1903 and first applied to state officers by amendment of the Oregon constitution in 1908. By 1914 the recall had been adopted by ten other states; since then only Wisconsin and Alaska have provided for the recall of state officials.[21] However, the recall has spread more widely on the local level, where it is available in some three-fourths of the states.

The steps in recall proceedings are similar to those involved in direct legislation, but a few important differences should be noted. A major distinction concerns the number of signatures required on a recall petition setting forth the grounds on which the recall of a particular officer is sought. Recall petitions regularly require a much larger number of signatures than either initiative or referendum petitions. The range is from ten to fifty-five per cent of those who voted for some designated officer at the last election; the most common requirement is twenty-five per cent. After the petition has been signed by the required number of voters, it must be filed with the appropriate official, who is responsible for determining the sufficiency and legality of signatures. Once everything is in

---

21. The recall is applicable to elective state officials in thirteen states: Alaska, Arizona, California, Colorado, Idaho, Kansas, Louisiana, Michigan, Nevada, North Dakota, Oregon, Washington, and Wisconsin. Only in Kansas are appointed as well as elected officers subject to recall. Some cities also subject appointed officials to the recall. In addition to the regular recall, Arizona uses the "advisory recall," a device by which candidates seeking election to Congress *may* file a statement indicating willingness or unwillingness to resign if not re-elected at a recall election. Candidates may refuse to file any statement. In any case, a recall vote itself cannot remove a member of Congress from office, since the U.S. Constitution does not recognize the procedure.

order, an election must be held within a specified time unless the officer in question resigns.

Although the procedural requirements for recall elections differ appreciably from place to place, there are three basic patterns. Under one arrangement, two elections are required. In the first election the people merely vote "Yes" or "No" on the question of removal. If the majority vote affirmatively, a second election is held, usually within thirty days, to choose a successor. An alternative arrangement enables the people to vote simultaneously on removal and for a successor. Thus each person who votes to remove the official also votes for someone to fill that place should the election result in recall. A third variation simply requires the person against whom a recall petition has been filed to run against other candidates whose names have been placed on the ballot. The first practice is to be preferred because the official "runs" against his or her record rather than against others seeking the position.

The recall has been used much less frequently than the initiative and referendum. The only instance of its successful use to remove officers elected on a statewide basis occurred in North Dakota in 1921, when the governor, attorney general, and secretary of agriculture were recalled.[22] Numerous unsuccessful efforts have been made, however, to remove state officeholders. On the other hand, many local officials have been removed by the recall.

Evaluation

As in the case of initiative and referendum, experience with the recall has justified neither the fears of its opponents nor the claims of its ardent advocates. It is undoubtedly true that the recall has been used in behalf of the public interest in some instances and to serve selfish, partisan interests in others. The fact remains that limited use has been made of the recall. All the reasons for infrequency of use are not readily apparent. Legal restrictions constitute a part of the explanation. In most jurisdictions, recall proceedings may not be started until an incumbent has been in office for a stipulated period, usually six months. Further, the law commonly provides that recall of an officer may not be undertaken more than once during a single term of office. The large number of signatures required on recall petitions probably contributes to the infrequency of their use. The major explanation for the fact that the recall is seldom used appears to be popular reluctance to resort to it.

---

22. Governor Frazier, oddly enough, was elected to the United States Senate the following year by the same electorate that had recalled him fron the governor's chair!

State and
Local Expenditures

13

Annual state and local direct expenditures now approximate $300 billion. Among the many services provided by the *states* with these funds, four are especially noteworthy. About three-fifths of all state expenditures go for the support of education, welfare, highways, and health and hospitals. Most of the remainder is spent for protection of persons and property, development and protection of natural resources, correctional institutions, debt retirement and interest payments, recreational facilities, general government, and insurance trusts. Major *local* expenditures are for public schools, public works including streets and highways, police and fire protection, and welfare.

TRENDS IN STATE AND LOCAL EXPENDITURES

The growth of public spending during the twentieth century has been impressive. Expenditures of state and local governments in 1902 totaled just under $1.1 billion and in 1922 barely exceeded $5.6 billion; by 1940 they approximated $11.2 billion, and in 1959 they totaled some $58.5 billion. The really explosive growth has occurred since 1960, as demonstrated by the fact that in fiscal 1971-72 state and local expenditures reached $190.4 billion and passed the $300 billion mark by 1980. But such figures are somewhat misleading when viewed by themselves. Population growth and changes in the gross national product, as well as fluctuations in the purchasing power of the dollar, must be considered. In 1902 these outlays amounted to $12.80 *per capita*; in 1922, $47.41; in 1940, $69.85; in 1959, $276.97; in 1972, $809.43; and by 1978 the amount had grown to $1,355.15. Thus while total expenditures increased about 350 times from 1902 to 1978, per capita amounts were multiplied just over one hundred times.[1]

1. See *Historical Statistics and Governmental Finances and Employment, 1977 Census of Governments* and *Governmental Finances in 1977-78.* Bureau of the Census.

Comprehension of governmental expenditures is more complete when viewed in relation to the gross national product, which is the value of the total output of commodities and services produced by the economy of a nation during a specified period of time, one calendar year. Thus the GNP consists of (1) all finished products such as consumer goods, capital facilities, and materiél for the armed forces; and (2) all services rendered by individuals, businesses, and governmental units. In other words, the GNP is the aggregate supply of goods and services resulting from the productive efforts of the nation's economy, and its value fluctuates from year to year. Table 13.1 indicates how great have been the changes in the GNP of the United States in recent times.

The more wealth a nation has, the more it can afford in the way of services. As wealth increases, larger governmental expenditures can be borne without increased sacrifice. Consequently, the ratio between the value of the GNP and the amount of expenditures by state and local governments is significant. The figures in Table 13.1 reveal that the percentage of the GNP accounted for by state and local spending between 1929 and 1978 ranged from a high of 12.8 in 1932 to a low of 3.6 in 1944. Several other interesting facts are worthy of attention in this regard. For one thing, the ratio of state and local expenditures to GNP was at its highest during the depression of the 1930's. Also, this ratio in recent years has not greatly exceeded the point reached in 1929. Therefore, state and local governments are not spending a great deal more than in 1929 in relation to the nation's wealth.

During the current century appreciable shifts have occurred in the *proportion* of funds expended by the national government on the one hand and state and local governments on the other. In 1902 state and local expenditures accounted for about sixty-eight per cent of total governmental outlay, and in 1923 the percentage stood at sixty-two. By 1940, however, state and local governments spent only about forty-eight per cent of the total, while the federal share had risen to approximately fifty-two per cent; and in 1948 the ratio stood at 32.5 to 67.5 per cent. Since that time a countertrend has developed, and state and local spending now amounts to about forty-four per cent of the total, leaving approximately fifty-six per cent for the national government.

CAUSES OF GROWTH IN EXPENDITURE AMOUNTS

Increased Demand for Services

A significant cause of higher governmental costs has been the steady public demand for more and better services. Of the factors producing this demand three are often stressed: a changing social and economic order, a changing theory of the proper role of government, and a changing

Table 13.1
State and Local Expenditures and Gross National Product
Selected Calendar Years 1929–1978

	BILLIONS OF DOLLARS				BILLIONS OF DOLLARS		
		STATE AND LOCAL EXPENDITURES[1]				STATE AND LOCAL EXPENDITURES[1]	
Year	Gross National Product	Actual	As % of GNP	Year	Gross National Product	Actual	As % of GNP
1929	$103.1	$7.6	7.4	1948	$257.6	$15.5	6.0
1930	90.4	8.3	9.2	1950	284.8	20.0	7.0
1932	58.0	7.5	12.8	1954	364.8	27.0	7.4
1934	65.1	6.5	9.9	1959	483.7	40.0	8.3
1936	82.5	7.4	9.0	1963	590.5	53.1	9.0
1938	84.7	8.2	9.7	1967	793.9	79.3	10.0
1940	99.7	8.5	8.5	1969	931.4	98.8	10.6
1942	157.9	7.9	5.0	1972	1,171.1	126.2	10.8
1944	210.1	7.5	3.6	1975	1,528.8	176.0	11.5
1946	208.5	9.9	4.7	1977	1,887.2	199.2	10.6
				1978	2,106.6	223.2	10.6

1. Excluding federal grants-in-aid.
Source: Tax Foundation.

conception of democracy. Rapid developments characteristic of the American social and economic order help explain demands for governmental activity. Automobiles require costly highways, streets, bridges, and police officers. Airports, beacons, radio beams, equipment inspection, and the licensing of pilots have followed in the wake of the airplane. Technological advances in jet travel and supersonic transport (SSTs) have produced an added demand on government. Radio and television, along with cable TV and video recording devices, have opened new fields of regulation. Early abuses of the public welfare and trust by public utilities as well as banking and insurance companies called forth governmental control. As the proportion of the population employed in industry grew, demands increased for public action to promote healthful working conditions, reduce accidents, and minimize conflicts between workers and employers.

Growth in urban population has spurred governmental activity. Concentrations of people in relatively small areas aggravate many problems, including those of health, welfare, transportation, and the protection of persons and property. The control of communicable diseases, the collection and disposal of waste materials, and the provision of pure water illustrate tasks involved in the protection of public health. Relief for the unemployed, assistance to dependent children, help for the aged, and care for the mentally and physically handicapped become more urgent and the need more apparent in cities than in rural areas. Transporting large numbers of persons safely and quickly to and from work, by private or public means, requires the construction and maintenance of streets, bridges, and similar facilities. Governmental operation of transportation systems is often necessary where private enterprise does not meet local needs. Heavy concentrations of people and property require costly protection, resulting in more police and fire fighters whose work involves the use of expensive equipment.

A second factor contributing to the increased demand for governmental activity has been a changing attitude toward the proper role of government. For many years after the founding of the Union, the consensus was that governmental functions should be held to a minimum in order to avoid encroachments upon individual freedom. As more and more public services were provided, the inadequacy of the laissez-faire theory of government became evident. Consequently, government came to be viewed as a positive force in promoting the general welfare.

Accompanying the changing idea of what government should do has been a change in the concept of democracy. Early emphasis was almost entirely on equality in political rights, including freedom of speech, press, religion, and assembly, a fair trial, and protection from double jeopardy, self-incrimination, and arbitrary seizure of property. Concern for economic as well as political equality has become increasingly evident. Demands for unemployment compensation, old-age insurance, minimum wage laws, and price supports reflect this trend. These and similar functions cost large sums of money and necessitate increased governmental expenditures.

Population Growth

Even if the urban-rural ratio in the population had not changed so spectacularly in recent years, the mere growth in number of people would have imposed additional demands on government. When the national Constitution was ratified, slightly less than four million perons lived in the United States. Within 100 years the number multiplied more than fifteen times. About the time of World War I the American population exceeded 100 million, and the 1950 census set the figure at slightly more than 150 million. In the early 1970's population exceeded 200 million and it now approximates 220 million. More people have required more services and at the same time called upon government to conserve the nation's resources of water, timber, minerals, and land—all exploited so freely in the process of rapid growth.

Inflation

During the twentieth century the purchasing power of the dollar has varied greatly; that is, prices have fluctuated widely. Consequently, a billion dollars expended one year might purchase much more or much less in the way of services and improvements than would be the case in another twelve-month period. In recent years, especially during the 1970's, the value of the dollar has been consistently and rapidly eroded by inflation. One study has estimated that inflation accounted for about three-fourths of the growth in municipal expenditures between 1973 and 1978.[2] Consequently, in order to maintain an established level of services, governments have found it necessary to increase their expenditures significantly.

FISCAL CONTAINMENT

As evidenced by the passage of Proposition 13 in California in June of 1978, strong opposition has developed against the continued growth of expenditures in many states and localities. By the mid-1970's, about three-fourths of the people in the United States were reported to feel that government wasted "a lot" of money, and some two-thirds believed taxes had reached the "breaking point." Not only have many voters come to distrust government and to question the efficiency and effectiveness with which it spends their money, their attitudes have given impetus to fiscal containment in some states and communities.

Several factors apparently have contributed to a recent slowing down in the growth of state and (especially) local expenditures. In the 1970's some two dozen states enacted constitutional or statutory limits on taxes or spending designed either to cut back existing levels of expenditures or to restrict future growth. Also, the rate of growth in funds transferred from the national and state governments to localities has slowed, and at the same time tax bases in many places have shrunk. Furthermore, there is some evidence to indicate that increasingly frugal voters have elected more "tightfisted" officials. Finally, there is no doubt that in recent years votes on state and local bond issues have evidenced growing fiscal conservatism. From 1969 to 1974, voters approved 53 per cent of the value of the issues on which they voted, a proportion that dropped to 29 per cent in 1975.[3]

MAJOR PROBLEMS

In order to meet the demands for expenditures imposed upon governments at all levels, certain problems must be faced. In meeting these problems,

2. See Anthony H. Pascal, M.D. Menchik, J. M. Chaiken, P. L. Ellickson, W. E. Walker, D. N. DeTray, and A. E. Wise, *Fiscal Containment of Local and State Government*, Rand, 1979, p. viii.
3. *Ibid.*, pp. 23–26.

consideration must be given to achieving effective controls over the purposes for which public money is spent, understanding economic growth, and improving intergovernmental fiscal relations.

Effective Controls

One maxim of sound financial practice which is often advocated but seldom practiced stresses the importance of flexibility in the allocation of state and local revenues. Achieving this flexibility is not easy, however, for legislators and the electorate are pressured by groups whose interests are served by earmarked taxes and statutory formulas that result in long-term commitments on expenditures. When pressures to commit funds are successful, collections from specified taxes are channeled in advance to designated functions and activities by direction of either statutory or constitutional provisions. A number of the states using the general sales tax provide that collections shall be used wholly or in part for specific functions. Similar situations exist with regard to taxes on tobacco and alcoholic beverages, and the bulk of income from gasoline taxes is earmarked for highways. As a consequence of this practice, over fifty per cent of the total tax collections in the states is expended without effective legislative review of needs as balanced against available funds.

Economic Growth

The importance of continued economic growth as a necessary condition to the support of expanding expenditures has been generally recognized. With varying degrees of success, states have sought to attract new industry and retain existing industries in a variety of ways. Low taxes are sometimes stressed as a means of promoting industrial development. However, it is questionable whether tax differentials are a major factor in promoting economic development, and their use is less common now than earlier. The manner in which tax money is spent seems to be more significant to business enterprises than total amounts collected. Considerations pertaining to such matters as geographical location in relation to markets, transportation facilities, and availability of adequate and relatively cheap power and labor resources are more crucial than tax rates.

Intergovernmental Fiscal Relations

The rapid population growth in urban areas during recent years has produced greatly increased demands for local services, particularly by municipal governments. In an effort to meet these demands local jurisdictions have taxed real property very heavily, in many instances reaching legal limits. Economic, political, and legal considerations have forced local governments to seek additional sources of revenue (see Table 13.2).

Table 13.2
State Aid for Local Uses: 1978
Total Aid: $67,287 million

	Millions	Per Cent
Education	$40,125	59
Public Welfare	10,047	15
General Support	6,819	10
Highways	3,821	5
Other	6,474	11

Although local taxes on income and sales have produced appreciable revenue in some jurisdictions, the most significant relief has come in the form of aid from the states and the federal government. State aid to local governments has multiplied many times in the last thirty years. Approximately eighty per cent of this aid to localities is for education, welfare, and highways. The states have not only provided assistance to local governments from their own revenue sources, they have also passed along some of the income they have received from the federal government in the form of revenue sharing. In addition, local governments, especially large cities, have obtained significant help directly from the national government.

The impact of federal grants-in-aid on state and local governments was studied by the Commission on Intergovernmental Relations a quarter-century ago, and the observations advanced at that time are still pertinent. Although an advisory committee of the CIR concluded that in general "the over-all impact of federal grants has had relatively little adverse effect in a majority of the States studied," it was agreed that in some states "Federal grants have produced shifts in State policies. In some instances, services were introduced which would not have been undertaken without federal aid." Furthermore, some functions receiving federal aid "were begun sooner and were done more extensively than would otherwise have been the case." Even though state functions not benefitting from federal assistance have not been "conspicuously neglected," according to the committee, there is considerable evidence to indicate that they have not been "equally well treated."[4] Differences appeared especially noticeable in poorer states.

Writing in 1953, Leonard D. White, a long-time student of American government, voiced the opinion that "if present trends continue for another quarter century, the states may be left hollow shells, operating primarily as the field districts of federal departments and dependent upon the federal treasury for their support."[5] Recent developments seem to

---

4. *The Impact of Federal Grants-in-Aid on the Structure and Functions of State and Local Government,* June, 1955, p. 12.
5. Leonard D. White, *The States and the Nation,* Louisiana State University Press, Baton Rouge, 1953, p. 3.

foretell a less inglorious future for the states. Noting that "the States and their subdivisions bear directly more than two-thirds of the growing fiscal burdens of domestic government," the Commission on Intergovernmental Relations has observed that "their activities have been increasing faster than the nondefense activities of the National Government." At the same time the Commission stressed the importance of strengthening state and local governments if they are to continue to play their vital role in the affairs of the nation.[6]

Revenue Sharing

In 1972 Congress enacted the State and Local Government Fiscal Assistance Act, commonly known as the "revenue sharing act." The law provided that $30.2 billion would be given to state and local governments over a period of five years. In 1976 Congress extended the life of revenue sharing to 1980, providing that approximately $6 billion would be distributed annually. In early 1980 the President announced his intention to seek a significant reduction in revenue-sharing funds as part of an anti-inflation package.

Distribution of revenue-sharing dollars has been determined by a formula that takes into account three factors: population, tax effort, and relative income level. This formula was designed to ensure that poorer, more heavily taxed communities would be favored in relation to more prosperous, lightly taxed ones and at the same time to guarantee that practically all multi-purpose local governments would receive some assistance. Two-thirds of the funds have been passed to local communities, while the states retained one-third. In the absence of restrictions on the purposes for which they may use their funds, the states have made part of their share available to local governments.

Originally, Congress imposed restrictions on the purposes for which local governments could spend revenue-sharing dollars, but in 1976 these limitations were removed. Consequently, the money has been used for a great variety of purposes. The law does stipulate that the money must not be spent so as to discriminate on the basis of race, color, sex, or ethnicity. In fact, local governments have spent most of their portions for public safety, public transit, recreational facilities, and general government. A few communities have used their share for rather trivial purposes.

The underlying idea behind revenue sharing has been that, given sufficient resources, states and local governments can identify the needs of their people more accurately than the federal government, and be more responsive to them. It was also designed to reverse the trend toward greater control by the federal bureaucracy associated with grants-in-aid. Revenue sharing has not replaced such grants (although some have been

6. *A Report to the President for Transmittal to the Congress,* June 1955, pp. 36 *ff.*

reduced)—it supplemented them in order to maximize local determination of priorities and minimize federal controls.

PURPOSES OF STATE EXPENDITURES

An appreciation of government spending requires not only an awareness of trends but also an understanding of what the money is spent for. The simplest way of accomplishing this purpose is to examine the financial reports of the states. There are, of course, varied systems of reporting, but expenditures commonly are classified according to *character* and *function*. Character reflects the nature of the expenditure regardless of the function, or functions, involved. Thus all money spent to pay interest on outstanding bonds is of the same character even though the bonds may have been issued to finance roads, hospitals, or school buildings. Function, on the other hand, refers to the nature of the activity such as road construction, public health, or education.

Expenditures According to Character

Major subclassifications under character are (1) current operation, (2) capital outlay, (3) insurance trusts, (4) debt service, and (5) intergovernmental. *Current operation* includes all direct expenditures for the compensation of officers and employees as well as for the purchase of supplies, matériel, and services other than capital items. *Capital outlays* are made for the construction of highways, public buildings, public works, and other improvements of a somewhat "permanent" nature. Included also are expenses for the purchase of real property and major items of equipment and for major alterations and additions to existing structures. Differences between expenditures for current operation and capital outlay are sometimes indistinct because items may be arbitrarily classified in one category or the other by different jurisdictions. Thus automobiles and typewriters, for example, are regarded as items of current expense, while road graders and electronic computers may be considered as capital outlays.

Insurance trusts include payments to retired employees, unemployment compensation, workmen's compensation, sickness insurance, and other social insurance programs. Costs of administering such trust activities and state contributions to these funds are *not* included. The major expenses under *debt service* involve the redemption of obligations such as bonds and warrants along with the payment of interest. The bulk of *intergovernmental* expenses stem from fiscal aid to other governments, especially grants and shared taxes.

In fiscal 1978 spending for current operation reached $86 billion, accounting for over forty per cent of total *state* expenditures. Capital outlay reached $16 billion, and insurance benefit payments passed $20 billion. During 1978 the states devoted about $22 billion to debt redemption and interest payments. State assistance to local governments increased to $67.3 billion during the same period. The tremendous growth in state payments to local governments during the current century is indicated in Table 13.3.

Expenditures According to Function

The most important groupings according to function are (1) education, (2) highways, (3) public welfare, (4) health and hospitals, (5) natural resources, (6) public safety, (7) general control, and (8) miscellaneous.[7] State allocations for *education* in fiscal 1978 totaled $69.7 billion, a sum significantly more than was spent for any other function. Aid to local governments for public primary and secondary schools reached $40 billion. The major portion of the remainder was used to support state colleges and universities. At the same time the states spent $18.4 billion for highways. About $3.8 billion went to local governments to help them finance their road building programs. The bulk of direct state disbursements for highways went for capital outlay, mostly in the form of payments to contractors.

In the field of *public welfare* the states function largely as middlemen. Of the $35.8 billion expended by the states for welfare programs in 1978, transfers to local governments totaled $10 billion. During that year the states received over $20 billion from the national government for public assistance. State spending for *health and hospitals,* the fourth major function, reached $13.8 billion in 1978. The bulk of these funds was used for hospitals and institutions for the handicapped.

Numerous programs are encompassed within the general category of *natural resources,* for which the states spent $4.6 billion in 1978. With this money the states sought to conserve, develop, and improve the utilization of such resources as soil, water, forests, minerals, and wild life. It is interesting to note that in 1902 the states spent only nine million dollars on natural resources. In 1978 the states spent $4.1 billion for correction and police functions, including general law enforcement, crime prevention, and prisons.

Expenditures for *general control* in 1978 barely reached $4.8 billion, financing the legislative and judicial branches, the offices of chief executives, and auxiliary and staff services in such fields as finance, personnel, purchasing, record-keeping, and public reporting. In addition to expenditures falling into standard "functional" categories, the states spent smaller sums for a variety of purposes, including housing and community redevelopment, water transport facilities, docks, terminals,

---

7. This breakdown of expenditures is adapted from the Bureau of the Census.

Table 13.3
State Expenditures for Selected Items
Selected Fiscal Years 1902–1978
(millions)

Year	SELECT DIRECT EXPENDITURES				Payments to local governments
	Current operation	Capital outlay	Interest[1]	Insurance benefits and withdrawals	
1902	$ 114	$ 2	$ 10		$ 52
1913	218	48	14		91
1922	562	302	45	$ 54	312
1932	982	786	114	63	801
1936	1,192	634	124	79	1,417
1940	1,570	737	130	601	1,654
1944	2,134	330	101	226	1,842
1948	3,837	1,456	86	1,020	3,283
1952	5,173	2,658	144	1,413	5,044
1956	6,758	4,564	311	1,984	6,538
1958	8,307	5,949	396	3,675	7,943
1961	10,384	6,865	584	4,701	10,114
1963	12,449	8,110	721	4,306	11,885
1965	14,930	9,307	822	4,170	14,174
1967	20,201	11,544	1,026	4,268	19,065
1069	27,052	12,696	1,271	4,911	24,779
1970	30,971	13,295	1,499	6,009	28,892
1972	39,790	15,283	2,135	8,938	36,759
1975	60,793	17,307	3,272	18,860	51,978
1977	75,857	16,793	5,136	23,426	62,460
1978	86,153	16,064	5,493	20,495	67,287

1. Does not include sums for repayments of debts.
Sources: Tax Foundation and Bureau of the Census.

airports, and miscellaneous commercial activities. (Table 13.4 indicates expenditures made by the states *directly* for certain functions, not including monies provided to local governments.)

PURPOSES OF LOCAL EXPENDITURES

Direct general expenditures by all local governments during fiscal 1978 approximated $183 billion, including income of some $84 billion from other governments. Major functions supported by these expenditures and the approximate amounts involved were as follows: education, $81.2 billion; highways, $9.9 billion; public safety, $14.4 billion; health, hospitals and sanitation, $22 billion; public welfare, $11.9 billion; general control, $8 billion; housing and urban renewal, $3.5 billion; parks and

Table 13.4
Direct State Expenditures for Selected Functions
Selected Fiscal Years 1902–1978
(millions)

Year	Total	Education[1]	High-ways	Public welfare	Health and Hospitals	Natural resources	General control[2]
1902	136	17	4	10	32	9	23
1913	297	55	26	16	53	14	38
1922	1,085	164	303	38	125	61	69
1932	2,082	278	843	74	215	119	114
1940	3,555	375	793	527	300	144	151
1948	7,897	1,081	1,510	962	663	344	266
1950	10,864	1,358	2,058	1,566	947	468	317
1956	15,148	2,138	4,367	1,603	1,470	670	477
1958	19,991	2,728	5,507	1,944	1,760	753	569
1960	22,152	3,396	6,070	2,221	1,896	842	654
1962	25,495	4,270	6,635	2,509	2,161	973	763
1964	29,616	5,465	7,850	2,796	2,464	1,185	871
1965	31,465	6,181	8,214	2,998	2,701	1,343	948
1967	39,704	9,384	9,423	4,291	3,358	1,801	1,175
1969	49,447	12,304	10,409	6,464	4,258	2,035	1,495
1970	56,163	13,780	11,044	8,203	5,053	2,223	1,749
1972	62,051	17,153	12,747	12,247	6,008	2,470	2,134
1975	86,326	22,902	14,258	17,457	8,968	3,368	3,205
1977	101,891	27,073	13,853	22,646	11,209	4,369	4,099
1978	112,515	29,577	14,658	25,729	13,769	4,644	4,815

1. Principally higher education.
2. Includes financial administration.
Sources: Tax Foundation and Bureau of the Census.

recreation, $4.3 billion. (See Table 13.5 for trends in local expenditures for selected functions.)

Total expenditures by local governments in 1978 amounted to $211 billion. Of this amount, municipalities spent $75.4 billion; school districts, $66.8 billion; counties, $43.2 billion; special districts and townships accounted for the remainder. Since a significant portion of the funds spent by municipalities went for education, it is apparent this function consumes the largest share of money spent locally, followed by police and fire protection; health, hospitals, and sanitation; and then welfare.

FINANCING EXPENDITURES

Once decisions have been made concerning the purposes for which public money shall be spent and the amounts to be allocated to individual purposes, then the big problem is, Where is the money coming from?

Table 13.5
Local Direct Expenditures for Selected Functions
Selected Fiscal Years 1902–1978

(millions)

Function	1902	1922	1948	1957	1967	1972	1975	1978
Education	$238	$1,541	$4,298	$11,793	$28,534	$47,734	$64,956	$81,181
Highways	171	991	1,526	2,941	4,510	6,263	8,270	9,951
Public Welfare	27	81	1,137	1,659	3,927	8,882	10,698	11,950
Health and Hospitals	28	133	566	1,549	3,283	6,858	9,878	12,632
Police and Fire	90	344	985	2,100	4,108	7,654	10,528	14,425
General Control[1]	118	244	614	1,195	2,139	3,753	5,435	7,595
Other[2]	207	853	2,372	5,492	12,601	24,803	34,348	35,677

1. Includes financial administration.
2. Includes natural resources, sanitation, recreation, interest on general debt, housing and urban renewal, nonhighway transportation, correction, local libraries, and other general government.
Sources: Tax Foundation and Bureau of the Census.

How is the necessary revenue to be raised? Answers to these questions are not easy. Many alternatives are open to legislators who are importuned from all sides by persons who claim their schemes are best. In general, no area of public policy is more loaded with political dynamite than decisions pertaining to taxes and debts. These matters are of vital concern to all citizens. The following chapter examines the means commonly used by states and local governments to raise revenue adequate to meet expenses.

Revenues and Debt

14

Benjamin Franklin once observed that the only sure things in life were death and taxes. Since the beginning of recorded history people have been concerned with taxes. The Egyptians had a well-developed tax system several thousand years ago. Taxes were a matter of real interest to Biblical writers. "Taxation without representation" was an issue in the American Revolution. Today the revenue of all governments in the United States, federal, state, and local, equals over thirty per cent of the total annual income in the United States.

In fiscal 1978 state and local governments raised about $302 billion directly from their own revenue sources, of which $171.6 billion were for the states. When allowance is made for intergovernmental transfers the picture is somewhat different: the national government provided states and localities over $69 billion, and the states paid about $65 billion to local governments. Thus in terms of the *final* recipient level of government, public revenues in 1978 were divided roughly in this manner: fifty per cent to the national government, thirty per cent to local governments, and twenty per cent to the states. Although the bulk of these funds came from taxes, significant amounts were derived from such other sources as charges for the performance of specific services, insurance trust revenues, utilities, state owned liquor stores, and interest earnings.

TRENDS IN STATE AND LOCAL REVENUES

Trends in amounts of state and local revenues necessarily have paralleled developments in expenditures—both have grown at a similar pace as revealed by a comparison of Tables 14.1 and 14.2. The factors basic to the growth of expenditures are equally significant with regard to changes in income. These trends and factors were discussed in Chapter 13. In addition to over-all growth in revenue, two other developments have been

Table 14.1
State Revenues by Source
Selected Fiscal Years 1902–1978
(millions)

Year	Total	FROM OWN SOURCES					Intergovern-mental[3]
		Total	Taxes[1]	Charges and misc.	Liquor stores[2]	Insurance trusts	
1902	$ 192	$ 183	$ 156	$ 25	$ 2	$ —	$ 9
1922	1,360	1,234	947	181	—	106	126
1932	2,541	2,274	1,890	266	—	118	267
1940	5,737	5,012	3,313	344	281	1,074	725
1953	17,979	15,218	10,552	1,198	967	2,051	2,761
1960	32,838	26,093	18,036	2,583	1,128	4,347	6,745
1967	61,082	46,793	31,926	5,856	1,470	7,541	14,289
1972	112,309	84,327	59,870	10,780	1,904	11,773	27,891
1975	157,033	119,206	80,155	16,629	2,219	20,393	37,828
1977	204,475	155,800	101,085	20,106	2,244	32,365	48,675
1978	225,011	171,550	113,261	22,757	2,389	32,562	53,461

1. Excludes unemployment compensation taxes.
2. Gross receipts from sale of alcoholic beverages in state monopoly systems.
3. Principally grants-in-aid and revenue sharing from the national government.
Sources: Tax Foundation and Bureau of the Census.

particularly noticeable during the twentieth century: changes in the relative amounts of income for state and local governments, and changes in revenue sources.

In terms of revenue from their own sources, local governments in 1902 collected nearly five times as much money as the states, and in 1922 the ratio was three to one. By 1940 nearly equal amounts were collected by state and local governments, and in more recent years the states have gained slightly on the localities. During the same period, the states have multiplied many times the aid given to local governments. Simultaneously, the states and local governments have been the recipients of increased assistance from the national government. Indeed, in recent years the states have received more money from the national government than from their most productive tax—the income tax.

Other major changes have occurred in revenue sources during the last half-century. The proportion of *state* income derived from *taxes* has declined steadily from eighty-one per cent in 1902 to twenty-seven per cent in 1978. During the same period taxes decreased as a per cent of *local* revenue from nearly eighty per cent to some thirty-five per cent, and the proportion of income provided by the property tax alone dropped from sixty-eight to approximately thirty per cent. Major proportional

Table 14.2
Local Revenues by Source
Selected Fiscal Years 1902–1978

(millions)

Year	Total	FROM OWN SOURCES								Intergovern-mental
		Total	TAXES				Charges and misc.	Utility and liquor stores	Insurance trust	
			Property	Sales and gross receipts	Income	License and other				
1902	$ 914	$ 858	$ 624	$ —	$ —	$ 80	$ 94	$ 60	$ —	$ 56
1922	4,148	3,827	2,973	20	—	76	476	266	16	321
1932	6,192	5,381	4,159	26	—	89	605	463	39	811
1940	7,724	5,792	4,170	130	19	178	510	717	68	1,932
1948	13,167	9,666	5,850	400	51	298	1,273	1,654	140	3,501
1953	21,007	15,323	9,010	718	103	523	2,331	2,357	280	5,684
1963	46,534	33,846	19,401	1,562	313	867	6,365	4,629	687	12,689
1969	79,274	53,192	29,692	2,470	1,381	1,239	11,080	6,176	1,155	26,082
1972	113,162	74,144	40,876	4,238	2,241	1,575	15,519	8,071	1,625	39,017
1975	159,731	97,757	50,040	6,468	2,635	2,116	23,047	11,205	2,194	62,074
1977	196,321	119,373	60,275	8,232	3,752	2,534	27,237	14,559	2,783	76,948
1978	214,518	130,464	64,058	9,326	4,072	2,925	30,349	16,662	3,073	84,053

Sources: Tax Foundation and Bureau of the Census.

increases in local revenue appeared in insurance trusts and revenue from the states and national government.

PRINCIPLES AND PROBLEMS OF TAXATION

Nature of Taxes

Although other sources have become increasingly important in recent decades, the bulk of revenue for most governmental units comes directly or indirectly from taxes. In the minds of many, all payments made to governments are taxes, but this idea is not correct. A tax may be defined as "a compulsory contribution, exacted by public authority according to some general rule, the expenditure of which is presumably for the common good without regard to particular benefits to individuals."[1] According to the United States Supreme Court, "A tax is an enforced contribution for the payment of public expenses."[2] These definitions, which are typical of many posed by students of public finance, stress the important characteristics of a tax: its compulsory nature, imposition by public authority on the basis of a general rule, and expenditure for the benefit of the public rather than individuals. Consequently, such payments as charges for specific services, special assessments, and income from governmental enterprises are not taxes.

Principles of Taxation

Since taxes constitute such a large part of state and local revenues, the development of "principles" or "criteria" to guide those who impose the taxes and to inform those who pay them is important. Such principles are even more significant and pertinent as they apply to a *system* of taxation rather than to a single tax. A system of taxation may be defined either as consisting of all the taxes levied *within* a governmental jurisdiction or all those levied *by* a government unit. The first definition is more important to the taxpayer and the second to the tax collector. Thus the system of taxation to which a resident of Gravel Switch is subject consists of all taxes levied by the city, county, special districts, the state, and the national government. On the other hand, Gravel Switch has its own system of taxation consisting of taxes levied by its authority.

Ideally, each governmental unit would construct its own tax system with consideration for all other systems to which its taxpayers are subject. Actually, governments pay too little attention to this problem,

---

1. Merlin H. Hunter and Harry K. Allen, *Principles of Public Finance,* Harper & Brothers, New York, 1940, p. 169.
2. *Houck* v. *Little River Drainage District,* 239 U.S. 254, 265 (1915).

although it is not entirely ignored. The trend among states to abandon the property tax in favor of local governments indicates awareness of the problem as does the reluctance of the national government to inaugurate a general sales tax. Because of restrictions imposed upon their taxing authority by state law, local governments normally must raise revenue as best they can with little or no consideration for the taxing practices of other governmental units. In terms of their meaningful application, canons of taxation are most significant as they relate to the taxes levied by each governmental unit.

Ability to Pay. Writing at the time of the American Revolution, Adam Smith, in his *Wealth of Nations,* stated emphatically that "The subjects of every state ought to contribute toward the support of the government, as nearly as possible in proportion to their respective abilities . . ." Although most tax systems evidence concern for ability to pay, none attempts to apply the concept strictly. The fact is that in spite of its popularity no accurate, objective means of measuring this subjective concept has been devised. *Progressive* taxation related to size of income or amount of wealth accords with a major social and political idea of modern times— that those who are "privileged" to have more money at their disposal should be more heavily taxed than those who are "underprivileged" and have less.[3] Furthermore, progressive income taxes have been found to be very productive, partially because they obtain "the most feathers with the least squawk"—a consideration that cannot be ignored even though it has not been elevated to a principle of taxation.

Diversity. Diversity in a tax system promotes stability and adequacy of yield. Demands on government revenues are changing constantly, and drastic adjustments are required in terms of emergencies such as wars and depressions. Relatively mild economic fluctuations, to say nothing of depressions or "booms," affect certain taxes appreciably. Lack of tax diversity caused serious difficulties for many local governments during the depression of the 1930's. Many persons, either by choice or necessity, failed to pay their property taxes, which constituted the chief and practically sole source of local revenue. Governments relying heavily on the income tax may experience unanticipated deficits or surpluses as a result of minor cycles of depression, prosperity, or inflation. Stability of yield is protected by the presence of other taxes less sensitive to economic fluctuations.

Economy of Administration. Although difficult to measure accurately, economy of administration is an important consideration. Collection costs add nothing to the public treasury. Thus a poll tax, which may consume

---

3. A progressive tax is one for which the rate increases as the base increases. A proportionate tax is one for which the rate remains the same regardless of changes in the base.

in the process of collection much of the revenue that it produces, is a poor tax in light of this criterion. Actual costs of administration are often hidden because they are not borne directly by the government imposing the tax. For example, much responsibility for the collection of a general retail sales tax rests with retailers. Expenses incurred by private persons who assist in the collection of retail sales taxes are sometimes not considered officially part of the costs of administration. Because it is so productive, however, the general retail sales tax is widely favored, and little concern is felt for economy of administration.

Simplicity and Convenience.   Since a favorable public attitude is important, taxes should be as easy to understand and as convenient to pay as possible. Even though many taxpayers long since have abandoned any effort to understand the complexities of the taxes they pay, changes and additions that confuse them are unwise. Ease of payment is a major consideration with regard to many taxes. Taxes "hidden" in the prices of commodities are especially convenient to pay. Efforts are made constantly by jurisdictions levying income taxes to make the process of self-assessment easier and more comprehensible through simplification of forms and required accounting practices. Also, provision is often made for payroll deductions and for time payments. In one sense there may be no such thing as a truly "convenient" tax, but taxpayer irritation may be decreased appreciably by procedures carefully designed and sympathetically administered.

Certainty.   The taxes due from each taxpayer should be definite and sure of collection. Uncertainty arises largely from two factors: poorly drawn tax legislation and ineffective administration. Tax laws full of loopholes permitting individuals to escape their tax burden violate this canon of taxation. Inefficient administration that permits some persons to evade their responsibilities while requiring others to assume their burden not only reduces the amount of revenue coming into the treasury, it also promotes public cynicism and disrespect. Much has been done in recent times to improve the administration of many taxes.

Sufficiency.   There is no more important test of a tax system than its adequacy to meet the requirements of public expenditures, or at least that portion not met by increased indebtedness. The sufficiency of revenue, including taxes, must be anticipated for each fiscal period. The adequacy of each source of income to meet its share of total expenditures must be estimated by those responsible for the preparation of budgets. If the best educated guesses indicate that an existing revenue system will not provide sufficient income, the chief means of meeting fiscal needs are to raise rates, provide new sources of revenue, go into debt, or reduce expenditures.

No single tax and probably no tax system accords perfectly with all six of the criteria discussed above. Furthermore, the significance of influence and expediency must not be overlooked. Influential groups may be the recipients of special favor in the construction of a tax system. Legislators, hard pressed to provide adequate revenue, may follow the course of least resistance by resorting to expedient tax measures or yielding to the pressures of special interests.

STATE AND LOCAL TAX PROBLEMS

In addition to whatever difficulties may be encountered in devising a tax system in keeping with good principles, legislators and other responsible public officers must face certain problems created by recent social and political developments. Included among the difficulties that aggravate the problems of state and local taxation are: (1) the increased total tax burden, (2) the growth of population and its increasing mobility, (3) inflation, and (4) weaknesses in the property tax. Despite the growth in national wealth in recent years, state and local governments in many instances are experiencing increasing difficulty in their efforts to raise revenue. One reason for this situation is the fact that the national government is first claimant on the taxpayer, relegating states and local governments to secondary roles.

The larger the population, the more insistent the demands for additional services of all kinds, including education, welfare, health, police, and environmental protection. Not only is the population growing, it is also moving. Some consequences of the outward flow of people to suburban communities are noted in subsequent chapters on local government. As a result of inflation, tax dollars buy less. Nevertheless, taxpayers often view their taxes in terms of a percentage or rate of growth in the number of dollars they must pay. Inflation has produced a special problem for local governments largely dependent upon the property tax. Not only is there popular resistance to increases in the tax rate, but also assessed values usually lag far behind market values in times of inflation. Inequities in assessment and poor administration further emphasize the weakness of the property tax.

MAJOR STATE TAXES

Growth of State and Local Revenue Systems

The early colonial governments needed small amounts of revenue and relied largely on allowances from England supplemented by fees and fines. As tax systems developed, they varied according to the economic characteristics of different regions. Since most people owned land and the distribution of property was fairly equal in New England, states in the northern portion of the country stressed the poll tax and levies on the gross produce of land. These levies developed into real property taxes and later into general property taxes. Because many townspeople were at first largely untouched by such levies, use was made of the "faculty tax," imposed at a fixed rate on various occupations.

In the southern colonies, with their landed gentry, large holdings, and slaves, little reliance was placed on real property taxes. Instead, excise taxes on imports and exports produced most of the revenue. By 1683 the property tax was well established in New York and growing in importance in other states. In colonial days taxes were commonly paid in commodities such as tobacco and corn. Thus at one time in Virginia each planter was required to send a bushel of corn to the public granary to help defray governmental costs, and a tax on land, horses, mares, cows, sheep, and goats was payable in tobacco.

By the time the Revolutionary War was won and the colonial period ended, numerous sources of revenue had been tapped by the states. Poll taxes and levies on property, both real and personal, were widely used. Earnings were taxed, and licenses were imposed on a variety of occupations. The beginnings of luxury taxes were apparent in the form of imposts on coaches. Collection procedures were greatly improved. Early in the nineteenth century the general property tax became the chief source of revenue for both state and local governments. The period from 1796 to the Civil War "witnessed the complete establishment of the American system of state and local taxation. The distinguishing feature of the system may be described in a single sentence. It is the taxation of all property. . . ."[4] Since Professor Ely penned these words in the 1880's, many changes have appeared regarding state and local revenues. Quantities, of course, have been multiplied, sources have become much more varied, and the relative importance of individual taxes has changed.

Tables 14.1–14.3 reveal some significant revenue trends during the present century in addition to increases in gross amounts. To begin with, seventy years ago the states relied much more heavily on their own sources of revenue than they do today. In 1902 they obtained less than five per cent of their income from other governments, principally grants-in-aid from the national government; in 1978 they received nearly twenty-five per cent of their income from this source. When taxes alone are considered, the change has been even more notable. In 1902 the states acquired over eighty per cent of their total revenue from taxes; in 1978 taxes accounted for only about fifty per cent of state revenue. In the meantime charges, liquor store revenues, and insurance trusts, as well as

---

4. Richard T. Ely, *Taxation in American States and Cities,* Thomas Y. Crowell Co., New York, 1888, p. 131.

Table 14.3
Major State Taxes
Selected Fiscal Years 1902–1978
(millions)

Year	General sales	Motor fuels	Alcoholic beverages	Tobacco products	Income[1]	Property
1902						$ 82
1922		$ 13			$ 101	348
1932	$ 7	527		$ 19	153	328
1940	499	839	$ 193	97	361	260
1948	1,478	1,259	425	337	1,084	276
1953	2,433	2,019	465	469	1,779	365
1962	5,111	3,665	740	1,075	4,036	640
1967	8,923	4,837	1,182	1,615	8,749	912
1972	17,619	7,216	1,684	2,831	17,412	1,257
1975	24,780	8,225	2,110	3,286	25,461	1,451
1977	30,896	9,088	2,297	3,500	34,667	2,260
1978	35,229	9,501	2,454	3,653	39,806	2,357

1. Both personal and corporate income taxes.
Source: Bureau of the Census and Tax Foundation.

intergovernmental revenue, had become important sources of income. Another significant development has been the dramatic decline in importance of the property tax at the state level. At the turn of the century the property tax supplied about forty-five per cent of state revenue; by 1978 this source accounted for less than one per cent of state income. Finally, the major state taxes today, those on general sales, income, and motor fuels were not used at the beginning of the twentieth century.

General Sales Taxes

Sales taxes are used by all levels of government—national, state, and local. Federal sales taxes, commonly called excises, are levied on a variety of commodities, including gasoline, automobiles, alcoholic beverages, tobacco, household appliances, and furs. Levies are also imposed on transportation, entertainment, and telephone service, to mention only a few. Since these taxes are imposed on *selected items,* it is said that the national government does *not* make use of a general sales tax.

More than any other type of governmental unit, the states have come to rely upon sales taxes, both selective and general. In fiscal 1979 these taxes produced nearly $40 billion for the states, or almost one-third of total state tax yield. Numerous variations exist, but a general sales tax may be defined briefly as a levy at a uniform rate on the sale of property at retail or wholesale. Since it is "general," such a tax applies to all sales not exempted by law. To most people a "sales tax" is a tax on retail sales at a rate of, say, three to five cents on the dollar.

The predecessor of the modern sales tax was the business occupation tax levied on sales, purchases, or receipts. A major difference between these taxes imposed by a number of states during the nineteenth century and the present-day sales tax was the use of fractional rates. Not until the twentieth century did any state realize an appreciable amount of revenue from such taxes; the first to do so was West Virginia subsequent to legislation enacted in 1921, followed by Mississippi in 1930. The urgent need for revenue during the depression of the 1930's accompanied by decreases in income from established tax sources hastened the adoption of sales taxes. Twenty-nine states imposed retail sales taxes between 1932 and 1937; six of these were allowed to expire within a short period.[5] In several other states sales taxes were enacted but defeated by popular vote before they became effective.

From 1937 to 1947 no state adopted or repealed sales tax legislation. Shortly after World War II, inflation and pressures for increased expenditures increased far more than income. Between 1950 and 1970 sales taxes were provided in sixteen states and the District of Columbia. Forty-five states now employ general sales taxes, which are basically retail sales taxes, applying to all or most sales at retail (see Table 14.4).

Administration. Contrary to opinion held in many quarters, sales taxes are not easily administered if the task is performed effectively. State laws require regular reports from businesses selling goods subject to a sales tax. However, successful administration requires extensive auditing in addition to routine office checks, a function that is often inadequately performed despite the lengthy experience that many states have had with the tax. It appears that the cost to the states of administering sales taxes averages around one and one-half per cent of the receipts. In addition, there are compliance expenses for which about half the states compensate retailers at a percentage of their tax liability.

Arguments for a General Sales Tax. Earlier in the chapter attention was called to certain criteria helpful in judging taxes. In light of these criteria proponents of a general sales tax advance the following contentions: (1) When used with other taxes, it diversifies a tax system and consequently promotes stability of income for the governmental unit employing it. (2) Since a general sales tax is highly productive, it can be adjusted to yield *sufficient* revenue to meet expenditure requirements. (3) It is a

---

5. If Indiana's "gross income tax" is counted, the total would be thirty. Although this tax was not a "true" sales tax, it imposed a levy at a flat rate on the receipts of all businesses, including retailers, as well as personal income. Effective in 1963, Indiana changed to a two per cent general sales tax.

Table 14.4
State Sales Taxes

State	Year of intro- duction	Tax rate	Major exemptions of consumer goods	Other major exclusions
Alabama	1936	4		Industrial machinery, fuel
Arizona	1933	4	Medicines	
Arkansas	1935	3		
California	1934	4.75	Food, medicines	
Colorado	1935	3	Medicines	Fuel
Connecticut	1947	7	Food, medicines	Fuel
Florida	1949	4	Food, medicines	
Georgia	1951	3		Industrial machinery
Hawaii	1935[1]	4		
Idaho	1965	3	Medicines	
Illinois	1933	4		
Indiana	1963	4	Food, medicines	
Iowa	1933	3	Medicines	Fuel
Kansas	1937	3	Medicines	Fuel
Kentucky	1960	5	Food, medicines	
Louisiana	1936	3	Food, medicines	
Maine	1951	5	Food, medicines	
Maryland	1947	5	Food, medicines	Fuel
Massachusetts	1966	5	Food, medicines, clothing	Fuel
Michigan	1933	4	Food, medicines	Fuel, industrial and farm machinery
Minnesota	1967	4	Food, medicines, clothing	
Mississippi	1930	5		Industrial machinery
Missouri	1934	3.13		
Nebraska	1967	3	Medicines	
Nevada	1955	3	Medicines	
New Jersey	1966	5	Food, medicines, clothing	Fuel
New Mexico	1933	3.75		
New York	1965	4	Food, medicines	Coal, farm implements
North Carolina	1935	3	Medicines	Coal, some industrial machinery
North Dakota	1935	3	Food, medicines	
Ohio	1934	4	Food, medicines	All production goods
Oklahoma	1933	2		Industrial machinery
Pennsylvania	1954	6	Food, clothing, medicines	Farm and industrial machinery
Rhode Island	1947	6	Food, medicines	Fuel
South Carolina	1951	4		Industrial and farm machinery
South Dakota	1933	5	Medicines	
Tennessee	1947	3	Medicines	
Texas	1961	4	Food, medicines	Farm machinery
Utah	1933	4	Medicines	

State Sales Taxes (*Continued*)

State	Year of intro- duction	Tax rate	Major exemptions of consumer goods	Other major exclusions
Vermont	1969	3	Food, medicines	Agricultural feed
Virginia	1966	3	Medicines	
Washington	1933	4.5	Medicines	
West Virginia	1921	3	Medicines	
Wisconsin	1962	4	Food, medicines, clothing	
Wyoming	1935	3	Medicines	Fuel

1. Hawaii used the sales tax for a quarter-century while a territory.

simple tax in the sense that it is easily understood by taxpayers and fairly *convenient* to pay once people become accustomed to it. (4) The amount of tax due is quite *certain,* and opportunities for evasion are minimal. Another argument in favor of a state sales tax is related to the fact that the chief alternative appears to be the income tax, which is so heavily emphasized by the national government. It is asserted that an important tax based on expenditures somewhat offsets the adverse affects on economic incentives produced by a highly progressive income tax. It is further maintained that sales taxes used along with income taxes enhance the overall *equity* of the tax structure.

Arguments against a General Sales Tax.   The chief contention advanced regularly against sales taxes is that they disregard ability to pay. Such a tax is said to be regressive or, more correctly, *regressive in effect* because it places a relatively heavy burden on those persons in the lower income groups whose expenditures on taxable items constitute a rather large portion of their incomes. This regressiveness can be lessened appreciably by exempting food and medicine, a practice followed in a number of states. The regressive effect of a sales tax may be somewhat offset by a progressive income tax with sufficient exemptions to exclude persons in lower income groups, particularly those with families to support. Also, arrangements may be made to "rebate" all or a portion of the estimated amounts paid in sales taxes by persons and families in low-income categories. These rebates may be in the form of credits against state income taxes or actual payments from the state treasury much like excessive income tax withholdings.

Motor Fuels Taxes

During the past fifty or so years taxes on motor fuels have become

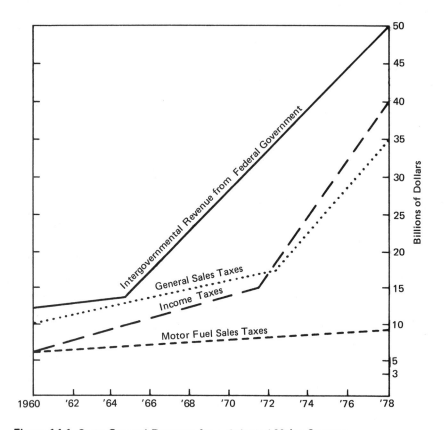

Figure 14.1 State General Revenue from Selected Major Sources

a very productive source of state tax receipts.[6] In fiscal 1979 the states realized about $10 billion from these taxes. The first state tax on gasoline was levied by Oregon in 1919. It proved so successful that by 1921 fifteen states were taxing gasoline; by 1929 all states had such a tax. In the early years rates varied from one to three cents per gallon. Rates now range from five to twelve cents on each gallon, with the most common levy at eight or nine cents. In 1980 Indiana and Kentucky approved laws changing their motor fuels taxes from a set rate to a percentage of the price of gasoline. Indiana imposed a limit of twelve cents per gallon in 1980, fourteen cents in 1981, and sixteen cents in 1982 and subsequent years. In Kentucky the limit was set at 13.5 cents per gallon by mid-1982, and in the following two years it will be indexed to ten per cent of the increase in gasoline prices.

6. The bulk of this revenue comes from the gasoline tax, which is so important that all taxes on motor fuels are sometimes loosely referred to as "gasoline taxes." However, other fuels, particularly diesel oil, are also taxed.

Taxes on motor fuels have been adopted with a minimum of opposition, and they continue to be among the most "popular" of taxes. This situation probably is due in large part to the fact that receipts most often have been earmarked for the construction and maintenance of highways. Since those who use the most gasoline pay the most taxes, there is a close correlation between benefits and payments. Another advantage of gasoline taxes is that they exact contributions from nonresidents in rough proportion to their use of a state's highways. About one-fourth of the state constitutions require use of gasoline tax receipts for highways only. Although the practice of earmarking taxes generally is open to question, it is well established with regard to motor fuels, and any effort to allocate such receipts to cover expenses other than those pertaining to highways inevitably meets stiff opposition.

Motor fuels taxes not only produce large quantities of revenue in good and bad times but are also collected easily, cheaply, and conveniently. Indeed, they are probably the cheapest of all major taxes to collect. States usually collect these taxes from wholesale distributors, who pass them on to retailers, who in turn collect them from consumers.

Some problems are associated with the administration of taxes on motor fuels. When adjacent states impose different rates, there is a temptation to "smuggle" gasoline into the state with the higher rate. By mutual agreements states may require exporters to report out-of-state deliveries and supply this information to the state of import. This arrangement has proved more satisfactory than efforts to patrol points along state borders where entry may be made. Other administrative problems relate to exemptions and refunds. Motor fuel not used on highways is commonly not subject to tax. Thus gasoline used in farm tractors, stationary engines, and airplanes may be exempt. Difficulties arise in determing how much gasoline is used in such engines and how much in motor vehicles when the same taxpayer owns both and purchases motor fuel in bulk. Such problems are especially significant in states with large farm populations.

Distributing the proceeds of fuels taxes among different political units has become a problem in states where receipts are shared with local governments. Increasingly, municipal and county officials have sought and obtained grants from the states to assist in constructing roads and streets. Local officials claim that since receipts are collected from persons within local jurisdictions who are operating vehicles on roads and streets built by the localities, the states should help in the construction and maintenance of such thoroughfares. The practice of sharing motor fuels revenues with local governments is widespread, but no uniformity as to the basis of distribution exists.

Income Taxes

In fiscal 1979 state income taxes yielded $44.9 billion—$32.8 billion from individuals and $12.1 billion from corporations. These taxes have become the most important source of state tax revenue. States used the income tax before the national government experimented with it during the Civil War. Following the panic of 1837 a few states adopted the income tax, but it did not spread significantly until the Civil War period. Early efforts at income taxation were not very successful, due largely to reliance on assessment by local assessors. In 1911 the first modern state income tax was inaugurated by Wisconsin. It was an immediate success as a revenue producer, and in 1917 four states followed Wisconsin's example. There were no further adoptions until 1929 when several states enacted income tax laws, followed by a score more states during the 1930's. Forty-six states levy taxes on personal or corporate income, or both.[7]

A few states tax only income derived from special sources, but usually all income with minor exceptions is taxable. With maximums of about ten per cent, personal income tax rates are progressive, although less so than at the federal level. The picture is different with regard to corporate income rates. Over three-fourths of the states using this type of tax impose flat rates.

A number of problems are associated with the administration of state income taxes. One concerns the geographical basis of taxable income. Some states tax only the income of residents from whatever sources it may be derived. Other states tax only income earned within their respective boundaries. Still others combine both of these practices. A major argument in behalf of taxing residents on their total income is that full effect is thereby given to graduated rates. A serious disadvantage of taxing residents only is that nonresidents who would otherwise be taxed go unscathed. Such people receive the benefits of public services during their working hours, and perhaps at other times also, without bearing their share of the costs.

Another difficulty associated with the progressive income tax is, in fact, a mixed blessing. In times of rapid inflation, individuals' incomes are pushed into higher tax brackets without their realizing any increase in purchasing power, and at the same time they are required to pay more taxes. As a consequence, the states' income is significantly increased. A remedy for this problem is to "index" the income categories in such a manner as to compensate for inflation. However, the states have been understandably reluctant to take such action and thereby reduce their income.

Certain difficulties surround the collection of income taxes. Traditionally, states have collected income taxes from recipients of income by requiring them to file a report of income by a certain date and to pay

---

7. States using neither type of income tax are Nevada, Texas, Washington, and Wyoming. Alaska is eliminating its income tax because of increasing revenues from the state's royalties on oil and natural gas leases.

at that time all taxes due. In recent years more and more states have resorted to collection at the source. When this procedure is employed, taxes are first collected from payers of income rather than recipients. Thus, taxes on wages are collected from the employer rather than the employee by means of deductions from the employee's paychecks. This action is supplemented by annual reports required of all persons subject to the income tax in order that they may pay additional sums due the state or obtain refunds due them. Collection at the source enhances convenience of payment and minimizes delinquency and avoidance. On the other hand, this practice has the disadvantage of imposing considerable costs upon employers resulting from the maintenance of records and the computation of deductions for each pay period. When these costs are considered, income taxes are not cheap to administer.

OTHER SOURCES OF STATE REVENUE

Now that the three major state taxes have been examined, a look at other sources of state revenue is in order. Although levies on general sales and gross receipts, motor fuels, and income are commonly considered as the "major" state taxes, they account for only about one-third of total state income. Other sources include intergovernmental revenue, license fees, miscellaneous taxes, charges and earnings, and insurance trust revenues. Most important among these in terms of the amount of money received are intergovernmental revenues.

Intergovernmental Revenues

Each year the states now receive about $53 billion from other governmental units (see Figure 14.1). With the exception of approximately three billion from local governments,[8] all of this amount comes from the national government in the form of grants-in-aid (especially for welfare, education, and highways) and revenue sharing. The national government possesses much greater financial resources than any state. In recent times Congress has taken the lead to expand governmental support for many important services traditionally considered to be state responsibilities.

More often than not, federal grants have been designed to stimulate state development and improvement of certain activities and services.

---

8. Funds paid by local governments to the states include payments for local shares in support of state administered programs, reimbursements for services performed by the states directly for local units, application on state debt issued for local benefits, and for repayment of loans made by the states to local governments.

The impact of such efforts by the national government in recent times has been particularly noticeable with regard to highways, welfare activities, public health, and development of natural resources. Although federal grants often are criticized on a variety of grounds alleging numerous deleterious effects on the states, the fact must be borne in mind that many of these programs were begun at least in part because of urgent requests by state officials for federal assistance. Indeed, it may be argued that the system of grants actually strengthens the states by utilizing them in the process of coping with problems of national scope.[9]

License Fees[10]

Although significant, license fees are much less important to the states than the sources of revenue already discussed. Licenses were among the early sources of state revenue. By the middle of the last century license fees were collected from auctioneers, peddlers, and slave traders as well as owners of ferries, toll bridges, circuses, and theaters.

Motor vehicle license fees are collected through the annual sale of plates, or "tabs" to go on old plates, which must be attached to vehicles. The fees vary appreciably from state to state, ranging for passenger cars from a few dollars to as high as $300. Some states impose a flat rate for all automobiles, but others vary the charges according to such factors as horsepower, age or "value" of the vehicle, and weight. Charging variable fees is defended largely on the ground that it gives some consideration to ability to pay in that the owner of a large, powerful, new automobile at least evidences more affluence than the owner of a small, older vehicle.

"Franchise" or "privilege" levies imposed on corporations in the form of licenses provide another source of state income. In most states domestic corporations are "taxed" simply for the right to exist and conduct business under state laws. Also, a corporation licensed in one state normally must pay an "entrance fee" in order to do business in another. Licenses on the manufacture, importation, and sale of alcoholic beverages provide income for the states as well as fees paid by persons wishing hunting and fishing licenses. Many other activities and privileges are licensed by the states upon payment of small fees, including many professions and matrimony.

Miscellaneous Taxes

As every citizen knows, the states tax many things in their search for revenue. Among the more important selective sales taxes are those on

---

9. See Thomas H. Kiefer, *The Political Impact of Federal Aid to State and Local Governments,* General Learning Press, 1974.
10. Sometimes called "license taxes." However, since levies considered here are made upon those who pay them in return for a special benefit or privilege, a distinction seems warranted.

alcoholic beverages, from which the states realized about $2.5 billion in fiscal 1979. These taxes are levied on distilled spirits, wines, and malt beverages. Rates vary not only according to the classification of beverages, but also according to alcoholic content. Even more lucrative are taxes on the sale of *tobacco products,* from which the states received $3.6 billion in fiscal 1979. Most of the imposts are on cigarettes, which are taxed at a flat rate per package. High levies on alcoholic beverages and tobacco products are defended on the ground that such things are luxuries and therefore "should" be taxed at a high rate.

Once the principal source of state income, the *property tax* has been relegated to a much less important role. In fiscal 1979 the states obtained around 2.3 billion dollars from property taxes. The trend in most states has been away from the property tax and toward an emphasis on selective taxes on specific types of property such as utilities and personal property, including automobiles, farm machinery, and livestock. A major reason for the move away from state property taxes has been recognition of the desirability of leaving general property taxation in the hands of local governments.

Nearly three-fifths of the states impose *severance taxes,* from which several hundred million dollars are obtained yearly. These taxes are imposed upon the privilege of taking or "severing" from the land certain resources, especially coal, oil, and timber. The base for such a tax is generally the quantity or value of the product. Thus the output of coal may be taxed by the ton, and the flow of oil by the barrel. Or a percentage of the value of each of these measures may constitute the tax. Since severance taxes are based on volume of production, they can be adjusted to encourage or discourage production. Consequently, they are sometimes considered as a means of conserving particular resources.

Practically all states tax estates or inheritances, and some tax both.[11] An *estate tax* is levied on the property of a deceased person without regard to shares belonging to relatives, friends, and others. An *inheritance tax* is imposed on the share received by each heir, subject to certain exemptions. Both these taxes are characterized by a bewildering complexity, and they defy more than general description. Inheritance and estate taxes were among early levies imposed by some of the states, but they were largely failures as revenue producers. The New York tax of 1885 appears to have been the first really successful one. During the last half-century most states have patterned their laws on the statutes of North Carolina (1901) and Wisconsin (1903), providing for progressive rates graduated according to the closeness of relationship between heirs and the decedent as well as the amounts of money and property involved.

Following the example of Oregon in 1933, many states have adopted *gift* taxes. These taxes are designed to supplement levies on estates and

---

11. Taxes on estates, inheritance, and gifts are often termed "death and gift" taxes.

inheritances in order to prevent evasion of **death taxes**. Generally, exemptions and exclusions permit transfers of property up to a certain amount, varying with the proximity of kin, over designated periods of time without taxation. Primary responsibility for the payment of gift taxes usually rests with the giver, but failure to pay may result in a levy against the recipient.

The states derive small quantitites of revenue from a variety of minor taxes. Taxes on various businesses and public utilities are widely used and are commonly imposed on the "gross receipts" of businesses. Levies are frequently placed on certain types of entertainment, such as pari-mutuels, horse and dog races, and boxing and wrestling matches. Fourteen states derive income from the profits realized from state lotteries.[12] However, these enterprises have not proved as profitable as generally hoped. In addition, off-track betting is licensed in New York. A few states tax document and stock transfers.

Charges and Earnings

The states realize an annual income of some $13 billion from charges and earnings of various sorts. A large share of these funds come from fees charged to students at institutions of higher education and patients in certain hospitals, as well as tolls imposed for the use of highways and bridges. Seventeen states realize profits from the operation of liquor stores. Earnings on trust funds also produce some income.

Insurance Trusts

The states collect large sums of money for the operation of social insurance programs of one kind or another. Most important are employee retirement programs and unemployment compensation. Income for the former consists of contributions required of employers and employees, while income for the latter usually derives from employer contributions. State-operated accident and sickness benefit systems and workmen's compensation schemes are also classified as insurance trusts. In addition, earnings realized on the investment of such funds are counted as trust fund income. Such funds must be held *in trust* by the states until disbursements are authorized to qualified persons in accord with appropriate statutes. In fiscal 1978 insurance trust revenues totaled $32.6 billion.

LOCAL REVENUES

The combined revenues of *local* governments in fiscal 1978 totaled $214.5 billion. Of this amount about $130 billion came from local reve-

---

12. These states are Connecticut, Delaware, Illinois, Maine, Maryland, Massachusetts, Michigan, New Hampshire, New Jersey, New York, Ohio, Pennsylvania, Rhode Island, and Vermont.

nue sources and some $84 billion from other governments. Of the total income *derived from their own sources,* local governments obtained about three-fourths from property taxes, charges, and utility revenues. About eighty per cent of local *tax* revenues came from property taxes alone. Although recent years have witnessed a struggle by local governments, especially large cities, to tap new sources of income, the major local sources of income remain much as they have been for years and years.

State Restrictions

The slow pace at which new sources of local income have opened up is partially attributable to restrictions imposed by state laws. Perhaps it is more accurate to say that the states have been reluctant to enlarge the taxing powers of local governments, and they have been particularly unwilling to sanction local use of taxes important at the state level since the practical abandonment of the property tax to local use. Local governments possess revenue-raising authority only to the extent that the states grant it to them.

In addition to limiting the sources of local revenue, states commonly restrict the amount of taxes that may be levied in a fiscal year. Such restrictions are especially noteworthy with regard to the property tax because of its great importance to local governments. Property tax limitations generally are expressed in terms of one of three factors: (1) a maximum percentage of the assessed value of the property subject to taxation, (2) a percentage increase over the previous year's levy, or (3) a maximum per capita levy. Fortunately, it is usually possible to exceed such limits by vote of the people. Local governments in some states have been further handicapped by the partial exemption of property owned by certain groups of people and organizations, such as homesteaders, partially disabled veterans, charitable and religious groups, and other governmental jurisdictions.

As noted in the previous chapter, new restrictions have been imposed recently on the revenue-raising capacity of local governments (and to some degree, the states as well) as a consequence of the "tax revolt" that has spread through many states. The archetype for the cutback approach was "Proposition 13" (Jarvis-Gann Amendment) adopted by the California voters in June of 1978. This drastic measure contained five major provisions:

(1) It rolled back the assessed value of each piece of property to its estimated 1975–76 market value (or its value at the last sale since 1975).
(2) It restricted increases in the assessed value of a piece of property to a maximum of two per cent a year. If the property is sold, it may be revalued according to its sale price.

(3) It limited property taxes to one per cent of the assessed value (except for taxes to pay off indebtedness incurred before the adoption of Proposition 13).

(4) It required a two-thirds vote of the qualified electors to enact new local taxes or to increase nonproperty taxes.

(5) It required a two-thirds vote of both houses of the legislature to increase state taxes.[13]

The chief immediate effect of Proposition 13 was to decrease annual receipts from the property tax by about seven billion dollars. Obviously, significant adjustments must be made to large reductions in income. In the case of California and some other states where fiscal limitations were adopted, their full impact was postponed by the availability of large state surpluses. Once these surpluses have been used up, local governments will be forced to cut services and/or seek new sources of income. Already both of these approaches have been used, resulting in a reduction in the number of employees (thus increasing unemployment) and the increased use of charges to defray the cost of services previously paid for out of taxes. Contrary to the claims of some supporters of cutbacks, it is not possible to absorb the loss of large amounts of income through increased efficiency.

MAJOR SOURCES OF LOCAL INCOME

The Property Tax

By far the most important single source of local revenue is the property tax. The ratio of revenue from property taxes to other sources of income varies appreciably for different classes of local governments. Special districts, including school districts, rely very heavily on them—as do most townships. Counties generally are less dependent than special districts and townships on property taxes, and municipalities enjoy a greater variety in their revenue sources than any other type of local government. Even big cities, however, continue to lean heavily on the property tax.

The property tax is no longer as "general" as it once was. Although the laws of a few states indicate that all property, except that which is specifically exempt, is *subject* to taxation, in fact no effort is made to levy taxes against many items of property. For purposes of taxation, property is divided into two major categories, *real* and *personal*. *Real property* consists basically of land and improvements, especially buildings. All other kinds of property are designated as *personal*. Personal property is subdivided into two types: tangible and intangible. *Tangible property,* as the name indicates, may be touched and seen—it has substance as

---

13. Adapted from Anthony H. Pascal, *et al., op. cit.,* pp. 58-59.

well as value. Included in this category are such things as stocks of goods in stores, livestock, grain, clothes, jewelry, furniture, household appliances, automobiles, and boats. *Intangible property* consists of legal rights to things of value. Mortgages, stock certificates, patents, copyrights, and various kinds of contracts illustrate the nature of intangible property.

Theory of the Property Tax. Property taxes rest on the assumption that the value of a person's property is a valid measure of the amount of tax he or she is able to pay. Such an assumption may have real validity in an agricultural community where property generally consists of the same items—land, buildings, livestock, and agricultural implements. However, the development of trade and industry complicates the picture because incomes are derived from sources other than property ownership.

Furthermore, all forms of real and tangible property do not indicate comparable taxpaying ability. Factories, farms, dwellings, cars, refrigerators, and radios are not equally indicative of taxpaying capacity. The most valid criterion of ability to pay taxes, as far as property is concerned, is productiveness. Some forms of property are not at all productive, while others may be very much so. Although ownership of nonproductive property, such as expensive jewelry or fancy automobiles, may be indicative of ability to pay, taxes other than those on property are better suited to measure this ability.

Administration of the Property Tax. The amount of property tax that a person must pay is determined by multiplying the assessed value of his or her property by the tax rate. Property tax rates may be expressed in *mills,* or in dollars and cents. A mill is one-tenth of a cent ($.001). Thus the tax on property assessed at $10,000 and taxed at a rate of forty mills would be $400. The same amount of tax would result from a rate of $4.00 per $100 of assessed valuation. Once the value of the property has been set, figuring the tax is a simple matter. The major problem is: How is the value of real property determined?

The *assessment,* or *valuation,* of real property is difficult. First of all, lists must be prepared of all taxable property. With adequate records and tax maps, this undertaking is not too troublesome. The second step, which is much more difficult, is determination of the value of each piece of property. Laws usually require the assessment of property to be based on a "fair," "reasonable," or "actual" value. Many techniques are used to arrive at appropriate valuations. Some are crude and others very involved.

For the bulk of real property, determination of the *assessed value* is usually accomplished in two steps. First, an effort is made to determine "actual" value for which the most common measure is "market" value— that is, the probable price at which the property might be sold on the open market. In times of rapid inflation, market value may be reduced in order to arrive at a more nearly "true" value. Determination of probable market value is not equally feasible for all property. What, for example, is the market value of the one or two mansions in a small town? Or the value of the Empire State Building in New York City? Other approaches to value-determination must be used in exceptional cases.

The second step in arriving at assessed value involves the use of an "assessment ratio." Once the "fair" or "market" value has been set, it is common practice to multiply that value by an arbitrarily established percentage. Perhaps the market value of a piece of property has been figured at $100,000. Local practice, resulting from law, administrative practices, or political pressures, may have established an assessment ratio for that particular type of property at fifty per cent. Accordingly, the assessed value would be $50,000. Assessment ratios often vary according to classes of property. One ratio may be set for industrial property, another for commercial property, and a third for residential property. Other classifications may, of course, be used.

Assessments are subject to review by a local agency, commonly called a board of review and equalization. *Reviews* may be automatic to correct clerical errors and add omitted property to the rolls. They may also result from complaints by individual property owners. Since review may result in raising or lowering assessed value, most property owners do not complain because they know that if any "error" has been made it is probably on the side of underassessment. *Equalization* involves "blanket" increases or decreases within a taxing jurisdiction. The purpose of such action is to guarantee that similar properties will be treated substantially alike. Thus, a board of equalization for a county consisting of four townships may order an increase in the assessment ratio in one township so that its residents will bear their share of county taxes and not benefit from competitive underassessment. Some states provide for review and equalization of county assessment practices by a state agency. Such an agency has proved helpful in many states by guiding, assisting, and training local assessors.

Although the discussion of property tax administration thus far has been concerned specifically with real property, much of what has been said is also pertinent to taxation of personal property. The biggest difference is that the problems of administration are aggravated in relation to personal property. Except when applied to selected items, such as automobiles, boats, airplanes, farm machinery, and livestock, it is impossible to administer the personal property tax efficiently. Visiting every home and place of business and setting a value upon the myriad items found there is a hopeless task. Reliance on declarations of ownership and value by individual taxpayers places a premium on dishonesty and has proved unreliable. Consequently, taxation of personal property has become increasingly selective and decreasingly important as a source of revenue.

The Case for the Property Tax

In spite of the weaknesses of the property tax, both theoretical and administrative, it continues as the major source of local revenue. What are the reasons for its continued importance? One major reason is the force of tradition. People throughout the country are accustomed to the tax, and they have purchased and sold property in anticipation of its continued use. A second consideration relates to the problems of local administration of major alternative taxes, especially income and sales. These taxes are not as easily administered on the local as on the state level. Third, the property tax has proved that it will produce revenue in large, dependable, and predictable quantities. Fourth, the property tax is easily adjusted to meet the needs of specific areas in that it can be applied accurately to property benefitting from a particular service or group of services, such as schools, water supply, and fire protection. Finally, property appears to many persons to be a justifiable basis for taxation. They reason that the property owners should pay for services rendered to them.

The tax on real property, in spite of its wide use, is often criticized as being "unfair." Although there may be some crude relationship between the value of property owned by an individual and his or her ability to pay taxes, this relationship does not always exist. Property may be inherited or purchased at a time when an individual's income is larger than it later becomes. If the property is productive, its productivity may decrease and the owner's income along with it. Or inflation may cause the value of the property to outstrip any increases in the owner's income. Also, an owner's income may significantly decrease because of retirement or disability. These problems have been somewhat alleviated in about half of the states by the adoption of some form of *circuit breaker* which goes into effect when property taxes exceed a certain percentage of the owner's income. Some states have sought to soften the impact of the property tax by rebating a portion of it from the general fund of the state, the proportion varying according to the income of the individual or family. Such an arrangement may also apply to renters. A few states have gone still further and provided for deferring payment of property taxes on homes occupied by persons over a certain age, usually sixty or sixty-five. These deferred payments come due when the property is sold or inherited.

Intergovernmental Revenues

In fiscal 1978 nearly 40 percent of all local governmental revenue came from other governments. State assistance to local governments takes two major forms: *grants* and *shared taxes*. Like federal grants-in-aid to the states, state grants to local governments are usually in the form of appropriations, ordinarily from the general fund, to assist local financing of designated functions. Grants are allocated to local governments according to some formula. Thus so many dollars may be provided to local school districts on the basis of the number of children in average daily attendance. Or funds may be allocated to enable poorer districts to maintain school facilities that meet state standards—often called the "equalization allocation." Through grants the states have utilized their superior taxing authority to relieve the burden upon local revenue sources. Local functions benefiting most from state grants are education, highways, and public welfare.

Shared taxes are collected by the state and apportioned among local governments according to fixed percentages of the yield. The income received by local jurisdictions from a shared tax depends on the yield from that tax, not on local needs. Conditions governing the distribution of shared taxes often require that the receipts of each local unit be in direct ratio to the amount of the tax collected there. Thus the revenue from liquor taxes returned to a city depends on the income from the tax collected within that city. Of course, the amounts probably are not the same since the state retains a portion of the tax—at least a sufficient amount to cover costs of administration. Occasionally, taxes are shared on a per capita basis, with local receipts determined by population. Shared taxes most often include those levied on motor fuels, liquor, incomes, and sales.

About 22 per cent of intergovernmental revenues received by local governments in 1978 came from the federal government in the form of grants-in-aid and revenue sharing. Great differences exist in the amounts of these funds as a proportion of local budgets. In some instances, the amounts are miniscule, while in others they are very important. Indeed, in recent years some major cities have received about half as much money from the national government as from local taxes. Although very helpful to the cities at times, this degree of reliance on federal largesse has placed the cities in a position of dependence that will cause severe withdrawal pains if and when major reductions are made in the national budget. Furthermore, the states may well be unable to offset the losses because of their dependence on federal dollars and the impact of the efforts at fiscal containment mentioned earlier.

Utility Revenues

Local governments realize about eight per cent of their income from *utility revenues*. Government owned and operated "business enterprises" have been numerous at the local level during much of American history. Local water, electric, gas, and transit utilities and liquor stores gross sizable sums, especially for municipalities. However, *net* income from such sources is generally small because the costs of purchasing, producing, or otherwise providing the facilities largely offset total revenues. Indeed, expenditures related to the operation of utilities sometime exceed revenues, and it becomes necessary to support them partially from the general fund. In a few instances, however, small localities have been able to subsidize other functions with income from an important enterprise such as a railroad.

Charges and Special Assessments

Local governments often impose *charges* for the performance of certain services. Prominent among activities financed partially or entirely by charges are sewage disposal, refuse collection, and parking facilities. *Fees* collected for the use of special facilities such as swimming pools, tennis courts, and golf courses also produce small amounts of income. *Fines* usually are not an important source of revenue, but occasionally a small community obtains significant amounts from the operation of a "speed trap." As noted earlier, reliance on this source of income is likely to increase because of limitations imposed on other sources of local revenue, particularly the property tax.

A *special assessment* is a levy against property made presumably in rough proportion to benefits accruing as the result of a specific service. Special assessments are used most frequently to pay all or part of the costs of paving streets, building sidewalks, installing water and sewer lines, establishing parks and playgrounds, and street lighting. Improvements financed in this way presumably make property more desirable to own and often more valuable as well.

A big problem in the use of special assessments is the determination of the amount of benefit received by each person or parcel of property. Paving the street in front of a house benefits not only the owner. Neighbors next door and persons living blocks away who pass the house each day or just on their way to church on Sunday also benefit. So do the delivery truck drivers who frequent the neighborhood. Obviously, assessments cannot be made against all these people. Recognizing that a "general" benefit also stems from paved streets, sidewalks, and similar improvements, cities often pay a portion of their costs from the general fund and assess the remainder against property situated in an arbitrarily determined "benefit district."

Sales Taxes

The first local sales taxes in the United States were enacted by New York City in 1934 and by New Orleans in 1936. Since that time some 5,000 local governments, mostly cities, have adopted general sales taxes. The only major city to try the retail sales tax and voluntarily abandon it is

Philadelphia. Many local communities also impose selective sales taxes on items such as gasoline, tobacco, and alcohol.

Aside from the fact that in many states local sales taxes are not permitted by law, other considerations have limited their adoption. Probably the most serious objection to the local sales tax is ease of avoidance and consequent shifting of sales to nontax areas. This problem is especially serious for small communities. If a small city adopts a sales tax, many residents will do their shopping, especially for major purchases, in nearby areas without such a tax. Municipal sales taxes also encourage the growth of suburban shopping centers. In an effort to counteract the economic consequences of large-scale buying outside their jurisdictions, some municipalities have resorted to a *use tax*. This type of tax is a levy on the use within the locality of taxable articles purchased outside. However, municipal use taxes are very difficult to administer and are practical only in relation to major purchases such as automobiles.

A more satisfactory approach to the problems of city sales taxes has been adopted in California and a few other states. In 1956 California counties received authority from the state legislature to levy one per cent sales taxes, provided they arrange for collection by the state agency that collects the state sales tax. Then each city within a county adopting such an arrangement could levy a sales tax up to one per cent and have it credited against the county tax. Thus, whenever a city tax is the same as the county's, all the revenue from the tax comes to the city, but if it is less, the county receives the difference. Sales in unincorporated areas and cities not using the sales tax are still taxed at one per cent, but all the proceeds go to the county. If a county chooses not to levy a sales tax, each city may impose and administer its own.

Income Taxes

Local governments have used income taxes sparingly in the United States. Levied by about 3500 jurisdictions in some ten states, local income taxes produced about $4 billion in fiscal 1978. The most widespread use of the local income tax is found in Pennsylvania, where Philadelphia pioneered its use in 1940. Since then many school districts, some cities, and a few townships in that state have adopted local income taxes. Outside Pennsylvania its use has been largely limited to cities.

Local income taxes differ from federal and state levies in two major respects: they are usually imposed at uniform, low rates rather than on a graduated scale,[14] and they generally do not allow exemptions. The most widely used rate is one per cent, although levies of one-half of one per cent are common. These two features, defended chiefly on the ground of administrative simplicity, demonstrate that local income taxes largely

---

14. In the District of Columbia and New York City the rates are mildly progressive.

disregard ability to pay, since no distinction is made among income levels and family responsibilities. Inequity is further aggravated by the fact that these taxes usually are imposed only on salaries and wages and do not include other types of income.

In addition to providing additional revenue, local income taxes generally possess two significant features that make them especially attractive: they are relatively easy and economical to administer, and they may exact contributions from nonresidents.[15] As a flat levy on all salaries and wages subject to collection at the source, income taxes are not easily evaded and at the same time are inexpensive to collect. Many people work in cities and live elsewhere. Such persons benefit from city services and should help to support them. A municipal income tax serves this purpose admirably. From both of these standpoints a local income tax appears more desirable than a sales tax.[16]

Other Sources of Income

Local governments, especially cities, obtain income from a variety of sources not yet mentioned. Parking meters produce significant quantities of revenue for cities in spite of the fact that they are justified chiefly on the ground that they regulate the use of public streets. Cities commonly license places of amusement such as theaters, cabarets, bowling alleys, pool rooms, dance halls, and restaurants. Fees charged for these licenses may produce sizable amounts of revenue, especially in large cities. A handful of cities in a few states, particularly Washington, California, and Alabama, impose taxes on the price of admission to various types of entertainment, of which the most important are moving pictures and theaters. Cities frequently tax mechanical amusement devices such as pinball machines, juke boxes, and skill-game devices.

Rather high license fees for places of amusement and heavy taxes on admissions and on amusement devices are easily justifiable from the standpoint of equity. Important also is the fact that directly or indirectly they reach nonresidents and transients who benefit from city services. Small communities must, of course, exercise care lest they drive places of amusement outside their boundaries and consequently beyond their regulation in most instances.

Many cities license a variety of businesses and commercial enterprises, including apartment houses, hotels, barber shops, beauty parlors, food stores, laundries, department stores, pawnshops, peddlers, taxicabs, and vending machines. Fees charged for licensing these and similar enterprises produce some revenue but often little more than the costs of administer-

15. Pennsylvania school districts cannot tax the income of nonresidents.
16. Of course, nonresidents making purchases in a sales-tax city contribute to the local treasury, but they can and probably will limit the value of such purchases.

ing the licenses. A few cities collect vehicle inspection fees charged for the examination of safety devices on motor vehicles. Local licenses for trailer camps have become increasingly common in recent years. Small amounts of income are realized from rents charged for the use of locally owned property and from interest on investments.

DEBT

When governments are unable or unwilling to finance their activities from current revenues, they may obtain money by borrowing. Debts usually are incurred for three major purposes: to obtain funds in anticipation of revenue, for expenditures arising from emergencies and exceptional circumstances, and construction of public improvements. Yields from taxes often do not come into the treasury in sufficient quantities early in a fiscal year to meet current expenses. As a result, governments must borrow in anticipation of income that will be received a short time later. This type of indebtedness is commonly called "short-term." Occasionally fires, floods, tornadoes, earthquakes, and other disasters require unanticipated expenditures that can be met only by borrowing. Also included in the second category are bonds issued in recent years by the states to finance veterans' bonuses.

By far the most significant purpose for which state and local governments borrow money is financing public improvements. Highways, school buildings, office buildings, city halls, courthouses, hospitals, sewage disposal systems, and airports illustrate the variety of projects often financed by issuing bonds. Best financial practice dictates that the maturity dates on bonds issued for such improvements should be arranged to provide for repayment within the useful life of an improvement. If such a requirement is not observed, taxpayers will not only pay huge amounts in interest, they will also have to begin paying for a new improvement before old obligations are met. Thus if the useful life of a school building is estimated at forty years, the life of the bonds issued for its construction should be somewhat less. Otherwise, it may be necessary to build a new school or thoroughly remodel the old one before the original investment is paid off. Debts for the construction of public improvements are designated "long-term."

Types of Bonds

Long-term debt is financed by three types of bonds: general obligation, limited obligation, and revenue. General obligation bonds, often called full faith and credit bonds, are guaranteed by the taxing capacity of the issuing government. In other words, a governmental unit pledges to use any and all of its revenue sources to pay off general obligation bonds as they come due.[17] Because of their safety as investments, such bonds normally have relatively low interest rates, assuming that the issuing authority has a satisfactory credit rating. Limited obligation bonds are guaranteed by income from specific taxes or more often by special assessments. Thus bonds issued to pave a street may be backed only by income from special assessments levied against benefited property.

Revenue bonds are issued to finance revenue-producing enterprises, and payment is guaranteed only from such income. This type of bond apparently was first used in the United States by Spokane, Washington, in 1897 to finance a water supply system. Since that time revenue bonds have been used widely by both state and local governments to finance such projects as toll roads and bridges, college and university dormitories, water works, sewer systems, public transportation facilities, housing projects, stadiums, and swimming pools. Since such obligations have no claim upon the general revenues of the issuing government, they are usually considered as less safe investments than general obligation bonds and consequently carry a higher interest rate. If a project financed in this manner fails to produce anticipated income, bondholders may suffer a loss. Revenue bonds are especially attractive to governmental units because their use is not restricted by general debt limitations. About half of the long-term debt of the states and forty per cent of local long-term debt has been financed in this manner in recent years.

Bonds are classified also according to arrangements made for their repayment. If all the bonds in an issue mature on the same date, provisions must be made to have sufficient money available at that time. Common practice is to establish a *sinking fund* into which money is paid at stipulated periods, usually yearly, so that with interest a sufficient amount will be on hand to pay off the bonds when they come due. Bonds amortized in this manner are called sinking-fund or *term* bonds. Interest on them is paid from current revenues.

Frequent mismanagement of sinking funds has caused *serial bonds* to grow in favor to the point where they are more widely used than term bonds. Two chief characteristics distinguish serial from term bonds: staggered maturity dates and payment from current revenues. Thus a twenty-year issue may be set up so that one twentieth of the debt is retired each year from current income. If arrangements are made to repay an equal fraction of the bonded indebtedness each year plus interest, the bonds are called *straight* serials. Since this practice results in larger total payments during the early years of repayment because of large interest charges, the governmental unit may choose to even out the payments. If this practice is followed, payments on the principal are

---

17. Rather than pay off bonds when they come due, a government may choose to "re-fund" them, that is, issue more bonds to replace them.

smaller during the early years of the loan and larger in later years when interest payments have been reduced. Bonds paid off in this manner are known as *annuity* serials.

Debt Limitations

Most states and local governments are limited in regard to the amount of debt they may incur. Such restrictions vary appreciably from state to state, with flat-sum limits ranging from $50,000 to a few million. In a few states limits are expressed in terms of a percentage of assessed valuation. A handful of states prohibit long-term borrowing. These limits are not absolute, however, for certain exceptions commonly are made to constitutional debt restrictions. Specific authority to exceed debt limits is granted most frequently for two purposes: to protect the state against invasion or domestic violence, and to refund existing indebtedness. Also, three procedures are widely used to avoid debt limits: popular referenda, revenue bonds, and special districts and authorities.

Exceptions to constitutional debt restrictions may be authorized by constitutional amendment, a step that requires a popular vote in all states except Delaware. Thus if a general limit of $50,000 is placed on state debt, the people may vote to amend the constitution to permit bond issues for a special purpose such as veterans' bonuses or highways. A separate maximum amount may be stipulated for such issues, constituting a special debt limit. Furthermore, a state constitution may authorize the incurrence of debts in excess of a general limit simply by a favorable popular vote on each indebtedness. The major difference between these two arrangements is that the latter generally involves a simpler procedure.

In states with strict debt limits a large portion of long-term debt is nonguaranteed, that is, it is payable only from specific sources such as income from revenue-producing activities. In a few states all long-term debt is of this variety. Courts generally have approved borrowing outside debt restrictions by means of revenue bonds on the ground that no state liability is created. Similarly, bonds payable solely from the proceeds of a specific tax, such as the gasoline tax when used for highway construction, are usually not subject to constitutional debt limitations.

Various types of independent authorities have proved highly useful in recent years as a means of avoiding debt limits, particularly for the construction of highways and public buildings and the provision of educational facilities. Debts incurred by such agencies, which are often set up as government corporations, are not considered debts against the state. State universities, for example, often issue bonds for capital improvements unaffected by constitutional restrictions. Sometimes bonds issued by such "independent" agencies are also exempt from limits because they are of the revenue type.

Local governments must operate within debt limits imposed not only by state constitutions but also by statutes and their own charters. Local debt restrictions are imposed to accomplish three major purposes: to limit the amount of borrowing, to prohibit borrowing for certain purposes, and to impose conditions on bonding practices. Most often the amount of indebtedness allowed a unit of local government is expressed in terms of a percentage of the assessed value of property located therein. The percentage may vary according to the manner in which the debt is authorized. A higher percentage often is permitted when a bond issue is sanctioned by popular vote than when it is authorized by legislative action. Indeed, no maximum may be imposed on borrowing approved by popular referendum. Debt limits quite regularly vary according to classifications of local governments, distinguishing, for example, among first-class cities, second-class cities, counties, unincorporated towns, and types of special districts. Although limiting the bonded indebtedness of local governments on the basis of the assessed value of property is not considered satisfactory by most students of public finance and local government, it remains standard practice.

In earlier years local governments borrowed money and then loaned it to railroads, public utilities, and other businesses, some of which proved to be poor investments. As a result of such unfortunate experiences, especially during the last century, states now forbid local loans to private enterprises or to individuals. Requirements pertaining to bonding practices sometimes impose a maximum on the life of bonds as well as on interest rates. Some states require local governments to levy taxes to cover all expenses connected with the use of sinking funds; others stipulate that only serial bonds may be used.

The Case of New York City

The financial difficulties that threaten our big cities have been dramatized recently by conditions in New York City that became acute in early 1975 when the city became unable to sell its bonds because investors doubted its ability to repay them. The state sought to rescue the city by lending it some $800 million and then creating the Municipal Assistance Corporation, known as "Big Mac," to function as a borrowing agent for the city. Even though backed by the state, "Big Mac" was unable to sell the city's bonds except at excessively high interest rates. By September of 1975, further action was required, and the state advanced the city $2.3 billion to tide it over for a short period. The state also established the Emergency Financial Control Board to supervise the efforts of the city to work its way out of its financial quagmire.

All these efforts proved insufficient. President Ford, although at first disinclined to do so, extended to the city loans up to $2.3 billion channeled through the Emergency Financial Control Board. At the same time New York City had to make drastic adjustments in its own budget.

Taxes on city residents were increased by $500 million; the city's work-force was cut by 55,000 people; and the wages of most of the remaining workers were temporarily frozen. The practice of providing tuition-free education at the city's institutions of higher learning was abandoned; transit fares were increased; and several public schools were closed, as were some city hospitals.

Although there has been considerable disagreement as to the causes for New York's financial difficulties, the essence of the problem lay in mismanagement. The city attempted to play Santa Claus to many of its residents and to its employees. Also, for a decade it had engaged in fiscal sleight-of-hand, sometimes called "creative accounting," in an effort to postpone the day of reckoning.[18] The case of New York City high-lights the fact that a major governmental unit cannot be allowed to go bankrupt since no one can accurately predict all the consequences, not only for the unit involved but also other governments, the bond market, and investors generally.[19]

18. For details, see Congressional Budget Office, *New York City's Fiscal Problem: Its Origins, Potential Repercussions, and Some Alternative Policy Responses,* U.S. Government Printing Office, 1975.
19. In 1978 Cleveland defaulted on $15.5 million in bank notes, but the amount involved did not pose a threat to the money market comparable to that of New York City.

Handling Public Money: Fiscal Management 15

It is important not only to understand how governments obtain money and the purposes for which they spend it, but also to be familiar with the techniques and procedures for handling public money. Fiscal management includes those operations designed to make funds available and to ensure their honest and efficient use. An exhaustive examination of the various aspects of fiscal management is beyond the scope of a single chapter. Instead, we will direct special attention to budgeting, auditing, and tax collection. Few governments adhere to any pattern exactly, but a general description provides a guide for understanding existing practices and serves as a sort of criterion by which to judge them. Every governmental unit that receives money engages in financial management, with practices ranging from the extremely crude to the very complicated.

ORGANIZATION FOR FISCAL MANAGEMENT

Excluding the legislature which grants the funds, organization for fiscal management includes (1) agencies in the executive branch that must have money in order to carry out their programs, (2) agencies organized primarily to implement the acquisition of funds and oversee their expenditure, and (3) agencies created to check on the fidelity and legality of disbursements after they have been made. Included in the first category are the great majority of agencies found in all multipurpose governments. State departments of all kinds, such as health, education, and highways, are vitally concerned with the management of funds allocated to them. The same is true of agencies at the local level concerned, for example, with the provision of police and fire protection, streets, and schools. The importance of arrangements found in local agencies often is overlooked in an examination of fiscal management. In view of the lack of close central supervision of fiscal procedures characteristic of many governmental units, the practices of spending agencies are especially significant. The trend, however, for some time has been toward increased central control, motivated in part by financial scandals prevalent among governments during the nineteenth century.

Fiscal Officers

The Chief Executive. Ideally, the chief executive—governor, mayor, or manager—is in a very real sense the chief fiscal officer. Although his or her authority in these matters is largely dependent upon constitutional, statutory, or charter provisions and consequently varies from place to place, the chief executive usually plays a major role in the fiscal process. The chief executive must assist in the allocation of funds by informing the legislative body and the people of the amount of money required to finance services and meet anticipated needs. Once the legislature has acted, it becomes the chief executive's responsibility to oversee spending and see that appropriate accounts are maintained to provide a record of the use of public money. Of all the fiscal responsibilities borne by the chief executive, those related to securing sufficient revenue are probably most important. They are discussed later in connection with the budget process.

The Treasurer. Although not as important a position as it once was, a typical treasurer still has a number of important, although somewhat routine, fiscal responsibilities. The great bulk of public funds are either received by or deposited with the treasurer by receiving agencies. For example, the receipts from a state income tax may be collected by a tax commission and then deposited with the treasurer. The treasurer is at least formally responsible for the custody and investment of public money. These duties, particularly that of investment, may be shared with other public officials. In a sense, the custodianship of funds has been shifted to the banks in which they are deposited. Treasurers also have the task of disbursing money upon proper authorization. In order to perform these and related duties satisfactorily, treasurers must maintain a system of accounts which may be quite complicated. They also prepare reports for the benefit of administrators, budget agencies, and the public.

The Budget Officer. In most states and many municipalities there is an official, commonly known as a budget officer, who aids the chief executive in preparing and executing the budget. Usually responsible directly to the chief executive or an appointed director of finance, a budget officer is in a position to affect profoundly the operations of agencies that come within his or her purview. If able to escape the "economizing orientation" that frequently appears to dominate those in that occupation, a budget officer may exert a constructive influence. The reputation of being a "nickel-nurser," whose chief aim is to cut expenditures, jeopardizes a budget officer's usefulness.

The Comptroller. As the chief accounting officer, the comptroller's job is to see that records are kept that accurately reflect the current financial status of a governmental unit and its major subdivisions. The comptroller not only maintains central accounts but also supervises the accounting systems of operating agencies. In this way uniform accounting procedures may be assured and a basis provided for comparing the financial status and practices of different agencies. Another duty frequently vested in a comptroller is the *preaudit,* by means of which proposed expenditures are compared with available money and authorized purposes. Proposals to spend are checked to determine whether they are legal and proper and whether sufficient money will be available to pay the bills. Individual agencies often perform the preaudit function within their own organizations in accord with procedures outlined by the comptroller.

The Auditor. When properly used, the term "auditor" designates a public official responsible for determining the *fidelity* and *legality* of the manner in which money has been used. This task is accomplished by examining the financial transactions completed during a fiscal period, usually a "fiscal year."[1] Occasionally, an official functions in an *ex officio* capacity as auditor. Thus in Oregon the Secretary of State is designated as state auditor by the constitution. Local governments, especially smaller ones, frequently hire private persons to audit their books. Auditors often are elected by popular vote, sometimes chosen by legislative action, and rarely appointed by the chief executive. Legislative selection is generally preferred by students of fiscal management because an auditor should and normally does report to a legislative body, either state or local.

The Purchasing Agent. During the last fifty years, state and local governments have made increasing use of centralized purchasing and property control. The older practice is still prevalent, however, whereby each governmental agency purchases all its own equipment and supplies. Centralized purchasing is designed to make a staff officer responsible for the purchase, storage, and distribution of items required by different departments, bureaus, divisions, boards, and commissions. Purchasing is never completely centralized. Specialized items, such as drugs for institutions and experimental equipment used in laboratories, are generally acquired by the agencies that use them. Also, emergency purchases must be made occasionally by line agencies when the central warehouse is unable to provide an item that is needed immediately and unexpectedly.

---

1. The fiscal year of most governments runs from July 1 to June 30; sometimes it is the same as the calendar year; rarely, some other period is used.

The Assessor. Administration of the property tax, the principal source of tax revenue for local governments, is usually the responsibility of an assessor. Consequently, the assessor is a major fiscal officer at the local level and has the task of locating, listing, and appraising or evaluating property, both real and personal. The adequate performance of these duties is important both to the taxpayer and to the tax collector. Popularly elected assessors often do not possess the knowledge and training necessary to do an adequate job, causing inequity and injustice in the distribution of the costs of government among taxpayers. Inadequacy on the part of the assessor can often be offset by competent personnel hired to work in the assessor's office.

Trends in Fiscal Organization

One of the striking trends in recent years in organization for fiscal management at both state and local levels has been towards an "integrated" system of finance under the chief executive. Such an arrangement brings together, or integrates, budgetmaking, revenue collection, the preaudit, accounting, central purchasing, and property management. Accordingly, an integrated system of fiscal management requires that the budget officer, treasurer or tax collector, comptroller, and purchasing officer be under the control of the chief executive. At the local level, the assessor should be part of the integrated structure. However, the auditor should *not* be included in order to enhance that officer's independence of the executive.

Procedures for handling financial affairs have been greatly improved in recent years at all levels of government. Fiscal leadership and supervision have been vested increasingly in chief executives and officers responsible to them and increased coordination is evident almost everywhere. Opportunities for mishandling public money have been appreciably decreased. Legislative procedures involved in reviewing requests for appropriations and in overseeing the manner in which they are spent have been strengthened, although improvements here have not been as noticeable as in the executive branch.

THE BUDGET PROCESS

One of the most important elements of fiscal management is an effective budget process. A budget is: "A comprehensive plan, expressed in financial terms, by which an operating program is effective for a given period of time. It includes estimates of: (a) the services, activities, and projects comprising the program; (b) the resultant expenditure requirements; and

(c) the resources usable for their support."[2] The term is also used in the sense of a "capital budget," involving a long-term program of capital improvements and operational programs. Discussion in this chapter is limited to a consideration of budgets prepared for specific fiscal periods.

Modern budgeting first developed in this country at the municipal level. All factors contributing to this occurrence are not entirely clear, but three were especially significant. The efforts of "Muckrakers" like Lincoln Steffens and Ray S. Baker at the beginning of the twentieth century aroused public indignation over widespread municipal corruption. Then in 1899 the National Municipal League, an organization active in local government reform, included in its model municipal charter provisions for a budget system. The New York Bureau of Municipal Research, a private organization that proved to be a powerful force in behalf of municipal reform, published in 1907 a study entitled "Making a Municipal Budget." This study contributed to improvements in fiscal management in New York City and later in other cities also.

Not long after improvements in budgetary practices appeared among municipalities, pressure began to build up for reform at the state level. Public interest was further promoted by the work of the Taft Commission on Economy and Efficiency at the federal level. The first state law providing for an executive budget was enacted in Ohio in 1910, and during the following six years eight states enacted similar legislation. According to Burkhead, the first state to adopt "a thorough system of executive budget-making" was Maryland in 1916; by 1920, budget systems had been established by forty-four states.[3] "As in the case of the cities, the 'friends of budgeting' were of two divergent groups: the reformers, who wanted to make governmental institutions more responsive, and organized taxpayer groups, who were promoting retrenchment in expenditures and reduction in taxation. Together, these groups were responsible for the rapid spread of the budget system."[4]

Before examining the steps involved in budgeting, it is important to understand the meaning of the term "budget cycle." A budget cycle involves three main steps that constitute a continuous process: budget making, budget adoption, and budget execution. The first step is an executive responsibility; it ends when the budget is ready for submission to the legislature. The second is the task of the legislature and is complete when appropriation bills are enacted. Responsibility for the third phase, budget execution, is divided between the executive who makes allotments and conducts a preaudit and the auditor who examines the records.

2. The International City Managers' Association, *Municipal Finance Administration*, Chicago, 1955, p. 61. (This organization has changed its name to International City Management Association.)

3. Jesse Burkhead, *Government Budgeting*, John Wiley & Sons, New York, 1956, p. 23.

4. *Ibid.*, p. 24.

Budget Making and Adoption

Agency Responsibilities. The process of building a budget begins when operating agencies prepare their expenditure estimates for the coming fiscal period. General instructions may have been prepared by the central budget office reflecting policies of the chief executive and communicated to the agencies. If these instructions have imposed a ceiling on increases for the next fiscal period, agencies must "hold the line" accordingly. Ceilings may be imposed, for example, in terms of a maximum percentage increase in requests over appropriations available for the preceding fiscal period. If no such limitations exist, each agency is free to make any requests it deems necessary or advisable in light of anticipated or proposed modifications of its program.

Requests for increases usually result from one or both of two factors: increased costs necessary to maintain an established level of service and expanded programs. In times of inflation governmental costs, like those in private industry, continue to rise because of increasing prices of equipment and supplies as well as advances in wage and salary levels. If allowances are not made for such increases, services must be reduced. As already noted, there have been continuous pressures for many years promoting growth in governmental services. These pressures have come both from inside and from outside government. Highway builders feel we need more and better highways; welfare workers are convinced of the importance of expanded programs; educators are sure they can do a better job with improved facilities and more qualified teachers; and so it goes. Although sometimes accused of "empire building," people dedicated to a function are naturally convinced of its importance. Without such dedication, they will not perform at their maximum level of effectiveness. Outside pressures for expansion come from special groups and from the public in general. Regrettably, some of the same people urge budgetary cuts—and of course, such reductions must always be made in *other* services.

Although responsibility for the preparation of an agency budget rests with the top administrator, as many persons as possible should be given a part in the undertaking. Budget time presents an excellent opportunity for employees to express their ideas concerning possible improvements in the program with which they are working. Large agencies commonly have budget officers to whom the task of budget preparation is delegated, subject to review by the agency head. These officers collect data from operating units, provide assistance in estimating cost increases, and prepare justifications for proposed program expansion. All work must be done in anticipation of the time when representatives from the agency will probably be called before a legislative committee to justify their requests.

The Central Budget Office. Once an agency has completed its budget estimates, they are usually sent to the chief executive or to a central budget office operating as part of his staff. In most states and large municipalities provision has been made for some type of central budget office, which has two major responsibilities, *program review* and *management improvement.* The former consists of an examination of the operations of each agency from a central viewpoint in order to place them in proper perspective in relation to other programs. The central budget office has a major responsibility at this point that is not shared with the operating agencies—namely, the preparation of an estimate of revenues that will be available to meet expenditure requests. A second major task of the budget officer relates to the most effective allocation of estimated resources in order to achieve desirable objectives. Involved here is a search for more effective methods of operation.

If it is to be successful, a central budget office must perform its responsibilities in cooperation with line agencies. A major obstacle to effective budgeting develops when line officers feel that the budget officer is attempting to usurp their prerogatives. People working in the field of public health, for example, resent attempts by a budget office to instruct them as to the best way to administer a public health program. The same is true of educators, firefighters, and all other specialists. Consequently, a wise budget officer seeks to assist specialists in "discovering" more efficient methods in the performance of their responsibilities. In the final analysis, a budget office must inform each agency under its jurisdiction as to the proportion of total anticipated income that will be allotted to it.

Within a unit of government not all activities are subject to central budget review. Usually, the expenditures of the legislature and the judiciary are excepted. Expenses involved in debt payments, in welfare and benefit programs, and funds required to match grants from another governmental unit are largely exempt. Also, central control does not apply to revenues from earmarked taxes, but it may limit expenditures from such sources.

It must be kept in mind that a central budget office usually functions as part of the chief executive's staff and supposedly speaks for the chief executive on policy matters. Because of their close relationship to the chief executive, budget officers must resist every temptation to "throw their weight around." At the same time, the chief executive must avoid becoming insulated from the line departments. Opportunities must exist to appeal budget decisions all the way to the top. After all, the budget, when completed, will be presented to the legislature as the chief executive's budget, not the budget officer's.

Legislative Authorization. When the chief executive submits the budget to the legislature, he or she normally presents a "budget message" at the same time. In this message the executive outlines expenditure and revenue proposals and seeks to justify them. The budget is then "divided up" and parceled out among various committees and subcommittees. Program changes and recommendations for new services are considered by appropriate "subject-matter" committees. For example, proposals to increase state aid to primary and secondary schools may be sent to a committee on education and welfare. The committee will probably divide itself into subcommittees, one of which will be instructed to report its findings and recommendations concerning increased aid to schools. Another subcommittee may consider requests for additional buildings at the state university. This pattern is repeated many times with relation to different governmental services.

A vital part of budget studies by legislative committees consists of public hearings at which governmental officials, organized groups, and all interested persons have an opportunity to present their ideas. It is at this point that the fact becomes evident that budgetmaking is a political process. Sometimes hearings are conducted in an honest effort to obtain information on all aspects of a question and weigh opposing viewpoints. When such is the case, policymaking functions in the best democratic tradition. At other times hearings are held as a matter of form, and committee members listen politely with closed minds—perhaps they have "heard from home," or perhaps in the absence of pressure they do not wish to be confused by the facts! The novice in legislative tactics soon learns that the important question often is not, *What* is wanted? Instead, it is, *Who* wants it?

When a budget is parceled out among committees, those items involving increased expenditures receive special scrutiny by a "ways and means" committee designated among the states by a variety of titles. Such a committee considers *all* requests for expenditures, attempts to decide where increases are most necessary and where decreases are feasible, arrives at recommendations for each agency, and computes a total. The total is likely to be less than that requested in the executive budget. Once the decisions of this committee are known, then a means of raising revenue necessary to finance the recommendations must be authorized. This whole procedure is complicated enough, but the fact that it may be substantially duplicated in a second house in a bicameral legislature makes it complex indeed.

Recommendations of both subject-matter and fiscal committees are transmitted to the respective houses of which they are a part. Sometimes joint committees are used, but they are the exception rather than the rule. Recommendations may be accepted quickly without change; they may be debated at length and accepted, or changed appreciably. If the membership of the house feels that additional committee work is desirable, a measure under consideration may be returned to the committee that worked on it, or it may be referred to a different committee. Reference to a different committee is sometimes sought by a minority of members who are unable to gain acceptance of their ideas at the time the measure is considered by the whole house. They may hope that a proposal more to their liking will come from a second committee, or they may seek to stall final action until late in the session in the hope that their chances of success may be better in the end-of-session rush.

The whole process of legislative action on budget requests is intertwined with oversight of administration. Governmental officials appearing before committees often get "cues" as to what is expected of them if they receive certain requests. Throughout the legislative process "understandings" of one kind or another are common. Such techniques of legislative supervision are not likely to be formalized in law, but failure on the part of administrators to honor them are very likely to produce unpleasant repercussions at later legislative sessions. One formal method of supervision relates to the *nature* of appropriations. If the legislature "itemizes" appropriations by specifying in detail the objects of expenditures, it thereby severely restricts administrative discretion by prohibiting transfers of money from one purpose to another. *Lump-sum* appropriations, on the other hand, reflect legislative trust of administrators and a willingness to allow them discretion in using public funds.

Although the foregoing description of legislative authorization of budget requests is couched in terms descriptive of procedures typical of state legislatures, a similar pattern exists at the local level. It is normally somewhat abbreviated and less formal, but the essential steps are similar. Local legislatures ordinarily use committees to consider budget requests. These committees hold hearings and make recommendations which are then acted upon by the legislative body. Legislative efforts to supervise administration are found at the local level as well as at the state level, but their intensity is affected by the form of local government. They are generally less noticeable, for example, in council-manager cities than in weak-mayor communities.

The Performance or Program Budget

Governments at all levels in the United States traditionally have prepared their budgets in terms of objects to be purchased such as equipment and supplies, and salaries to be paid. Classifications in such budgets are in terms of what is to be bought rather than what is to be accomplished. In recent times a few governments have turned to the *performance or program budget,* which is prepared in terms of services to be performed or programs to be achieved rather than items to be purchased. Interest in this type of budget was stimulated by the first Hoover Commission, which advised:

> We recommend that the whole budgetary concept of the Federal Government should be refashioned by the adoption of a budget based upon functions, activities, and projects: this we designate a "performance budget." Such an

approach would focus attention upon the general character and relative importance of the work to be done, or upon the services to be rendered, rather than upon the things to be acquired, such as personal services, supplies, equipment, and so on. These latter objects are, after all, only a means to an end. The all important thing in budgeting is the work or the service to be accomplished, and what that work or service will cost.[5]

The performance budget has proved to be especially adaptable to municipal governments, and a number of cities have adopted it, including Los Angeles, Cleveland, Denver, Detroit, and Phoenix. Its use at this level of government has resulted largely from the interest of some local officials and from the nature of certain municipal functions. Changes in the form of government in some cities, especially to the manager type, have been accompanied by experiments with performance budgeting. Also, it is relatively easy to identify the end product of certain municipal activities. Thus the results of garbage collection and street cleaning are more easily reduced to measurable units than education or welfare.

A few states have incorporated the performance concept in their budgets. Among these states are California, Connecticut, Illinois, Maryland, Michigan, New York, Oklahoma, and Oregon. A major argument in behalf of the performance budget is that it provides a means by which governmental agencies are able to explain to legislators and citizens their contributions to the community.

Zero-Base Budgeting

Although not a new idea, zero-base budgeting has recently become the latest fad in governmental budgeting. ZBB is intended to require justification by each agency of every proposed expenditure in every year's budget rather than the traditional incremental approach. When Jimmy Carter assumed the governorship of Georgia in 1971, he saw the state's budget process operating in this manner:

> No one had made any attempt to assess the worth of the budget requests or to arrange them in any sort of priority. . . the only analysis of funding requests were those for new and expanded programs. No method existed for the analysis on an equal basis for old and perhaps obsolete programs which had been ensconced within the governmental bureaucracy years ago. . . . Once a bureaucratic entity had been established, it was almost immune from later scrutiny.[6]

Shortly afterward, Governor Carter learned of a type of budgeting installed by Peter Pyhrr at Texas Instruments Incorporated called zero-base budgeting. He then hired Pyhrr as a consultant to help introduce ZBB into Georgia. Governor Carter was enthusiastic about starting budgets

5. Commission on Organization of the Executive Branch of the Government, *Budgeting and Accounting,* Washington, 1949, p. 8.
6. Jimmy Carter, *Why Not the Best?* The Broadman Press, Nashville, Tenn., 1975, p. 127.

from scratch. When he became President, Mr. Carter vowed to innaugurate ZBB at the national level. He even installed his formed Highway Commissioner, Bert Lance, as head of the Office of Management and Budget to facilitate the introduction of the changes he desired.

In spite of this testimony in its behalf, ZBB has not taken the country by storm at any level of government. The "volume problem" poses a serious obstacle to the implementation of ZBB in large organizations. Although it may cause people to think more carefully about what they are doing, efforts to translate these self-critiques into budgetary policy are very costly. Merewitz and Sosnick describe the problem quite well:

> The purpose of zero-base budgeting is to discourage agency heads from taking program perpetuation for granted and to encourage them to reallocate funds as they think appropriate. However, . . . zero-base budgeting makes an impossible demand of these men, provides no help in deciding whether the allocation of funds could be improved, and tells them to discard some information [the previous year's appropriation] that might help.
> . . . [T]o exclude reference to previous years' appropriations is self-defeating. A request for funds whose relation to the current appropriations is unclear is needlessly hard to evaluate. . . . If a request for funds is not expressed as a change from the current appropriation, reviewers cannot relate the request to their impressions of the program's current operations and cannot compare the requests with their earlier conclusions as to an appropriate scale for the program. [7]

As a consequence of the significant difficulties inherent in any serious attempt at zero-base budgeting, its implementation is often superficial, involving no more than changes in terminology. Little seems to have changed at the federal level as a consequence of its adoption. [8] Undoubtedly, the difficulties at the national level are compounded by the size of the budget. Although the costs are real and the net benefits questionable, steps have been taken in about half of the states and numerous local governments to implement some form of ZBB.

Budget Execution

Subsequent to legislative authorization of budgetary requests, the next important phase in the budget cycle is execution or administration. This task belongs to the executive, and a major objective is to preserve legislative intent with regard to expenditures. If they are to assist in the realization of program goals, expenditure controls must be flexible and not allowed to degenerate into a routine application of rules and regu-

7. Leonard Merewitz and Stephen H. Sosnick, *The Budget's New Clothes*, Markham, Chicago, 1971, pp. 62–64.
8. See Robert N. Anthony, "Zero-Base Budgeting Is a Fraud," *The Wall Street Journal*, April 27, 1977; and Allen Schick, "The Road from ZBB," *Public Administration Review*, March/April 1978.

lations. Nevertheless, certain basic practices are generally recognized as essential to effective budgetary control, the most important of which are *allotments, preaudit,* and *postaudit.* As noted earlier, the postaudit is not properly considered an executive function, but it is an essential step in fiscal control.

Allotments. One of the most useful devices for controlling expenditures is the allotment by which funds are made available to a spending agency at intervals. They are usually made on a monthly or quarterly basis and provide a means of keeping expenditure programs under constant review to prevent too rapid disbursements early in the fiscal year resulting in later deficits. Like appropriations, they may be itemized or lump-sum. Also, allotments provide a means whereby economies may be effected as a result of changes in work loads or improved management techniques.

The Preaudit. The preaudit may be defined briefly as a procedure for determining the propriety of a proposed expenditure. In determining propriety, two major considerations are involved: sufficiency of funds to pay an obligation, and legality of a proposed obligation. Obviously, the officer responsible for the preaudit must maintain accounts that reflect the financial status of each agency and subdivision. Sometimes more than one preaudit is required. One may be administered by the spending agency and another by a central fiscal officer. In general, the duplication of effort involved in such procedure is unreasonable and causes excessive delay in financial transactions. Also, government personnel are hampered in performing their duties and merchants are annoyed by the red tape.

The Postaudit. The postaudit, which comes at the close of a fiscal period, is concerned with the honesty and legality of transactions and the accuracy of accounts as well as program effectiveness. The officer or private person responsible for conducting this audit normally has the duty of reporting all findings to a legislative body. State laws may require the accounts of local governments to be audited at specified intervals. Such audits are occasionally performed by a state official but more frequently by someone designated by the local legislature. Postaudits are absolutely essential as a guarantee that public funds are handled in an honest, legal, and effective manner.

ASSESSMENT AND COLLECTION OF TAXES

In the context of fiscal management, "assessment" has two meanings that should be distinguished. In one sense, assessment refers to the process of determining the value of something, particularly income and property, for the purpose of taxation. It also means the procedure of fixing the amount of a tax. Assessment is accomplished in one of three ways: (1) by self-assessment, (2) automatically, or (3) by governmental action. The personal income tax, as used by the national and state governments, is administered basically through a process of self-assessment. Taxpayers are responsible for determining the value (amount) of their income and the exact tax they are obligated to pay.[9] Of course, this action is subject to review by a governmental agency. Many taxes are assessed automatically. Probably the best known examples are retail sales and excise taxes. When a person knows that two cents must be added to each dollar spent for a purchase, the tax is automatic. The same is true of gasoline taxes, which are included in the price of each gallon. Hidden taxes incorporated in the prices of items, such as food and clothing, without being identified as such are generally termed excise taxes, and they, too, are assessed automatically. Among those taxes to which governmental assessment is applicable, the most important is the property tax. Responsibility for determining the value of property and for fixing the amount of the tax rests with governmental agencies. Because of the importance of governmental action, the significance of the property tax as a source of local revenue, and the problems related to its administration, assessment of the property tax demands special consideration.

The Personal Property Tax. As described in an earlier chapter, property is generally classified as real or personal. Real property consists of land and improvements, while all other property is considered personal. Although decreasing in importance, local jurisdictions and some states continue to receive revenue from the personal property tax. Taxes on personal property are selective, that is, they apply to some kinds of property and not to others. Tangible personal property, including such things as automobiles, furniture, appliances, farm machinery, and livestock, is more easily subjected to taxation than intangible property which consists of stocks, bonds, mortgages, patents, copyrights, and similar evidences of wealth. The latter are much more easily concealed than the former. Since taxes on intangibles are very difficult to administer and tend to penalize the honest taxpayer, they are used much less widely than they once were.

In earlier days the assessment of personal property was based almost entirely upon declarations submitted by taxpayers. Some supplementary information was provided by assessors on the basis of their general but rather haphazard knowledge of property within their respective jurisdictions. In recognition of the inadequacy of such procedure, assessors

---

9. The fact that some jurisdictions provide for "collection at the source" whereby deductions are made from pay checks does not mean that each person is relieved of responsibility for determining the amount of tax due. At some date, each recipient of taxable income must still file a return indicating the amount of tax he or she is obligated to pay.

have resorted to personal visits to view taxable tangible property and record information concerning its quantity, quality, and valuation. Each taxpayer is usually visited only once every two, three, or more years since time and staff do not permit annual visitations in most places. Assessment of the assets of business firms other than real property must be based largely on accounting records, which may be subject to more or less thorough and regular checks.

The Real Property Tax. Much as in the case of the personal property tax, the assessment of real property requires discovery, listing, and valuation. The problems are different, however. Land and buildings are much more easily discovered and listed than most varieties of personal property. Nevertheless, as a result of poor administration considerable amounts of real property have regularly escaped taxation because they have not been placed on the assessment rolls. The cure for this situation lies in a system requiring that land be surveyed and property lines be recorded on scale maps which must be kept current on the basis of alterations in property lines and changes in ownership. In addition to land maps (commonly called lot and block maps in cities), information must be recorded concerning improvements on each parcel of land. An actual viewing of each piece of property by someone from the assessor's office is the only satisfactory method of accomplishing this purpose. Assistance may be obtained from aerial maps.

Maintaining current records pertaining to improvements is much more difficult than with regard to the parcels of land themselves. Each year buildings are constructed, and old ones modified, torn down or moved. Unless building permits are required, chief reliance must be placed on personal observation to keep abreast of such changes. Even where building permits are required and serve as the major source of information for the assessor, personal viewing cannot be abandoned since changes may be made by property owners who neglect to obtain permits.

The most serious difficulties in the administration of the property tax are associated with valuation. Some of the major reasons for these difficulties are: (1) No two parcels of property are identical because they cannot have identical locations, and the location of property is a major factor in determining its value. (2) Sales of real property often occur too infrequently to provide adequate data on value. (3) Since land is irreplaceable, there are no reproduction costs that may be used in the valuation process. (4) Since land and buildings generally exist over long periods of time, estimates pertaining to income and depreciation are difficult to make. (5) Too often assessors and their employees, insufficiently trained in the techniques of assessing property, must rely on the routine application of rate-scale formulas.

Nevertheless, local assessors are required by law to arrive at a taxable value for most property within their jurisdiction.[10] Even under the best circumstances this is a difficult task. When approached unsystematically, property valuation is characterized by inadequacy, inequity, and even chicanery. In an effort to provide assistance to assessors, the National Association of Assessing Officers has developed the concept of "constructive market value" as a guide in determining real property values for purposes of taxation. Constructive market value has been defined as "an approximation of market value arrived at through the application of reasonable rules and procedures of appraisal, such as corner influence and depth rules, building classification and cost schedules, and physical depreciation schedules."[11] An examination of the import of this definition is beyond the scope of this chapter, but one important fact should be noted. Reference is made to an "approximation of market value" through the use of "reasonable rules and procedures." Thus valuation is recognized as an *estimate* based on reason reinforced by standard methods of procedure. Since an estimate smaller than true value is generally preferred to one that is larger, underassessment is the rule. From the viewpoint of a popularly elected assessor, overassessment must be avoided at all costs.

Review and Equalization. Due process of law requires that all taxpayers have the right to a hearing before taxes on their property become final. The standard practice is to establish an administrative agency, commonly an *ex officio* board, to *review* individual assessments against real or personal property, and raise or lower them or uphold the assessor's valuation. The number of appeals to such bodies is kept to a minimum partially by the usual practice of underassessment. Where the distribution of state property taxes among counties or of county taxes among smaller units of government is involved, arrangements must be made for adjustments by the central units to facilitate equitable distribution of such taxes. The procedure whereby these adjustments are made is called *equalization,* and it is intended to minimize inequalities in the administration of the property tax. Equalization is not concerned with adjusting inequalities in the assessment of individual properties. Instead, it is intended to make adjustments in the level of assessments within jurisdictions like townships, villages, and cities. Thus if the assessor in one township is valuing property appreciably higher than the assessor in another township, the county board of equalization may make them more comparable.

Recent years have witnessed increased state activity with regard to the equalization of property assessments. In many states a "tax commission"

---

10. Some types of property, such as that belonging to utilities and railroads, are assessed by a state agency.
11. Quoted in International City Managers' (Management) Association, *op. cit.,* pp. 230–231.

is empowered to review and equalize assessments among counties and to assess public utility properties directly. Generally, these commissions use persuasion and education in their efforts to improve the quality of local assessments. They may advise local assessors and conduct schools for them. If such procedures prove inadequate, the state agency may order reassessments by local officials in accord with state rules and regulations, or it may direct local boards of review to correct inequities.

Common Defects.   Many of the difficulties associated with the property tax stem from defects in administration. First and probably most important, local assessors are often inadequate in relation to the demands of the job. Popular election, which is the rule, emphasizes the need for gaining favor in the eyes of voters rather than fearless application of the best assessment techniques. Short terms of office further stress the importance of keeping popular favor. In most states no formal qualifications are required of assessors. As a consequence, valuation may be based largely on guesswork; some property escapes taxation; and there is little incentive to install modern procedures. Of course, it sometimes happens that a well qualified assessor is elected, and his office is a model of effectiveness and efficiency.

Defects in property tax administration also stem from the fact that assessors often are provided insufficient funds to perform their duties. Even if they are familiar with modern practices and wish to install them, assessors may be prevented from inaugurating changes by lack of money, and they may be severely limited in the number and quality of personnel they may hire. One of the major causes of poor assessment is the entirely unwarranted assumption that almost anyone can do the work.

Tax Collection

The collection of taxes for any governmental jurisdiction is usually scattered among a number of officers and agencies. Treasurers collect some taxes; separate boards or commissions collect others; and sheriffs may collect still others. The variations are legion, but there has been a trend in recent years toward improvement. It was not uncommon at one time for a taxpayer to have to pay part of the property tax to a county collector; part to a township collector, part to a city collector, and part to a school district collector. Today the collection of the local property tax is usually centralized in a county official who is responsible for allocating to the other jurisdictions their appropriate shares. Practically all states have established a central agency, often a commission, to collect a variety of state taxes. The collection of earmarked revenues may rest with the agencies authorized to spend them.

Where assessment of a tax is a governmental responsibility, economy and efficiency would seem to dictate combining assessment and collection in the same agency. Such an arrangement is seldom found, however—a fact that may be partially explained by the different skills and abilities required of those persons responsible for these functions. A major consideration in the collection of a tax is that the procedure should be economical, as Adam Smith observed nearly two centuries ago. Today it is generally conceded that no tax is good if it eats itself up in costs of collection. Whatever official is responsible for collecting a tax should also possess the authority and responsibility to follow up cases of delinquency and collect delinquent taxes whenever possible. In order to insure the safe custody of public funds, all persons involved in their collection should be bonded.

Department of Revenue. A few states, including Oregon, Georgia, and Alaska, have organized departments of revenue. Advocates of a state department of revenue argue that the enforcement of major tax laws as well as the collection, custody, and management of state moneys should be brought together under a single authority in the name of efficient and economical management. Opposition comes largely from agencies with vested interests in the administration of certain aspects of a state's finances and from those who have a special interest in the use of specific state funds. Thus a liquor commission with authority over collecting and spending alcoholic beverage taxes may oppose a department of finance, and sportsmen may fight against taking control over the income from hunting and fishing licenses from the fish and game commission. These and other pressures have succeeded in defeating most proposals to create a state department of revenue.

Staffing State and Local Governments: Personnel Management 16

In earlier chapters, stress was placed on the importance to good government of sound structural arrangements and adequate financial resources. Important as they are, these factors alone cannot produce effective government. Qualified, industrious, loyal people are essential. The magnitude of personnel management problems experienced by state and local governments is reflected in part by the fact that they now employ some thirteen million persons, necessitating payroll costs in excess of eleven billion dollars per month.

Around the close of the eighteenth century, government employment was considered a privilege. This viewpoint, coupled with the relatively simple governmental activities characteristic of the times, produced a group of public servants who performed their duties satisfactorily. During the first quarter of the nineteenth century, the "spoils system" infested state and local governments generally throughout the nation. In the eyes of the spoilers positions in the public service were viewed as booty for the party in power. Accordingly, a change in party resulted in a wholesale turnover of public employees because "to the victor belong the spoils."

Under the spoils system, now as then, persons are appointed to positions on the basis of party and personal considerations. Elected officials reward fellow partisans and personal friends by providing them with jobs at the taxpayers' expense. Little attention is paid to such matters as ability and competence. Many people in the early days of the nineteenth century probably thought the spoils system a less serious threat to democratic institutions than a "bureaucracy" resulting from the retention of employees for long periods of time. Any effort to justify the practice today on such grounds is doomed to failure. Nevertheless, the spoils system is still widespread in state and local governments.

In 1877 public-spirited citizens organized the New York Civil Service Reform Association, the first of many such groups. This organization contributed materially to the enactment in 1883 of the federal civil service act (Pendleton Act) and to the passing of the first New York state civil service law. Massachusetts followed suit in 1884. No other state passed similar legislation during the next twenty-one years. Now some three-fourths of the states have provided for "general" coverage under civil service or merit system laws. Most of the other states have enacted laws applying to employees of selected departments. Because of federal requirements, every state has required that employees handling funds provided under grant-in-aid programs must be chosen according to civil service or merit system procedures.

At the local level the quality of personnel management varies greatly. Most cities with populations in excess of 100,000 operate under civil service laws or a merit system, as do many smaller communities. In counties and some other units of local government the picture is discouraging. Only a small minority of the nation's counties have such laws or are included under state statutes designed to provide general coverage, and in many cities such regulations apply only to personnel in certain departments, particularly police and fire.

However, statistics on merit system coverage are deceptive as they merely indicate the presence of such systems "on the books," but they provide no information about their administration. Local tradition may support practices designed to strengthen merit or to undermine it. The existence of civil service or a formal merit system does not guarantee good personnel management. Legislatures (state or local) may fail to appropriate sufficient money to implement laws effectively; responsible officials may be hostile; the public may be indifferent; or provisions of the law may be unworkable. On the other hand, it is possible to have efficient personnel management without civil service or formal merit system arrangements.[1]

TERMINOLOGY

Frequently, in discussions of personnel management in the public service, terms appear that are misunderstood. Some of these will be defined and discussed later in the chapter, but attention should be directed to certain concepts at this point. Students often are confused concerning the differences between "civil service," "merit system," and "career service." Although it may be impossible to distinguish them completely, some differences can be noted. As used in this text, *civil service* refers to a system of personnel management *formalized* by a government through laws, rules, and regulations. The term is also used to refer to the employees subject to such a system. Originally, civil service laws were enacted primarily to keep the rascals and incompetents out of public office. Em-

1. See Jay M. Shafritz, Walter Balk, Albert Hyde, and David Rosenbloom, *Personnel Management in Government: Politics and Process,* Marcel Dekker, N.Y., 1978.

ployees were to be chosen on the basis of competence or "merit" rather than political affiliation or personal friendship. As a result, the terms "civil service" and "merit system" often have been used interchangeably.

An arrangement for managing personnel in which various actions, such as hiring, promoting, and firing, relate closely to the individual employee's fitness and performance qualifies as a *merit system,* whether in public or private employment. Thus any government unit that emphasizes individual fitness for the job may be said to operate on a merit system. The basic difference between civil service and a merit system lies in the fact that civil service *must* rest on laws, rules, and regulations that spell out in considerable detail permissible personnel practices, while a merit system *may* be informal. Confusion is compounded by the fact that laws may specifically provide for the establishment of a "merit system" and stipulate that certain procedural requirements be observed that are similar to those under civil service.

The third term, "career service," is not so difficult to distinguish. "By a *career* is meant a life work. It is an honorable occupation which one formally takes up in youth with the expectation of advancement, and pursues until retirement. A *career service* in government is thus a public service which is so organized and conducted as to encourage careers."[2] Accordingly, in a career service competent young people are recruited with the expectation that they will have long tenure in an agency or governmental unit. Advancement is along recognized promotional ladders, and very few persons fill intermediate or higher positions unless they have "worked their way up." It is probably correct to state that at the present time no governmental unit as a whole operates on the career principle. Young people do not accept employment in a state or city, for example, with any clear idea of the path of advancement open to them as employees of that *unit* of government. Instead, at best they must think in terms of promotion with a particular agency, such as a department of health or welfare. Even then, their future may be quite uncertain because of the absence of clearly established career ladders.

Employees of a governmental unit are often divided into three categories: "classified," "unclassified," and "exempt." Generally, those positions over which the central personnel authority has jurisdiction are in the *classified service.* Their selection, advancement, removal, etc. are governed by rules and regulations issued by the central agency. The *unclassified service* normally encompasses such personnel as private secretaries, deputies to executive officers, lawyers, doctors, and staffs of educational institutions. In the *exempt service* are usually found popularly elected officials, members of boards and commissions, department heads, judicial officers, and employees of the legislature. The allocation of per-

---

2. Commission of Inquiry on Public Service Personnel, *Better Government Personnel,* McGraw-Hill Book Co., New York, 1935, p. 25.

sonnel to the unclassified and exempt services is normally a matter of legislative discretion.

SOURCES OF PERSONNEL POLICIES

Formal sources of personnel policies include state constitutions and local charters, state statutes and local ordinances, and the rules and regulations issued by the central personnel agency. State constitutions and local charters often contain brief statements concerning the creation, nature, and powers of central agencies for the administration of civil service or merit systems. More detailed provisions are reserved to statutes and ordinances that outline the basic purposes and policies to be observed in personnel management, including such items as requirement of competitive examinations, prohibitions against political assessments, and procedure for the dismissal of employees. Additional details are normally set forth in rules and regulations prepared by an administrative agency.

ATTRACTING GOOD PEOPLE

Public Attitudes. In a democracy the public service is what the people make it. At least two considerations support this conclusion. In the first place, a democracy draws its public servants from the people, and they constitute a reasonably good cross section of the population. Hence, their basic ideals, aspirations, and beliefs are much the same. In the second place, the conditions under which public employees work, as well as their responsibilities, are determined at least in broad outline by the people through their representatives. Too often the canard is voiced that public employees "do not work as hard" as those in private employment, although no substantial evidence ever has been advanced to support such an assertion. Wherever peculiar circumstances lend support to that viewpoint, the explanation probably lies in lack of incentives.

Competition. Especially in periods of prosperity, governments must compete among themselves and with private employment in order to attract competent employees. Although this necessity is recognized in theory, it is often overlooked in practice. As a group, governments are *not* model employers. Consequently, it is important for each jurisdiction to follow two courses of action to obtain able employees. They must stress their strong points and strengthen their weak ones. They cannot expect their advantages to balance their disadvantages. Thus, a superior retirement program will not effectively counterbalance an inferior pay plan. It is important that the whole program of personnel management be attractive in order to be generally competitive. Furthermore, it is imperative that those persons responsible for shaping such programs *not* accept the fatalistic idea that governments are unable to compete effectively with private employment. Such a philosophy contributes to the creation of a second-rate service.

Recruitment. Recruitment encompasses those processes and practices designed to discover and attract talent into the public service. It is complete once an applicant has filled out an application blank. Although it will not always result in obtaining the most highly qualified personnel, the crucial importance of a good recruitment program is widely recognized. In the words of one acute observer, "The ultimate possibilities of solving problems of government lie in the nature of the men and women who compose the institution."[3] A poor recruitment program is likely to attract applicants who are, as a group, mediocre at best.

Although it is true that for the "selling" campaign to be successful, there must be something worthwhile to sell, the importance of techniques of salesmanship cannot be disregarded. The best recruitment practices will not produce miracles, but they play a vital role in attracting qualified people. Increasing recognition has been given recently to the validity of this assertion. For many years public jurisdictions generally followed a pattern of "passive" recruitment, characterized first by the preparation of uninteresting, unattractive announcements of job openings, followed by limited distribution for display on bulletin boards and for the files of employment agencies. Sometimes announcements appeared in the classified advertisements of larger newspapers. A good recruitment program must be designed to discover and develop sources of potential employees and to sell the public service to them. Most jurisdictions, however, have been unwilling to appropriate sufficient funds to underwrite costly recruitment efforts.

One technique possessing great potential as a recruitment device often is not classified as such. Some public jurisdictions have developed programs through which young persons still in college are brought into the service for short periods, usually during the summer. This practice is one of the soundest recruitment devices for certain types of jobs, particularly those requiring college or other specialized training. Its scope is restricted by available money and by the willingness of responsible officials to appreciate its value. At the same time it has an advantage possessed by no other practice in that it enables the recruit to get a "taste" of the service under relatively favorable circumstances.

Effective recruitment is affected adversely by lengthy delays between contact and employment, delays sometimes so long that they cause the whole process to partake of the nature of an endurance contest. A "suc-

3. Herman Finer, *The Theory and Practice of Modern Government,* rev. ed., Henry Holt and Co., New York, 1949, p. 609.

cessful" candidate for public employment often must have patience, time to spare, and a lack of attractive alternatives. These factors may result in the loss of the most highly qualified candidates. A significant advantage enjoyed by recruiting teams from private industry compared with those from public agencies is their ability to make job commitments at the time of contact. Although it may not be feasible for public agencies to emulate this practice, every effort should be made to shorten the time between arousing the interest of good applicants and offering them jobs. A 1970 study of the New York City civil service concluded that the lengthy waiting period characteristic of the selection process regularly resulted in choosing relatively weak applicants.[4]

PUTTING THE WORKER ON THE JOB

Position Classification. Included among the most important elements in any well-developed program of personnel management is a system of position classification. Although it is not important that students of state and local government be familiar with the details of this highly specialized function, a general understanding of its nature is helpful. Position classification involves the orderly arrangement and definition of categories of employment on the basis of work performed. Major groups or *classes* of positions are identified, such as clerks, stenographers, carpenters, and statisticians. Individual positions are assigned or "allocated" to the appropriate classes on the basis of the duties and level of responsibilities involved. Each class, then, includes all positions sufficiently alike to be designated by the same descriptive title, such as clerk-typist, stenographer, or budget analyst. These classes are further refined on the basis of rank, as reflected in the titles "Clerk-Typist I," "Clerk-Typist II," and "Clerk-Typist III." Incumbents of each class are expected to possess substantially the same qualifications and to receive the same scale of pay.

Although position classification does not eliminate inequities, it does diminish them appreciably. Individual inequities may be explained largely on two grounds: inaccuracy in original classification of a position, and inadequacy of procedures for reclassification. Errors are inevitable, especially in view of the necessity of frequently exercising *judgment* throughout the entire process. More important as a source of difficulty, however, is the absence of adequate reclassification procedures. Positions change as duties are added or taken away, and changes may warrant moving a position from one class to another. Even in the absence of a significant change in duties, "upgrading" a position may be required in order to retain experienced, efficient employees. Although personnel

---

4. E.S. Savas and Sigmund Ginsburg, "The Civil Service: A Meritless System?" *The Public Interest*, Summer 1973.

technicians commonly decry such action, it may be wise in terms of the effective performance of work in an agency.

In order to keep a classification plan up to date, periodic surveys are needed. Thus changes in jobs can be noted and appropriate reassignments made throughout the service, instead of being confined to agencies where officials make the loudest complaints. Only rarely do central personnel agencies have sufficient staff to perform this important task. Since they are less pressing than the demands of day-to-day tasks, surveys are often postponed indefinitely.

Examination. Once applications have been accepted for a particular opening, they must be "sifted" to check the completeness of data and to determine whether applicants possess the legal qualifications necessary for eligibility. Those who pass this first screening are then admitted to an examination. A great variety of examinations have been used in an effort to determine the fitness of applicants, and they may be classified in many ways.

Examinations are classified as *assembled* and *unassembled.* Actually, they are frequently a combination of both. When applicants are required to meet in groups for purposes of testing, the examination is designated as assembled. When an unassembled examination is used, applicants' qualifications are determined on the basis of training and experience. For certain types of positions, particularly those requiring professional training or administrative experience, the unassembled procedure is generally preferred. For others a combination may be desirable. For positions that do not require professional training or much varied experience, reliance may be placed entirely on the assembled examination.

The varieties of assembled examinations are legion, but in general they may be divided into three major types: written tests, oral interviews, and performance tests. Although written tests are subdivided into "objective" and "subjective" types, these terms are misleading. Multiple-choice, true-false, and short-answer questions are classified as *objective* because the answers do not have to be evaluated—they are definitely either "right" or "wrong." Such tests, however, are subjective in their construction, that is, in the choice of questions. Essay questions, on the other hand, are *subjective* both as to selection and grading.

A specialized variety of the written examination is the *personality* test, which has been used much more widely in industry than in government. The value of this type of test is questionable because its ability to test what it is supposed to test has not been demonstrated. Whenever evaluation of the personal traits of candidates is considered essential, the formal *oral interview* is standard practice. The oral examination normally does little more than formalize *impressions* of individuals. It is most useful as a means of observing how people react to certain stimuli under conditions of stress. A significant weakness of the oral test stems from the tendency of raters to generalize on the basis of such reactions. Thus it may be assumed that a candiate who becomes disturbed under questioning will evidence "instability" on the job. Not only may this be a false assumption, but a further difficulty arises from the fact that "stability" in this sense may not be an important qualification for the particular position. Interviews may partake of the nature of "fishing expeditions" in which interviewers make random efforts to discover unrelated bits of information about applicants. Recently, restrictions have been placed by law on questions that may be asked.

The performance test, sometimes called a "practical" test, is especially useful in measuring physical abilities and skills. Such tests usually reproduce work situations, such as those encountered by stenographers, carpenters, and cooks. Designed to discover how effectively an individual will perform under specific conditions, the performance test indicates nothing about an applicant's potential. A major disadvantage of this type of test is that it is time-consuming and often expensive to administer.

Certification and Appointment. Following examinations, the names of those who have "passed" are placed on lists of *eligibles*. When a vacancy occurs, a *requisition* is forwarded to the agency responsible for maintaining the lists, and the names of a number of eligibles are *certified* to the appointing authority. The number of eligibles that may be certified at any one time is usually limited by law, which often stipulates the "rule of three." According to this rule, only the names of the three persons receiving the highest scores on the examination for a particular type of job are certified. In some jurisdictions only the top person on the list may be certified, a practice that places great faith in the accuracy of the examining process; in others a larger number may be certified. The appointing authority may reject the first list "for cause" and request another group of eligibles. "For cause" implies that some reasonable explanation of the rejection must be given. Although this procedure may be abused, some flexibility is desirable to diminish the likelihood of appointing persons who will be "misfits" because of working conditions peculiar to a particular position.

Sometimes when a vacancy occurs no current eligibility list exists for that position. It is impossible to maintain lists of eligibles for all possible openings at any one time, perhaps with the exception of classifications in which there are a large number of positions characterized by a relatively high turnover, such as clerks and typists. Consequently, provision is normally made for *provisional* or temporary appointments until examinations are held and applicants qualify. Unless constant vigilance is exercised, temporary appointments may become permanent, even in the absence of satisfactory performance. Of course, temporary appointees should be given the opportunity to take the appropriate examinations and qualify as permanent appointees.

Veterans' Preference

Since World War I, public jurisdictions generally have followed the practice of giving priority to persons who have served honorably in the nation's armed forces.[5] A variety of methods have been used to implement this policy, but the most widespread has been to add a number of points to the veteran's examination score—usually five or ten. Disabled veterans are given more "bonus" points than those who are not handicapped. Preferred practice dictates that extra points shall be added only to passing scores, although they are sometimes added to all test results. Veterans, particularly those who are disabled, may be accorded preference ahead of all other applicants, after they have passed entrance examinations.

Controversy has centered around the use of veterans' preference. Viewpoints on the issue often are founded on emotions rather than impartial analysis. The nature of the problem has been well stated by O. G. Stahl: "In essence there are two basic philosophies underlying veteran preference in public employment: (1) the idea of preference as a continuing reward for service to the country and (2) the concept of preference as a readjustment aid to help veterans adjust to civilian life."[6] In terms of their consequences for public employment, these views are quite different. If the reward idea is accepted, the veteran is accorded a permanent privilege insofar as public employment is concerned. This practice is subject to criticism from many standpoints, not the least of which is the fact that it is diametrically opposed to the idea that civil service employment should be on the basis of merit as evidenced by fitness to fill a position and by potential for future growth. Acceptance of the readjustment concept implies the granting of such privilege only on a temporary basis, and its implications are consequently not so serious from the standpoint of efficient personnel management.

Affirmative Action

States and local governments throughout most of our history have been able to operate their personnel systems with minimal interference by the national government. As a consequence of Congressional legislation, executive action, and federal court decisions, this situation has changed. The Equal Employment Opportunity Act of 1972 brought state and local governments under the provisions of the Civil Rights Act of 1964. This act provided the statutory basis for the federal government's equal employment opportunity program, prohibiting discrimination on the basis of race, religion, sex, and national origin.

As a consequence of executive interpretation of the statutes, state and

---

5. The practice of granting preference to veterans has long been used in this country. However, it did not become widely established by law until the period following World War I.
6. O. G. Stahl, *Public Personnel Administration*, Harper & Brothers, New York, 7th ed., 1976 p. 157.

local governments have been required to do more than refrain from discrimination on prohibited grounds in their current hiring practices. They have been required to innaugurate programs designed to compensate for past deficiencies—programs designated as *affirmative action.* Supporters of these efforts claim that public employers should make special efforts to hire members of those segments of society that have experienced discrimination in the past, especially on racial, ethnic, or sexual grounds. Not only do they deserve special consideration in regard to employment opportunities but also in relation to opportunities to get ahead. Opponents maintain that there should be no "lowering of standards" to compensate for the past. They allege that such action will cause the efficiency and effectiveness of government to deteriorate. This concern is based on the assumption that it is likely to be impossible to find qualified minority candidates and women, and in some instances it is impossible to do so. However, affirmative action has promoted a wider search for talent than was previously the practice. AA was never intended to require hiring unqualified persons.

Implementation of affirmative action has involved the use of "quotas" and "goals." A quota may be defined as a specific share of a total that is due to a person or a group. Hence, the idea that certain portions of persons hired over a period of time should be blacks, women, or Spanish-Americans. A goal, on the other hand, involves a long-range commitment to create a workforce whose characteristics (especially as they relate to race and sex) reflect the characteristics of the employment market.[7] Although the statutes do not refer to quotas and goals, both have been sanctioned by the courts.

In a number of instances, minority hiring quotas have been imposed by the courts, as illustrated by *Carter* v. *Gallagher,* where a federal court ordered the Minneapolis Fire Department to hire one minority person for every three whites until a minimum of 100 minority applicants were employed.[8] Similarly, in *NAACP* v. *Allen* the federal district court required that one black trooper be hired by the Alabama Highway Patrol for each white one until the force was approximately 25 percent black.[9] More recently, some cases have brought such actions into question. For example, in *Hiatt* v. *Berkeley* a California court voided a requirement of racial quotas in city departments matching the racial composition of the local population. The court asserted that such a demand violated both the federal Civil Rights Act and the Fourteenth Amendment of the U.S. Constitution.[10]

---

7. It is interesting to note, however, that in *Rias* v. *Steamfitters Local 638*, the court asserted that a temporary numerical requirement should be viewed as a "goal" rather than a "quota" because the latter implies permanence. 501 F.2d 622 (1974).
8. 452 F.2d 315 (1971).
9. 493 F.2d 6111 (1974).
10. 149 Cal. R. 155 (1978).

THE WORKER ON THE JOB

Orientation. It is common practice for new appointees to undergo a *probationary* period of six or twelve months during which they are "on trial" to determine their suitability for the job. At any time during this period their services may be terminated. Good personnel management requires that new employees be observed carefully and *oriented* to their positions. Public jurisdictions are often negligent with regard to these matters—even more so than private employers. The attitude of new employees toward their jobs and their co-workers may be determined largely by the manner in which they are introduced to each other. Haphazard orientation is not conducive to enthusiasm, and time consumed in an adequate program of orientation is well invested. The probationary period may well be considered essential to adequate selection procedure. Responsibility for its success rests with those who directly supervise new employees.

Evaluation of Performance. Adequate determination of the effectiveness of each employee relative to the demands of the job is very difficult. Few aspects of personnel management have caused more dissatisfaction. A huge variety of methods and devices have been used to measure job effectiveness, but no generally satisfactory scheme has been devised.[11] Distrust and skepticism relative to "merit ratings" is widespread, and the obvious fallibility of many systems provides some justification for such an attitude. The failure of many rating procedures to produce the desired results has motivated the proposal that they be abandoned. Such a simple solution to the problem is not feasible because *everyone who manages people performs the act of evaluation.* The act may be formalized or completely informal and irregular. Evaluations may be based on conscientious efforts to assess the quality of employees' work and their value to the service, or they may be founded entirely on personal prejudice. The alternative to formalized systems of rating is dependence on judgment unguided by formal criteria.

Merit ratings should not serve as the *sole* basis for personnel actions, including promotions, transfers, salary changes, layoffs, and discharges. Even though they may not provide a "scientific" basis for such actions, ratings may be administered in such a manner that those concerned will *feel* that emphasis is placed on fairness and impartiality. Beyond question, evaluation devices may help to identify factors pertinent to employees' effectiveness and focus attention on their strengths and weaknesses. Such information may be used in setting up training programs and indicating how each individual may obtain the greatest benefit from them.

11. Such devices are commonly called "service ratings," "efficiency ratings," "merit ratings," or "performance reports."

In any event, it is imperative that the results of ratings *not* be filed away and seldom, if ever, consulted. If they are, employee evaluation becomes a routine task, performed as quickly as possible with a minimum of effort and reflection.

In recent years, the courts (especially federal) have insinuated themselves into the area of performance evaluation. In *Allen* v. *City of Mobile,* the court declared that service ratings used by the city in its police department were discriminatory and spelled out in considerable detail the procedures that should be followed in their administration.[12] In *Harper* v. *Mayor and City Council of Baltimore*, the court held the city fire department to be in violation of the Equal Protection Clause of the Fourteenth Amendment to the Constitution of the United States by requiring a certain time in grade to qualify for promotional exams, alleging specifically that seniority requirements penalized black officers.[13] Taking note of the fact that black employees had a lower average than whites on a subjective evaluation scheme that had not been demonstrated to be a predictor of performance, the court in *Wade* v. *Mississippi Cooperative Extension Service* found the state extension service to be in violation of the law and required modification in its system of evaluation.[14]

Promotions and Transfers. A major deterrent to effective personnel management is a feeling among many employees that there is "no place to go." The incentive of advancement resulting from superior qualifications and performance is significant for efficiency. Although many difficulties are inevitably encountered in its establishment and application, a *definite promotion policy* is vastly superior to the practice of considering promotions individually as the opportunities arise. Such a policy may be opposed because it limits the opportunity for arbitrary discretion on the part of administrators.

The use of *promotional examinations* is common in large jurisdictions operating under civil service. Although these examinations may test with reasonable accuracy the knowledge necessary to perform duties associated with a particular position, they have not yet succeeded in measuring capacity for administrative responsibility and personality traits that may be important. Promotional exams should, and usually do, include not only formal, written portions, but also an evaluation of an employee's record and experience. In combination such procedures are not entirely satisfactory, but they may be administered with better results than can be obtained by informal selection.

Although *seniority* is seldom relied upon exclusively, it should be given serious consideration along with other factors when a promotion is con-

12. 331 F. Supp. 1134 (1971).
13. 359 F. Supp. 1187 (1973).
14. 372 F. Supp. 126 (1974).

templated. Emphasis on seniority is favored generally by employees, and their viewpoint is not without foundation.[15] Reliance on seniority reduces discord and favoritism in that it is most subject to accurate, impartial measurement. Too great emphasis on this factor, however, may produce complacency and result in the advancement of mediocrity. The basic difficulty in the use of seniority as the ground for advancement is that it can reflect only quantity, not quality, of service. Used in combination with a reasonably good rating system, seniority should be given weight in a promotional program. Where the number of persons eligible to fill a vacancy is quite large, formal examinations may also be desirable.

Transfers not involving change in rank are generally used ineffectively in public jurisdictions. Nevertheless, they may be useful in meeting a variety of personnel problems such as getting employees out of "blind alley" jobs, counteracting major fluctuations in work loads, alleviating personal frictions, relieving monotony, and implementing training programs. Although the management of a large administrative unit may be able to develop a good internal program of transfers, such action should be taken in cooperation with the central personnel agency.

Compensation.   In spite of the difficulties that inevitably arise in determining salaries and wages, it is imperative that some *plan* be developed and administered as fairly as possible. If this goal is to be accomplished effectively, cooperation among the legislature, the executive branch, the central personnel agency when one exists, and the employees themselves is essential. The role of employees in determining compensation has been greatly enhanced by the growing importance of unions in the public service. A wage plan must be constructed and maintained so as to attract and retain a working force of able, efficient people.

A governmental unit's pay plan must be competitive in relation to those of other jurisdictions, both public and private. Certain disparities have existed traditionally between private and public compensation plans, especially with regard to high-level positions. Salaries and wages for employees performing routine activities in the public service have been much more competitive with private employment. Serious disparities often develop regarding professional, technical, and management personnel—crucial areas from the standpoint of program effectiveness. Low salaries accorded to top-level personnel like department heads tend to "freeze" the compensation of subordinates. Thus a public health department may experience difficulty obtaining doctors because of the low salary provided for the director of public health.

Not only should a pay plan be competitive, it should also be internally

15.   However, as noted earlier, seniority may be challenged as discriminatory against minorities who have not had equal opportunity for lengthy service. *Harper* v. *Mayor and City Council of Baltimore*, 359 F. Supp. 1187 (1973).

consistent. In some ways, this is the more crucial requirement insofar as the majority of employees are concerned. An employee may not be aware of the pay received by a counterpart in some other jurisdiction, but very probably will be aware of the compensation of co-workers. Pay inequities are regrettable, but the implication of unfairness on the part of management that stems from them is serious for morale. During periods of inflation, regular cost-of-living increases are necessary. Otherwise, the employees subsidize the employer through losses in real wages. On the average, such increases have not kept pace with inflation in the last few years.

Other Incentives. The level of compensation is recognized as a major incentive to good work, but other important ones should not be overlooked. Employees are much concerned about such matters as hours of work, vacations, leaves, suggestion programs, grievance procedures, and retirement provisions. In most jurisdictions with civil service, hours of work, vacations, and leaves have been largely standardized. Reasonably liberal policies in these areas help to offset inadequacies in pay. Vacation periods ranging from two to four weeks per year depending on length of service are common. Government policies with regard to vacations are often more liberal than those in private employment.

Until recent years, the removal of public employees because of age or disability was often handled in a haphazard and unjust manner. Consequently, "payroll pensioners" were retained on the job or allowed to become public charges, and employees injured in the line of duty became objects of charity. The federal Social Security Act has provided impetus toward improvement in public retirement practices in order that they might be somewhat competitive with private employment.[16] Most states now have retirement programs covering all full-time personnel, many of them participating in Social Security. All states have retirement programs covering selected groups of employees. A somewhat comparable situation exists on the local level, but small jurisdictions operate under a severe handicap because of an insufficient number of employees to establish a sound retirement program. Statewide systems in which local governmental units may participate are highly desirable.

When both the employer and the employee make formal contributions toward the employee's retirement, the system is said to be *contributory*. When such responsibility rests solely on the employer, the system is termed *noncontributory*. In recent years, an increasing number of governmental jurisdictions have begun to make the full contribution to employee

---

16. Retirement systems existed much earlier in some states and municipalities. Massachusetts adopted the first general state retirement law in 1911, followed by Connecticut, Maine, New York, New Jersey, and Pennsylvania during the succeeding dozen years. The first municipal pension fund was established for New York City policemen in 1857. All of the early systems applied only to selected groups of employees.

retirement programs. These systems may operate under a *cash-disbursement* plan, in which money is appropriated by the government during each fiscal period to cover the benefit payments anticipated during that time. The longer the plan is in existence, the larger the appropriations must be. Others are administered by means of an *actuarial reserve,* or "pay-as-you-go" plan, in which contributions are made regularly to a fund that is built up for each employee during employment. Money in this reserve is then invested, and the contributions and earnings are figured to anticipate and provide for future retirement payments as well as withdrawals resulting from changes in employment and death. In the more adequate systems, retirement payments average at least fifty per cent of an employee's income over a specified period of time, such as the last five or ten years of employment. Membership in retirement systems usually is compulsory for all eligible employees.

Employee Conduct.   The position of government workers differs from that of other persons because in a sense they are a repository of public faith and trust. Accordingly, the public employees' attitudes and behavior are more subject to popular reproach than is the conduct of the ordinary citizen, and the seriousness of their ethical and moral deviations is magnified. General distrust and suspicion of government may result, at least temporarily, from one or a few instances of unwise conduct in the public service.

Every government has the unquestioned right to specify in detail the conduct expected of its employees *on the job.* Attempts to regulate conduct *off the job* are different. Illegal conduct cannot be condoned. Efforts to require private conduct on the part of public employees that is significantly different from that expected of people in general tends to place public servants in a category apart, an undesirable situation in a democratic society. Potential recruits to the public service may hesitate to place themselves in such a position.

A major problem of public employees, particularly those under civil service and certain merit systems, is the extent to which they may participate, if at all, in political activity. *Political neutrality* on the part of civil servants in the performance of their duties is generally considered desirable. At the same time, participation in public affairs by interested and informed citizens strengthens democratic institutions. Logic dictates that some of those most able to participate intelligently are among public servants. The basic query is, "To what extent are public employees to be limited politically?" No easy answer to this question, whether positive or negative, can withstand critical analysis.

Through the Hatch Acts and other requirements, the national government has made strenuous efforts to "neutralize" federal civil servants.[17]

17.   Provisions of the Hatch Acts extend to state and local personnel paid from federal funds.

Most state and local governments have not found it necessary or wise to go so far, although civil service and merit system laws generally provide some restrictions on the political activities of employees. Discretion should be the rule. Some limitations on political activity are desirable, but too great severity makes public employment unattractive to many persons who are vitally interested in public affairs.

Training. Although training programs for public employees are frequently neglected, no program of personnel administration can be considered complete unless it gives much attention to the development of employees. Conceived broadly, training occurs regularly as a result of increased familiarity and facility with the duties of a position. In the usual sense, training is apart from routine work. The basic steps in a formal training program are: identification of needs, development of programs and choice of techniques of execution, implementation of program, and checking on reactions and results.

In spite of its importance, formal training has been traditionally neglected in public jurisdictions, much more so than in large private concerns. Reliance has been placed on the costly practice of learning by doing. Today many varieties of programs and techniques are included under *in-service training.* Formal courses, institutes, demonstrations, apprenticeships, and internships are included, to name only a few. Especially valuable are programs designed to improve opportunities for promotion. Development and implementation of such undertakings in large jurisdictions require the services of specially trained persons, for whose salaries legislatures often are unwilling to appropriate money. A successful training program requires cooperation from all concerned, not only the efforts of training specialists.

REMOVING THE "WRONG" PEOPLE

Necessity for Occasional Removals. In all organizations, regardless of the care with which employees are selected, it is sometimes necessary to remove incumbents from their positions. Contrary to a popular misconception, employees are frequently discharged at all levels of government. Uninformed persons may assert that it is impossible to dismiss someone who has "tenure," but the fact is that all jurisdictions provide for separation *when the work situation demands it.*

Unregulated "firing" of employees under civil service and merit systems is generally not permitted. Procedural requirements are designed to guarantee that persons shall be recruited, examined, appointed, paid, and promoted with careful regard for job responsibilities. It is only logical that the same principle apply to dismissals. Consequently, laws and regulations stipulate that certain procedures be observed in discharging employees, both for their benefit and for the benefit of the service.

Open vs. Closed Back Door. Most jurisdictions set forth at some length the procedural requirements that must be followed in removals, including formal, written notice stating the grounds for discharge, and an opportunity for a hearing. Laws require review of dismissals allegedly made on racial, political, or religious grounds, and they empower central personnel agencies to reinstate any employee whom they find was removed on such grounds. When employees are dismissed "for cause" as required by law and no questions pertaining to race, politics, or religion are raised, authority to make the final decision may be vested either with the employing agency or with the central personnel agency. If final responsibility rests with the employing agency, the *open back door* is said to exist; if it rests (on appeal) with the central agency, the arrangement is referred to as the *closed back door.*

Even with the open back door it is possible for a central personnel agency to review cases of removal "for cause." Where this procedure is provided, the function of the agency is to consider the sufficiency of the stipulated grounds for discharge and to make recommendations as to the best course of action. Responsibility for the final decision rests, nevertheless, with the employing agency. The open back door is generally preferred by operating officials, and employees prefer the closed back door because it provides them with additional protection against possible arbitrary action. Despite opinions often voiced to the contrary, the fact is that appeals systems have resulted more often in approving rather than in reversing removals.

Transfers. Circumstances indicating a need to move an employee from a particular position may not justify dismissal. Instead, a change of surroundings may be in order, and a *transfer* may serve the purpose admirably. In this way an employee may move to another position in the same class situated in another organizational unit. Unfortunately, transfers without change in rank are generally not used effectively in public jurisdictions. This fact is explained in part by the reluctance of a supervisor to accept someone who is transferred from another position because of the implication of lack of success in the former job. Such prejudice may be decreased by a program of regular, planned transfers among agencies for the benefit of employees, who may in this way increase their potential for advancement. Personnel in small agencies are especially handicapped by a lack of opportunity to transfer.

EMPLOYEE ORGANIZATION

Importance of Organization. Free people tend to combine in order to further their interests and objectives. Public employees are no different in this regard, in spite of a widespread feeling that they should be. A major function of personnel management is to establish a cooperative relationship with employee organizations and attempt to arrive at solutions to any clashes and disagreements that occur. The rapid increase in the number and size of organizations among public employees in recent years reflects a general feeling that their common interests and needs can best be met through organized effort.

Although the detailed objectives of public employee organizations differ from time to time and place to place, certain major categories may be identified: (1) establishing and strengthening the merit and career concepts, (2) emphasis on seniority and tenure, (3) improvements in wages and hours, (4) more adequate retirement programs, (5) improved machinery for handling grievances, and (6) "fringe benefits." All of these are entirely legitimate objectives, and their realization results in making the public service more attractive.

A major concern of many public employee organizations has been more widespread recognition of the importance of merit and career practices. Many such organizations have lobbied before legislative bodies for improvements in personnel practices. (It must be admitted, however, that their programs have been motivated sometimes by selfish interests contrary to best personnel practices.) Also, employee groups have functioned to bring attention to legitimate grievances of public employees. Complaints supported by organizations representing large numbers of employees and presented by competent people are more likely to receive favorable consideration than the "gripes" of individuals.

In recent years a number of states have passed laws authorizing collective bargaining or similar procedures for their employees. Over half of the states have granted the right to organize and bargain collectively to some or all employees. (Collective bargaining is the process whereby employees and management participate mutually in making decisions concerning conditions of work.) Some of the states have imposed upon management the obligation to engage in collective bargaining and have created machinery to guarantee that such efforts shall be undertaken in "good faith." A few states, including Alaska, Hawaii, Minnesota, Oregon, and Pennsylvania have extended to their employees the right to strike.

Right to Strike. Strikes by federal employees are forbidden by law. Similar legislation is found in many states and localities, but a policy of silence has been observed in some jurisdictions. This situation is probably explained by the fact that "A study of judicial decisions relating to the right of public employees to strike . . . leads to the conclusion that there is no inherent right to strike against the government, and it would appear that a statute prohibiting such strikes is unnecessary."[18] Furthermore, the constitutions of some public employee organizations explicitly disavow the use of the strike.

---

18. H. Eliot Kaplan, *The Law of Civil Service*, Matthew Bender & Co., New York, 1958, p. 325.

In spite of legal restrictions and unsympathetic public opinion, many strikes by public employees have occurred. Furthermore, in recent years there has been a notable increase in the frequency of strikes, especially at the local level, among such professional personnel as teachers, nurses, and welfare workers, as well as employees of sanitation departments. Arguments advanced against permitting public employees to strike usually stress the sovereign nature of government and the urgency of its functions. Emphasis on sovereignty in this context harks back to the outmoded concept that "the king can do no wrong." The alleged life-or-death character of all governmental activities was refuted by L. D. White years ago:

> The inconvenience caused by a public service strike . . . is not necessarily so great as that which would be involved in a stoppage in some privately managed undertakings. A strike on the nation's railroads . . . would bring instant disaster to the whole country . . . a strike of milk handlers would be as grave as a strike of almost any group of municipal employees. The relative inconvenience of a strike of street maintenance men, or of public welfare case workers, or of seamen on a government-owned barge line is clearly less.[19]

A realistic distinction between those workers who may strike and those who may not must rest on the nature of their work rather than on the nature of their employer. Whether in private industry or the public service, the potential dangers and discomforts associated with strikes can be forestalled by good personnel management. Equitable working conditions, a spirit of teamwork between employees and management, recognition of the right of collective representation by employees of their needs, and adequate grievance procedures are far more effective in building an efficient organization than restrictive measures designed to curtail employee activities.

ORGANIZATION FOR CENTRAL PERSONNEL MANAGEMENT

Bipartisan Commission. Where general civil service laws exist, responsibility for personnel management is divided between a central agency and operating or "line" agencies. Impetus for this arrangement stemmed originally from the desire to remove personnel administration from "politics." The belief was that this goal could be best accomplished by creating an independent commission that could withstand attacks from spoilsmen. Consequently, the *bipartisan commission* or *board* is the traditional and still dominant organizational pattern for central personnel management. Commission members in most instances are appointed by the chief executive with senatorial approval for long terms, staggered to promote continuity of policy and to curtail control by the appointing authority.

---

19. L. D. White, "Strikes in the Public Service," *Public Personnel Review,* January 1949.

Conceived to implement the negative goal of "keeping the rascals and incompetents out of public office," bipartisan commissions undoubtedly have contributed much to the improvement of public personnel management. They have several weaknesses, however, that tend to make them ill-suited to implement the modern emphasis on positive objectives that necessitate strong leadership. In this regard, attention is usually directed to the emphasis on political allegiance in choosing members, and the lack of expert knowledge of personnel matters on the part of commissioners, often resulting in indecision and lack of decisive action. These difficulties can be largely overcome, but a serious, often neglected problem remains, namely, inadequacy of time available to the commissioners. Standard practice has been that commissioners are chosen from among persons who have achieved prominence in some field such as law, education, or mass communication. They are busy people who may experience difficulty in allocating sufficient time to a sideline—even an important one like serving on a civil service commission which may meet only twice a month. Consequently, the knowledge and leadership needed to meet personnel problems are not forthcoming.

Obviously, such multimembered bodies cannot administer directly the details of personnel management. In order to meet this need, commissions follow the practice of appointing someone, often called a director, to administer their policies and all pertinent laws. The director may be required by law to be a "career person" in the sense that competence in the field of personnel management must have been demonstrated. In any event, the duties of such a position require impartiality and nonpartisanship as well as technical competence if civil service is to function most effectively.

Single Director.   Under the single director arrangement, central administration of personnel matters is lodged entirely in one individual appointed by and responsible to the chief executive. Although found in a few localities and in Illinois and Maryland, this organizational pattern has not been widely adopted. The main arguments in its favor are that it centralizes personnel management under the chief executive and facilitates quickness of action when necessary. It is argued that by placing responsibility with the chief executive, leadership is facilitated. Thus, if the governor favors a program to improve the compensation of civil servants, the position of a personnel director *of the governor's choosing* is greatly strengthened with the public, the legislature, and with members of the governor's party.

Single Director with Commission.   The Model State Civil Service Law advances a proposal designed to combine the advantages of both of the structural patterns described above and at the same time to overcome their weaknesses. Provision is made in the Model Law for a director of personnel who shall be appointed by and serve at the pleasure of the chief executive. The director is empowered to direct all administrative and technical activities of the personnel department. The law also provides for an advisory board appointed by the chief executive, subject to legislative confirmation. Members of this board may be removed only "for cause" following an opportunity for a public hearing.

In the Model Law provision also is made for separation of administrative responsibilities, at least partially, from those designated as *quasi-judicial*. The law provides for a hearing officer, to be appointed by the advisory board. This officer may be removed by the chief executive only "for cause," following an opportunity for a public hearing. The hearing officer reviews employee appeals resulting from alleged adverse employer action, including but not limited to demotions, dismissals, and suspensions, and then forwards recommendations to the chief executive for "appropriate action."

It is impossible to say that any one form of organization for personnel management is universally preferable. The most desirable type depends upon the major functions that the central agency is supposed to perform. Also, the total environment in which the system must operate requires consideration. Local attitudes, beliefs, practices, and customs vitally affect the way in which any system operates. If emphasis is on negative "police" functions, the bipartisan board or commission may serve satisfactorily, assuming appointment by the board of someone competent to administer the activities required by law. Whenever the need is for a "positive" program designed to attack and solve operational problems, a single director appointed by the chief executive and assisted by an agency created to hear appeals and to participate in rulemaking presents an attractive alternative. Under such an arrangement, it is especially important for chief executives to pledge unqualified determination to maintain an effective public service through support of the merit idea. This consideration further emphasizes the importance of competent, well-informed chief executives.

The Nature and Legal Position of Local Governments

17

While the spotlight of citizen interest focuses on national and international affairs and shines less intensely on the activities of state governments, the functions of local governments may be obscured in the shadows. Many factors combine to produce this situation, not the least of which is a difference in the dramatic quality of the tasks involved. "No incumbent mayor or city councilman will ever sign a treaty of peace ending all war; no city engineer will ever build a hydrogen bomb; no police chief will ever command a victorious United Nations Army; but these local officials . . . will determine whether the several communities in which we live will remain relatively civilized and decent."[1] People tend to take their local governments for granted and to forget that they provide such essential services as public education, welfare and health programs, utilities, streets and roads, fire and police protection, airports, and waste disposal. Without these local activities, the nature of American society would be drastically altered. Hardly anyone would maintain that the change would be an improvement.

Interest in local affairs occasionally becomes very strong. As a result of outbursts of civic virtue and the strenuous efforts of small groups of practical reformers, tremendous improvements have highlighted the history of local government during the twentieth century. Lincoln Steffens wrote of widespread municipal corruption in 1902 and 1903, and he concluded that the greatest need was an awakening of the people's conscience.[2] Stirred by the disclosure of Steffens and other "muckrakers" and spurred on by the efforts of groups dedicated to civic reform, the people demanded and obtained improvements in municipal government.

1. S. K. Bailey, H. D. Samuel, and S. Baldwin, *Government in America*, Holt-Rinehart-Winston, New York, 1957, p. 455.
2. Written as a series of articles in *McClure's Magazine*, Steffens' observations were published in the well known volume entitled *The Shame of the Cities*, McClure, Phillips and Co., New York, 1904.

Graft, corruption, and bribery still exist, but they are no longer regarded as inevitable accompaniments of local government.

What Is a "Unit of Local Government"?

According to the U.S. Bureau of the Census, a unit of local government must exhibit three qualifications. First, it must exist as an *organized entity,* possessing organization and some minimum powers such as the right to enter contracts and own property. Second, it must have *governmental character* as an agency of the public, to whom it must be accountable. Its officers must be elected or appointed by elected officials. Third, it must possess *substantial autonomy,* particularly as reflected in the right to prepare a budget and raise the revenue necessary to meet it. In his study of governmental units, Professor Anderson has identified seven characteristics: (1) territory, (2) population, (3) organization, (4) separate legal identity, (5) a degree of legal independence, (6) authority to exercise governmental powers, and (7) the power to raise revenue.[3] Viewed in the light of *all* these requirements, administrative areas such as judicial districts, election districts, police precincts, and city wards do not qualify as "governmental units."

NUMBER AND VARIETY OF LOCAL UNITS

The serious study of local government is greatly complicated by the multiplicity of units. In 1977, the Bureau of the Census counted 79,913 units of local government in the United States. This figure included 3,042 counties, 18,862 municipalities, 16,822 towns and townships, 15,174 school districts and 25,962 other special districts. In the last decade, the number of local units has remained quite stable, declining less than two per cent. Since 1942, however, there has been a significant decrease of about forty-one per cent, attributable almost entirely to a steady reduction in the number of school districts through consolidation. Understanding the nature of these local governments requires a brief examination of each type.

Counties

Most people in the United States live within the boundaries of a county. No organized counties exist in Connecticut, Rhode Island, and the District of Columbia.[4] Also, the inhabitants of some three dozen of the larger

---

3. William Anderson, *The Units of Local Government in the United States,* Public Administration Service, No. 83, Chicago, 1949, pp. 8–10.
4. In Alaska counties are called "boroughs" and in Louisiana "parishes."

cities in Virginia are not subject to county government. Although counties traditionally have been primarily units of rural government, they regularly provide services to urban dwellers. In legal terminology, counties often are designated as "quasi-municipal corporations," reflecting their nature as administrative subdivisions of a state, created to administer functions of statewide concern, such as law enforcement, justice, and welfare. Since counties also provide services of special interest to their residents, such as libraries, recreational facilities, and record maintenance, they partake of the nature of a municipality.

Although counties are found almost everywhere in the United States, they are not uniformly important. New England counties perform very limited functions because of the primacy of the town. In about one third of the states, located in the northern portion of the country, counties share their responsibilities with townships. In the South and the West the county has no peer as a unit of rural local government.

Municipalities

No precise, universally accepted definition of "municipality" or "municipal corporation" exists. The Bureau of the Census takes the position that a municipality is an incorporated political subdivision of a state within which a government has been established to provide services for a concentration of population within a defined area. Several implications in this definition need to be spelled out. Like counties, municipalities are political subdivisions of the states in which they are situated. Unlike counties, however, municipalities are organized (incorporated) primarily to provide services desired by *concentrations of population.* But municipalities are *not* organized *solely* for this purpose. They also act as agents of the state in providing certain services to their inhabitants, such as law enforcement and health protection. An important consideration with regard to municipal corporations not clearly indicated in the Bureau's definition is that municipalities normally are created at the behest of their residents rather than by the desire of the state legislature.

Cities. Depending on local custom and statutory provisions, municipalities may be known as "cities," "towns," "villages," or "boroughs." The meaning of these terms varies among the states. Larger municipalities everywhere are designated as cities, but the laws of some states provide that all municipal corporations organized in a certain manner shall be known as cities regardless of size. Thus New York is a city, and so is Greenhorn, Oregon, with a 1970 population of three. Although laws regularly stipulate that a minimum number of persons must live in a given area before a municipality may be organized, later shifts in population may reduce it to little more than a "ghost town."

Towns. Much confusion is associated with the use of "town." The term sometimes is used to refer to a unit of rural government more properly called a "township." Unincorporated settlements with no governmental organization of their own may be called "towns." Basic units of general local government in the New England states are "towns."[5] In popular usage in some states, any small municipality may be referred to loosely as a "town." In order to qualify formally as a type of municipality, however, a town must be *incorporated,* that is, certain steps taken as required by law to bring it into legal existence for the purpose of providing services to its inhabitants.

Villages. The smallest of municipalities are commonly known as villages. Indeed, the concentration of population in a village may be so small that it is in reality a unit of rural government. On the other hand, quite populous places may continue to be designated as villages because the official action required for change to some other designation is not taken. Suburban communities, located near large cities, may be organized as villages. Generally, the governmental organization of a village is rather simple, and its powers are less extensive than those of larger municipalities.

Boroughs. In Connecticut, New Jersey, and Pennsylvania, certain municipalities are designated as boroughs. They differ in no essential respects from incorporated towns and villages in other states. Boroughs were established in New Jersey and Pennsylvania during the colonial period and were modeled after the English borough; lawmakers in these states have chosen to continue the use of the term. The first borough was organized in Connecticut in 1800, and about a dozen boroughs now exist there. These units of government are not to be confused with the Alaskan borough, which is a substitute for the county.

Towns and Townships

In almost half of the states there are governmental subdivisions known as towns or townships.[6] Although the Bureau of the Census classifies all of these governments as townships, some distinctions can be made. New England towns generally are not municipal corporations and have been created directly by state statutory provisions. Except for cities, towns are the chief units of local government in the New England states. Their importance stems from the fact that they administer functions performed elsewhere by counties and by small incorporated towns and villages. Consequently, a New England town may function as a unit of rural or urban government and sometimes as both.

---

5. Classified as townships by the Bureau of the Census.
6. These "civil" townships must be distinguished from *congressional townships,* which are areas for land surveying and are not governments.

In a band of states running westward from New York and New Jersey, townships are significant units of rural government.[7] Although townships occasionally are active in highly urbanized places, particularly in New York, New Jersey, and Pennsylvania, they normally provide a number of services such as roads, poor relief, and property assessment in rural areas. Commonly, such activities are shared with counties. Townships often serve also as election districts. Recent years have witnessed a trend for townships to lose responsibilities to the counties in which they are located.

Special Districts

As the name indicates, a special district is organized for the provision of a *special* function.[8] Hence, a special district is characteristically a unifunctional unit, providing only one service to the people residing within its boundaries. Occasionally, two or three related functions are provided, such as water and fire protection. Although most special districts are small in area, some are quite large and many include several counties. Great variety in organizational patterns characterize these governmental units, which as a group provide many services, including education, water, sanitation, flood control, street lighting, recreational facilities, and fire protection. Special districts (including school) account for just over one-half of all local governments in the United States.

Complexity of Picture

Because of sheer numbers, local governments present a complicated and confusing picture. Other considerations such as difference in powers, variations in structure, and relations with the parent state and other local units contribute to the difficulties involved in any attempt to describe their nature and their role in relation to the people who live under them. The picture is further complicated by the fact that the typical citizen lives under at least five or six "layers" of government: national, state, county, municipal, town or township, and at least one special district. This number may rise easily to ten or more when several special districts are superimposed. Often the multiplicity of governmental units under which citizens live is not appreciated by them because of the lack of impact these units have on their lives.

7. These units are called "towns" in New York, but they are functionally like townships in other states and unlike New England towns. The township states are Illinois, Indiana, Kansas, Michigan, Minnesota, Missouri, Nebraska, New Jersey, New York, North Dakota, Ohio, Pennsylvania, South Dakota, Washington, and Wisconsin. Not all the territory of each of these states is divided into townships.
8. As a result of this characteristic, special districts are sometimes described as *ad hoc* districts, indicating that they are created "for this purpose."

City dwellers are constantly aware of the existence of their city because of its ever-present physical manifestations, such as streets, police-officers, parks, and water supply. They may at the same time almost forget that they are county residents because county services are not so important to their day-to-day existence—at least until they receive their tax bill. Urbanites, and perhaps rural residents, may overlook the activities of a sanitary, park, library, flood control, or utility district in which they live, thinking that such services are provided by the city or the county. The reality of the typical multiplicity of layers is further obscured by the fact that the citizen commonly receives a consolidated property tax bill from the county, a bill which includes levies imposed by several governmental units.

The usual pattern of local government across the country is complex, and it is greatly complicated by numerous exceptional situations. A few examples are illustrative. Cities are normally located within counties, both legally and geographically, but the counties of Bronx, Kings, New York, Queens, and Richmond are subdivisions of New York City and are not considered as separate governments. Some three dozen "independent" Virginia cities are legally outside counties and constitute "islands" of government surrounded by county areas. Similar situations exist with regard to Baltimore and St. Louis. Although still in existence, Iowa townships are so lacking in functions that they are no longer considered as governmental units. California, Montana, and North Carolina have no township governments, but counties are divided into townships that serve merely as election districts. Michigan cities are outside townships, but villages remain in them. In New England, cities are usually excluded, while villages are within the jurisdiction of town government.

It is very difficult to acquire complete, detailed knowledge of even a major portion of all local units. It is feasible, however, to obtain sufficient information and insight to understand their general nature, appreciate their importance, and become familiar with their problems. Armed with such knowledge, a citizen is equipped to participate intelligently in the public affairs of the community.

LEGAL STATUS OF LOCAL GOVERNMENTS

Each of the fifty states is a *unitary* government. Consequently, each possesses complete authority and control over local governments within its boundaries. As "creatures of the state," local units are created by and derive their powers from state law, either constitutional or statutory. The accuracy of this observation is more readily apparent in relation to quasi-municipalities than in relation to "true" municipal corporations. The former, particularly counties and townships, function as administrative subdivisions of their states.[9] The latter are organized at the behest of local residents and have as their chief responsibility the provision of services to their residents, but they are still created under the authority of state law.[10] The states follow a variety of procedures in the creation of municipal corporations.

CHARTERS

Special Charters

Immediately following independence from England, the first state legislatures assumed responsibility for organizing local governments. Each municipality was organized and granted powers by a separate, special legislative act called a charter. This practice was standard procedure for about three-quarters of a century, and it still exists in a few states.[11] Although special charters provide flexibility to whatever degree the legislature is willing to sanction, they subject municipalities to regular, continuing, and detailed legislative supervision. Occasionally, legislatures have taken advantage of the opportunity to dictate by controlling local services and the construction of public buildings.

Inadequate, ill-considered, sometimes punitive laws caused a reaction against special laws of all kinds, and most states have included provisions in their constitutions designed to prohibit or severely curb their enactment. Constitutions sometimes prohibit special legislation whenever a general law can be made applicable. A more satisfactory type of restriction, and the one most widely employed, itemizes subjects upon which special laws are specifically forbidden, usually including certain local affairs. Instead, other methods of organizing and controlling municipal corporations were devised.

General Charters

Reflecting a strong reaction against special local acts, some states went to the opposite extreme and provided that all municipalities should be organized under the same laws. Providing the same form of government and the same powers for all cities prevented discrimination and created uniformity—in fact, too much uniformity. It is not feasible to govern all

9. County home rule, provided in some twenty states, does not basically change this relationship. In these states, counties are granted by state law more freedom in certain areas, especially with regard to governmental structure. See Chapter 19.
10. For a classic statement of this rule by the U.S. Supreme Court, see *Barnes* v. *District of Columbia*, 91 U.S. 540 (1875). See also Eugene McQuillin, *The Law of Municipal Corporations*, 3rd ed., Callaghan and Co., Chicago, 1949, sec. 4.03.
11. The use of special legislation to provide municipal charters is still common in the New England states, Delaware, Georgia, and Tennessee.

communities alike. Differences in size produce differences in needs and problems. Governments of large, complex cities require more varied authority than the governments of small, relatively simple ones. Local preferences vary, and the people in one place may prefer a form of government quite different from that of their neighbors in a nearby community. The needs of some cities may change rapidly while those of others may remain rather static.

Classified Charters

In an effort to give recognition to different local needs, states have adopted plans whereby municipalities, especially cities, are classified into groups on the basis of population. Localities within each class are treated alike, each operating under a charter enacted by the legislature and applicable to all local units within a certain class. For example, the cities of a state might be classified into six groups according to population as follows: I—over 500,000; II—100,000 to 500,000; III—50,000 to 100,000; IV—25,000 to 50,000; V—10,000 to 25,000; VI—under 10,000. All cities within the same group or class would be governed by the same statutory provisions, with those in Class I enjoying greatest authority and those in Class VI the least. Of course, some powers would be common to all, such as regulating traffic, paving streets, and building city halls.

Designed to minimize discrimination and at the same time to provide flexibility, classification systems have proved generally superior to special acts or general charters. Special treatment for individual cities, especially the largest ones in a state, is possible under a classification system. In terms of the six hypothetical classifications set forth in the preceding paragraph, one charter would be applicable only to city A and another applicable only to city B if they were the only cities in groups I and II, respectively. It is possible for a legislature to construct a classification scheme specifically in order to give special attention to certain cities. It is fairly common practice to have the largest city in a state occupying a class by itself, and occasionally other classes cover such a small population range that only one city is affected.

A basic weakness exists in all schemes for classifying municipalities, even those that are administered in the fairest manner possible. Every such arrangement must be based on the assumption that communities of approximately the same size have similar needs. They may, or they may not. Differing social and economic conditions, rate of growth, and age are illustrative of many factors that impose different demands upon local governments. An allied problem stems from the fact that a city may be required to change its form of government when it moves from one population class to another. Under some circumstances a change may be desirable, but under others it may only serve to disturb well balanced working arrangements.

Optional Charters

A noteworthy modification of traditional classification practices is provided by use of the optional charter. This device, used in a few states, makes available to all cities, or those within each population group, alternative forms of government that are spelled out in detail by statutory provisions. For example, residents of Class III cities may be able to choose among three types, while the inhabitants of Class I cities may have only two options. The number and variety of choices may be the same for all cities, or they may differ from some or all classes. Sub-options may also be allowed, providing minor variations within a major type. In this way a rather wide range of choices may be available from which the people of each community may choose, but no modifications may be made in any plan. Each option must be accepted or rejected in its entirety.

Home Rule Charters

Some forty states provide a significant modification of traditional practices for the provision of local charters through home rule, either constitutional or statutory (see Table 17.1). "Constitutional home rule is a form of state-local relationship in which local governmental units are granted, by state constitutional provision, authority to exercise certain local powers free from control by the state legislature."[12] Under statutory home rule, a comparable relationship is established by legislative act. Since a legislature may take away whatever authority it gives, statutory home rule is different from constitutional—so different that "home rule" is sometimes ascribed only to those states where it is based on constitutional provisions.

In spite of variations in detail, constitutional home rule is always intended to increase the freedom and authority of those units of government to which it applies.[13] This freedom relates to two areas of responsibility, structural and functional. Uniformly, the residents of home rule communities are empowered to prepare and adopt charters and provide the form of government they prefer. Home rule is also supposed to provide local control over matters primarily of local concern as distinguished from those in which the state has paramount interest. Although this statement of the functional significance of home rule may be helpful as a guide, it is pregnant with difficulties. Specifically, what matters are of local concern and what matters are of state concern? Who is to make the decisions?

12. Clyde F. Snider, *American State and Local Government,* Appleton-Century-Crofts, Inc., New York, 1965, p. 72.
13. The fact that a state has home rule does not mean that *all* local governments of any given type enjoy its advantage. In about one fourth of the home rule states specific minimum population requirements exist for cities, commonly ranging from 2,000 to 10,000, and only communities of stipulated size enjoy home rule privileges.

Table 17.1
Municipal Home Rule

I. CONSTITUTIONAL HOME RULE STATES

State	Date	Application
Alaska	1959	First class cities
Arizona	1912	Cities of 3,500 or more
California	1879	Cities and city-counties of more than 3,500
Colorado	1902	Cities and towns of 2,000 or more
Hawaii	1959	All political subdivisions
Illinois	1970	Any municipality over 25,000
Iowa	1968	Any municipality
Kansas	1960	All cities
Louisiana	1952	Any municipality
Maine	1970	Any municipality
Maryland[1]	1954	Cities and towns
Massachusetts	1966	Cities and towns
Michigan	1908	Each city and village
Minnesota	1898	Any city or village
Missouri	1875	Any city over 5,000
Montana	1972	Incorporated cities and towns
Nebraska	1912	Any city over 5,000
Nevada	1924	Any city or town
New Hampshire[2]	1966	Cities and towns
New Mexico	1970	Municipalities
New York	1923	Cities, towns, and villages
Ohio	1912	Any municipality
Oklahoma	1908	Any city of 2,000 or more
Oregon	1906	Every city and town
Pennsylvania	1902	Cities, towns, and boroughs
Rhode Island	1951	Every city and town
South Dakota	1962	Any municipality
Tennessee	1953	Any municipality
Texas	1912	Cities over 5,000
Utah	1932	Any incorporated city or town
Washington	1889	Any city of 10,000 or more
West Virginia	1936	Each municipal incorporation over 2,000
Wisconsin	1924	Cities and villages
Wyoming	1972	Cities and towns

II. LEGISLATIVE HOME RULE STATES

State	Date	Application
Connecticut	1951	Any city, town, or borough
Florida	1915	Every city and town
Georgia	1947	Any municipal corporation
Indiana	1971	Every city
North Carolina	1917	Any municipality
South Carolina	1899	Any city or town
Vermont	1969	Any municipality

1. Home rule for Baltimore only was adopted in 1915.
2. Legislature permitted to authorize cities and towns to adopt charters.

Any effort to allocate municipal functions on the basis of primacy of local or state interest is doomed to failure. Local interest may be considered paramount in such matters as terms and qualifications of local officials, procedure for the enactment of ordinances, recreational facilities, standards for street cleaning and lighting, municipal utility services, and zoning ordinances. State interest may be conceded as paramount, on the other hand, with regard to municipal debt limits and major taxes, jurisdiction of local courts, procedure for annexation of territory, and regulation of private utilities. Both levels of government usually exercise considerable authority in relation to education, welfare, sanitation, the police power, and certain types of physical planning. Such an arbitrary and incomplete division of responsibilities does not describe the situation in any particular state, but it provides concrete illustrations of the complexity of the problem.

Who makes the decisions concerning the allocation of responsibilities in a home rule state? The people themselves and state agencies do so, with their determination taking the form of specific constitutional provisions, statutes, court decisions, or acquiescence in the assumption of functions by local governments. If a favorable climate of opinion exists toward local self-government in the courts and the legislature of a state, chances for the effective implementation of home rule are excellent. On the other hand, if unfavorable or hostile attitudes exist, no conceivable constitutional provision will provide effective self-government for localities. Since attitudes and traditions differ from state to state, similar constitutional provisions produce dissimilar results.

Rarely have all communities within any state received their charters in the same manner. In a state with general classification statutes, cities may continue to operate under charters granted earlier by special act of the legislature. In an optional charter state, a municipality may function under a charter granted by special act or provided under a general classification law. Municipalities entitled to acquire home rule charters may choose to retain charters granted by special law, by classification statute, or by optional charter procedure. Such home-rule communities, however, may amend their old charters by local action without replacing them. Regardless of the manner in which it is acquired, every charter must be in harmony with the state constitution and general laws.

STATE ADMINISTRATIVE CONTROL AND SUPERVISION

A major aspect of the recent history of local government in the United States has been the continuing struggle, particularly on the part of municipalities, to reduce legislative domination and interference with regard to local affairs. At the same time, it has been generally recognized that each state, having an interest in many local activities, may exercise reasonable control and supervision. When such control takes the form of statutory provisions, such as a specific debt limit, enforcement must normally be sought through the courts. Not only does a restriction of this type possess the disadvantage of rigidity, its enforcement is cumbersome. As the number and variety of governmental activities have increased rapidly during the past generation or so, the need for frequency and flexibility of supervision has grown. Activities and policies of a local government may affect not only its own residents but also people outside its jurisdiction. For example, a substandard health program may threaten the welfare of residents, visitors, and persons who live nearby.

Since increased supervision of any type runs contrary to demands for local self-government, it is often opposed by local residents and officials. Nevertheless, the necessities of modern living have dictated increased control in certain areas, control sufficiently adequate and flexible to meet the needs of each individual community. Seven methods or procedures are especially noteworthy: (1) advice and information, (2) reports, (3) grants-in-aid, (4) inspection, (5) review and approval, (6) state appointment and removal of local officers, and (7) instructions to local agencies. Viewed legally, the first three of these techniques are noncoercive in that no enforcement procedures are associated with them, and the localities may accept them or ignore them. The last four are normally accompanied by some means to compel acquiescence.

LEGAL LIABILTIY

As noted earlier, local governments function in a dual capacity as state agencies and as means of providing services to local residents. Although blurred, this distinction is important in determining whether a person may successfully sue a locality for damages. Unlike the national government and the states, local governments may be subject to suit without consenting to be sued. Such suits arise from acts involving *torts*[14] and *contracts*. The law of tort liability is very confusing, and its principles can be sketched here only in the broadest outlines. Where valid contracts are involved, the rule is that local governments are responsible for observing their provisions and are subject to legal action for any breach of contractual obligations. Regardless of the nature of the function, the local unit is liable to civil suit for breach of contract.

Tort Liability. Actions in tort against local governments most often stem from injury sustained by someone because of the manner in which a local function has been performed. Thus a suit for damages may be instituted by someone who falls into a manhole because the cover has

14. Briefly defined, a tort is a private wrong not arising from a contract.

been removed and no warnings or barricades have been put up. A person injured on the icy steps of the city hall may seek redress. A bystander wounded by the police in pursuit of a criminal may be unable to recover damages from the city, but may sue the policeman. Although it is impossible adequately to blanket these and comparable circumstances with a general rule, the following judicial statement serves as a guide:

> Those acts which are done by a municipal corporation in the exercise of powers for the benefit of the people generally, as an arm of the state, enforcing general laws made in pursuance of the general policy of the state are "governmental" acts, from the negligent manner of doing which no liability follows; while those acts which are done in the exercise of the powers of the municipal corporation for its own benefit, or for the benefit of its citizens alone, or the citizens of the municipal corporation and its immediate locality, are corporate or ministerial actions which are governed by the same rules that govern private corporations.[15]

The courts generally accept the proposition that the powers of municipalities may be viewed as "governmental" or "corporate."[16] The common law rule is that damages may be recovered by persons harmed or injured as a result of the performance of functions considered as corporate, but in the performance of governmental activities municipalities are free from suit.[17] This distinction is founded on the dual role of municipal corporations as agents of the state and as organs for the satisfaction of local needs. Functions considered governmental in most states include fire and police protection, public health, hospitals, poor relief, education, traffic regulation, and the management of jails and similar institutions. Activities generally classified as corporate include municipally owned and operated utilities, transportation facilities, and other enterprises operated for profit. Considerable difference of opinion exists with regard to functions such as construction and maintenance of airports, quarries, cemeteries, sidewalks, bridges, sewers, parks, and recreational facilities in general.

Although the logic of the distinction between governmental and corporate activities is somewhat obscure, its existence must be recognized. Further application of this distinction is found in the fact that quasi-municipal corporations may be held not to be liable in tort in connection with any of their functions. In 1961 the California supreme court ruled that a patient in a hospital maintained by a hospital district could recover damages for injuries allegedly caused by the hospital staff, even though the district was a state agency. The court expressed the opinion

---

15. *City of Mobile* v. *Lartigue*, 223 Ala. App. 479, 127 So. 257, 259 (1930).
16. Governmental functions sometimes are called "political" or "public," and corporate activities are referred to as "proprietary" or "private."
17. The importance of the common law rule arises from the fact that in some states this matter is not covered by statutory provisions. For an expression of judicial refusal to follow this rule, see *Kaufman* v. *Tallahassee*, 84 Fla. 634, 94 So. 697 (1922).

that the "rule of government immunity from tort liability must be discarded as mistaken and unjust."[18] Municipal corporations may also be made subject to suit by state statute. Reluctance to extend the liability of local governments has stemmed in part from the fear that excessively large and frequent awards might be made by juries whose sympathies lie with the plaintiffs rather than with the taxpayers. In an effort to forestall fiscal difficulties associated with possible damage awards, some municipalities have resorted to liability insurance.

Employee Liability.   An example of a tort mentioned earlier concerned the wounding of an innocent spectator by police in pursuit of a criminal, and reference was made to the fact that the offending policeman might be sued. Performance of a governmental function would not protect the local officer although it would probably prevent a suit against the city. Although the municipal official or employee is liable as an individual for his torts, negligence or culpability must normally be proved to justify an award of damages against the employee. Superior officers may be considered a party to the negligence if it can be proved that they were aware of former actions by employees indicating that they might abuse or wrongfully use their authority.[19] From the standpoint of an injured person, employee liability is not a satisfactory alternative to governmental liability because employees may be "suit proof" due to lack of financial resources. The infrequency of awards against local employees probably reflects in part a realization that the constant threat of such action would not foster effective performance of duties. On the other hand, the possibility of civil action for damages is conducive to the exercise of care by employees.

18. *Muskopf* v. *Corning Hospital,* 359 P. 2d 457.
19. *Fernelius* v. *Pierce,* 22 Cal. 2d 226, 138 P. 2d 12 (1943).

Municipal Government 18

URBAN GROWTH

The size of urban populations and the rapidity of their growth during the past century have imposed tremendous demands on urban governments. In 1790 only about five per cent of the people were urbanites, and the largest city, Philadelphia, boasted 42,000 souls. By 1850 urban dwellers composed barely fifteen per cent of the country's population. The next sixty years witnessed such rapid urban growth that by 1910 about half of America's population was urban, and recent trends indicate that the urban-rural ratio will soon be three to one. Today nearly three-fourths of the population of the United States is urban. Although the causes of this growth are numerous and complex, a few major ones should be examined briefly.

Factors Contributing to Urban Growth

Important factors contributing to urban growth include improvements in agricultural practices, advances in techniques of production, growth of commerce and trade, changes in methods of transportation, advances in medical science, and new engineering techniques. Before people can gather in large numbers to engage in manufacture and trade they must be freed from the soil. By increasing the productivity of agricultural practices, the ratio of farmers to nonfarmers can be appreciably diminished. Erstwhile farmers can then seek their fortune in other endeavors; they can heed the lure of the city.

Urban growth has depended also upon advances in technology. The use of steam to provide power to run machinery made possible the growth of the factory system, which in turn demanded increasing numbers of workers concentrated in proximity to the factories. Then "the baker, the butcher, and the candlestick maker," along with many others, set up business in order to meet the needs of the factory workers. As means of transportation improved, markets widened, demands for manufactured goods increased, and more workers were needed. Railroad centers grew in importance along with ports. The proximity of important natural resources, such as iron, coal, and water, has made some places especially attractive as centers of industry and trade. Dangers from diseases of all kinds are greatly increased whenever people congregate in large numbers. Plagues that ravaged ancient and medieval cities posed a constant threat to the lives of urban dwellers and at more or less frequent intervals reduced their numbers appreciably. Advances in medical knowledge and improvements in methods of sanitation have made cities more attractive and accelerated their growth. The modern city is also dependent upon the application of engineering techniques to build skyscrapers, to construct water distribution systems, to dispose of sewage, and to provide other amenities of community living.

Consequences of Urban Growth

The concentration of large numbers of persons into relatively small areas has produced many problems and increased the severity of others. Provision of new services and improved performance of traditional ones are inevitable consequences of urban growth. Urban living would soon become unsafe without more police protection than can be usually provided by county sheriffs and state police. This situation stems not from characteristics of the urbanite, but from the increased opportunities for crime in the city. There are simply more houses to be burglarized, more people to be robbed and swindled, and more traffic to be regulated. The suppression of crime, along with the provision of a great variety of services, means that there must be many more police officers per capita in the city than in the country.

The proximity of residential, commercial, and industrial property in urban areas requires fire protection facilities totally different from those found in rural areas. Large sections of cities, if not entire communities, would be devastated by conflagrations if trained personnel and specialized equipment were not available at all times to fight fires at their inception. Although not as spectacular as fighting fires, combatting disease is also an important local function. Since major reliance is placed on private physicians, urban residents are not as dependent upon government in this area as in many others. Certain local functions performed to promote public health are generally classified as public works, including water supply systems and sewage disposal facilities.

Some of the most troublesome municipal responsibilities relate to the transportation of people and goods. Urban residents move about a great deal, traveling to and from work as well as for purposes of shopping and recreation. Many cities, especially the larger ones, provide public transit systems. All cities build and maintain streets on which people travel. Also, they regulate the flow of traffic by means of signs, lights and police officers. These functions by no means exhaust the range and variety of tasks demanded of municipalities today.

STATE RESTRICTIONS

Legally, each unit of local government is a creature of the state in which it is located. All states impose restrictions, explicit and implied, on the powers of local governments, including municipalities. The traditional pattern of these limitations is revealed in the oft-quoted "Dillon's rule":

> It is a general and undisputed proposition of law that a municipal corporation possesses and can exercise the following powers, and no others: First, those granted in express words; second, those necessarily or fairly implied in or incident to the powers expressly granted; third, those essential to the accomplishment of the declared objects and purpose of the corporation—not simply convenient but indispensable. Any fair, reasonable, substantial doubt concerning the existence of power is resolved by the courts against the corporation, and the power is denied.[1]

The implications of "Dillion's rule" have been somewhat modified in those states that have extended home rule powers to municipalities, particularly where such powers have been granted by constitutional provision.

Although local affairs are no longer run from the state capitol as they once were, practically every state legislative session considers questions pertaining to local governments. During the nineteenth century, legislative concern with local matters characteristically took forms that would now be condemned as "meddling." Legislatures sometimes went so far as to change the powers of cities according to the political party in power! If the majority in the legislature and the majority in the city government were of the same party, additional powers might be granted. A change in political complexion on either level could result in a reduction of local authority. Making appointments to specific local offices, changing municipal boundaries, authorizing the construction of local public works, and granting utility franchises illustrate legislative interference in local affairs characteristic of earlier years. Although similar legislative actions occasionally occur today, they are not nearly so common. City fathers continue to chafe under restrictions, but the trend in recent years has been toward increased powers for local governments.

1. John F. Dillon, *Commentaries on the Law of Municipal Corporations,* 5th ed., Little, Brown & Co., Boston, 1911, I, Sec. 237. Some question as to the correctness of the assertion that cities are merely creatures of the state is implied in *City of Tacoma* v. *The Taxpayers of Tacoma,* 357 U.S. 320, 78 S. Ct. 1209 (1958).

MAJOR FORMS OF GOVERNMENT

Although the existence of some 19,000 municipalities results in a multitude of variations in the details of governmental machinery, most of these governments display the basic characteristics of one of three major types of municipal government: mayor-council, commission, and council-manager. Consequently, it is possible to describe city government in general and consider certain of its strengths and weaknesses by analyzing these types. Although some well known commentators, including Alexander Pope and Lincoln Steffens, have minimized the importance of structure in determining the effectiveness of government, most students of government agree that good organization *and* good people produce better government than either alone.

MAYOR-COUNCIL GOVERNMENT

Eighteenth-century local government in the United States was patterned after that of England, resembling the English borough, with authority vested in a "common council" composed of the mayor, recorder, aldermen, and councilmen. In those days, the burden of responsibilities on urban governments was very light. Few ordinances were enacted, and limited administrative activities were carried out by the council as a body, often acting through committees. The mayor, recorder, and aldermen, as justices of the peace, formed a local court of limited jurisdiction.

As urban problems grew, the need for leadership became increasingly apparent, and the position of mayor assumed greater importance. Mayors came to be popularly elected rather than appointed by governors or chosen by local councils as in the past. Popular election did not result in a sudden and appreciable increase in the mayor's formal authority. Nevertheless, it separated the "chief executive" from the legislative branch. This application of the principle of separation of powers endured, becoming a basic characteristic of mayor-council government. The people of the United States repeatedly have affirmed their confidence in this principle and have embodied it in the governments of the nation and the states. Popular acceptance of the desirability of separation of powers undoubtedly accounts in part for the fact that mayor-council government is the oldest and still the most widespread form of city government.

The Mayor

Selection. City charters regularly impose minimum qualifications on the office of mayor, a number of them being implied in the requirement that candidates be qualified voters in the community. Occasionally, other age and residence requirements are imposed. In order to be elected mayor, a person must possess numerous qualifications not reflected in law. Like a gubernatorial candidate, a mayoral candidate must be "available." Those qualifications that produce "availability" differ in detail from community to community. In general, however, they must result in acceptance by those groups in a community that play a dominant role in influencing public opinion with regard to political issues and more especially with regard to candidates for public office, including party organizations, business leaders, and nonpartisan political groups.

Although mayors in a few small cities are still chosen by the council, the usual method of selection today is popular election. In those cities with partisan election, some formal procedure for the nomination of candidates is necessary so that the elements within each party may unite in support of its slate of candidates. The caucus, the convention, and the direct primary have been widely used for this purpose at different times; the direct primary is used in most communities today. In order to get his or her name on the primary ballot, a candidate may file a declaration of candidacy and pay a token fee or obtain a stipulated number of signatures of qualified voters on a petition. [2] In some states a choice of methods is open to candidates, while in others no option is available.

In recent years, increasing use has been made of nonpartisan elections for city officials. The major difference between partisan and nonpartisan election is simply that the names of candidates are placed on the ballots of primary and general elections without party designation. Placement of names on the nonpartisan primary ballot may be accomplished by the same means used with regard to the partisan primary. Usually, among contestants for an office the two persons obtaining the highest number of votes in the primary run against each other in the final election. Sometimes, a candidate receiving a majority of the votes cast for the office sought is declared elected, and there is no further contest. Nonpartisan election does *not* mean that the voters are unaware of the political affiliation of candidates. With a minimum of inquiry a person may discover the party allegiance of most candidates and then vote party preference just as in partisan elections.

Popular election of mayors is sometimes criticized by those who prefer an appointed chief executive on the ground that election is not the most reliable means of picking someone endowed with administrative ability. This contention is unquestionably correct. An obvious rejoinder is that a mayor *should not* be chosen solely, or perhaps even mainly, because of administrative capacity. The most important role of a typical mayor, especially in large cities, is that of political leader—not necessarily a

---

2. In a few cities, candidates may get their names on the *election* ballot by petition, thus avoiding the primary. This method is criticized because it may result in the election of a "plurality" candidate, that is, one who has received more votes than any of his opponents but less than all others combined.

partisan leader, however. Some really great mayors of large cities, like Fiorello La Guardia of New York, Brand Whitlock of Toledo, and Charles Taft of Cincinnati, were first of all molders of public opinion and leaders of diverse groups interested in good government. Had they not succeeded at this task, their administrative abilities alone would never have raised them to the heights they achieved. In some big cities like New York and Los Angeles recognition has been given to the need for placing administrative responsibilities in the hands of someone other than the mayor who can then perform tasks of community leadership. [3]

Powers. The mayor-council form of government is commonly divided into sub-types known as "weak-mayor" and "strong-mayor" according to the degree of authority granted to the mayor. Until the present century, local governments almost uniformly had "weak" executives, and many still do. In general, weak executive arrangements possess four significant characteristics: (1) a strong legislative body, most often called a "council" in cities, possessing not only law-making authority but also power to appoint and perhaps to remove a number of administrative officers: (2) popular election of several administrators; (3) very limited appointive and legislative power in the hands of the chief executive, often including absence of the veto; and (4) short terms of office, commonly two years.

No fine line can be drawn to divide municipalities neatly into two groups on the basis of the strength of the chief executive because strength is a matter of *degree*. Some mayors are very weak and others are very strong, but the great bulk are in between these extremes. In general, strong mayors exercise relatively extensive authority to appoint and remove administrative officials, perhaps with consent of the council, and they regularly possess the power to veto ordinances passed by the council. They frequently serve longer terms in office, often four years. Few administrators are elected by the people or chosen by the council in a strong-mayor city. Under such circumstances, local residents may logically hold the chief executive and legislative body responsible for the manner in which local needs are met.

The distinction between weak-mayor and strong-mayor governments may be further blurred because the *fact* of strength and its *form* do not necessarily exist together. The mayor of a city may be strong even though the structure of the city's government indicates the position of the mayor is weak, or vice versa. Chicago has proved an excellent example of a strong mayor with a weak formal structure. As a consequence of his dominant position in the Democratic Party, Mayor Richard Daley functioned as a

---

3. By providing an administrative assistant to the mayor, the performance of many routine tasks may be delegated. San Francisco provided for a general manager of this type in 1932, and since then several large cities have adopted the idea, including Boston, Chicago, Louisville, Newark, New Orleans, and Philadelphia. A number of smaller cities also have created such an office.

very strong chief executive in spite of the fact that his formal authority was quite limited. On the other hand, a mayor may be unable or disinclined to use the powers available to him or her in an effective manner and consequently be "weak" although considerable formal authority is vested in the office.

In addition to the powers directly concerned with day-to-day supervision of city affairs, mayors have a variety of other duties. Responsibility for the preparation of a budget and its submission to the council commonly rests with the mayor in a mayor-council city. The mayor may propose other measures for consideration by the council and may preside over meetings of that body. As head of the city, the mayor is expected to deliver frequent addresses to civic organizations, service clubs, political assemblies, and meetings of all types. Many persons impose upon a mayor's time daily with complaints and proposals, and the mayor cannot adopt a "closed-door" policy, especially if he or she has political ambitions.

Removal. Four methods of removing mayors have been adopted in the United States: (1) action of the council, (2) recall, (3) judicial action, and (4) action of the state governor. Parallel to the practice at the state level, the most common method available for removing local chief executives is impeachment. Since almost all city councils are unicameral, the same body brings charges, decides guilt or innocence, and votes on removal. An extraordinary majority is usually required to accomplish removal. Since its inclusion in the charter of Los Angeles in 1903, well over 1,000 cities have provided for the recall by which officials may be voted out of office.[4] Easily subject to abuses, the recall generally has been used with restraint. Common practice provides that local officials shall be removed from office upon conviction of a felony, and courts are occasionally empowered to remove persons for malfeasance or misfeasance in office. In a few states, the governor may remove mayors. For political and other reasons, this authority has seldom been used.

The Council

The legislative bodies of most municipalities, particularly cities, are known simply as "councils." Practically all local councils today are unicameral.[5] Following the American Revolution, cities began to use the bicameral council, and by the middle of the nineteenth century it was in general use. During the last quarter of the past century, the unicameral council grew in favor, and the shift to this arrangement developed very rapidly during the first three or four decades of the current century. The single house of

---

4. For a discussion of the recall, see Chapter 12.
5. The governing body of New York City consists of a "Council" and a "Board of Estimate," but the latter is concerned only with fiscal matters.

most city councils today is considerably smaller than either house of the old bicameral councils. Very few cities have more than a score members on their councils, and many have less than half that number.[6]

Selection. Two major trends in the selection of councilmen are especially worthy of note: election at-large, and nonpartisan selection.[7] At-large election of council members has been used increasingly. Traditionally, cities have been divided into *wards,* and one or more council members have been elected from each ward. Advocates of the ward system argue that it guarantees that the interests of sections and neighborhoods will be represented and considered in the deliberations of the council. Critics maintain that the promotion of sectional interests should be discouraged by requiring all council members to seek election at the hands of all the voters in a city. "The chief weakness of the ward plan is that the members of the council often work for the interest of their own wards rather than those of the city as a whole. It brings into the municipal field the 'pork barrel' system of legislation."[8] This criticism is especially relevant to large cities. In the spirit of compromise, some communities elect part of their council members at-large and the remainder from wards. Also, a few cities nominate candidates by wards or districts and elect them at-large. More and more cities recently have turned to nonpartisan nomination and election of council members. Proponents of nonpartisan selection argue that "there is no Democratic way to pave a street or Republican method of laying a sewer." Also, they maintain that partisan issues and cleavages should not be extended to questions relating to municipal services such as improvements in police and fire protection and more adequate recreational facilities, as well as many other matters that should be settled on more objective grounds. Those who favor retention of partisan selection claim that many matters, such as changes in taxation and the provision of new municipal services, may properly become issues between parties. Furthermore, it is asserted that formal separation from local issues will weaken political parties at the "grass roots" and thereby impair their effectiveness at all levels of government.

Organization. Due to the small size of most city councils, their organization is relatively simple. Provision is always made for a presiding officer, who may be the mayor, an independently elected "president," or some-

6. The range among cities over 500,000 is from fifty councilmen in Chicago to seven in New Orleans—a wider range than is found among smaller cities.
7. An innovation used in a few cities is proportional representation—commonly called "PR." For excellent discussions of this device see Charles M. Kneier, *City Government in the United States,* Harper & Brothers, New York, 1957, pp. 226-236; and Arthur W. Bromage, *Introduction to Municipal Government and Administration,* Appleton-Century-Crofts, New York, 1957, pp. 227-233.
8. Charles M. Kneier, *op. cit.,* p. 225.

one chosen by the council from among its membership. Commonly, the city clerk or recorder serves as clerk to the council. Municipal councils often perform much of their work through committees, and many decisions pertaining to council action on major as well as minor issues are made by them. Although subject to abuse, the use of committees may be very helpful. Most council members do not possess the time or inclination to become well versed with regard to all municipal functions. Instead, they develop interest in certain areas, such as public works, police, or finance. The needs of a community are better served by enabling each council members to devote special competence to particular local problems. To prevent "government by committee," the council must restrain its committees from meddling into the responsibilities of administrative departments and agencies.

Powers. Within limitations imposed by state and federal law and local charter provisions, local councils determine city policy, subject to possible veto through the referendum. All powers possessed by a city and not conferred by law upon some other officer or agency belong to the council. Although governments of limited powers, municipalities provide many services and impose numerous regulations that are of vital concern to local residents. Fire and police protection, recreational facilities, water, refuse collection and disposal, and street construction and maintenance are illustrative. Regulations are imposed, for example, in relation to health, traffic, use of property, and the conduct of many kinds of business. The very existence of these activities and their quality depend largely upon decisions made by local councils. Also, of course, determination of the amount of money to be spent for municipal functions is a responsibility of the council.

In addition to their ordinance-making authority, local councils have numerous other responsibilities. Investigations must be conducted. They may be concerned with uncovering information pertaining to proposed projects or changes in policy, or their purpose may be to determine the efficiency with which municipal affairs are being administered. Long-range plans must be considered, especially with regard to public works such as streets, water supply, and sewage disposal. Contracts and franchises must be reviewed. Petitions from individual citizens and organized groups within the community must be given attention. Careful consideration needs to be given, at least occasionally, to appointments to municipal offices. Although by no means exhaustive, this list of responsibilities provides some insight into the variety of tasks imposed upon municipal councils.

Removal. Although members of municipal councils are seldom removed from office prior to the expiration of their terms, such action is occasionally desirable. Three methods of removal are common: recall, expulsion by the council, and conviction of crime. Where permitted, removal by recall requires the circulation of a petition setting forth the charges and the acquisition of a certain number of signatures of legal voters on the petition, followed by a vote on removal. Usually, a special election is called for this purpose. Some city charters empower councils to expel members. Persons convicted of a serious crime during their term of office must normally relinquish their position on a local council.

COMMISSION GOVERNMENT

The stepchild among the major varieties of city government is the commission form, which grew in favor during the first quarter of the twentieth century but has been on the decline ever since. This type of government received widespread attention as a result of its adoption in Galveston, Texas, following a tidal wave that killed thousands of persons and destroyed millions of dollars worth of property.[9] The mayor-council government of Galveston proved unable to cope with the serious situation produced by the disaster. A committee of civic leaders drew up a new charter and requested the Texas legislature to adopt it as the basic law for Galveston.[10] The legislature complied, and commission government was established in 1901.

During the next dozen or so years, between four and five hundred communities adopted commission government. Although accurate figures are not available, the high point in the number of adoptions of this form of government appears to have occurred around 1920. Since then the trend has been downward. Less than 100 cities over 5,000 population now use the commission form. Very few cities have adopted the plan in recent years, while many have abandoned it. On April 19, 1960, the people of Galveston voted commission government out in favor of the council-manager plan.

The Nature of Commission Government

Most notable among the features of commission government is the concentration of major legislative, executive, and administrative responsibilities in a single body, the commission. Consequently, there is a fusion rather than a separation of powers. Although details vary from community to community, three major features are characteristic: (1) a small, popularly elected commission, sometimes known as the "council," (2) a mayor

9. The commission form of government was used by a few cities during the nineteenth century, including Sacramento, California (1863), New Orleans, Louisiana (1870), Memphis, Tennessee (1878) and Mobile, Alabama (1879). Washington, D.C., has operated under a type of commission government for three-quarters of a century.
10. This was a "special act" charter.

who is usually a member of the commission and is often chosen by that body to serve as "chief executive," and (3) members of the commission serving individually as top-level administrators in charge of major departments. This arrangement is structurally simple, but it has proved complex in operation.

The Commission. Membership on the commission or council rarely exceeds seven; three or five members are most common. Collectively, the commissioners serve in a legislative capacity and perform duties comparable with those belonging to council members in the mayor-council system. In other words, the commission decides issues of public policy and enacts the ordinances necessary to implement its decisions. Most often, commissioners are selected on a nonpartisan basis from the entire city.

Executive Officers. In commission cities various methods are employed to designate the chief executive, a position normally carrying little more authority than belongs to individual commissioners. The mayor usually does not possess the veto power. He or she may be chosen by popular vote as mayor, or the commissioner who receives the largest number of popular votes may automatically assume that position. In many cities the commissioners choose one of their own number to serve as mayor, who then heads a major city department, usually the one including fire and police services. As a consequence of being "first among equals" and as titular head of the city government, the mayor enjoys more influence, if little more formal authority, than other commissioners. In some commission cities, the position of mayor is rotated among the commissioners.

Since commissioners serve individually as administrators of major departments, there is no organizational distinction in commission government between policymaking and policy-execution. A commissioner may be elected to head a particular department, but more often the commissioners allocate the departments among themselves. In a few communities, the mayor is empowered to designate the department for which each commissioner will be responsible. Because the number of major departments is limited by the number of commissioners, each department is responsible for a variety of duties, many of which may be functionally unrelated. Depending on the size of the city and the predilections of the commissioners, professional personnel are hired to supervise each of the subdepartments. Thus a police chief, a fire chief, an engineer, and a recreation specialist may be placed in immediate charge of functions for which they are specially trained.

Assessment of Commission Government

Although generalizations concerning the effectiveness or desirability of a particular type of government are fraught with danger, a brief review of the claims of proponents and opponents of commission government is in order. The major advantages of this type of government are alleged to be: simplicity, small size of commission, concentration of authority and responsibility, and close relation between policy-making and administration. Structural simplicity is unquestionably characteristic of commission government, which substitutes a single small body for separate executive, legislature, and independent administrative officers. On the other hand, the variety of functions lodged in a single agency may create difficulty for citizens when they attempt to pinpoint responsibility for the manner in which a particular task has been performed or for failure to meet certain needs of the community.

The chief advantage associated with a small commission is a short ballot. However, the short ballot is in no sense peculiar to commission government, since small councils and few elected administrative officers may be provided in any type of municipal government. It is sometimes maintained that the small number of commissioners combined with the importance of the responsibilities attaching to each position attracts superior personnel. This claim appears to be entirely in the realm of conjecture.

That official authority and responsibility are concentrated in a few hands in commission government is undeniable. That such concentration produces good government is debatable. Since responsibility for the administration of local affairs is placed in the hands of a *group,* opportunities for "buck-passing" are always present. Whenever anything goes wrong in a department, the commissioner in charge may attempt to avoid unpleasant consequences by asserting that his or her actions are controlled by the majority of the commission.

Location of responsibility for making policy and administering it in the same hands is favored by some persons and criticized by others. Proponents of this arrangement maintain that the combination of responsibilities reduces legislative-executive friction and minimizes opportunities for mutual misunderstanding of the problems faced by each branch of government. However, one astute student of local government has observed, "To entrust these divergent processes to the same body is to invite confusion. . . . Making policy calls for a different type of ability from the conducting of administration. The amateur may be desirable in the former but never in the latter role. . . . In principle, the commission idea errs in its merger of legislative and executive operations."[11]

Critics of commission government usually emphasize the following points: (1) absence of a chief administrator, (2) inexpert administration, (3) joining of politics and administration in the same hands, (4) rigid departmental organization, and (5) inadequate provision for political leadership. Effective administration of municipal affairs requires coordin-

11. Arthur W. Bromage, *op. cit.,* p. 285.

nation. "Everybody wants coordination, at least on paper, but nobody wants to be coordinated in practice. Every agency wants to go its own way and have other agencies build around their own program. Unless there is strong leadership at the top, leadership with ability to induce different departments or units to work as a team, then in all probability these units will be proceeding simultaneously in all directions."[12] Structurally, little or no provision is made in commission government for such leadership.

It has been said often that "experts should be on tap and not on top." Expert administration of governmental services is very much needed today. Political leaders seldom have the time or inclination to acquire knowledge and techniques necessary for effective administration of fire and police departments, public works programs, and other important municipal activities. Commission government, particularly in smaller communities where it is most common, seeks to combine political finesse and technical *expertise* in the same persons. Such a combination is rarely found. Since commissioners must be elected, their primary emphasis must be on politics.

Combining policymaking and policy-execution in the same hands contributes to "horse-trading" among commissioners, according to critics. Commissioners are primarily concerned with their own individual administrative responsibilities; and in order to win approval of policy proposals, each commissioner is inclined to treat the suggestions of other commissioners sympathetically. Consequently, commission government has been likened to "a spending machine without a brake." Although somewhat inaccurate, this observation reflects difficulties inherent in any system that places responsibility in the same hands for determining how much shall be spent and for supervising actual expenditures.

Since the number of major departments cannot exceed the number of commissioners, all governmental activities must necessarily be allocated to a predetermined number of departments. If commission government is to retain its characteristic advantage of a small council, the number of departments must be strictly limited regardless of the size of a city. Combinations of unrelated, or at best remotely related, functions are inevitably found in most if not all departments. Detailed supervision by one person of such varied activities is difficult at best.

A major criticism of commission government is that from the viewpoint of *structure* it makes inadequate provision for political leadership. However, the same criticism can be leveled against all forms of municipal government with the exception of the strong-mayor type. Furthermore, it is possible for mayors in commission communities to *assume* positions of leadership. A popular mayor with a strong personality and a determi-

---

12. W. Brooke Graves, *Public Administration in A Democratic Society*, D. C. Heath and Co., New York, 1950, pp. 66-67.

nation to "get things done" may accomplish more under commission government than a mayor without these qualities in a strong-mayor city.

COUNCIL-MANAGER GOVERNMENT

The third major variety of municipal government, the council-manager form, was inaugurated in Staunton, Virginia, in 1908.[13] As in the case of commission government, a natural disaster brought manager government to prominence. The Miami River flooded portions of Dayton, Ohio, in 1913, drowning many and destroying large amounts of property. The government of Dayton was so ineffective in meeting the resultant problems that the city was placed under martial law, and a group of business men took responsibility for overhauling local services. A proposal to "put business in government" by adopting council-manager government was approved in late 1913, and a new charter became effective on January 1, 1914. Municipalities using this type of government have increased steadily and now number more than 3,000 including Dallas, Kansas City, Phoenix, San Antonio, and San Diego. Over half of American cities of more than 10,000 population have managers. This form of government is especially popular in middle-class suburbs with 25,000 to 250,000 people.

The Council

Responsibilities of the council in council-manager government are, with one major addition, much the same as in mayor-council government. That addition is the task of choosing a manager.[14] The manner in which this responsibility is handled largely determines the success or failure of this type of government. In council-manager cities legal authority to run city affairs is definitely located in the council. The council not only determines policy, but it also selects the top-level administrator empowered to implement that policy. Furthermore, the council normally has authority to terminate the manager's services at any time.[15]

Although many variations exist, council-manager cities typically have a small council of five to nine members who are elected at-large on a nonpartisan basis. Terms of office are commonly two or four years and occasionally six. Council members often serve without compensation except

13. Sometimes called "city-manager government," but the designation used here is preferred. The first city to adopt council-manager government by charter amendment was Sumter, S.C., in 1912.
14. Very rarely, the manager is appointed by the mayor.
15. Occasionally, managers are hired for fixed terms, a practice that is opposed by the International City Management Association. Some charters provide that the manager shall be removed only for "cause," but any council wishing to remove a manager can develop reasons for the action.

for payment of expenses, and where pay is provided it is usually nominal. Monetary remuneration is not a major concern of public-spirited citizens who spend hours each week investigating, considering, and hearing citizen viewpoints on the many problems of local government.

The Mayor

Mayors in council-manager cities may be popularly elected or chosen by the council from among its membership. Since administrative responsibilities are separated from the office, the mayor is concerned with policy-making and ceremony. Ideally, a mayor provides the political leadership in which a manager may not dare indulge. Usually the only popularly elected executive officer, mayors occupy a position of potentially significant influence. Their knowledge of public sentiment and their effort in "selling" projects and programs may provide invaluable assistance to the council and to the manager. Although possessing little responsibility for the administration of city functions, the mayor's role need in no sense be insignificant.

The Manager

Selection and Tenure. Beyond prescribing "executive and administrative ability," most local charters say nothing about the qualifications of a manager. Consequently, councils are legally free to choose anyone who appears best suited to meet community needs. Such intangible qualities as honesty, tact, energy, foresight, resourcefulness, and a sense of humor must always be considered. Experience in the public service in some professional capacity, preferably on the local level, is usually demanded. Although a council may consider local talent for promotion to the position of manager, someone from outside normally is brought in to fill the position, particularly where it is a full-time job.

The opportunity to move from community to community promotes professionalization of city-manager work. It is estimated that the average tenure of managers today is five to seven years. Although managers occasionally are dismissed by council action, the great majority of separations are voluntary. Especially since World War II the demand for qualified managers has exceeded the supply, and when a larger city needs a manager it looks to smaller communities. The higher salaries and greater challenges offered by the large city are attractive to many administrators who have begun their careers in small cities and towns.

Duties. Although their duties necessarily vary from city to city, managers should have full responsibility, subject to council approval, for the administration of city affairs. In order to accomplish this task, the manager must have control of most, if not all, departments implemented by authority to appoint and remove their heads, along with responsibility for preparing an annual budget and submitting it to the council. The manager must submit proposals to the council on any and all matters that he or she feels should be brought to their attention and must prepare information and recommendations on questions raised by the council. The manager should prepare an agenda prior to each council session so that members may anticipate matters that will be brought before them. Finally, a major portion of the manager's time needs to be allocated to the implementation of a "public relations" program designed to keep interested persons and the public in general informed about the operations of city government.

Arguments in Favor. The major arguments in behalf of council-manager government may be summarized briefly. Although legal responsibility for the conduct of local affairs rests with the council, adequate provision is made for separation of legislative and administrative functions. Managers normally are chosen on the basis of training, ability, and experience rather than political considerations. Because of the conditions surrounding selection and tenure, the manager is less subject to political pressure than a popularly elected official. Council membership involves relatively fewer demands on incumbents than in other forms of local government, thus encouraging civic-minded persons to seek membership. Reduction in the number of elected officials shortens the ballot. Managers possess authority commensurate with responsibility for overseeing local activities. Opportunities for "buck-passing" are reduced to a minimum. Finally, communities using this form of government generally praise it as providing increased efficiency.

Arguments Against. Opponents of council-manger government stress a number of considerations. Too much authority is placed in the hands of an appointive official, and manager government is consequently less democratic than those types in which the chief administrative officer is popularly elected. Since the supply of qualified managers is limited, municipalities, particularly small ones, experience serious difficulty in their efforts to secure and retain capable, experienced managers. Separation of responsibilities between the council and the manager may be clear in theory, but in practice it is difficult to maintain. Councils tend to interfere in matters of administration, and managers become involved in major policy decisions.[16] Inadequate provision is made for effective political leadership. Salary costs required to attract and keep competent managers are excessive. Several communities have tried the plan and abandoned it.

16. See Ronald A. Loveridge, *The City Manager and Legislative Policy,* Bobbs-Merrill, Indianapolis, 1971.

Basic to council-manager government is a division of responsibilities between the council and the manager, a division that is not easily realized in practice. Although final authority to make decisions on major questions of policy is lodged with the council, many persons other than councilmen participate in the process, including the manager and subordinate administrative personnel, the mayor, and various groups in the community. From these and other sources councils receive information, suggestions, and recommendations, all of which influence their deliberations. But once a decision has been made, the manager must see that it is carried out in the most effective and expeditious manner possible. Selection and supervision of personnel is the manager's responsibility, and many local charters specifically prohibit council members from seeking to influence the manager in regard to such matters. If the council as a body concludes that the affairs of a community are not being adequately administered, it has the legal and moral duty to obtain a new manager.

Some of the most vexatious problems in council-manager communities pertain to political leadership. There appears to be no reason why a popularly elected mayor *cannot* fill this important need. However, experience shows that mayors often do not assume this responsibility. Where they are chosen by the council, the inability or reluctance on the part of mayors to assume leadership is understandable. Studies indicate, however, that even elected mayors may be willing to allow leadership to emanate from other sources such as the manager, prominent administrators in various city departments, and leaders of pressure groups in the community. Problems inherent in the assumption of leadership by the manager are reflected in the assertion by a former mayor of Philadelphia to the effect that "top leadership in American politics is never hired; it is always elected. . ."[17]

Hybrid Forms

Figures 18.1–18.4 are diagrams of the major varieties of municipal government, and depict each type in its "pure" or "ideal" form. Governments in many communities do not fit any of these patterns. Thus the prominence of an appointed chief administrator is the central characteristic of council-manager government, but a similar arrangement is found in some mayor-council cities. The "chief administrative officers" in these cities are appointed by the mayor and function to assist him or her in various capacities. This arrangement originated in San Francisco in 1932 and has been used in a number of large cities, including Boston, Los Angeles, Louisville, Newark, New York, New Orleans, and Philadelphia. Advocates

17. Quoted in Dorothee Straus Pealy, "The Need for Elected Leadership," in "Leadership and Decision-Making in Manager Cities," *Public Administration Review,* Summer 1958, p. 214.

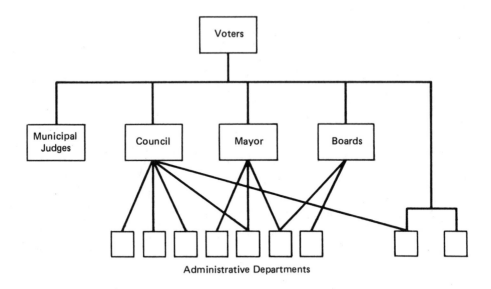

Figure 18.1 Weak-Mayor and Council Government

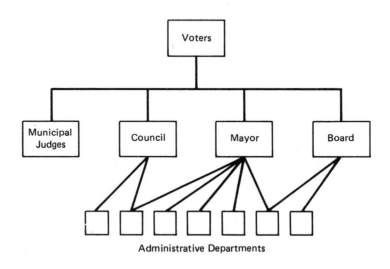

Figure 18.2 Strong-Mayor and Council Government

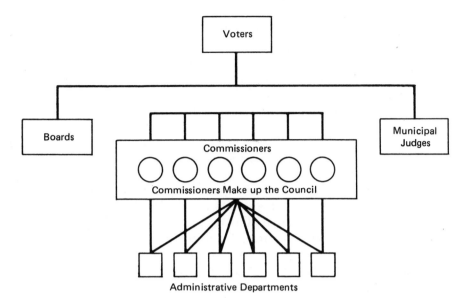

Figure 18.3 Commission Government

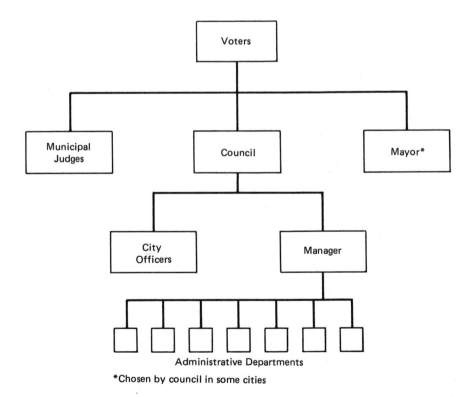

*Chosen by council in some cities

Figure 18.4 Council-Manager Government

of the plan stress its combination of a strong, elected chief executive with a professional administrator.

Innumerable minor variations appear from community to community. In some manager cities certain department heads are not subject to appointment and removal by the manager. They may be selected by the mayor, by popular vote, or even occasionally by departmental personnel. The last arrangement is most common among volunteer fire departments. In a few manager communities the legislative bodies are called commissions rather than councils. The voters in "true" commission cities occasionally elect important administrative officials in addition to members of the commission. Consequently, in these municipalities some functions are assigned to departments or agencies not under the immediate supervision of a commissioner. Such illustrations could be multiplied many times. The governmental structures found in many municipalities do not fit any pattern exactly. This fact is not too significant, however, since these patterns still serve as guides for the deliberations of those responsible for determining the form of government in each community.

MAJOR MUNICIPAL FUNCTIONS

Public Safety

Some of the most important activities of municipal governments are related to the promotion of public safety. Police and fire protection, traffic engineering, street lighting, and building inspection are important illustrations. Beginning with the night watch in colonial times, cities have had important responsibilities for the protection of persons and property. From New York City with over 25,000 police officers to hundreds of small communities with one or two members in their police forces, municipalities spend major portions of their budgets for the apprehension of criminals, recovery of stolen property, suppression of vice, crime prevention, and traffic control, to name some of the more common activities.

Americans annually spend millions of dollars to man and equip local fire departments. Although not so dramatic as fire-fighting, fire-prevention activities are assumiing increasing importance. Particularly in larger communities, it is important that fire fighters be mentally alert, physically agile, and professionally trained. Training schools for fire fighters have proved their worth in reducing fire losses and property damage.

Although sometimes considered as part of planning rather than public safety, traffic engineering is vitally important to the safety of citizens, especially in congested areas. Laying out thoroughfares, widening streets, designating one-way arterials, locating lights, and setting speed limits indicate the close relationship between traffic engineering and safety.

Adequate street lighting is important to traffic control, but it also bears a close relation to crime detection and suppression. Dangers to persons and property lurking in poorly lighted areas have stimulated many local councils to provide more modern facilities. Review of plans for the construction of buildings, industrial and commercial as well as residential, and inspection of wiring, plumbing, fire escapes, elevators, heating systems, structural strength, and many related matters contribute significantly to public safety.

Health and Welfare

Because of the necessity of controlling communicable diseases in heavily populated areas, cities have long assumed responsibilities relating to the protection of health. In earlier times, pesthouses and quarantines were established to isolate those seriously ill. With the growth of medical knowledge, the importance of sanitation was recognized. Cities began to construct sewage disposal systems and dispose of garbage and other wastes. Responsibility for the provision of an adequate supply of pure water has long been a major municipal function. Cities occasionally have vaccinated and innoculated large numbers of their residents against certain communicable diseases. Municipal hospitals have been established in many communities. A new area of concern for municipal public health authorities is pollution, which creates many health problems.

Until recent times cities played a major role in the provision of welfare services, and a few still do. Municipal almshouses and poor farms cared for indigent aged, invalids, orphans, and other persons mentally and physically disabled. During the last quarter-century or so, responsibility for the provision of welfare has been assumed by the national and state governments, with counties generally serving as the primary agencies for local administration. Since the depression of the 1930's the concept of welfare has expanded to encompass those persons temporarily out of work and in need of assistance to "tide them over" until they resume gainful employment. Cities have cooperated with the national and state governments in support of programs for slum clearance and public housing.

Utilities and Transportation

Many municipalities provide service that may be classified broadly as utilities, including electricity, water, gas, airports, auditoriums, port facilities, and public markets. Also sometimes considered as utilities are transportation facilities. Municipal streetcar and bus systems have been a familiar part of the local scene for many years. Most public transit systems today are either operating at a deficit or on a very narrow margin of profit because of greatly increased use of private automobiles. Fewer public transit passengers cause higher rates, which in turn mean fewer passengers. The energy crisis has increased the need to strengthen public transit.

Planning and Zoning

Most American cities have grown largely without plan, but fortunately increasing attention is now being given to the future. Although other types of planning have not been entirely ignored, attention has been given primarily to physical planning. Planners with an eye for the future are increasingly concerned about such matters as street patterns, parking facilities, water and sewer systems, mass transportation, parks, airports, schools, public buildings, and sites for industrial, commercial, and residential developments. This list by no means exhausts the areas of concern to planners, but it indicates the difficulty of their task, which is further complicated by the necessity of relating projected population growth and financial resources to physical needs.

Planning and zoning go hand in hand. The best laid plans for the orderly development of a community may go awry unless legal restrictions are imposed on indiscriminate uses of property. Zoning is intended to implement the orderly development of a community by regulating the use of land and buildings within precisely defined districts. Restrictions are imposed upon the size of buildings as well as the uses to which they may be put, the proximity of structures to each other, and the density of population. Zoned cities are usually divided into industrial, commercial, and residential areas with subcategories within each. Thus residential areas may be subdivided into one-family districts, two-family districts, and multiple-family districts, controlling the number of families that may reside within each residential building. Except in areas developed after the adoption of a zoning ordinance, some nonconforming uses normally exist in each zone. For example, a few multiple-family dwellings may be located in a section zoned for single-family residences, or vice versa. Through "spot-zoning" small segments of land are set aside for special uses different from those authorized for the zone in which they are situated. In this way, for example, neighborhood commercial areas may be permitted to encroach upon residential zones.

Judicial Functions

All states have granted to municipal courts limited authority for the administration of justice in both civil and criminal cases arising within their territory. The number and variety of these courts often bear a close relation to the size of the city. The charters of large cities may establish a variety of courts, including special courts dealing with domestic relations, juveniles, small claims, and traffic offenses. In many small cities the jurisdiction of municipal courts is limited largely to violations of local ordinances, particularly those pertaining to traffic, punishable by small fines and short jail terms. These courts must not be confused with state courts that happen to be physically situated within the environs of individual municipalities. The jurisdiction of state courts, in terms of types of cases and geography, is much broader than that granted to municipal courts. The importance of city courts must not be measured solely in terms of their jurisdiction, however. The fact that many citizens have their only contact with the judiciary in these courts gives them an importance that is often overlooked.

The County

19

The American county is a direct descendant of the English shire established in the ninth century. At that time "the affairs of each shire were managed by a semiannual court, composed of the representatives of each township and the individual landowners . . ."[1] The chief function of the court was the administration of justice. Officials of the shire were the earl, the shire-reeve or sheriff, and the bishop. Shortly after the Norman conquest earls and bishops disappeared as administrators of shire business; shires came to be called counties, and the sheriff became the dominant officer in county affairs as the representative of the King.

When our English forebearers settled this country, they naturally established governmental forms with which they were familiar. In Virginia the English system of local government was followed closely, and as early as 1634 that state was divided into eight shires or counties. Counties were established in Massachusetts in 1643, Maryland in 1650, Connecticut in 1663, and Rhode Island in 1703. Similar developments took place in other states about the same time.

Following the Revolution, state constitutions made frequent reference to counties, and considerable authority for self-government was granted. Increases in local authority were apparent in regard to local influence over the choice of county officials formerly appointed by the governor or other state officials. By the end of the first quarter of the nineteenth century the basic characteristics of county governmental structure as they exist today were taking form. Throughout the last century increased local control by virtue of more widespread popular election of county officers characterized developments at that level of government.

---

1. John A. Fairlie, *Local Government in Counties, Towns and Villages,* The Century Co., New York, 1906, p. 5. Information for this section on historical background is drawn largely from Dr. Fairlie's volume.

PRESENT STATUS OF THE COUNTY

The county is the most nearly universal unit of local government in the United States. In name at least, almost the entire area of the country is included in the 3,042 organized counties.[2] Organized county governments are found in every state except Connecticut and Rhode Island, where areas known as "counties" have no governments. There are three "unorganized" counties in South Dakota, five counties in New York City, several that have merged with their central cities and lost separate existence for all practical purposes, and the city-counties of Denver, San Francisco, and Honolulu. There are also some three dozen cities, the District of Columbia, and Yellowstone National Park that lack county government. The number of counties per state ranges from three in Delaware to 254 in Texas, and in size they vary from 20,117 square miles in San Bernardino County, California, to twenty-six square miles in Arlington County, Virginia.

Counties are legally geographical subdivisions of a state for the administration of certain governmental activities of statewide concern, such as construction and maintenance of highways and other roads, conduct of elections, and the application of justice. Accordingly, the area and governmental organization of counties are determined by state constitutional or statutory law.[3] Counties are also primarily units for rural government in most places. Although not so universally true as earlier the fact remains that county functions considered as a whole are more vital to people living outside city boundaries than to urban dwellers. At the same time, rapid population growth in suburban areas around many cities has imposed upon counties the responsibility of providing urban fringe dwellers with certain municipal services. A third fact worthy of note is that county boundaries in most instances were determined many years before the advent of modern means of transportation. In earlier years it was important to have the county seat near all parts of a county so that residents having business at the courthouse could make the trip in a day or so.

The importance of the county varies considerably in different parts of the country. In New England the town overshadows the county to the point that responsibilities allocated to county governments are meager. In a dozen or so states outside New England, certain functions are divided between counties and townships. In the remaining states, particularly in the South and the Far West, the county is the dominant unit of rural local government. Although counties have been called the "dark continent of

---

2. Included in this number are the parishes of Louisiana and the boroughs of Alaska, which are legally and politically comparable with counties.
3. Even in those states with county home rule, county charters are adopted pursuant to provisions of state law.

American politics," they play a vital role in our system of government. Indeed, recent years have seen a notable increase in the responsibilities and functions assigned to counties.

As mentioned above, counties have been regarded traditionally as political subdivisions of the states. Legal sanction was given to this doctrine by the supreme court of Ohio well over a century ago:

> Counties are local subdivisions of a state, created by the sovereign power of the state, of its own sovereign will, without the particular solicitation, consent, or concurrent action of the people who inhabit them . . .
>
> A municipal corporation proper is created mainly for the interest, advantage, and convenience of the locality and its people; a county organization is created almost exclusively with a view of the policy of the state at large, for purposes of political organization and civil administration . . .[4]

This viewpoint has been repeated by courts in other states and is accepted as a settled point of law.

County Home Rule

Traditionally, direct control by state legislatures has extended to matters of county organization. State constitutions and statutes usually specify what officers shall be responsible for county government, the manner in which they shall be chosen, and their terms of office as well as their duties. In a few states the people have in recent years extended to individual counties increased freedom with regard to organization. In some instances this goal has been accomplished by means of optional-charter provisions authorizing counties to choose among alternative patterns of organization set forth more or less in detail by statutory provisions. The basic purposes of such optional-charter laws are to enable counties to adopt a type of organization better suited to the new demands placed upon counties and at the same time to keep control over the structure of county government in the hands of the state legislature.

Some two dozen states extend even greater freedom of action to counties than that granted by optional-charter laws. The constitutions of Alaska, California, Florida, Georgia, Hawaii, Illinois, Louisiana, Maryland, Michigan, Minnesota, Missouri, Montana, New Mexico, New York, Ohio, Oregon, Pennsylvania, South Carolina, South Dakota, and Washington provide for *county home rule.* As in the case of cities, a major purpose of home rule for counties is to permit the people to determine by popular vote the form of government they want. Basic to this privilege is the authority to frame and adopt their own charters.

Although home rule is supported by some as a significant means of improving county government, experience with it has proved somewhat

---

4. *Commissioners of Hamilton County* v. *Mighels,* 7 Ohio St. 109 (1857).

disappointing. Many charters have been drafted and then failed to obtain the popular vote required for adoption. The most distinctive feature of home-rule charters adopted by counties is that in many of them provision has been made for a chief executive officer, either appointed by the county governing body or popularly elected.

In fairness to advocates of county home rule, it should be noted that the small number of counties availing themselves of the opportunity to adopt their own charters and rearrange their governmental structures does not prove the idea defective. In those counties where it has been tried, people appear to be generally well satisfied with the arrangements created under home-rule authority. The fact remains, however, that experience thus far indicates that the presence of provisions in a state constitution making home rule available to counties will not result in appreciable improvement in county government on a statewide basis. The small number of home-rule charters in states where they are available may be due in part to public apathy and indifference. Yet, many of the same people who have been indifferent to county home rule have taken advantage of municipal home rule.

ORGANIZATION OF COUNTY GOVERNMENT

Since county governmental organization is characterized by diversity, detailed examination of the many existing variations is impossible here. Instead, a description of the "typical" county will be undertaken (see Figure 19.1). As has been aptly observed, if any "principle" could be distinguished in American county government, it is the principle of confusion.

Governing Bodies

In most counties the governing body is composed of several members, ranging from three to fifty. Most commonly, this body is designated as the board of commissioners or board of supervisors, often referred to simply as the "county board." Titles vary among the states, including county court, commissioners court, fiscal court, policy jury, board of freeholders, and commissioners of roads and revenue. In spite of the variety, it is possible to distinguish four major types of county governing bodies:

1. board of commissioners or supervisors,
2. board composed of township supervisors,
3. board composed of one judge and commissioners,
4. board composed of one judge and justices of the peace.

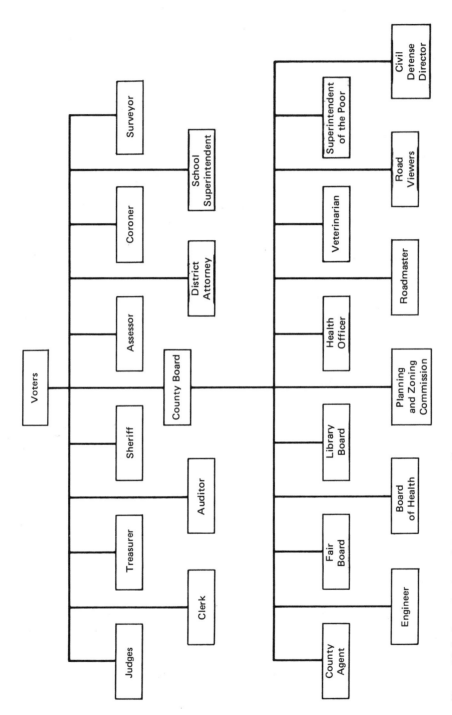

Figure 19.1 Organization of Typical County Government

Approximately two-thirds of county governing bodies belong in the first category. Members of boards in this group are elected specifically to perform the duties belonging to these bodies collectively, and they normally hold no other public office. Members of boards of the second type are chosen from townships composing each county and regularly have responsibilities as township officers in addition to those that they possess as county officials. Boards in the third group differ from those in the first largely in that their chairman is also a judicial officer who has duties other than those belonging to him as a member of the county governing body, duties not shared by the other members. In the fourth category are those boards where not only the chairman is a judicial officer, since other members are justices of the peace.

With very few exceptions, members of county governing bodies are popularly elected. They are usually chosen from districts or governmental subdivisions of the county rather than at-large. According to the Census Bureau, less than twenty per cent of the counties elect all members of their governing bodies from the county as a whole. Election from subdivisions of a county is defended chiefly on the ground that membership will be distributed geographically and local interests adequately represented. This claim has some validity for counties that are not homogeneous in character, but election from subdivisions entails the very real danger that members of a governing body may fail to appreciate county needs as a whole because of preoccupation with the wishes and demands of their immediate constituents.

Although terms of office for members of county governing bodies vary from one to eight years, the great majority are elected for four years. Members usually are paid an annual salary or a per diem allowance, with salaries ranging from a few hundred dollars to several thousand per year. County boards usually meet at least once a month, but meetings may be held less often in rural counties and more frequently in populous ones. In some states a certain number of meetings per year is prescribed by law, while in others the frequency of meetings is left to determination by the board. In all instances, special sessions may be called as needed.

The powers of county governing bodies are determined by state constitutional and statutory provisions. All powers conferred by law upon a county, and not specifically delegated to some other county officers, are normally exercised by the county board. County boards commonly exercise legislative, administrative, and judicial powers, an arrangement contrary to the principle of separation of powers characteristic of American government generally. The most important legislative powers pertain to finances. A county board levies taxes, make appropriations, and incurs debts for the county, subject to restrictions imposed by provisions of the state constitution and statutes. County boards also possess a variety of minor legislative powers, particularly in the regulatory field. Counties license and regulate businesses situated outside the boundaries of incorporated municipalities, such as liquor dispensaries, dance halls, circuses, and sporting events. They may also enact health and zoning ordinances as permitted by state law.

Subject to varying amounts of state control and supervision, county boards exercise a wide variety of administrative functions. Probably the most important single function of a "typical" county board is supervision of the road and highway program. Another important duty concerns the control of county property. Administration of the courthouse, jail, poor house, county hospital, and various recreational facilities may rest with the county board. The board oversees the purchase and sale of property, construction and repair of buildings, and the general maintenance and upkeep of all county property. The county board may be responsible for the administration of elections and the supervision of poor relief, subject to control by state law. In addition, the board appoints certain officers, assistants, and deputies of many kinds, as well as a number of employees. It may also fix the salaries of county officers and employees, often subject to limitations imposed by state laws.

The judicial powers of most county boards today are insignificant. In some states these bodies have the legal status of judicial tribunals in spite of the fact that they perform few if any judicial functions. In other states county boards cannot be vested with judicial authority. Despite such restrictions, individual members of county boards may have judicial responsibilities when acting as county judges or justices of the peace.

Collateral Agencies

A practice has long existed in county government of establishing a variety of inferior boards and commissions, usually unifunctional, to administer or supervise such functions as welfare, health, property assessment, libraries, elections, and hospitals. Further complicating the picture is the fact that there may be more than one special agency responsible for different aspects of a single function. The existence of boards and commissions engaged in such activities as planning, land use regulation, airports, recreation, and personnel reflects recent developments in county government, often involving the addition of new functions. Such new functions are significant with regard to the nature of county government today because they are primarily of *local* interest. Because of the increasing importance of such activities, counties can no longer be correctly viewed almost exclusively as subdivisions for the administration of state programs. Occasionally authority over county financial affairs may be lodged in an agency other than the county board.

Officers and Employees

The Sheriff. The most time-honored and universal county officer is the sheriff, who is nearly always elected by popular vote. The term of officer is usually two or four years. Although the law in some states provides that sheriffs may not succeed themselves, such a provision does not prevent their spouses from being elected to the office and their serving as chief deputy! Traditionally, the sheriff has served as conservator of the peace in the county. Although legally the chief law enforcement officer in the county, the modern sheriff has devoted less and less time to this responsibility, a trend due largely to two factors. First, increased urbanization has placed more and more policing responsibilities in the hands of municipal police. For several reasons sheriffs are willing to leave crime control in incorporated areas to city police officers and town constables even though their legal authority to enforce state laws and county ordinances extends into all units of government in their respective counties. Second, many law enforcement activities formerly in the hands of sheriffs have been transferred to state police. Nevertheless, the county sheriff and deputies still constitute an important agency for law enforcement in counties generally.

In addition to being conservator of the peace, the sheriff is an officer of the courts of record in the county. The sheriff or a deputy is required to attend court sessions and perform a variety of duties as directed, including the service of warrants, summonses, and subpoenas. The sheriff also conducts foreclosures and confiscates abandoned and illegal property. In addition, the sheriff is responsible for persons being held in jail pending indictment or trial, for taking convicted persons to institutions to which they are committed by court action, and frequently for the custody of persons who have been sentenced to the county jail. Sheriffs in some states are required to perform functions not directly related to law enforcement, such as collecting taxes and issuing licenses.

County jails occasionally are administered by the sheriff on the basis of fees. Especially reprehensible is the practice of allowing the sheriff or jailer a stipulated sum per day for each prisoner. Not only does this arrangement serve as an incentive to keep the jail filled, it also constitutes an ever-present temptation to provide substandard meals and inadequate care for prisoners. Knowledge of the evils of this system is widespread, but it is often impossible to arouse sufficient interest on the part of citizens to make changes. In recent years the fee system as a means of financing county jails has been abolished in many jurisdictions, and provision is made in some counties for a separate jailer.

The Prosecuting Attorney. Another county officer intimately associated with law enforcement is the prosecuting attorney, who is known by such titles as state's attorney, district attorney, or solicitor. This official, who may serve more than one county, is essentially a state officer, although popularly elected on a local basis in some three-fourths of the states. When a crime is committed, it is the prosecuting attorney's job to investigate, collect evidence, institute formal proceedings against suspected persons, and represent the state at the trial. Although there may be a staff for purposes of investigation, it is important that the prosecuting attorney work in close cooperation with sheriffs and other local police officers. The prosecuting attorney may also be responsible for giving legal advice to county officers and conducting civil cases to which the county is a party, a task performed in some counties by an attorney retained by the county governing body.

From the standpoint of effective law enforcement, it is difficult to overestimate the importance of the prosecuting attorney. Without the cooperation of this officer, effective law enforcement is impossible. To begin with, grand juries which in a majority of the states are responsible for indicting persons suspected of serious crime, usually consider only evidence presented to them by the prosecuting attorney. As an alternative to grand jury indictment, the prosecuting attorney in many states may bring criminal charges directly by a process known as "information." Whether a grand jury is used or not, the prosecutor largely determines who shall and who shall not be prosecuted for crime.

After a person has been charged with crime, the prosecuting attorney is responsible for conducting the prosecution. Once again the role of this officer is critical. Legally responsible for prosecuting the guilty, a prosecutor also is obligated to seek justice, and this task involves acquitting the innocent. When a prosecuting attorney is doubtful about the sufficiency of evidence to prove a person guilty of a specific charge, he or she may refuse to prosecute or may engage in "plea bargaining" with the accused person's lawyer in order to obtain a guilty plea to a reduced charge. Plea bargaining may also stem from the fact that the prosecuting attorney has insufficient staff to prosecute all offenders. Failure to prosecute may also be explained by personal or political reasons. In spite of the great importance of the office, it is often held either by a young lawyer seeking by this means to become more well known and at the same time gain some experience, or by an older attorney whose career in private practice has not been outstanding.

The Coroner. Only slightly less ancient than the office of sheriff is that of the coroner, who is often popularly elected. The coroner's principal function is to hold inquests to determine the cause of deaths occurring under violent or suspicious circumstances. A few states require coroners to be physicians, but they may be undertakers whose official fees are determined by the number of corpses they bury. Usually there is only one coroner per county, but in a few localities there may be two or more. In some counties, especially more highly urbanized ones, the coroner has been supplanted by a medical examiner who is required to be a physician. Even this arrangement is not entirely satisfactory, however, since the duties of the office involve legal as well as medical questions and decisions. Rare is the person who possesses training desirable for handling both types of problems. As a consequence, it is often necessary that the medical examiner and prosecuting attorney maintain a close working relationship. Although subject to much criticism and the object of proposals for its abolition, the office of coroner performs a significant function in counties across the nation.

The Clerk. The office of county clerk is found in about half of the states, and the incumbent is usually chosen by popular vote. The duties of county clerks may be divided into three major categories: (a) preparation and custodianship of records, (b) issuance of warrants against the county, and (c) administration of elections. The clerk serves as secretary of the county board and "clerk of court" for many local courts of record. The office is commonly the repository for all books, records, and papers of the county and often of special districts located in the county. Deeds, mortgages, leases,[5] plats, marriage certificates, divorce records, birth certificates, adoption papers, and similar documents may be filed with the county clerk. The clerk may also issue passports and naturalization papers in accord with procedures specified by federal law.

When issuing warrants against the county treasury, the county clerk is sometimes called the "auditor," if there is no separate officer with that title. Prior to the issuance of a warrant, a claim must be allowed by the county board. Once it has been prepared by the clerk, the warrant is countersigned and paid by the county treasurer. In practice, actual determination of whether a claim will be allowed against a county often lies with county clerks. This situation stems from the fact that they have available the records to determine the validity of a claim, and their recommendations are likely to be accepted by the board.

The county clerk typically performs important functions with regard to the administration of elections, for example, registering voters where there is no separate registrar to perform this important task. The clerk prepares ballots, receives nominating as well as local initiative and referendum petitions, establishes election precincts, canvasses the vote, and issues certificates of election to local officers. In addition, the county clerk is often responsible for issuing licenses, such as those required for marriage, hunting, fishing, and operation of certain types of businesses.

The Treasurer. Most counties have a treasurer, who may be popularly elected or appointed by the county board. The duties of this office fall into three major categories: (a) receipt of county revenues, (b) custodianship of county funds, and (c) disbursement of money as directed by proper authority. Although certain revenues are received by other officers in

---

5. In about half of the states provision is made for a recorder or register of deeds, and documents relating to property transactions are entrusted to the care of that officer.

many counties, some authorities believe that the collection of all county income should be centralized in the treasurer.[6] Such an arrangement simplifies administration of financial affairs and facilitates the preparation of adequate reports. Furthermore, it may be advisable for the treasurer to collect income due governmental subdivisions within a county, particularly special districts.

When revenues are received by other county officers such as the sheriff or the clerk, they are usually turned over to the treasurer.[7] Earlier in history, county treasurers often retained for their own use any interest paid on county bank deposits, a practice generally recognized as intolerable today. Treasurers usually are required to provide an indemnity bond as a guarantee against any possible loss or misuse of public funds. The third major responsibility of the treasurer is to disburse funds as directed, usually on order of the county board.

The Assessor. Administration of the property tax involves determination of the value of property, a task commonly placed in the hands of the assessor of a county, township, or city. Most often the county assessors evaluate all taxable property within their jurisdiction, and their assessments are accepted by other governmental units for purposes of taxation. In some places assessment of property is lodged with the township assessor. The importance of the assessor is indicated by the fact that much of the revenue of local governments is largely derived from the property tax. Serious problems may result from the election of persons not qualified adequately to perform the assessment function. In an effort to overcome difficulties associated with such a practice, some states have provided that only individuals certified by a state agency as qualified appraisers may actually set the value of real property. Such a requirement means that elected assessors frequently must hire persons qualified to do the work for which they are responsible.

The Superintendent of Schools. The county superintendent of schools may be elected or appointed.[8] The duties and responsibilities of this office vary greatly from state to state. In the fifteen or so states that use the county-unit plan[9] for providing primary and secondary education, the responsibilities of this officer are especially important because most schools are managed on a county-wide basis. In the other states the

---

6. Alternative arrangements have been adopted in a few states whereby the treasurer's office has been merged with some other office or abolished, and banks have been designated to serve as depositories and disbursing agents.
7. Fees received by county officers for the performance of certain particular functions constitute an exception.
8. The office is not found in all states.
9. The county-unit system provides for financing and administering most of the schools, if not all, by county authorities. City schools are sometimes not under direct county supervision and have their own school boards and superintendents.

duties of the county superintendent are less numerous, and he or she serves primarily as an agent of the state department of education in seeing that state requirements are met. This generalization does not mean that in the states without the county-unit arrangement the responsibilities assigned to the county superintendent are unimportant. Duties often include assisting in the development of improved curricula and methods of teaching, encouraging parental interest in the schools, observing physical conditions in school plants, advising school district authorities, making reports to state agencies, and keeping records on all teachers in the county.

Miscellaneous Officers. The foregoing list of county officers is by no means complete. Many others are found in counties across the United States. For purposes of illustration, mention may be made of the *surveyor*, who is usually popularly elected and compensated by fees. A surveyor's chief task is to conduct land surveys and determine boundary lines, a job that can be done equally well by private surveyors. Many counties have an *engineer*, often on a part-time basis, who is in charge of the location, design, and construction of roads and bridges. In addition, there may be a county *roadmaster* who supervises the actual construction and maintenance of county roads, as well as *road viewers* charged with the task of establishing the most feasible route for a proposed road. Some counties have an *auditor*, who may be responsible for preparing budgets and maintaining accounts. Another important function of the auditor is the preaudit of claims against the county to determine their validity and the existence of funds available for payment. Seldom does this officer perform a postaudit to determine the fidelity with which public funds have been handled. Many other county officers exist, but their number and variety are too great to examine here.

Employees. Although an adequate distinction between officers and employees is difficult to make, the general consensus seems to be that an officer is an individual who holds an office or position created specifically by law and who is responsible for the performance of certain duties set forth by law. An employee, on the other hand, is a person hired by an officer or agency to perform tasks specified by superiors.

A problem of county government today is that the spoils system is widespread. Thus, many county employees are appointed on the basis of party and personal allegiance. It is *not impossible* to have efficient government without a merit system, but it is difficult. Although no authoritative list exists, probably no more than fifteen per cent of our counties have established civil service procedures for the selection and appointment of employees on the basis of demonstrated merit.[10] A large part of these counties are situated in New York and Ohio, where

---

10. This number does not include school employees.

counties are required to operate under a merit system. Otherwise the largest percentage of counties with a merit system is found in California. In most other states only a few of the more populous counties have taken similar action.

Even in counties that make no provision for a general merit program, certain employees are under a merit system. Those engaged in administering welfare programs are commonly selected on the basis of merit. This situation is *not* due to a widespread voluntary decision by county authorities to place welfare workers in a different category from other county employees. Instead, it is attributable to a federal requirement that personnel administering welfare funds received from the national government must be employed under some sort of merit plan. Consequently, counties have been forced to make provision for a merit system for such people in order to receive federal monetary assistance.

STRUCTURAL REORGANIZATION

Consolidation

Many proposals have been made for the modernization of county government. In addition to home rule, discussed earlier, a proposal that has received some support is county consolidation. Many counties are too small and possess inadequate financial resources to be effective. Numerous studies have been made with consolidation in mind, and serious proposals have been advanced in several states, but very little has been accomplished. Many factors have contributed to the rarity of county consolidations, but the basic reason is probably reflected in this highly perceptive statement: "Consolidation often seems to be a logical solution, but political decisions are often illogical. The people of one county may be willing to merge with another, providing the *other* county gives up its county seat, courthouse, and officeholders."[11] County officials, politicians, and many citizens look with disfavor upon the idea of losing their identity as residents of *their own* county.

Another type of consolidation that has experienced more success is city-county consolidation, involving the merger of city and county governments. Well known instances are found in Baltimore, Denver, Honolulu, St. Louis, and San Francisco.[12] Partial mergers have been undertaken in

---

11. Marguerite J. Fisher and Donald G. Bishop, *Municipal and Other Local Governments,* Prentice-Hall, New York, 1950, p. 627.
12. Denver, Honolulu, and San Francisco are known as city-counties, while Baltimore and St. Louis are designated simply as cities. Technically, these cities were separated from the counties of which they were once a part. The boundaries of the city-county of Honolulu include the island of Oahu and all nearby islands not assigned to another county. In 1962 a consolidation of the governments of the city of Nashville and Davidson County, Tennessee, was approved by the voters, creating the Metropolitan Government of Nashville and Davidson

Baton Rouge, Boston, New Orleans, New York City, Philadelphia, and Jacksonville, Florida. A special situation exists in Virginia, where cities with 10,000 or more people are legally separated from the counties in which they are situated and perform both city and county services for their residents. No pattern has emerged from the actions taken in different localities; each consolidation has been unique in certain of its aspects. Accordingly, this device is generally viewed not so much as a means of improving county government as of meeting the problems of metropolitan areas.

A Chief Executive

One outstanding weakness of county government in general is the absence of a chief executive. There are far too many independent "executives" and department heads whose activities are subject to no effective supervision and coordination. Recognition of the weaknesses of this arrangement has been widespread, and efforts at improvement have taken three major forms: (a) adoption of the county-manager plan; (b) provision of an appointed chief executive with less authority than is usually granted to a manager; and (c) an elected chief executive. Since the first two of these arrangements are similar in form, they are sometimes not distinguished.

County-manager government is organized in essentially the same manner as the city-manager form.[13] (See Figure 19.2 for a graphic presentation of county-manager government in its "pure" form.) Its basic feature is appointment by the county board of a manager who serves as the county's principal administrative officer. Duties of the manager include enforcement of the official policies of the board, appointment and removal of administrative officers, preparation of budgets, and provision of advice and recommendations to the board. Under this arrangement, *legal* responsibility for the conduct of county affairs rests with the county board, which vests *administrative* responsibility in the hands of a person chosen supposedly without regard to political considerations.

Only a few dozen counties operate under the manager form of government. Unsuccessful efforts have been made in other counties to adopt manager government, which is opposed on a variety of grounds, many of them rather specious. The allegation is often made that manager government is "undemocratic." The popularity of this claim stems from the belief that in order for a government to be democratic, the people

County. A different type of merger was accomplished in Virginia in 1963 when Norfolk and Princess Anne counties became the cities of Chesapeake and Virginia Beach. The Indiana Legislature consolidated Indianapolis and Marion County in 1969. In 1972 voters in Lexington and Fayette County, Kentucky, approved a charter consolidating the two governments. The cities of Anchorage, Glen Alps, and Girdwood were consolidated with the Greater Anchorage Area Borough in 1975.

13. For a discussion of the council-manager type of city government, see Chapter 18.

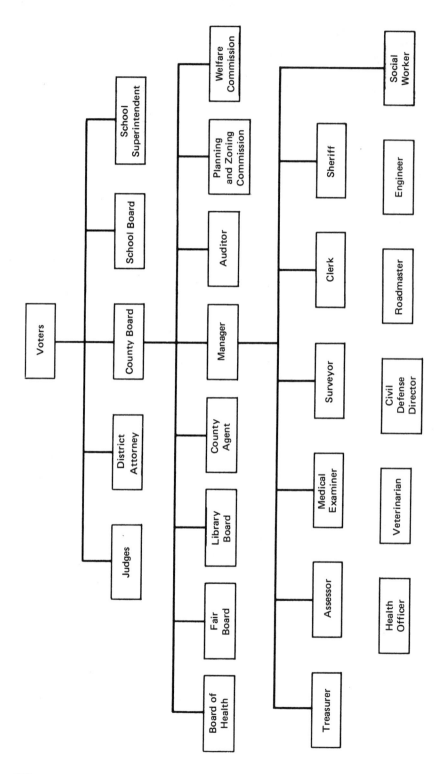

Figure 19.2 County Manager Government

must elect those officers responsible for the execution of public policy as well as those responsible for its formulation. Persons advancing this argument against the manager system disregard the fact that basic responsibility continues to rest in the hands of popularly elected officials. It must be admitted, however, that appointed officials sometimes actually make decisions that appear to be made by representative bodies.

Adoption of the manager form of government is sometimes opposed on the ground that there is too little county business to justify hiring a manager. Even in rural counties where this claim may have some merit, arrangements may be made for hiring part-time managers as is done in some cities. Another possible means of meeting this problem is to put the manager directly in charge of certain county functions, thus eliminating some positions.

More common than managers are *chief administrative officers* who have less power than is normally granted to managers, especially with regard to making appointments and preparing budgets. Chief administrative officers may be limited to making recommendations on appointments to the county board, which retains final appointing authority over officers not elected. In respect to budgets they are usually responsible merely for collecting annual departmental estimates and submitting them, perhaps accompanied by suggestions, to the board. The chief administrative officer constitutes a sort of compromise between the no-executive arrangement traditional in our counties and the strong manager system.

The third alternative followed in some counties that have reorganized their administrative structure is the elected president or supervisor, an arrangement very similar to the mayor-council form of city government.[14] Again, variations in titles and organizational details abound. Efforts directed along this line began during the last century. Among the first counties to provide for an elected president was Cook County, Illinois, where the president is popularly elected as a member of the county board. In addition to being chairman of the board, the president possesses powers of appointment and veto. A majority of the chief county officers are still popularly elected.

Popularly elected chief executives called county supervisors are found in Essex and Hudson counties, New Jersey, where they have been authorized for first-class counties since 1900. Although supposedly responsible for supervising the activities of county officials and employees, these supervisors are without effective authority because they lack control over appointments and budgets. Consequently, their effectiveness as executive officers is quite limited. In Nassau and Westchester counties, New York, elected county executives possess greater control over county affairs since they are empowered to appoint and remove a number of important county officers as well as to prepare budgets. A similar pattern

14. For a discussion of the mayor-council form of city government, see Chapter 18.

is found in St. Louis County, Missouri, where the elected supervisor exercises more administrative control than in most counties with this form of government. Elected county executives have also been established in Baltimore County, in Jefferson Parish, Louisiana, in Milwaukee County, Wisconsin, and in Howard and Montgomery counties, Maryland.

In an effort to overcome some of the difficulties resulting from the lack of a county executive officer, a few counties, especially in Wisconsin, have strengthened the position of the county clerk. The degree to which the clerk's powers are broadened depends largely upon the wishes of the county board. If the members choose to rely upon the clerk in a variety of matters, they may in effect make the officer *primus inter pares,* first among equals. Since such an arrangement involves no reorganization of governmental structure, it does not qualify as constituting a significant change in the traditional pattern of county government.

COUNTY FUNCTIONS

Of the many functions performed by the county some are required by state law, while others are optional; some are traditional, while others are new. Considered generally, those required by state law are the traditional functions, while optional activities are the newer ones. In the former category belong such duties as law enforcement, administration of justice, public welfare, construction and maintenance of roads and highways, assistance to agriculture, and responsibility for phases of public education, a particularly important function in certain parts of the country.

Law Enforcement

From the time of their beginning in England, counties have had responsibilities with regard to preserving public peace and order. While the prevention of crime and the apprehension of criminals now rests in large part with municipal and state police, the sheriff and his deputies usually constitute the only local police force with county-wide jurisdiction. In spite of the fact that the sheriff's office is often poorly prepared to cope with modern crime, he is still responsible for many law-enforcement activities outside municipal boundaries. Two important officers, other than the sheriff, concerned with law enforcement are the prosecuting attorney and the coroner, whose duties have been briefly described above.

Administration of Justice.   One of the most important county functions involves provision of courts and other agencies for the administration of state civil and criminal laws. Although local courts are viewed legally as components of the state judicial system, responsibility for their organization, staffing, and financial support often rests with counties. The interrelations existing in this area are stressed by the fact that local judicial officers may serve as members of county governing bodies. Throughout most of the rural United States, a person who commits a minor infraction of the law or who wishes to institute a minor civil suit must go into a justice of the peace court. The justice of the peace is a traditional county officer.[15] At a time when the law was not yet developed into the many refinements associated with a complex social and economic order, and ordinary people were competent to settle the controversies among their neighbors, much could be said in behalf of this office.

Persons committing more serious infractions of the law or wishing to institute a major civil action commonly begin proceedings in a "court of general jurisdiction." Known most often as circuit, district, or superior courts, the geographical jurisdiction of these courts is often coterminous with county boundaries. More often, however, special judicial districts are provided by state law. These districts frequently comprise two or more counties, each of which is required to supply funds for the support of the court; and the court must hold sessions in each county at prescribed intervals. Although popularly elected in over three-fourths of the states, judges of such courts generally must be qualified both as to training and experience.

Provision is sometimes made for a trial court intermediate between the justice of the peace and the general trial court. The county commonly constitutes the geographical jurisdiction of such a court, which may hear criminal cases more serious than those taken into a justice of the peace court and less serious than those that must go into a general trial court. Some states permit only counties with a specified minimum population to establish such a court. A fourth type of court found in some counties is the probate court, whose chief duties involve supervision and disposition of the estates of deceased persons. In those counties without probate courts, the administration of estates is generally performed by courts of general or limited jurisdiction as described above.

One phase of the administration of justice that is poorly handled throughout most of the United States is the defense of persons accused of crime who are financially unable to hire capable legal talent. In more serious cases involving such individuals, it is the duty of the court to see that defense counsel is provided. The traditional method of meeting this requirement is through the device of assigned counsel, whereby the court designates a lawyer to represent the defendant. This practice is generally unsatisfactory either because the better lawyers do not draw the assignments, or if they do, the accompanying fees are insufficient to arouse their best efforts. In an attempt to make "equality before the law" a

---

15. Justices of the peace often are chosen for smaller areas, such as the township or special district.

fact as well as a slogan, a few counties and cities have made provision for the office of public defender, who is required by law to defend the accused just as the prosecuting attorney is required to prosecute him.[16] Of course, persons able to do so must still provide their own counsel.

Public Welfare

The care of dependent poor is a traditional function of American counties. Although the *portion* of the public welfare burden borne by local governments has decreased appreciably in recent times counties still play a vital role in the administration of welfare services; they are the major local agencies through which so-called "outdoor" assistance is usually provided.[17] Outdoor assistance, sometimes called home relief, consists of grants of food, clothes, fuel, medical supplies, utilities, shelter, or in some cases the provision of funds for the purchase, by the recipient, of such necessities. Counties also share in the administration of assistance to the aged, the blind, and dependent children, although most of the money for these programs comes from the federal and state governments. Recent years have witnessed greatly increased state supervision of county welfare activities, a development stemming in large part from provisions of federal law requiring effective administration of federal welfare funds in all political subdivisions of a state.

Roads and Highways

Provision of ways for public travel is another traditional function of counties and other units of local government. Indeed, it was not until World War I that all states participated in the construction of highways. In most states, responsibility for this important activity is now divided between the state and local units. Rural public ways are commonly classified as primary or secondary highways and farm-to-market roads. Highways of the first class are generally designed to facilitate cross-state or interstate traffic. Secondary highways, referred to in many localities as county highways, are designed to link small towns and to feed traffic into first-class highways. As their name indicates, farm-to-market roads are designed chiefly to carry traffic to and from farms and in turn to feed traffic into highways of the first two classes.

Everywhere, states have assumed most of the responsibility for con-

16. First provided in Los Angeles County in 1914, the office of public defender has spread to many California counties and municipalities, along with a sprinkling of others across the country.
17. "Indoor" assistance, typified by the county almshouse or poorhouse, has been of decreasing importance in recent years. Many persons earlier commited to such institutions are now cared for in state institutions, while others are kept out of institutions by improved programs for outdoor relief.

struction or supervision of the construction of primary highways. Generally, chief responsibility for secondary highways rests with counties, which in recent years have been increasingly responsible for farm-to-market roads that were formerly constructed and maintained by towns or townships. Although they carry only a small part of the total traffic, secondary highways and farm-to-market roads comprise some seventy-five per cent of the total road mileage in the United States. Despite the fact that construction and maintenance of roads in these categories are vested in counties and other units of local government, more than half of the necessary money is provided by the states, largely in the form of allocations from gasoline taxes.

Assistance to Agriculture

Agricultural extension work is found in most counties in the United States. Often called "cooperative extension," this program is financed by the national government, the states, and counties. Its basic purposes are to provide farmers and other rural dwellers with practical information on agriculture and home economics and instill in them a desire to use that information to increase productivity and improve their standard of living.[18] Actual administration of the program rests with county extension offices working in close cooperation with state agricultural colleges. Each extension office is under the supervision of a "county agent," who usually has a home-demonstration agent and sometimes a 4-H Club agent working alongside. These agents may be appointed by the county board, subject to the approval of other governmental units sharing the cost of the program. At present the national government bears over forty per cent of the costs of extension work, the states something over thirty per cent, and the counties slightly under twenty-five per cent, with a small amount coming from farmers' organizations.

Education

In nearly one-third of the states the county is the dominant governmental unit in the administration of public education on the primary and secondary levels. Under this arrangement, the schools in a county are financed and administered on a county-wide basis, although city schools may be separately controlled. Major arguments in behalf of the county-unit system are that it promotes uniformity of educational opportunities throughout a relatively large area and that by pooling the resources of this area the likelihood of better educational facilities is enhanced. However,

---

18. The efforts of extension workers are not limited to these undertakings. Particularly in recent years, they have branched out into social and recreational activities as well as adult education programs designed to promote interest in community, national, and international affairs.

there exists in many places a strong desire on the part of the people to keep control over schools "close to home," and local school districts accord with this wish. In counties not under the county-unit arrangement, county school officials may still serve an important function, particularly in enforcing the rules and regulations of state departments of education.

Newer County Functions

Contrary to the frequently repeated views of some skeptics, counties in recent years have demonstrated their capacity to assume a variety of new functions. Included among these newer responsibilities are health protection, parks and recreational facilities, libraries, and zoning. This list is in no sense complete, but it serves well the purpose of illustration. Assumption of these activities has been largely a matter of necessity, resulting from the rapid growth of heavily populated areas outside municipal boundaries.

Although much emphasis has been placed on "healthful" country living, deaths from certain diseases, such as malaria and typhoid fever, are higher today in rural areas than in cities. Many problems complicate the development of adequate health programs in counties across the nation. A large portion of the rural counties are financially unable to create and maintain adequate health departments. Efforts along this line were given impetus by the Social Security Act of 1935, which made federal funds available to assist in establishing and maintaining local health services. On occasion counties have cooperated to provide joint health programs. County health organizations have accomplished much in the areas of disease-control, sanitation, and health education. Also, many counties have performed an important service by establishing hospitals.

Many counties own and operate parks and other recreational facilities such as playgrounds, swimming pools, golf courses, and camping and picnic grounds. These facilities serve not only county residents, but city dwellers as well. Failure on the part of many cities to plan for adequate recreational facilities within their confines has increased the need for county action. County libraries for the benefit of both city and rural dwellers have been established in many localities. In some instances counties have entered into contracts with city libraries or other county libraries to provide service to their rural residents, or they may have joined with a city to establish a joint city-county library. In recent years, increasing use has been made of regional libraries established cooperatively by two or more counties, especially poorer, less populous ones.

Zoning has been a generally accepted practice in cities for many years, involving the creation of districts in which only specified land uses and building arrangements are permitted. The authority under which counties are able to zone derives from state enabling legislation. Under such permissive statutes, a county may, by means of a zoning ordinance, impose reasonable restrictions upon the use of real property. Wisconsin, in 1929, was the first state to provide for full-fledged rural zoning. Over three-fourths of the states have passed laws granting zoning powers to counties or townships.

Rural zoning is intended basically to conserve natural resources and prevent wasteful scattering of rural population on unproductive land. Ordinances designed to accomplish these purposes commonly provide for three types of districts: recreational, forest, and agricultural. Lands in recreational and forest districts may be put only to certain specified uses, including playgrounds, parks, hunting and fishing, cottages, and growth of forest products. Agricultural land, on the other hand, may be put to any lawful use. Through zoning, privately owned land may be reserved for particular uses as specified by law. Zoning serves in part as an alternative to public ownership. Linked with a program of submarginal land purchase by government, zoning can effectively change a wasteful and unproductive pattern of land use into one that will bring material benefits to a county.

Although financial and legal limitations generally stand in the way of the assumption of new activities by counties, a major reason for their failure adequately to meet many needs has been public indifference and even hostility. A number of studies in different states have concluded that the county is the logical unit of government to provide many services and controls necessary for the "good life" in rural and suburban areas. Counties may even assist cities in providing typically municipal services to urban residents, as has been done to a considerable extent in Los Angeles County. Too often, however, counties are dominated by an attitude as antiquated as their administrative structure. Rural residents particularly may be slow to see advantages accruing from increased governmental activity. Suburbanites often move into the "country" to get away from the city, and they oppose extension of urban controls and services. Many of them prefer to drink unsafe water, travel on poorly paved and inadequately lighted streets, and live with insufficient police and fire protection.

PROSPECTS FOR THE COUNTY

Counties and municipalities are the dominant units of local government, and there is a trend to grant counties many powers formerly exercised almost exclusively by cities. One reason for the increasing importance of the county is that the national government has found the county more convenient than the municipality as a base for certain grant-in-aid programs. Another reason for recent growth in the importance of the county lies in the rapid development of urban fringe areas over which no other unit of local government has general authority. Where the county is unable or unwilling to act, the needs of such areas often become acute. In order that the county may prove equal to the responsibilities thrust upon it, some changes are badly needed, since the organizational structure and powers of most counties were designed to meet the needs of the rural society of a century or more ago.

Other Local Governments

Three types of local governments often not clearly differentiated in the public mind are the New England town, the township, and the special district. At least three distinct types of governmental units are known as *towns*. Generally outside New England, New York, and Wisconsin, a town is a small urban place that may or may not be incorporated. In a few states, particularly New York and Wisconsin, units of government known elsewhere as townships are officially designated as towns. In the six New England states, *towns* are the *principal units of local government* except in the more populous urban areas that have been incorporated as cities or in some instances as villages.

Townships generally function to provide certain services to the inhabitants of relatively small areas without regard to population concentration. Townships commonly provide services largely if not exclusively to rural residents, but they sometimes perform functions for the benefit of persons living in urban areas that are not incorporated as municipalities.[1]
Special districts, occasionally called *ad hoc* districts, are found throughout the United States. Typically, a special district provides only one service, such as schools, water, or fire protection. It is not uncommon, however, for two or three closely related functions to be performed by a single district.

NEW ENGLAND TOWNS

Most of the area of New England is divided into towns, each usually encompassing between twenty and forty square miles. These towns frequent-

---

1. The civil township discussed in this chapter must not be confused with the congressional or survey township, which is not a governmental unit. The latter was created by Congress under the Articles of Confederation in 1785 as a means for surveying land in the Northwest Territory.

ly include both rural and urban territory—much like counties in other states. As will be noted later, New England towns perform a variety of important governmental functions. Their unique character stems not so much from their structure or their powers as from the manner in which they conduct local business.

Organization of Town Government

The Town Meeting. New England towns afford the outstanding example in the United States today of a governmental unit that operates as a direct democracy instead of employing a representative body to make policy decisions. All voters are eligible to attend and participate in their own town meeting. Many voters, particularly in large urban towns, do not attend the meetings, and decisions are made by a small minority of residents. In an effort to meet the problems inherent in this situation, some larger towns, especially in Connecticut and Massachusetts, have established the representative town meeting. This arrangement requires the popular election of a number of voters from "districts" or "precincts" within each town to serve as "town meeting members." Although voting at the town meeting is restricted to such elected members, all voters are still eligible to attend and voice their opinions.

Important decisions are made at town meetings. Ordinances or "bylaws" are enacted; appropriations are voted for the following year; taxes are levied; borrowing is authorized as necessary; and town officers are elected. Other important matters are also considered, such as the construction and repair of roads, the purchase of individual items of property and equipment, street lighting, improvement of library facilities, and employee salaries. The necessity of having to make decisions on such a variety of matters undoubtedly causes some citizens to absent themselves from town meetings. The increasing complexity of government has caused the town meeting to lose much of its "pristine vitality."

The Selectmen. An important task of a town meeting is the choice of selectmen,[2] in whose hands rests the executive authority of the town. The board of selectmen, most commonly consisting of three members, is responsible for the conduct of town business between town meetings. Consequently, the board performs a variety of routine functions, such as issuing licenses, awarding contracts, conducting elections, and supervising the maintenance of town property, the repair of streets, and the construction of sewers—to list a few. One selectman frequently assumes a position of leadership on the board and may function much like a "mayor" in spite of the fact that all authority is formally vested in the board as a

2. Selectmen may be chosen at separate town elections.

body. Selectmen also make the rules and regulations necessary to govern a town between town meetings.

Other Town Officers. Among other important town officers is the town *clerk,* whose responsibilities are comparable to those of the county clerk outside New England.[3] Although official duties are primarily concerned with record-keeping, the town clerk is typically the chief source of help and information concerning town affairs, a situation resulting in part from the long tenure characteristic of the office. The town *treasurer* is the recipient and custodian of town funds, from which payments are made upon proper authorization. The same person often serves both as clerk and treasurer. Judicial functions of the town are generally performed by the *justice of the peace.*[4]

Evaluation of property for purposes of taxation is the duty of town *assessors* or *appraisers,* of whom there are commonly one to three per town. The town law enforcement officers are the popularly elected *constable* and *attorney.* The duties of these officers have decreased in importance in recent years, as law-enforcement activities have been assumed increasingly by state, city, and county officials. Popularly elected *auditors* check the books of small towns, while larger ones usually hire professional help. Responsibility for the condition of rural town roads rests with the *road commissioner,* who most often has learned the trade by experience rather than training. Minor officers found in some but not all towns are *overseers of the poor; fence viewers* who settle disputes between farmers concerning the proper location of fences; *sextons* who look after cemeteries; and *water commissioners* with responsibility to maintain an adequate supply of pure water. Some towns recently have provided for civil service commissions and planning boards.

Among the more recent and important additions to town government is the *town manager* whose duties are similar to those of the city manager.[5] Subject to the requirements of state law, typical procedure is for the town meeting to instruct the selectmen to hire a manager who is answerable to them. The manager is responsible for seeing that state laws and local ordinances are enforced. It is common practice for a manager to assume the duties of some of the other officers, often including the treasurer, the road commissioner, the water commissioner, and overseer of the poor. In addition, the manager usually acts as purchasing agent for the town. In order to obtain the benefits of manager government, some small New England towns have hired managers jointly with other units of local government. These joint efforts may involve two or more towns or in some instances towns and villages.

3. For an examination of the duties of the county clerk, see Chapter 19.
4. Although justices of the peace are technically state officers, they are generally elected by the voters of each town and are identified with town government.
5. For a discussion of the duties of city managers, see Chapter 18.

Functions of Town Governments

The foregoing discussion of the organization of town government reveals the major functions of New England towns. Functioning in a capacity somewhat similar to that of counties elsewhere, New England towns perform many duties that vary according to the needs and demands of local residents. In general, towns are concerned with roads, education, libraries, parks, sanitation, water supply, health, recreation facilities, and police and fire protection, as well as the assessment and collection of taxes. Towns, particularly the more urbanized ones, may provide many municipal services. Consequently, the distinction between an urban New England town and a city may be more of form than of substance.

TOWNSHIPS

Townships exist as functioning governmental units in fifteen states outside New England.[6] As noted earlier, these governmental units are officially designated "towns" in New York and Wisconsin.[7] Townships are numerous in some states and scarce in others. Only in the state of Indiana does township government encompass the entire area of the state. In a few states, establishment of township government is optional with each county. Some states include municipalities within the jurisdiction of townships, while others exclude them.

Organization of Township Government

Township Meetings. Like their New England prototype, township meetings are in theory composed of all qualified voters. Attendance is generally very poor, however, and township government has lost much of its early vitality. Often no one attends except officeholders. Those who do attend have important matters to consider. They levy taxes, provide appropriations, authorize bond issues, enact ordinances and bylaws, and elect township officers. They may also perform a variety of less important duties such as authorizing acquisition of property for various public uses, entering into contracts for the provision of goods and services, and receiving reports from various officials. Recent years have witnessed a gradual decrease in the powers of township meetings.

---

6. The fifteen states are Illinois, Indiana, Kansas, Michigan, Minnesota, Missouri, Nebraska, New Jersey, New York, North Dakota, Ohio, Pennsylvania, South Dakota, Washington, and Wisconsin.
7. In a few states, Minnesota and Pennsylvania for example, the terms, "town" and "township" are interchangeable in popular usage with reference to township governments.

Township Boards. Every township has a board known variously as the board of trustees, board of supervisors, board of auditors, or just simply the township board. Members of such boards, usually three or five, may be elected directly to membership or they may acquire membership as a result of some other office which they hold. Persons in the latter category are said to be *ex officio* members. Township clerks, treasurers, and justices of the peace often serve in an *ex officio* capacity. About half of the township boards are composed of both *ex officio* and elective members; all members of the others are directly elected. Terms of office are usually two or four years. Regular meetings are held monthly in some states and only two or three times a year in others.

Where township meetings exist, duties of township boards are largely administrative, including preparation of budgets for presentation to the meetings. In the absence of a township meeting, the board may be both the legislative and administrative authority, an arrangement somewhat similar to the commission form of city government.[8] The similarity is especially striking where individual board members are responsible for supervising certain town functions such as road construction and maintenance or the assessment of property. Townships occasionally are divided into sections, with each board member responsible for administering affairs in one of the sections.

Other Township Officers. A noticeable parallel exists between officers of townships and those of New England towns. Great variety is evident among townships as to the number of officers, their duties, and the methods of their selection. Provision is made regularly for a *clerk,* a *treasurer,* an *assessor,* a *constable, justices of the peace,* and *road commissioners,* whose duties are much like those of their counterparts in New England towns. Among the less important township officers are *fence viewers, overseers of the poor, poundkeepers,* and *weed commissioners.* The last two officers, respectively, are concerned with impounding stray dogs and livestock and with eradicating noxious weeds.

In about half the township states provision is made for a chief administrative officer in each township who is known by a variety of titles, including *supervisor* and, *trustee.* This officer is usually a member of the township board. Some comparison may be drawn between this officer and a mayor in the commission type of city government, since the officer typically combines the roles of legislator and administrator. First and foremost a politician by necessity, the supervisor is seldom a professional administrator. Nevertheless, this arrangement is preferable to the headless administrative structure characteristic of many townships.

---

8. For an explanation of commission government, see Chapter 18.

Functions of Township Governments

Township activities differ from state to state and even within individual states. Urban townships may provide such a variety of functions that they resemble municipal governments. The great bulk of townships, however, are units for rural government, and their most important activities generally relate to roads, welfare, education, and law enforcement. Undoubtedly, the most important of these is the construction and maintenance of roads. Although townships are too small to function economically and efficiently in this area, the desire of local residents to keep control of roads "close to home" has deterred shifting the task to counties. Nevertheless, such a shift has occurred in a few states. Townships occasionally serve as administrative units for the distribution of welfare funds under supervision by state agencies. In a few states the township rather than the school district serves as the basic agency for providing public education. Township police officers are normally active only in the enforcement of township traffic ordinances. Other services provided by some townships include fire protection, public health programs, recreational facilities, cemeteries, licensing and regulating certain businesses, planning, and zoning, as well as the construction of public works like sanitary sewers, disposal plants, and waterworks.

Future of Township Governments

Over forty years ago Professor Lane W. Lancaster observed, "There is not a function now performed by the township which could not be better performed by other units."[9] But the township continues to play a significant role in rural government in nearly one-third of the states. In spite of the passing of pioneer days for which townships were well suited, many persons prefer to adhere to time-honored arrangements. So long as the people in township states maintain an attitude of toleration or even admiration toward its institutions and practices, the township will survive.

Recent events point toward the eventual demise of the township, but the process is certain to be slow. Modern means of communication and transportation have rendered small township areas somewhat anachronistic. Township organization for the provision of services such as roads and welfare overlaps and duplicates comparable arrangements in other governments, especially counties. Recognition of this duplication is reflected in major transfers of some township functions to counties. This shift has been most noticeable in relation to roads and welfare, but it has also occurred with regard to education, property assessment, and law enforcement. Another factor that has weakened the townships

9. Lane W. Lancaster, *Government in Rural America,* D. Van Nostrand Co., Inc., Princeton, 1937, p. 77.

has been the incorporation of portions of their area either by annexation to existing cities or by creation of new municipalities, particularly villages. Incorporation is especially detrimental to townships where state law provides that incorporated areas shall be severed from township jurisdiction.

SPECIAL DISTRICTS

Early in the century the county was dubbed "the dark continent of American politics." It is appropriate, says John C. Bollens, to describe the special district as the "new dark continent of American politics."[10] The number and variety of special districts make any effort at general description difficult. In 1977 the Bureau of the Census counted 41,136 special districts in the United States, including 15,174 school districts, which were enumerated separately. The Bureau found special districts in every state except Alaska and the District of Columbia and noted the absence of a consistent pattern relative to their organization and financing.

Reasons for the Growth of Special Districts

In a thorough study of special districts, Professor Bollens has identified five major reasons for their growth: (1) unsuitability of other units of local government, (2) desire for independence, (3) advocacy by existing governments, (4) expediency and finances, and (5) unadorned self-interest.[11] When the need for a particular service such as fire protection or soil conservation becomes evident to the people residing in a given area, no existing, general-purpose local government may be able, ready, and willing to take steps necessary to meet the need. Area is a major problem because the boundairies of established governments such as counties and cities often are not coterminous with the area of need. Thus when urban fringe dwellers desire fire protection they may be unable to obtain it from an existing government. Since they are outside the city, it has no duty to serve them, and counties and townships generally do not provide such services. The easy and quick solution is to create a fire district by vote of the residents, levy a tax on the property in it, and then establish a fire department or contract with a nearby city to provide protection.

The unsuitability of established governments may stem from factors other than area. Expansion of services may be restricted by financial and functional limitations imposed by constitutional or statutory provisions. Thus the residents of a city may wish to expand the recreational

10. John C. Bollens, *Special District Governments in the United States,* University of California Press, Berkeley, 1957, p. 1.
11. *Ibid.,* pp. 6-15.

facilities of their community. At the same time the city may have reached or come close to a legally imposed tax or debt ceiling, and no other means of raising revenue may be available. A possible solution may be the creation of a park district to levy the necessary tax and provide the desired facilities. Variations of this hypothetical situation are almost unlimited in practice. Another problem arises from the lack of authority of general governmental units to provide needed services. Counties and townships, for example, may not possess authority under state law to provide fire protection and a supply of water to residents, who then seek to solve their problems by creating special districts.

Even when financial and functional restrictions do not prohibit action, established local governments sometimes promote the creation of special districts because of their administrative inability to assume the burden of expanded services. Elected officials, often concerned primarily with keeping the tax rate down, may be reluctant to expand activities. Furthermore, the quality of administration may be so poor that an extension of services may be impractical and undesirable. Such an extension might lead to a complete breakdown of established practices and would be unlikely to provide the level of service desired by those seeking a solution to their problems.

Another major reason for the growth of special districts has been a desire for independence. Persons strongly interested in the success of a particular activity or program commonly seek to give it some sort of independent status. An excellent example of this tendency is the school district. In the great majority of states public education is provided partially, if not entirely, by school districts. A major consideration leading to the establishment of these districts has been the conviction on the part of educators, legislators, and the public in general that such an important function should not be entrusted to a general-purpose governmental unit. This attitude is often expressed in terms of keeping education "out of politics." The implication is that where "politics" dominate, professionalism and efficiency must suffer. A related concern is the feeling that a relatively small, single-purpose unit is more responsive to the wishes of the people than a larger one. Although the accuracy of this idea is debatable, it has unquestionably contributed to the proliferation of various types of special districts.

Advocacy for special districts has also come from existing governments. Jealousy among local governments may generate support for the creation of a new government rather than the augmentation of one already in existence. Thus township authorities may promote special districts to provide services to certain areas rather than support annexation to a city, especially if incorporated areas are not within township jurisdiction. On the other hand, efforts to organize special districts may stem from a conviction in the minds of local officals that only in this way can needed services be provided. A city may recognize the importance of extending fire protection to surrounding areas, and a special district may appear to be the only feasible method of meeting the need. Also, support for special districts may arise from national and state laws designed to enhance the provision of particular functions, usually by means of financial support. The large number of soil conservation districts attests to the impact of national legislation.

Expediency and financial condition constitute important factors in explanation of the growth in number of special districts. The simple fact that it is often more expeditious to provide a governmental service by creating a new district rather than setting up the required machinery within an established unit explains the existence of many special districts. Another consideration is that an area with limited population and financial resources may need and be able to afford only a few functions that it cannot obtain from a general-purpose government. Under such circumstances, the obvious solution is to create a low-cost government capable of providing the limited functions required, that is, a special district.

Self-interest on the part of small groups may be decisive in creating special districts. Businesses interested in selling supplies and equipment may also induce some persons to favor the establishment of a new government. Another, probably somewhat more important selfish consideration, has been noted by Emmett Asseff, who expresses the opinion that "the special district has a psychological attraction, for there a specific tax is applied to a specific function and area" in which the taxpayer is especially interested.[12]

Formation and Organization of Special Districts

Details pertaining to the organization of special districts are spelled out in the statutes of each state.[13] Quite naturally, great variations exist, and generalization is difficult. Individual districts occasionally are formed by special legislative act, but in most instances they are organized by local residents according to the provisions of general statutes. Three major steps are usually required to set up a special district. First, a petition must be circulated among those to be affected, stipulating the type of district to be created and defining its area, and a specified number of signatures of residents or property owners must be secured. Second, the petition must be filed with some governmental agency, commonly the county board. The board may simply pass on the legality of the petition, or it may possibly determine the desirability of the district and grant or deny the petition. Most often, a third step in the formation of a special district is a local referendum.

12. Emmett Asseff, *Special Districts in Louisiana*, Bureau of Government Research, Louisiana State University, Baton Rouge, 1951, p. 3.
13. Rarely, special districts are organized directly under the authority of constitutional provisions.

The variety of organizational patterns found in special districts defies general description. Nevertheless, it is important to get an idea of the manner in which they are organized. The governing body of a district is generally a board composed of three, five, or seven members. These persons, variously known as commissioners, directors, trustees, or supervisors, may be appointed or elected. Only rarely is a single officer made responsible for the affairs of a district. Among school districts common practice dictates that policymaking shall be in the hands of a popularly elected board, which in turn hires a professional administrator, or superintendent, to oversee the affairs of the district. Terms of office for board members are usually two, four, or six years.

An outstanding characteristic of many special districts is their informality in organization and procedure. This is not surprising in view of the fact that about one-third of all nonschool districts have no paid personnel, and very few have a payroll of 100 or more persons. School districts employ over nine-tenths of all special district employees. District boards normally possess practically unlimited discretion in hiring and firing employees. Teachers may enjoy "tenure," but this status does not constitute very effective protection against removal by the board. Civil service is practically unknown. In the smaller districts, officers often perform their duties and maintain records in a desultory and haphazard manner.

Finances

Property taxes, special assessments, service charges, and grants from the states and federal government constitute most of the income received by special districts. The relative importance of these sources varies appreciably with the type of district. School districts obtain almost all of their income from local property taxes and state grants. On the other hand, water, sanitary, and similar districts acquire most of their revenue from special assessments against benefited property and service charges collected from those using district facilities. Some special districts, especially soil conservation districts, must rely for their revenue entirely on contributions from other governmental units and residents within their boundaries. Most special districts possess authority to issue bonds, usually subject to approval by the voters. Strict limits are generally imposed by state law upon the taxing and bonding capacity of districts.

Taxpayers often fail to appreciate the impact imposed upon their pocketbooks by special districts within which they live. It is not uncommon for a person, particularly someone living outside a municipality, to be taxed by four or five special districts. For example, many people live at the same time in a school district, a water district, a fire district, and a sanitary district. All of these districts may levy property taxes, and commonly all of the levies are incorporated in the tax bill prepared by the county. The share of taxes paid to the county treasurer and actually remaining with the county may be very small. In this way the county serves as a collection agency for special districts within its boundaries.

Quasi-Special Districts

Scattered across the country are many subordinate agencies that do not possess sufficient administrative and fiscal autonomy to be classified as separate governmental units. Often known as "districts" or "authorities," these agencies are generally dependent for their creation and continued existence upon some government such as a state, county, or municipality. Thus, California has created fish and game districts, game refuge districts, and highway districts, all of which function as adjuncts of the state government and engage in no independent action. Florida counties have established sanitary, water, and zoning districts, as well as airport, bridge, and port authorities. Each of these agencies is created by the county in which it is located, and they function under the direct and immediate supervision of the respective boards of county commissioners. New York municipalities similarly use garbage and refuse districts, water districts, and parking authorities. Municipal park, sewer, and zoning districts exist in South Dakota. Such examples could be multiplied many times.[14]

Like true special districts, quasi-districts may be organized so that their boundaries are coterminous with the area in which a particular service is needed or desired. Thus zoning districts may be desirable in only a few, scattered sections of a county. Possessing authority to establish such districts, the county board can take steps to provide the necessary machinery for the enactment and administration of zoning rules and regulations in selected areas. The county board probably would serve *ex officio* as the governing body of each zoning district, an arrangement typical of the practice in most quasi-districts. A significant consideration in favor of quasi-districts is that they do not require the establishment of separate governmental units. Consequently, the people do not have to elect additional officers and be burdened further with the multiplication of governments.

---

14. Occasionally, authorities are established by the cooperative efforts of two or more governments. Probably the best known example is the Port Authority of New York and New Jersey.

Metropolitan Areas

WHAT IS A "METROPOLITAN AREA"?

One consequence of the rapid increase in urbanism has been the growth of the *metropolitan area,* sometimes called the metropolis. Although large "urban aggregations" have been the subject of much study and concern in recent years, metropolitan areas are not easily defined. They are large social, economic, and cultural communities characterized by a complex governmental pattern. A metropolis may be a "concept that is foggy in spots and fuzzy around the edges," but it definitely implies the presence of a large, heavily populated urban area that transcends the borders of numerous governmental units, including cities, towns, special districts, and often even states.

Recognizing the need for precise, even though arbitrary, terminology, the United States Bureau of the Census in 1949 established criteria for a *standard metropolitan area.* Except in New England, such an area consisted of a county or group of counties containing at least one city of 50,000 population or over. Counties without cities of this size but contiguous to a county possessing such a city were included within a standard metropolitan area if they were "socially and economically integrated with the central city" and not essentially agricultural. In New England the town was substituted for the county as the basic governmental unit for determining the geographical boundaries of standard metropolitan areas.

About three-fifths of the country's population lived in the 174 standard metropolitan areas in the United States in 1957, which contained about fifteen per cent of the nation's local governmental units. In June, 1959, the official designation for metropolitan areas was changed from "standard metropolitan area" to "standard metropolitan statistical area." As a result of changes in designation, eight new areas were added to the list, raising the total to 188 within the continental United States, plus three in Puerto Rico and Honolulu, Hawaii. In 1967, there were 226 standard metropolitan statistical areas in the continental United States, plus one in Hawaii and three in Puerto Rico. By 1977, the number of SMSA's in the fifty states had reached 272, plus four in Puerto Rico. The largest, of course, was the New York area with 11.5 million persons, followed by the Los Angeles—Long Beach and Chicago complexes with over seven million persons each.

Most of the nation's increase in population since 1950 has occurred in the metropolitan areas, chiefly in the suburbs and fringe areas around the central cities. Care must be taken in discussing the characteristics of metropolitan populations, however. One complication arises from the fact that not all residents of metropolitan areas are classified as urban. The Bureau of the Census considers places of 2,500 or more population and closely contiguous areas as urban. Since the county is the basic unit for determining the boundaries of standard metropolitan statistical areas, some rural population is included within them. Consequently a state may have more metropolitan than urban residents!

Useful though it is, the standard metropolitan statistical area is not an entirely satisfactory concept as a basis for studying metropolitanism. From the practical standpoint, the important task is to identify the problems resulting from the rapid growth of large urban areas and to develop means of meeting them. The difficulties associated with water supply, police protection, waste disposal, and transportation, to name only a few, are not restricted to cities with 50,000 or more residents. Indeed, the problems of urban growth in and around a community with 35,000 people, for example, may be more complex than in one of 50,000 or more.

Recognition of the Metropolis

Serious study of the growth, characteristics, and problems of the metropolis is largely a product of the last forty or so years. An early study published in 1933 under the direction of the President's Research Committee on Social Trends combined three approaches to the metropolitan community which may be identified as the governmental, the sociological, and the economic. Comprehensive understanding of the metropolis requires the best efforts of the political scientist, the sociologist, and the economist. Some studies of metropolitan problems have been oriented largely, if not exclusively, toward only one of these disciplines. Fortunately, others have sought to combine them. By its very nature, a textbook on state and local government must stress the governmental aspects of metropolitanism, but it is important that the student be aware that they by no means constitute the whole picture.

CONSEQUENCES OF METROPOLITAN GROWTH

Governmental Inadequacy

Luther Gulick has offered an incisive analysis of causes for the "breakdown" of local government in metropolitan areas. He suggests four major reasons: (1) a governmental vacuum, (2) fractionalization of assigned duties, (3) political and economic imbalance, and (4) lack of political leadership accompanied by inadequate recognition of the nature of the overall problem.[1] A governmental vacuum exists, according to Gulick, because in each metropolitan region there usually is no governmental body with authority to cope with the major problems of the area, whether they be water supply, air pollution, or transportation. Governments functioning in metropolitan areas are usually inadequate in terms of geographical jurisdiction, functional authority, or both. Thus central cities are always geographically inadequate since their powers are essentially limited to their boundaries; in the circumstance where a county encompasses the critical area it probably lacks power to exercise general control of such necessary functions as public transportation and police protection.

Fractionalization of duties results from the independent operation of numerous governments within an area that has in many ways become a unit. For example, cities situated miles apart may construct their separate sewage disposal facilities and draw up their own plans for orderly growth. Once grown together, each disposal facility may not only be inadequate but may actually contaminate the source of water for the other city. Their street and land-use plans may not fit together at all. Fractionalization may result also from failure to appreciate the nature of a problem currently at hand, which produces difficulties in such matters as air pollution, health, fire protection, crime control, traffic flow, and taxation.

A third reason for governmental inadequacy in metropolitan areas is political and economic imbalance. Assuming that the presence of some sort of "balance" of forces and interests is important to an effective governmental unit, the tendency for some communities to become predominantly upper or lower class in terms of economic status is disturbing. The outward flow of people and commercial establishments to suburbs not only deprives central cities of an important portion of their tax base, but it also removes persons from whom community leadership is normally expected. On the other hand, suburban communities may be rich in leadership but poor in taxable resources. "Democracy needs balanced constituencies, balanced leadership groups, balanced economic interests, balanced taxable resources, and powers of government which are balanced and appropriate to these other elements."[2] Obviously, not every minor

---

1. Luther Gulick, *Metro: Changing Problems and Lines of Attack,* Governmental Affairs Institute, New York, 1957.
2. *Ibid.,* p. 15.

constituency can be balanced in this sense, but Gulick's point is that in an area of the size and complexity characteristic of a metropolis such balance is important to effective governmental action.

The inadequacy or even total absence of area-wide political leadership in metropolitan regions is largely due to the fact that elected public officials are unlikely to have the entire area as their constituency. Candidates for office in a city do not have to dwell on matters of concern to residents of surrounding areas and nearby cities. Few community problems, regardless of their nature, are effectively handled unless impetus is provided by persons who can rally public support for their cause.

Duplication and Overlapping

Taxpayers everywhere, aware of the high cost of governments, deplore unnecessary duplication and waste. Yet few appreciate the costliness of many independent agencies, side by side, providing parallel services. If anyone were to suggest the establishment of two or three police or fire departments, planning commissions, or departments of public works within a municipality one would not be taken seriously for obvious reasons. Nevertheless, comparable situations exist in metropolitan areas. The residents of each municipality support such agencies and many others like those of their neighbors in other cities. Simultaneously the same people support county, district, town, and township agencies with responsibilities related to police, fire, planning, public works and many other services. Too often various governmental officials proceed with duties within their own limited jurisdictions without concern for the efforts of their neighboring counterparts, who may even be housed in the same building!

Unevenness of Services

Within a metropolitan region many levels of service exist in regard to individual governmental functions. Residents of one section may receive excellent fire and police protection while those living in other sections may be served in a fair, poor, or totally inadequate manner. Disposal of wastes may not be a problem in some places while in others the inadequacy of this service may pose a real threat to health. Some streets may be adequately lighted, and others may have no lights at all. This list of examples could be greatly lengthened, but it illustrates the unevenness of services characteristic of metropolitan areas.

Disparity and inadequacy of services are especially noticeable in so-called "fringe areas." These zones, located outside municipal boundaries, are generally unable to turn to any unit of local government possessing responsibility for meeting their needs. Water supply, sewage disposal, fire and police protection, drainage, street lighting, and zoning are often inadequate in fringe areas. The picture is further complicated by the fact that the quality of services differs greatly among various fringe zones, a situation explained largely by the relative adequacy of special district arrangements. Fringe areas are an especially fertile breeding ground for special districts.

Fiscal Inequity

Since metropolitan areas are major centers of income and wealth, fiscal problems stem largely from inadequate machinery for the effective use of financial resources. The problem was summarized in this way many years ago:

> The policy of providing city-wide services on the basis of need rather than the fiscal resources of each block, precinct or ward is not extended in the great majority of instances to metropolitan areas. Instead, the individual governmental unit relies upon a small amount of territory for its local financial resources. Thus some units are wealthy but have relatively few needs; others are extremely poor and have extensive needs. Such disparity between needs and resources is particularly apparent in the central cities, which must furnish services to many nonresidents but cannot tap the financial resources of the localities in which these people reside. The broad variations between needs and resources make for gross inequalities in financial burdens.[3]

Problems faced by some smaller communities are equally as great if not more severe than those of central cities. "Bedroom" communities housing low- and middle-income groups are illustrative. Property valuation in such places is rather low, but at the same time the need for services is high. At the other extreme are "wealthy tax colonies," where only the well-to-do reside. Neither of these types of communities benefits from the tax base supplied by large commercial and industrial enterprises.

Another major cause of fiscal difficulties in metropolitan areas arises from the many revenue and debt limitations imposed upon local governments by state laws. Local governments are generally able to levy only those taxes authorized by state law, and most state legislatures have been jealous of revenue sources (excepting the property tax) and unwilling to relinquish them to subordinate governments. The problem is further compounded by the fact that some localities are too small for effective and economical administration of revenue sources. Taxes may be avoided through changing residence by a few blocks or going to a nearby community to shop.

3. The Council of State Governments, *The States and the Metropolitan Problem*, Chicago, 1956, p. 20.

SUGGESTED SOLUTIONS TO METROPOLITAN PROBLEMS[4]

Responsibility of State Legislatures

In an earlier chapter attention was directed to the fact that local governments are creatures of the states in which they are situated. Before effective local action to meet the needs of metropolitan areas is possible, important changes in state constitutions and statutes may be necessary. Old restrictions, procedural as well as substantive, require modification. Laws pertaining to the incorporation of cities or annexation of territory to them may require modernization. New sources of local revenue await legislative authorization. Restrictions on municipal forms of governments need to be repealed. Counties require more varied powers. These examples serve to stress the crucial role of the state legislatures.

For many years it was generally assumed that malapportionment of state legislatures contributed significantly to their reluctance to take action designed to alleviate metropolitan problems. Decisions by the U.S. Supreme Court, especially *Reynolds* v. *Sims,*[5] were viewed as harbingers of better days for urban areas throughout the country. However, several studies conducted in states whose legislatures were reapportioned on the basis of "one man, one vote" indicate that the expected consequences have not materialized.[6] The fact seems to be that urban legislators do not vote as a bloc. The concerns and policy preferences of representatives from suburban communities may not be at all in harmony with those of representatives from the central cities. Indeed, the conflicts and dissimilarities between them may well be even greater than between the urban and rural legislators, partly because suburbanites may view the big city with its problems as a direct threat to their chosen way of life.

Annexation

Viewed historically, the standard method of providing increased service to expanding urban areas has been to add these areas to a central city through *annexation,* which is the process of adding territory to an established government. When created, most cities were much smaller than they now are; their growth has resulted from the annexation of contiguous, unincorporated territory—usually in a piecemeal, haphazard manner. The

---

4. See James F. Horan and G. Thomas Taylor, *Experiments in Metropolitan Government,* Praeger, 1977; and Howard W. Hallman, *Small and Large Together,* Sage, 1977.
5. 84 S. Ct. 1362 (1964).
6. See Thomas R. Dye, "Malapportionment and Public Policy in the States," *Journal of Politics,* August 1965; David Derge, "Metropolitan and Outside Alignments in the Illinois and Missouri Legislative Delegations," *American Political Science Review,* 1958; and Herbert Jacob, "The Consequences of Malapportionment: A Note of Caution," *Social Forces,* December 1964.

great bulk of nineteenth-century annexations were accomplished by legislative act, a fact that helps to explain their frequent use.

The twentieth century has witnessed a decline in annexation as a means of seriously attempting to meet the needs of rapidly urbanizing areas. Although it is difficult to isolate factors accounting for the decline, these have been significant: (1) ability of fringe-area dwellers to obtain desired services without annexation; (2) hostility of fringe-area dwellers toward the central city and their consequent determination to take advantage of increasingly stringent procedural requirements governing annexation; (3) incorporation of satellite communities; and (4) reluctance on the part of central cities to assume the expense required to increase services and facilities in newly annexed areas to a level comparable with that existing in the remainder of the community.

Particularly through the use of special districts and in some instances by means of increased county activity, fringe-area residents have satisfied their desire for municipal-type services such as pure water, fire protection, and waste disposal. A consequent reduction in the urgency of annexation has occurred. Alternative methods for obtaining services without annexation have been authorized by state legislatures whose members viewed such methods as easy "solutions" to vexatious problems. Hostility toward core cities is widespread among suburbanites. Because of fear of increased taxes, dislike for city regulations, or concern over loss of local identity, people living near a city on which they are dependent may not wish to become part of it. Of all the factors contributing to the decrease in municipal annexations, antipathy toward the central city is among the most important.

Typically, annexation proposals must be subject to a popular vote in the area to be annexed. Action on the part of the annexing city may be accomplished by council action or by popular vote. Where approval by city voters is required, a favorable majority usually must be obtained separately within the city and in the area to be annexed. Favorable council action or popular vote within a city is often negated by an unfavorable vote outside. In this way "local control over local matters" has hindered the orderly development of many communities. In a few states, particularly Missouri, Ohio, New Mexico, Texas, and Virginia, annexations may be accomplished without popular vote.

A technique sometimes advocated as a means of reducing suburban opposition to annexation is the *tax differential*. This device enables a municipality to enter into an agreement to the effect that upon annexation and for a period thereafter residents of a newly added area will be taxed at a rate different from that applied generally throughout the city. The theory behind such an arrangement is that for some time following annexation an area cannot receive full advantage of all municipal services and consequently should enjoy a lower tax rate. In view of its importance as a source of municipal revenue and its susceptibility to adjustment, the property tax would probably be scaled down in some manner to achieve the desired result.

Although a promise of lower taxes for a period of time may serve as an inducement to encourage fringe dwellers to accept annexation, the fairness of this practice from the standpoint of city residents is questionable. Granting reduced tax rates to newly annexed areas disregards the fact that the costs of improvements and services in such places are generally greater in proportion to assessed valuation than in other parts of the city. Occasionally, cities have accepted this premise and assessed higher taxes for a short time in new additions or required payment of some sort of entrance fee. Intended to discourage annexations, such a policy is feasible only when outside areas desire to join a city that is not especially interested in extending its boundaries.

The record clearly indicates that annexation has proved inadequate as a means of meeting the problems of rapidly growing urban areas. Urbanization outruns annexation. Since urban growth does not respect legal boundaries, county lines and state boundaries are crossed. State laws may not allow municipalities to expand across county lines, and annexations across state boundaries are not permissible because such action would involve surrender of territory by one state to another. Furthermore, the incorporation of small satellite communities around a large city seriously impedes annexations. Annexation of incorporated territory is nearly always cumbersome if possible at all. A favorable vote is usually difficult to achieve within a community marked for absorption, and arrangements concerning the disposition of the assets and liabilities of the disincorporated municipality are complicated.

Extraterritorial Jurisdiction[7]

One approach to the metropolitan problem is to empower municipalities to extend their authority beyond their boundaries for certain purposes. Specific territory is a necessary attribute of a municipality, and municipal powers are intended chiefly for use within municipal boundaries. Cities regularly extend their activities beyond their geographical limits for many purposes which may be considered in terms of two broad classifications: implementation of services and acquisition of facilities for the benefit of city residents and provision of services to fringe areas which are usually unincorporated. Municipalities frequently must go outside their bound-

7. "Extramural" is often used in place of "extraterritorial." Extramural means literally "beyond the wall." In the Roman language and practice this term was applied to powers exercised beyond the territory of a municipality. The boundaries of major Roman cities were marked by walls, and the area around such cities for a certain distance beyond the walls was under municipal jurisdiction. For additional information on the historical aspects of municipal extraterritoriality, see Russell W. Maddox, *Extraterritorial Powers of Municipalities in the United States,* Oregon State College Press, Corvallis, 1955, pp. 6–8.

aries to obtain water, locate parks and sewage disposal works, build bridges, and operate airports. At the same time they supply water to non-resident consumers, provide fire protection for nearby property, extend transportation facilities to surrounding areas, and regulate the subdivision of property within a specified distance beyond their limits.

Municipalities can exercise only those extraterritorial powers permitted them by their respective state legislatures.[8] Some states have been more generous than others, and within a single state jurisdictions over various functions have been treated differently. "Accuracy requires recognition that most municipalities possess a *number* of 'jurisdictions.' A municipality may extend its powers over one territory in order to acquire water and over another in order to inspect dairies that supply milk for its residents; it may acquire property for sewage disposal facilities within one area and for parks in another; it may be able to collect taxes only from its residents and at the same time provide a variety of services to nonresidents."[9]

Extraterritorial jurisdiction for cities has proved unsatisfactory as a means of meeting metropolitan needs for a number of reasons. Although cities are permitted to extend services beyond their limits, they exercise very little regulatory authority and usually no taxing power over nonresidents. Under such circumstances, no city can administer a plan to control the development of an area because its authority and resources are not commensurate with the need. A basic obstacle to the expansion of extraterritorial regulatory power is that it is "government without the consent of the governed" since nonresidents have no direct voice in city government. Another complication arises from a conflict of jurisdictions. Competition among cities and with other local governments for spheres of control and influence may produce rivalry and disharmony rather than cooperation.

Intergovernmental Cooperation

Cooperation among local governments involves minimum disturbance to established patterns and relationships and consequently does not encounter the hostility directed toward some other suggested means of solving metropolitan difficulties. Cooperative arrangements take a number of forms which may be divided into two major categories: (1) Counties may provide services for governments within their borders. (2) Two or more governmental units may undertake joint efforts. A third category, extension of services by a central city, has been considered above under extraterritorial jurisdiction.

---

8. Such powers may be expressed or implied. For example, the power of eminent domain may be implied in a specific grant of power to provide an adequate water supply or construct sewage disposal facilities.
9. Russell W. Maddox, *op. cit.*, pp. 88–89.

County Services. Strengthening counties and extending the scope of their services constitute a potentially significant means of alleviating metropolitan problems for several reasons. First, the territories of counties more nearly approximate the limits of metropolitan regions than do the boundaries of other local governments. Second, recent years have witnessed numerous increases in authority vested in counties by state law. Third, using county governments is probably more feasible than attempting to create other general-purpose governments. Usually, however, reorganization of county government is essential prior to any appreciable increases in authority and responsibility.

A few states have enacted general laws empowering counties to perform any municipal function for local governments within their jurisdiction. Most states have expanded the authority of counties activity by activity, usually to a limited extent. Functions performed by counties in lieu of action by other local governments include, for example, property assessment and tax collection, public health and welfare, library service, sewage disposal, and fire protection. In no other place have county services to local governments developed to an extent comparable to the practice in Los Angeles County, where the county provides a variety of services for many cities within its boundaries.

Joint Undertakings. Joint undertakings involve arrangements among governments whereby ownership and control of facilities as well as program supervision remain at least partially in the hands of all participants. Cooperation between cities and counties as well as among cities is especially significant. Services provided in this manner include purchase of equipment and supplies and the construction and maintenance of recreational facilities, hospitals, airports, sewage-disposal systems, bridges, and a variety of public buildings. Police radio facilities, fire protection, and aspects of personnel management are also provided cooperatively.

A major problem facing most governments pertains to ways of procuring materials and equipment at minimum costs while maintaining adequate standards of quality. Although cooperative purchasing among local governmental units can save significant amounts of money, lack of uniformity in the laws governing purchasing procedures for individual governments is an obstacle to joint efforts. Another difficulty stems from the usual desire on the part of local officials in each government to enjoy independence of action in spending "their" money.

Recreational programs are often financed and administered jointly by cities, school districts, and counties. City-county hospitals and public health units exist in many communities. City-county cooperation in the construction and maintenance of airports is common. Some cities have resorted to joint development of sewage disposal systems. Courthouses, office buildings, and jails in a number of communities are the products of city-county cooperation.

Although joint efforts represent progress in meeting some problems, they have proved to be too slow an approach to the great problems of metropolitan areas. Legal restrictions and financial limitations accompanied by a mutual lack of determination on the part of local officials to work cooperatively have seriously hampered progress. The multiplicity of governmental units characteristic of metropolitan regions constitutes an additional obstacle. It seems major progress toward a solution of the problems of these regions must be sought along other lines.

Federation

Metropolitan federation appears, at least theoretically, to be among the more promising approaches to metropolitan area problems. In a federated metropolis, authority to administer certain matters of regional concern would be transferred to a "central" government. Local governments would continue to exist and maintain control over certain functions. Representation on the governing body of the metropolitan authority would probably be guaranteed to each government within its jurisdiction. The resemblance between such an arrangement and the federal system on the national level is apparent.

Interest in metropolitan federation was heightened appreciably in 1954 when the Municipality of Metropolitan Toronto (Canada) began to function. This new unit of government had been created the previous year by act of the Ontario provincial legislature. Included within its boundaries were the City of Toronto and twelve suburban municipalities, all of which continued to function. The law creating the metropolitan municipality specified that it should assume responsibility for the following functions: water supply, sewage disposal, arterial highways, metropolitan parks, housing and redevelopment, certain health and welfare services, and over-all planning. It was also empowered to appoint the governing body of the Toronto Transit Commission, provide a courthouse and jail, assist in financing education, review and issue bonds for member municipalities, and set a uniform assessment rate for all taxable property within its jurisdiction. Municipalities within Metropolitan Toronto continued to administer law enforcement, fire protection, most public health services, public relief, libraries and building regulations—to name only the more important functions.

Hailed as "a bold new development in metropolitan government," the accomplishments of the Municipality of Metropolitan Toronto have been too numerous to review here, and on balance the achievements of the new government have been favorably received by its residents. Nevertheless, the experiment has been criticized on several counts. It is asserted that some functions retained by the individual municipalities should be in the hands of the federation and that its geographical jurisdiction is inadequate to meet the needs of a rapidly growing urban area. Some critics claim that representation on the metropolitan governing body is inequitable and that the administrative structure is top-heavy. However, these criticisms relate to matters of detail and do not reflect basic weaknesses in the concept of a metropolitan federation.

In 1955, a plan of "federation" for Dade County (Miami), Florida, was approved by a board created to study the problems of the area. A constitutional amendment authorizing federation was submitted to the state legislature, which altered it to make the board of county commissioners the metropolitan governing body. This amendment was approved by popular vote in 1956 along with a home rule charter for Dade County. Since the federation boundaries are limited to Dade County which is designated as the metropolitan government, there is some question as to whether this arrangement is a "true" federation.[10] Instead, it is sometimes referred to as an "urban county" approach. Dade County is not geographically coterminous with the heavily urbanized area around Miami, even though it does encompass the bulk of it. Nevertheless, the experiment in southern Florida may be viewed as the closest approximation to federation at the local level in the United States.

Success in Dade County and Toronto heightened interest in federation as a means of attacking metropolitan problems. In 1958, the voters of Davidson County (Nashville), Tennessee, and of King County (Seattle), Washington, defeated proposals for metropolitan government. In the same year, the Quebec Provincial Legislature created the Montreal Metropolitan Corporation, which was described as "a limited and skeleton form of Metropolitan Government." Too little authority was granted to the Corporation, however, to classify it as a federation although it represented a halting step in that direction. In 1959, the voters of Knox County (Knoxville), Tennessee, defeated a charter creating The Knoxville-Knox County Metropolitan Government providing a federated approach to some of the major problems of that area. During the same year metropolitan plans were also defeated in Cleveland and St. Louis. In 1960, the Metropolitan Corporation of Greater Winnipeg was created by the Manitoba provincial legislature followed in 1968 by the establishment of a federated government in Ottawa.

City-County Consolidation or Separation

City-county consolidation consists of a partial or complete merger of the area and government of a county with the area and government of a city or cities. City-county separation consists of detaching a city from its county so that the city performs most if not all county functions within

10. For a detailed analysis of the Dade County arrangement, see Edward Sofen, *The Miami Metropolitan Experiment,* Indiana University, Bloomington, 1963. See also, Richard Carpenter, "Is Dade County Plan Applicable to the California Experience?" *Western City,* November 1958.

its territory. This arrangement has found little use in the United States except in Virginia where every city upon reaching a population of 10,000 is separated completely from its county. An obvious difficulty associated with this practice, particularly in heavily urbanized regions, is the reduction in taxable resources suffered by the county.

An early instance of city-county consolidation in the United States occurred in New Orleans in 1813, when the state legislature authorized the city to perform within its boundaries certain functions assigned to parishes (counties). A similar arrangement became effective in Boston in 1822. The boundaries of the City of Philadelphia were made coterminous with those of the County of Philadelphia in 1854, and twenty-eight local governments in the county became part of the City of Philadelphia. Consolidation was partial because a number of county officers were continued in existence.

Probably the best known example of city-county consolidation is found in New York City. In fact, a number of consolidations have taken place, the first occurring in 1730, the second in 1894, and the third in 1898 when the boundaries of New York City were extended to encompass four counties (five when the Bronx was divided from the County of New York in 1912). Most county functions were turned over to the city government. A unique feature of the New York plan is the arrangement whereby local areas, called boroughs, are permitted administrative powers and representation on the legislature of the consolidated government, the city council. Representation actually is granted to the boroughs on the Board of Estimate, which is the "upper chamber" of the council.

A few consolidations have occurred during the present century. The city and county of Honolulu were consolidated in 1907. Today the entire island of Oahu is organized as one unit of local government, namely, the City and County of Honolulu. Consolidation was accomplished in Baton Rouge, Louisiana, in 1949. At that time, East Baton Rouge Parish was divided into an urban area, two industrial areas, and a rural area. The boundaries of Baton Rouge were defined to encompass only the urban area. Partial consolidation was accomplished in 1951 between Atlanta and Fulton County, Georgia. Consolidation received favorable popular votes in Nashville and Davidson County, Tennessee, in 1962, and in Jacksonville and Duval County, Florida, in 1967. In 1969 the Indiana legislature voted to consolidate Indianapolis and Marion County, without calling for a popular vote. During the last decade efforts at city-county consolidation were successful in four localities: Lexington-Fayette County, Kentucky, in 1972; Greater Anchorage Area Borough in 1975; Anaconda-Deer Lodge County, Montana, in 1977; and Butte-Silver Bow County, Montana, also in 1977.

Less frequently advocated as an approach to the solution of metropolitan problems, city-county separation has been effected in more communities than city-county consolidation. With the exception of those found in Virginia, most city-county separations were achieved during the nineteenth century. The separation of Baltimore and San Francisco from their counties was accomplished during the 1850's, followed by the separation of St. Louis in 1876. Denver was officially separated from its county in 1902 by terms of a constitutional amendment, although litigation postponed its effective operation for about ten years. Virginia is the only state where systematic use has been made of city-county separation.

Numerous difficulties are associated with city-county consolidation and separation. The characteristic determination of small communities to retain their identity leads their residents to vote against any constitutional amendment or local referendum measure authorizing or implementing consolidation or separation. Furthermore, if consolidation or separation is accomplished with a view toward future growth and problems, some rural land must be included within the city-county. Residents of such areas also regularly oppose consolidation. Territorial circumscription has posed another problem. Consolidations have been based on the area of individual counties and consequently have provided no assistance in the solution of inter-county problems. Experience has demonstrated that it is very difficult, if not impossible, to enlarge the original boundaries of the consolidated area. The same problem exists in regard to city-county separations. The boundaries of St. Louis and San Francisco are the same as when they were separated from their counties, and only very limited additions have been made to Denver. Of the three examples of separation mentioned above, only Baltimore has increased appreciably in territory, but each annexation required a special act of the state legislature. Since annexation is a judicial process in Virginia, separated cities have been able to add appreciably to their territory.

The City-State

The most radical proposal for dealing with metropolitan problems involves the creation of city-states. Proponents of this idea advocate the separation of large urban areas from their states and the admission of such areas as new states in the Union with powers and privileges equal to all other states. Each city-state would be free to work out its own salvation under the Constitution of the United States. A little reflection reveals the thoroughly fanciful nature of such a proposal. The U.S. Constitution forbids the creation of a new state within an existing state or by joining parts of two or more states without the consent of the state legislatures concerned as well as of Congress. No state legislature is likely to agree to such a proposal!

Special Districts

Since special districts were discussed in an earlier chapter, they will be considered only briefly here. However, a few comments are in order concerning the use of special districts as means of handling certain metropolitan problems. It appears that a special district was first used on what might be called a "metropolitan basis" in 1790 when a special district was established in the Philadelphia area to administer prisons. Special districts were created in the New York area to administer the police function in 1857, fire departments in 1865, and public health in 1866. The growth of special districts in metropolitan areas and elsewhere has been especially rapid during the last generation or so.

Metropolitan special districts have been used quite frequently to provide port facilities, sewage disposal, water supply, and parks. They also operate bridges, tunnels, housing projects, airports, libraries, and transit facilities; furnish public health services, power, ice, gas, and coke; and develop regional plans. Some of these districts are truly big government. The oldest active independent metropolitan district in the United States, the Metropolitan Sanitary District of Greater Chicago, covers about 500 square miles and includes about fifty percent of the area of Cook County. The Metropolitan Water District of Southern California contains approximately 2,700 square miles and serves millions of people living in five counties.

Although the cumulative effect of increasing use of special districts is to complicate governmental structure, this disadvantage does not outweigh their several advantages, including these: (1) their creation does not disturb the existence of other governmental units; (2) they may cross county and even state lines; (3) they may circumvent tax and debt limits imposed by state law; and (4) they are easily organized. The fact is that of all the approaches to metropolitan problems, particularly as they pertain to the provision of services, the special district has been most widely used. However, the special district has not been used as a comprehensive solution to metropolitan problems.

Evaluation of Solutions

Victor Jones, a widely known and highly respected student of metropolitan regions, has developed a number of propositions as guides for the evaluation of various approaches to metropolitan problems. His propositions provide such an excellent basis for critical insight that they are quoted here in full.

(1) Metropolitan communities are growing so large and becoming so complicated that the effort to find solutions to their problems should be shared by federal, state, and local governments.
(2) Whenever possible, a metropolitan government responsible to the inhabitants of the area is preferable to direct federal or state administration.
(3) It would be undesirable to attempt to govern the modern metropolis with its large area, huge population and many divergent interests as if it were a small, compact, homogenous city.

(4) A metropolitan government should be devised that will provide effective services, guidance and controls where desired over the whole of the metropolitan area, that will equalize the burden of supporting such governmental functions, and that will facilitate effective citizen control of governmental policies which affect them at their places of work and recreation, as well as their places of residence.

(5) There should be an area-wide government with sufficient authority to make policy decisions about, and to administer, those matters that the community considers to be of metropolitan interest and concern.

(6) All or part of a governmental function might be assigned to a limited metropolitan government (a) when coordination of a function over the whole area is essential to effective service or control in any part of the area; (b) when it is desired to apply the ability-to-pay theory of taxation to the area as a whole, instead of allowing each part to support its own activities at whatever level its own economic base will permit; (c) when services can be supplied more efficiently through large-scale operations and when the advantages of large-scale operations are desired; and (d) when it is necessary in order to assure citizens a voice in decisions that affect them in other parts of the metropolitan area, as well as the part in which they reside.

(7) There should be a network of submetropolitan governments, perhaps existing counties and municipalities, to legislate and administer those matters that the metropolitan community does not consider to require uniform treatments throughout the metropolitan area.

(8) The metropolitan government should be a *general* government with responsibility for enough functions so that it can weigh the claims of one function against those of other functions. Only a general government can, in planning and administering the government of a metropolis, take account of the delicate and intricate relations among governmental and private services and controls.[11]

No solution thus far suggested accords completely with all these criteria. Metropolitan areas provide a sort of frontier in society today. New problems, new dangers, and new threats to established ways of doing things are appearing all the time. Only through ingenuity, resourcefulness, and informed effort on the part of leaders and citizens can large communities prosper.

11. Victor Jones, "The Organization of a Metropolitan Region," 105 *University of Pennsylvania Law Review* 538, February, 1957, pp. 551–52. Copyright © University of Pennsylvania Law Review. Reprinted by permission of University of Pennsylvania Law Review and Fred B. Rothman & Company.

Health, Safety, Welfare, and Housing

22

Social problems very often are, or may become, governmental problems. This statement is dramatically borne out by the course of development of government in the United States. During the colonial period and early statehood, American governments were essentially "negative" in character. That is, they did very little by way of providing services to the people or regulating private affairs. Over the years, however, government became increasingly "positive," doing more and more for its citizens and paying more attention to their problems.

PUBLIC HEALTH

Governmental concern for matters of general health reflects a very real connection between public well-being and the obligation of government to provide for the general welfare. Epidemics, poor sanitation, lack of hospitals and laboratory facilities, and the like are not only serious problems themselves—they also create other problems. There is no doubt that health problems can result, for example, in economic loss and dependency. Viewed in this light, governmental action in the health field is both reasonable and justifiable.

Although organized governmental efforts in public health can be traced to the final years of the eighteeth century,[1] they did not become significant until after the Civil War. There had been local activities before that time, but from mid-century on the states became increasingly active. Federal concern dates back to the first decade of union but did not assume prominence until the last generation.

The tardiness of meaningful governmental effort in regard to public

---

1. Wilson G. Smillie, *Public Health Administration in the United States,* 2nd ed., The Macmillan Co., New York, 1940, p. 369, reports local boards of health in Massachusetts in 1797.

health was not due to arbitrary refusal to act. Public officials were mindful of the ravages of disease. Scourges such as smallpox, yellow fever, and tuberculosis elicited governmentally imposed quarantines and such sanitary measures as were thought necessary. The major difficulty was lack of medical knowledge. It was not until Louis Pasteur's discoveries in 1866 on the causes of disease that truly effective strides could be taken. After that date public health programs based on preventing ills rather than curing them began to develop.

The National Role

The United States Constitution does not give the national government express authority to engage in public health activities. Consequently the power to protect the public health is a reserved power lodged in the states. Even so, the national government has managed, through its implied powers and by means of grants-in-aid, to carry on extensive health activities itself and at the same time promote broadened programs in the states.

Of all federal agencies engaged in health work, the most important is the Public Health Service. Dating from 1798 when it was created as a hospital for American seamen, the Public Health Service has expanded until now it administers most national health programs. It operates hospitals and outpatient clinics, administers grant-in-aid programs, trains researchers, cooperates with private research agencies, assists states in drawing up health legislation, and maintains the National Institutes of Health. The contributions of the Public Health Service have been characterized by one eminent health authority as having "raised the level of work performed in every county, city and state health department with which it has had even indirect contact."[2]

It would be difficult to say exactly how many national agencies are involved in public health activities. Some are directly involved, but others created to perform tasks considered outside the health field certainly *affect* public health work. Thus the Food and Drug Administration, medical agencies of the armed forces, and the Veterans' Administration's medical department may be classed as health agencies. At the same time it would be unrealistic to assert that the Federal Trade Commission, National Bureau of Standards, and research agencies of the Department of Agriculture do not also contribute to improvement of national health.

State Health Agencies

As noted earlier, general health programs at the state level did not take

---

2. Harry S. Mustard, *Government in Public Health,* Harvard University Press, Cambridge, 1945, p. 59.

form until after the Civil War. In 1855 Lousiana created a state board of health in the wake of a yellow fever epidemic, but within a few years it became inactive. The first board of health to become a permanent part of state organization was created in Massachusetts in 1869. California established a health organization the following year, and in the next ten years more than two dozen states followed suit. By 1909 every state had set up a department to administer health laws of statewide application.

Practically all states maintain boards of health composed of members appointed by the governor. Serving four to six year overlapping terms, they are responsible for all policy decisions in the administration of programs under their jurisdiction. Serving under the board is an executive officer, known as the state health officer, health commissioner, director of public health, or some similar title. This officer is chosen by the governor in over forty states and serves an indefinite term. The state health officer supervises day-to-day administration and enforcement of state health laws.

The functions of state health organizations vary from one state to the next. Such factors as geographical location, size and character of population, climate, and occupational pursuits of the inhabitants result in differing health problems in different states. However, there is enough similarity in the various programs to warrant general classification of health activities. These functions, which include the principal areas of concern in public health, are discussed later in the chapter.

Local Organization

Most routine health services rendered to the general public are performed by personnel of local health organizations. Yet, it is at the local level that the most glaring inadequacies are found. Despite the existence of a large number of local health agencies administering comprehensive programs, it is nevertheless true that many Americans reside in areas where health services and facilities are demonstrably inadequate or totally lacking.

Despite the fact that local health organizations appeared in the first decade of the nineteenth century, more than a hundred years elapsed before full-time, permanently staffed local organizations came into existence. In fact, prior to World War I most local organizations consisted of private physicians serving part-time. In view of these facts it is surprising that during the past fifty years local health services have developed as rapidly as they have.

Local health units exist in many forms. When considered in detail, administrative variations seem endless. Nevertheless, basic patterns of organization similar to those at the state level can be delineated, with both boards and single administrators being used. Local organization is often based on the county, or as an alternative, the township or town. Sometimes two or more counties band together, sharing costs of health services. Cities commonly operate health units, with the more competently staffed and better equipped ones found in the larger cities around the nation. Another general type of health organization is the health district that combines several counties and is administered under direct supervision of the state health department. The pronounced trend in recent years toward district organization has been occasioned largely by the difficulties experienced by local governments in meeting the costs of securing competent personnel and modern equipment.

The functions of public health at the local level are no different, in principle, from those of the states. In most instances, however, local governments confine their activities principally to disease control, particularly to checking the spread of communicable ills. The main reason for such restricted activity is the expense of a general health program.

PUBLIC HEALTH FUNCTIONS

Areas of concentrated health activity vary widely among the states as well as at the local level. Nevertheless, it is simple to list the major categories into which most public health efforts can be classified. Generally considered, the most important areas are: collection and publication of vital statistics, disease control, sanitation, and sanitary engineering. These functions comprise the heart of a state public health program. In addition, states commonly undertake such activities as provision of diagnostic laboratory services, health education, industrial hygiene, maternity and child hygiene, dental health, public nursing, and public school nursing.

Vital Statistics

Health statistics are indispensable to an effective public health program. Consisting of data on births, deaths, causes of death, incidence of disease, and the like, these statistics are measurements of the effectiveness of health programs and indications of areas in which future efforts should be concentrated. The value of such information can be illustrated in countless ways. Tabulations on mental illness and hospital space available forewarn shortages in that area. "Keeping books" on communicable diseases may foretell possible epidemics; records of infant mortality may point the way to necessary changes in nursing and maternity and infant care.

Disease Control

The first public health departments, state and local, were organized primarily to fight the spread of communicable diseases. Epidemics of smallpox, typhoid, and yellow fever were combatted largely through the imposition of strictly enforced quarantines. Today these diseases and others such as diphtheria, pneumonia, polio, syphilis, and gonorrhea are countered with a vastly superior arsenal of medical weapons. New medicines, improved techniques, better hospitals, rapid reporting, and emphasis upon prevention have brought these diseases more nearly under control. Today more money is spent to control contagious diseases than ever before, but the expenditure is a smaller percentage of the total health outlay.

A great deal of effort is concentrated on diseases that, while not communicable, disable or claim the lives of many Americans. Cancer, heart ailments, and mental diseases head the list of ills that are subjected to intensive research by government health specialists. National and state organizations are especially active in this field.

Sanitation and Sanitary Engineering

Promotion of sanitation has long been a major function of public health organizations, particularly since the causes of disease have been more fully understood. All levels and units of government have enacted laws, ordinances, and regulations designed to eliminate unsanitary conditions that endanger public health. Many such laws are administered by health officials, of course, but enforcement authority, especially at the local level, is often lodged in other officers. Illustrative of the broad range of sanitation laws are those designed to protect the purity of water and milk supplies, assure cleanliness of food handlers, prevent pollution of rivers and other bodies of water, provide safe means of garbage disposal, eradicate rodents and insect pests, eliminate unsanitary conditions in public recreation facilities, require safe methods of sewage disposal, and prevent or correct air pollution.

The term sanitary engineering refers to the profession of developing methods and programs to eliminate and prevent the dangers to health that lack of sanitation involves. In recent years, for example, air pollution in industrial centers has proved a thorny problem. Improved methods of treating raw sewage, safer and more economical ways of providing supplies of potable water, and more effective application of plumbing skills are constant challenges.

Other Functions

A standard function of state departments of health is to provide diagnostic laboratory services for local health units as well as private physicians and hospitals. Assistance is rendered to expectant mothers and infants through maternity and child hygiene programs that include operation of clinics, prenatal instruction, training midwives, care of premature babies, and nursing assistance. Industrial hygiene programs promote more healthful working conditions to prevent occupational diseases. Public health nursing, particularly in low-income areas, is a usual health activity. Public school nurses often are provided by school districts, but some are supplied by health departments. Both health units and school districts provide for dental inspections and treatment. Every state department of health, and most local ones as well, conduct health education programs in the valid belief that a public well informed on health matters is better able to protect the public health.

PUBLIC SAFETY

The governor of each state is constitutionally charged with the responsibility of seeing that all laws, civil and criminal, are executed,[3] and must, therefore, be regarded as the principal official in implementing public safety measures. Obviously no one individual, regardless of how learned and competent, could personally supervise and guide all state programs. There are simply too many things that have to be done. The function of public safety alone, involving widely varying agencies and programs, would prove too much for a single director. Consequently, state efforts to provide for public safety are not performed by a single, central agency but represent instead the activities of numerous officers and agencies.

Attorney General

The chief legal officer of a state is the attorney general, whose principal function is to represent the state or state agencies in suits to which they are parties, advise the governor and other executive officers on legal matters, and in many states supervise local prosecuting attorneys. In actual practice the attorney general personally does not have time to tend every duty of the office. Depending upon the size of a state and the volume of legal business to be handled, the duties are shared with a number of assistant and deputy attorney generals.

The attorney general does not play a prominent part in criminal law enforcement. Conducting local prosecutions is a responsibility of the attorney general only in Delaware and Rhode Island—the two smallest states. Although usually vested with authority to function at the local level, an attorney general rarely does so because prosecutions are con-

---

3. Typically, state constitutions echo the phrase of the U.S. Constitution, Article II, Section 2, which states that the President shall "take care that the laws be faithfully executed." Even when such clauses do not appear, as in the Ohio and South Dakota constitutions, the duty of the governor is clear and unmistakable.

ducted by district or county prosecuting attorneys. Only in cases of extreme importance does an attorney general undertake prosecution locally, since possible conflicts with local prosecutors are dangerous both professionally and politically.

State Police and Highway Patrols

Except in Hawaii where organization is on an island-county basis, each of the states maintains a police organization to assist in the enforcement of its criminal laws. These units may be classed as state police, with broad powers of law enforcement; or as highway patrols, with functions generally limited to the enforcement of traffic laws. Of the organizations found in the states today, half can be regarded as true police forces. Variations in size are pronounced across the nation. In some of the more populous states the police forces consist of several thousand officers and employees, in many other states the personnel rolls list up to a thousand, and the remainder range downward to a few dozen patrolmen.

The first modern police system was established by Pennsylvania in 1905, although other states had established state agencies with limited law enforcement functions in earlier years. Forerunners of today's state organizations date back to 1835 when Texas, then an independent republic, created the Texas Rangers for patrol duty along the Mexican border and to Massachusetts' system of state constables organized in 1865. At the turn of the present century Arizona, Connecticut, and New Mexico also established police agencies, but each was severely limited in its jurisdiction.

At the head of a state police force is usually a director or superintendent chosen by the governor, although in some states administrative control is vested in an administrative board. State police authority extends to all parts of a state, including the area within incorporated municipalities. However, in order to avoid conflicts with municipal forces, state police generally confine themselves to rural areas. When it is necessary to enter a city on police business it is common practice for state patrol officers to contact the municipal police department. Experience has shown that tactless "invasions" of municipalities by state police cost dearly in terms of state-local police cooperation.

Military Force

Inasmuch as the states may not maintain military forces without congressional consent, national law has, since 1792, set the pattern for state military organization. Under present law state military forces exist in the form of the National Guard, ostensibly commanded in each state by the governor. Actual command in day-to-day administration is exercised by an adjutant general, and all gubernatorial appointments must be nationally approved. That the National Guard is, for all practical purposes, a unit of the national armed forces is forcefully indicated by the extent of national control. Size of the National Guard, types of units to be maintained, qualifications of officers, periods of enlistment, and salaries are nationally determined. Equipment is provided by the national government to all Guard units, which may be summoned into national service by the President.

Basically, the function of the National Guard is to help provide for military security, but it also serves, in a stand-by capacity, as an agency of law enforcement. At the direction of the governor, National Guard troops may be called upon when violence erupts or is threatened during strikes, racial conflicts, or other civil disorders. The most frequent use of the Guard, however, occurs during emergencies occasioned by natural disasters.

Administrative Agencies

Although they are not designed as criminal law enforcement bodies, administrative agencies render valuable service in the field of public safety. Agencies of all descriptions implement legislation that involves virtually every aspect of social intercourse. Through their regulations these agencies strive to maintain or establish standards of performance and integrity in their respective areas of concern. Public health personnel, for example, work constantly to check disease. Bank examiners keep banking practices under perpetual surveillance. Licensing and examining officials have the duty of preventing incompetents, quacks, and charlatans from masquerading as physicians, lawyers, engineers, and the like. Agricultural inspectors, utilities commissioners, insurance inspectors, and other such officers perform duties in the public interest.

Disciplinary techniques available to administrative officers and agencies vary widely. Revocation or suspension of a license, refusal to certify a product as salable or edible, or imposition of a quarantine may be all that is necessary to secure compliance with statutes or regulations. In some cases monetary penalties can be assessed. Failing of success by these means, more drastic steps usually can be taken. For example, an agency may obtain a judicial order directing compliance with an administrative decision. Refusal by an offender to obey them becomes contempt of court, an offense punishable by the court issuing the order. Another method of enforcement often available is the bringing of criminal charges by an administrative agency. When this occurs the state becomes the prosecutor as in other criminal cases. Finally, an agency may, if it has no authority to institute criminal proceedings and no other remedy is available, enlist the aid of the attorney general or a local prosecuting attorney in civil litigation.

PUBLIC SAFETY AT THE LOCAL LEVEL

At the grass roots level public safety figures prominently in the functions of many officers and agencies. Public health offices, licensing boards, building inspectors, planning bodies, fire departments, zoning commissions, and maintenance crews are among agencies performing meaningful functions in the area of public safety. Some agencies are purely local, some work closely with state counterparts, and some are branches of state departments. Probably the most important of them all, and certainly the best known, are the local agencies of criminal law enforcement: the sheriff, the prosecutor, and the municipal police.

The Sheriff

Local law enforcement in rural areas is primarily the responsibility of the sheriff, an elected official. The duties of the office vary considerably from state to state, but a sheriff has jurisdiction to enforce state laws on a county-wide basis. Since sheriffs do not enforce municipal ordinances, and because the chance of conflict with municipal police forces is constantly present, sheriffs and their deputies nearly always confine their activities to rural areas. There the sheriff shares jurisdiction with the state police with whom probability of conflict is slight since relatively few state police attempt to enforce all laws.

The quality of law enforcement achieved by sheriffs varies tremendously both among the states and within a single state. In some places, such as Los Angeles County, the sheriff's office is a highly effective, vigorous organization. At the other extreme the sheriff of a small, sparsely populated county may be little more than a process server and keeper of the county jail.

The Public Prosecutor

Bringing criminals to justice involves more than detection and arrest; they must be prosecuted before a court. This task forms the basic function of the public prosecutor who is known by such titles as district attorney, county attorney, county prosecutor, state's attorney, and solicitor. Jurisdiction usually covers a single county although several counties may be combined into a district. In the more populous areas of the nation the prosecutor's office includes a staff large enough to handle the preparation of cases as well as to conduct investigations and to gather evidence.

The importance of the office is indicated by the fact that the effectiveness of local law enforcement depends largely upon the success of the prosecutor. It is the prosecutor's duty to seek or to bring formal accusations against persons suspected of crime, and to decide whether to prosecute or to continue a prosecution already in progress. Obviously, an inept prosecutor can nullify good police work, and a corrupt one can easily sabotage the best efforts at law enforcement.

Municipal Police Departments

Most incorporated places in the United States, whether called cities, towns, or villages, maintain agencies whose primary function is law enforcement.[4] These municipal police departments, ranging in size from about 30,000 in New York City[5] to the many small departments consisting of only a few officers, are with few exceptions locally chosen, financed, and administered. State operation of local police departments was in vogue a century ago, but lack of anticipated improvements resulted in reestablishment of local control in all but a few large cities.

Municipal police departments staffed by professional career police officers originated in New York City in 1844. The idea quickly spread to other large cities and in due time to municipalities throughout the country. Municipal police enforce both local and state criminal laws, ranging from prohibitions against jaywalking and overparking to the most serious offenses against state law, including murder, rape, arson, and robbery. Police departments sometimes are assigned a variety of other duties such as elevator inspection, dog pound management, licensing bicycles, censorship of motion pictures and night club shows, and operation of emergency ambulance services.

Police department organization varies, of course, but the larger cities follow much the same basic pattern. Administrative boards were once in common use and are still found in a few cities, but they have been largely abandoned in favor of a single administrator usually called the police commissioner. Immediately below the commissioner is the chief of police, ordinarily a career person with several years of service. The pattern of intradepartmental organization depends upon the number and nature of tasks assigned a given department. In smaller cities the office of commissioner usually does not exist, and small town departments frequently consist of a mere handful of patrol officers.

Today the merit principle is widely accepted as the best way to recruit personnel for a police force, and promotion is frequently dependent upon passing a qualifying examination. Dismissal is in most cases controlled by the chief although appeals may be taken to a commissioner or civil service board, a procedure criticized by some students of police administration as

---

4. Unincorporated places, many small rural communities, and some municipalities located adjacent to large cities do not support police departments. In the first two instances reliance upon the county sheriff is considered adequate. Small incorporated municipalities in metropolitan areas may depend upon a combination of the sheriff and police services rendered by larger cities on a "contract" basis.
5. The actual breakdown is approximately 25,000 officers and 4,700 "civilian" employees.

detrimental to discipline. Special training schools for recruits are conducted in some cities, supplemented by on-the-job instruction. Small cities are at a disadvantage in this regard due to lack of funds and facilities for training.

The record of American municipal police departments has suffered because of instances of corruption in decades past, and even today an occasional scandal is unearthed. Of course police officers are human; some of them succumb to the temptations which their jobs hold, but it is regrettable if scandals exposing corruption among some police officers cause the many honest police officers to be held in disregard. Far more serious as a criticism is the chorus of objection to brutality, particularly against members of ethnic minorities. A sufficient number of documented instances of such treatment has resulted in the establishment of civilian review boards in some of the larger and more racially troubled cities. Such boards are not the answer, however, for even when they are able to facilitate the correction of some injustice, they are essentially punitive in nature. The ultimate solution to the problems which gave rise to their creation in the first place lies in raising the level of competence of police officers, and that is a goal that can be achieved only through better training, improved equipment, and more adequate salaries.

FIRE PROTECTION

An aspect of public safety that is of fundamental importance to every individual is protection from personal injury and property losses by fire. The magnitude of the problem is indicated by the fact that each year in the United States more than two billion dollars' worth of property is consumed by fire, and thousands of lives are lost. Consequently, national, state, and local governments administer fire prevention and protection programs.

National efforts in fire protection are not as extensive as those of state and local governments. National properties, national forests, and shipping facilities are the principal objects of federal efforts. Probably the most valuable federal services consist of research on matters relating to fire prevention and control. Many federal agencies such as the Department of Education, Bureau of Mines, Bureau of Standards, and the Forest Service render valuable assistance to state and local governments by disseminating information on fire prevention and control techniques.

State contributions in the field are varied, but they rarely involve fire fighting as such. The criminal laws of every state make arson—the deliberate and malicious setting of fires—a crime punishable as a felony. Statewide building codes, civil defense legislation, and fire hazard laws on handling of combustibles and explosives represent other areas of state concern in fire protection. About forty states have created the office of fire marshal, an officer who investigates causes of serious fires, conducts fire prevention educational campaigns, and enforces all state fire laws that are not specifically assigned to other state officials.

Local governments perform the basic function of protecting lives and property from damage and destruction by fire. Virtually every community provides some organized effort to control fires. In small towns and cities fire-fighting forces are usually composed of volunteers, often supplemented by a few full-time, paid fire fighters. Several small governmental units may be included in a fire control district; a town or county fire department may be maintained; or a large city may, by formal agreement, provide protection to smaller, neighboring communities. Fire departments of large cities employ professional, full-time fire fighters involving in cities like New York and Chicago, thousands of personnel. The larger the community, the more varied are the types of property to be protected, and consequently the more specialized must be the training and equipment.

When compared to European countries the record of American fire losses is high. Even after allowances are made for the greater amount of property involved and its higher value in dollars, the American record does not measure up to European efforts. The difference is emphasized further by the fact that fire-fighting equipment used in the United States is superior and more abundant than in any other country. The difference seems best explained by general attitudes toward fire prevention, with Americans typically exhibiting indifference unless exhorted by such campaigns as "fire prevention week" or sobered by experience with a destructive blaze.

PUBLIC WELFARE

Society has always been plagued by poverty and its consequences. In good times and bad there are those who, because of such factors as sickness, physical handicaps, old age, mental condition, and economic disruptions, are unable to make their way unaided. Provision of assistance to these people today is regarded as a proper function of government. Indeed, assuring minimum conditions of subsistence is looked upon as a *duty* of government.

The Modern Approach to Welfare

The concept of public welfare held by Americans today is the culmination of a development reaching back to the Elizabethan poor laws of sixteenth- and seventeenth-century England. According to Elizabethan theory, responsibility for welfare activities rested with the individual, the family, and local governments. The influence of this line of thought upon American practices is indicated by the fact that down to the present century the national government had very little to do with public welfare, and the states were not organized to administer general welfare programs.

For the first three decades of the twentieth century the largely local situs of welfare functions was not disturbed. During the 1930's, however, the catastrophic Great Depression wrought fundamental changes in outlook. With at least a fourth of the labor force idle, long bread lines, and little promise of improvement, local governments were unable to meet demands for welfare assistance. In turn some states virtually exhausted their resources trying to cope with the situation. Out of sheer necessity the national government entered the welfare picture, at first modestly and later on a grand scale. Many federal welfare programs of the thirties were temporary, but out of that era a whole new system of national-state cooperation evolved—a system still in effect today.

During the critical 1930's the national government first extended loans to state and local governments for relief purposes. Outright grants were made in 1933, and the earlier loans were written off. Throughout the rest of the decade numerous agencies and programs designed to lighten individual hardships were inaugurated. Most important was the Social Security Act of 1935, which today forms the heart of the federal-state system of public welfare. This basic law established an old-age insurance program and set up grants-in-aid under which the national government and the states administer programs of old-age assistance, unemployment compensation,[6] and aid to dependent children, the blind, and the disabled.

Welfare Organization

Prior to the passage of the Social Security Act, state welfare organization was for the most part a jumble of agencies, boards, and commissions. Since there was no concerted pressure for centralized administration, common practice was to establish a separate board for each welfare function. Although some states, following the lead of Illinois in 1917, had unified most welfare activities in a single administrative authority by the time of the Depression, most unification occurred after 1935 in view of the requirement of the Social Security Act that participating states provide administrative agencies acceptable to the national government. However, since the Act pertained only to certain forms of public assistance, many states still have not placed *all* welfare activities under one department.[7]

Historically, the county has been important as a local welfare unit,

6. Although a case may be made for the fact that payment of unemployment compensation is a form of welfare, it is considered in this volume in conjunction with labor problems. See Chapter 24.
7. Nor is it wise always to do so. For example, the education or training of mentally retarded public charges should probably be controlled by state education officers. By the same token, rehabilitation of criminals is ordinarily a function of correctional personnel, and medical treatment of indigent persons is assigned to health officials.

maintaining poor farms, almshouses, orphanages, and dispensing direct relief. Large cities and New England towns also provide such services. Since the advent of the Social Security Act local welfare agencies, particularly those in the counties, have taken on new significance. Commonly, they function as field extensions of the state welfare agency in administering federally aided programs. As such they are subject to close supervision by the state agency. In addition, local agencies also perform other welfare functions that may be assigned to them by the states.

The Problem of the Aged

Prior to inauguration of the present system of social insurance and public assistance, retirement for great numbers of the aged was a period of deprivation and hardship. Without savings accumulated over the years, insurance annuities, support contributed by friends or relatives, or some other help, many aged persons were without the necessities of life. Many were forced to seek public assistance. The Great Depression dramatized the needs of the aged whose problems are made even more evident by longer life expectancy. The Social Security Act was designed to ameliorate these difficulties by establishing broad programs of public assistance and social insurance.

Old-Age, Survivors and Disability Insurance.   In the strictest sense, OASDI is not a public welfare undertaking. The benefits received under this program are based upon contributions paid in the form of taxes levied in equal amounts upon participants and their employers. The program is, in fact, a system of compulsory retirement and disability insurance administered by the Social Security Administration in the Department of Health and Human Services.

Now covering the vast majority of employed persons in the country, the program is financed by a tax levied equally upon employees and employers. The payments are made to the national government which credits the social security accounts of employees. Benefits are payable at age sixty-five, or at reduced rates, as early as sixty-two. The benefits are payable irrespective of age in the event of disablement. Surviving dependents, such as a widow and children under eighteen, are entitled to the benefits a deceased worker would have received.

OASDI was begun too late to be of much help to workers nearing retirement when the Social Security Act was passed. Also, the coverage of the act was not extended to millions of others until later amendments were added. Help was provided to these individuals in the form of federally aided state public assistance programs.

Old-Age Assistance. Payments of money to the needy aged were first undertaken on a statewide basis over half a century ago. In 1923 Montana established the first such program, and by 1935 thirty states had done so. Both coverage and benefits were generally inadequate, however, and it was not until the states took advantage of the public assistance provisions of the Social Security Act that anything like satisfactory systems came into operation.

From 1935 to 1974 the states administered the assistance program with matching funds from the national government. However, with the implementation of the Supplemental Security Income program in 1974, in accordance with provisions enacted two years earlier, the assistance program became more nationally oriented. Under this approach the states may opt to administer the program or leave that responsibility to the Social Security Administration in the national government—which three-fifths of them have done. The program is financed mainly with federal funds although the state supplement has amounted to about a fourth of the total outlay.

In the United States today about one of every eleven persons over the age of sixty-five receives old-age assistance payments. Although this proportion is lower than in many recent years, one may still wonder why there are so many in view of the existence of OASDI. Several reasons may be cited. First, OASDI was not begun in time to benefit many already aged persons and others approaching retirement. Second, coverage was not extended to certain large groups of workers, notably farm workers, domestic employees, and the self-employed, until a few years ago. Finally, the modest OASDI benefits may be inadequate because of increasingly high costs of living. The expectation is that eventually participation in the OASDI program will all but eliminate reliance upon welfare payments.

Medical Assistance. Among the many problems besetting the needy aged is that of securing adequate medical care. With meager financial resources the aged poor find it difficult to receive needed treatment. To reduce the severity of this problem Congress, in the closing days of its 1960 session, passed the Kerr-Mills Act, which established a cooperative federal-state system of medical care for the indigent aged. Revised and expanded in 1965 into the Medicaid program, it is now a system which involves two basic kinds of assistance. The first is in reality an extension of the old age assistance program, and the second involves aid to persons who are medically indigent, although not receiving welfare assistance. In both areas funding is accomplished through matched grants-in-aid, with the major costs borne by the national government.

Further action was taken by Congress in 1965 when it voted in favor of the Medicare program, which went into effect the following year. The legislation established a program of medical care for the aged as part of the OASDI system. First proposed by the late President Kennedy and later by President Johnson, the program is a compulsory system administered directly by the national government through the Department of Health and Human Services. Like retirement benefits, Medicare is financed through taxes paid in equal amounts by both employers and employees. The state and local governments are not involved with Medicare as they are with Medicaid.

Dependent Children

Federal law declares that a dependent child is "a needy child under the age of eighteen, who has been deprived of parental support." Included are those whose parents are living but who, for one reason or another, do not support or care for their offspring. Prior to the Social Security Act, dependent children commonly were cared for in institutions such as orphanages. Today the trend is to preserve or construct the home situation by extending aid to mothers, near relatives, or foster parents who care for these children. The emphasis is apparent in that the aid, while primarily for the support of children, is known as aid to families of dependent children. These programs, administered by state welfare departments, are financed by state appropriations and federal grant-in-aid funds. Payments may be made not only for the support of dependent children but also for the support of those who care for them.

Other Programs

It is remarkable to note that since the 1930's, the decade of the Great Depression, welfare programs in the United States have grown from the modest beginnings of that era to the present day broad range of offerings. In addition to the basic programs discussed in the foregoing pages there are literally dozens of others. Some are broadgauged, designed to benefit the general population; others are quite narrow in scope and intended for the welfare of a specific segment of society.

Included in the panoply of welfare programs is provision for the adult blind and disabled, a program fully implemented by 1950 and administered today under terms of the Supplementary Security Income reforms of 1974. Among the best-known welfare undertakings is the food stamp program begun in 1965, and revised in 1977, as a means of improving the diets of the poor. Recipients are issued scrip, the amount based upon need, which can be used to purchase staple foods. Still in operation but not as prominent as in former years are the so-called poverty programs inaugurated in 1964 by the Equal Opportunity Act. Rent supplementation, designed to assist the poor in obtaining adequate housing, has been of particular benefit to the elderly. Under an array of statutory provisions a great many "social services" are also provided, including individual and family counseling, day care and other types of child welfare assistance, employment services, and varied special benefits for the aged.

PUBLIC HOUSING

Until recent years government took little direct action in regard to housing problems. Regulation through building codes, sanitation laws, and zoning ordinances, all of which are still used, were the usual modes of governmental action through the first quarter of the twentieth century. With the coming of the Great Depression, housing problems assumed a new importance, and governmental participation in the housing field took on a different character. The pressing need for new housing, particularly of the low-rent type, was so great that the national government entered the field.

To some people, governmental efforts to promote or provide housing are somehow "improper." Such actions are in reality profitable investments when measured against costs occasioned by substandard slum areas. When adequate housing is not available, slums and depressed areas inevitably develop, and such areas are costly in terms of police and fire protection, health services, and welfare assistance. Normally, taxes on slum property and other taxes collected from slum dwellers are but a fraction of the cost of the public services they require. Further, since the great need is for low-rent housing that low-income families can afford, some sort of subsidy is required. Private capital cannot sustain such housing. The logical solution is government help.

Governmental activity in housing represents a departure from the usual pattern of intergovernmental programs. Usually, federally aided ventures involve grants-in-aid to the state with administration centered in a single state agency. Housing problems, however, are basically local in nature. Thus public housing programs are primarily federal-local undertakings. With the exception of a few states the primary role of the states has been to enact legislation authorizing their local governments to participate in federally assisted housing programs.

There are two general facets to public housing ventures supported by the federal government: the construction of low-rent housing projects and the rehabilitation or clearance of slum areas. The construction of new public housing is facilitated by loans and grants made by the Housing Assistance Administration, an agency within the Department of Housing and Urban Development, to local housing authorities. The Renewal Assistance Administration aids in the redevelopment of slum areas, through grants and loans. In meeting the problems of reclaiming or rehabilitating the worst areas of urban blight, Congress in 1966 established the Model Cities Administration, authorizing it to grant funds to selected cities for the purpose of urban renewal. In each of these programs, as well as others not directly involved with public housing as such, the national agency is essentially the center of control and sets the standards.

Education

23

Democracy as it is known in the United States requires participation in the governmental process by most of the citizenry. Since political activity for its own sake is of doubtful value, the quality of that participation is a matter of prime importance. Political activity of a kind that strengthens rather than weakens democratic institutions presupposes mental, social, and emotional competence on the part of the citizens. At a time when almost nine out of ten young people between six and seventeen years of age are enrolled in public schools, a major share of the responsibility for such an accomplishment rests with the primary and secondary schools, as well as colleges and universities, that are publicly supported and administered. Of course, other institutions, such as the family and religion, have an important share in this great undertaking.

According to Henry Steele Commager, schools have made self-government work; they have created a national unity, swiftly made Americans of immigrants, and taught the equality of individuals.[1] In the early years of American history the fortunate few who were the beneficiaries of formal education received their training in private schools. Far into the nineteenth century public schools were commonly considered as schools for the underprivileged. Although provisions pertaining to education were included in six of the original state constitutions, the idea behind them was that government should supplement private facilities, and these provisions were later revised to indicate clearly that public responsibility was limited to the provision of some type of minimum training for those unable to pay the price of a private education.

A great expansion of educational opportunity occurred during the nineteenth century, and basic features of modern public education emerged. Legal responsibility was recognized as belonging to the states, but geographical necessity and political mores kept actual control of education

1. H. S. Commager, "Our Schools Have Kept Us Free," *Life*, October 16, 1950, pp. 46–47.

at the local level. During this period the typical school was an individual enterprise unconcerned with the programs of other schools and largely unencumbered by state controls. By 1900, half of the population between five and seventeen years of age attended school an average of about seventy-two days per year. However, only twelve per cent of those of high-school age were in school. An even more rapid increase occurred during the first half of the twentieth century, so that by 1950 eighty-two per cent of the young people between five and seventeen were in school, average school attendance was 150 days a year, and seventy per cent of those of high-school age were enrolled. Now some ninety per cent of school-age young people are enrolled.

PRIMARY AND SECONDARY EDUCATION

Local Responsibility

Throughout the history of America, public education has been primarily a local responsibility. Costs have been met in large part by some unit of local government with authority to construct buildings, provide equipment, hire teachers and administrators, and control curriculum content. Increasingly, local authorities have been required to accept controls imposed by state law, a development that has accompanied increased state financial support of primary and secondary schools. There is no doubt as to the legal right of each state to regulate all aspects of public education within its domain, but the wisdom of greatly augmented control is questioned by many who feel that the more effective approach is to strengthen local systems.

The Special District. Five types of local governments are concerned with providing education: special districts, counties, municipalities, New England towns, and townships. The district system appears to have originated in Massachusetts, where by the middle of the eighteenth century "a multitude of petty local boards and 'directors' ruled supreme in their infinitesimal districts. Each district was a law unto itself; of uniformity and system there was none."[2] The district pattern spread to other states and was carried into frontier regions where pioneer conditions provided fertile ground for its growth. Scattered neighborhood settlements had to provide their own educational facilities if there were to be any, and the school district, locally organized, controlled, and financed, served the purpose.

In over half the states responsibility for public primary and secondary

---

2. William C. Webster, *Recent Centralizing Tendencies in State Educational Administration*, Columbia University Press, New York, 1897, p. 24.

schools rests with school districts which are locally organized governmental units. Each district has a school board, known variously as the board of education, the board of directors, or the board of supervisors. Board members are popularly elected in most instances, and important responsibilities are vested in them, including constructing and maintaining physical facilities, hiring teachers, arranging curriculum, purchasing supplies, providing transportation for some pupils, and approving financial claims against the district. School boards commonly appoint superintendents to whom responsibility for these and other functions is delegated, and whose decisions are generally subject to board approval. In some small, rural districts board members are still burdened with many routine chores.

Inadequacies so painfully evident in many small districts over the years have promoted their consolidation into larger units. In 1942 there were over 108,000 independent school districts in the United States, a number now reduced to some 15,000. The consolidation movement has resulted largely from action at the state level. Some states have enacted legislation designed to compel consolidation, while others have sought to reach the same goal by providing incentives for "voluntary" consolidation. Often the incentives have taken the form of cash subsidies made available to districts of a certain size (measured in terms of area, valuation, or some other criteria) and withheld from others. Because of increased financial resources, consolidated districts are able to provide better school plants and improved curricula and to attract more highly qualified teachers.

The County-Unit. The plantation system in the South early favored the county as the chief unit of local government. When education was recognized as a public function in the South, the county became the principal unit for its administration. Many states still employ the county-unit to administer some or all schools. The county-unit plan calls for the administration and financial support of all or most primary and/or secondary schools on the *county-wide* basis. Occasionally, high schools are under county-wide administration while elementary schools are controlled by districts within the county, and schools located in large municipalities may be operated independently of county-unit administration.

Relationships between public schools and the county governing body under a county-unit arrangement differ significantly from state to state. Officials administering schools normally enjoy considerable independence. The fact is reflected in the term "county-unit school district," commonly used to designate the agency responsible for providing public education under the supervision of the "county board of education." These districts are quasi-corporations recognized by state law as enjoying an existence independent from the county. The degree of independence, particularly in regard to finances, varies from state to state. Typically, a county governing body exercises very little control over the county board of education.

The Municipality. Urban school districts are commonplace in most parts of the country. Much like county units, these districts normally are quasi-corporations whose boundaries are usually coterminous with those of the city or village with which they are identified. In earlier times, cities frequently encompassed numerous school districts, much as most counties do at the present time. In most cities today all schools are administered by a single district. Indeed, many districts include urbanized territory outside city boundaries along with the city itself. Under such circumstances, the administration of the district and the government of the city are usually completely separate. Although most urban school systems are independent of the city government, a few function as municipal departments. Occasionally, control over city schools is divided between the district and the municipality.

The Town and the Township. Only in the six states of New England and in New Jersey is the town the principal governmental unit for school administration. In all the New England states except New Hampshire town school districts are fiscally dependent upon town government, while township districts are as a rule fiscally independent of the township. In New England and New Jersey large municipalities frequently possess independent school districts. Like counties, towns and townships are more adequate administrative and financial units for the provision of public education than many small districts that are unassociated with a general purpose government. Of course, use of the town or township as the basic administrative area does not guarantee the elimination of small and inadequate schools, a fact reflected in the elimination of township schools in several states.

State Responsibility

During the first century of American independence, state activity in regard to public education was minimal and did not assume significant proportions until the end of the nineteenth century. According to a New York law of 1812, the state superintendent of common schools was authorized to prepare plans for improving public schools, to report the manner in which school money was used, and to provide information concerning schools to the legislature. By 1850, many states had provided for state superintendents who often were *ex officio.* Their chief duties were to administer certain state funds and oversee the manner in which they were spent by local school authorities.

By the end of the nineteenth century, state supervision had been extended in some states to such matters as textbooks, courses of study, selection of teachers, educational methods, and construction standards for buildings. Throughout the twentieth century there has existed a definite trend toward centralization in education. This trend has been evidenced by a greatly increased number of statutory provisions and by an appreciable growth in professional leadership emanating from state agencies. Local school administrators voluntarily seek the assistance of specialized personnel in state agencies. In Delaware and Hawaii the administration of education is sufficiently centralized for these states to be classified as state-unit systems.

State Board of Education. Most states have a board of education which exercises some control over elementary and secondary schools. Board members are selected in a variety of ways, but the great majority are either *ex officio* or appointed by the governor. The use of *ex officio* members, such as treasurers or attorney generals, is in part a carryover from earlier days when supervision of public school lands and custodianship of state aid money were the chief responsibilities of the board. Gubernatorial appointment subject to legislative approval is generally considered by students of education as the preferable method of selecting board members today. A number of states provide for popular election, and other methods of selection are employed in a few states.

The state board should be the dominant statewide agency concerned with public education, particularly at the primary and secondary levels. In many states, state boards of education have been slow to develop into important, responsible educational agencies. If this situation is to be remedied, state legislatures must grant more authority and discretion to their state boards of education, reduce the number and power of competing authorities, and place in the hands of the board the authority to chose a chief state administrative officer, usually known as the superintendent of public instruction.

The Superintendent of Public Instruction. The chief state administrative officer immediately concerned with the supervision of public education generally has the title of superintendent of public instruction, but other designations are used, including commissioner of education, director of education, and state superintendent of schools. The impact of this officer and accompanying staff, commonly called the department of education, on the operation of schools stems not so much from formal controls as from assistance extended to local units. Although conditions surrounding the early development of the superintendent were not auspicious, no position has greater potential for the unification and leadership of education in each state.

The great majority of state superintendents of public instruction are either popularly elected or chosen by the state board of education, while a handful are gubernatorial appointees. All of those popularly elected or appointed by a governor serve definite terms in office, while some chosen by a board serve definite terms and others at the pleasure of the board. In nearly half of the states the superintendent is a member of the board, and in about an equal number this officer serves as secretary to the board. As a consequence, the superintendent may function both as a policymaker and as an administrator. Such a combination of responsibilities, especially in view of the fact that they often result from popular election, decrease the probability that the superintendent will be a skilled professional administrator and educator. People of the desired calibre often are deterred from seeking office because of the risks involved in popular election.

The Department of Education. A strong state department of education, under the leadership of an able professional superintendent, engages in a variety of functions of great importance to public education. Such departments originally performed routine tasks like compiling statistics, making reports, publishing state laws pertaining to education, and apportioning state aid money to local schools, but today they perform a variety of responsibilities important to the quality of education throughout the state.

Major activities of state departments of education include planning, research, appraisal of present conditions and future needs, presentation of needs to legislatures and the people, provision of leadership to the teaching profession, and administration of regulations. Only a state agency can gather and interpret pertinent data pertaining to all aspects of public education in a state so as to provide a comprehensive picture of current conditions and relate resources to anticipated needs. It is important for school authorities in each state to know, for example, the number of classrooms in existence and their capacity as well as their structural condition; they also need to know the number of teachers on hand, the number potentially available, and the qualifications they possess; school administrators must also have up-to-date information on population trends. These examples merely serve to indicate the variety and importance of plans and supporting data made available to local educators by central agencies.

Plans for the future are of little value unless they can be effectively presented and interpreted to those persons able to implement them. If they are to be effective in promoting the kind of education they feel is desirable, state departments of education must constantly explain their programs to legislators and to the public in general and enlist their support. Implementation of plans rests, in the final analysis, upon those persons who are "on the firing line." In the field of education these people are the teachers, and it is imperative that a central agency inspire them to improve their teaching methods, advance their educational qualifications, enhance their pride in their profession, enrich the curricula where possible, and in every way seek to perform their mission more effectively. The regulatory responsibilities of state departments of education, although important, are likely to be of a routine nature. Included in this category are such functions as certification of teachers, inspection of sanitary facilities and fire escapes, review of curricula to ascertain that state requirements are met, and apportionment of state subsidies, especially when conditions are attached.

State Financial Assistance. A major development in recent times has been the rapid increase in the relative importance of state money used to assist in paying the costs of primary and secondary education. Traditionally, most of the costs of public education have been defrayed by local governments. Little change occurred in this pattern until the depression of the 1930's when revenues, coming largely from property taxes, decreased sharply. Rather then allow education to be crippled almost irreparably, public opinion favored state aid. A sharp upturn in state assistance occurred around 1930 and has not abated.

Factors causing the growth in state aid are numerous and complex. One underlying cause was the change in the nature of the economy from an agricultural to an industrial one. As industrialization spreads, disparities in taxpaying capacity of localities become increasingly evident. The more highly industrialized a state is, the more severe the discrepancies. Thus the taxpaying capacity of the area around Detroit is much greater than that of the upper peninsula in Michigan. The same is true of the areas around Philadelphia and Pittsburgh as contrasted with many sections of Pennsylvania. Although local differences exist in states like Iowa, Mississippi, and Nebraska, they are not so great. If revenue is to be collected from areas of concentrated wealth and spent in proportionately larger sums in less wealthy communities, responsibility for the undertaking logically rests with the states.

Intertwined with the collection of money in one locality and spending it in another is the problem of equalization of educational opportunities. Few persons now claim that because a child is born in a "backwoods" community he or she should be deprived of educational opportunities at least broadly comparable with those of fellow state citizens who enter the world in a more prosperous locale. Absolute equalization may be neither practical nor desirable, but steps in that direction have constituted a major reason for the increase in state aid. Related to equalization has been increasing acceptance of the idea that each state should assume responsibility for acquiring or encouraging *minimum* standards for *all* schools within its jurisdiction. For example, a state may stipulate that no local school may receive certain state aid unless it remains open at least nine months in each year; or a state may withhold state assistance if a school is permitted to become excessively crowded, or if the ratio between pupils and teachers exceeds a stipulated maximum.

Motivation for state aid has stemmed from many other considerations, including a desire to establish new services such as guidance, to enrich existing programs, to equalize the tax burden, to improve organizational arrangements, or to encourage research and experimentation in educational practices such as special curricula for exceptional children. As an alternative a state could, of course, assume direct responsibility for the provision of all public education, but there has been and continues to be a strong demand for retaining basic responsibility at the local level.[3]

It has been said, "He who pays the piper calls the tune." This homely observation points to the heart of a major question in public education today. How should control be divided among local, state, and federal authorities? When schools were financed locally, they were also controlled locally. Increased state financial support has been accompanied by increased state regulation, a situation now generally accepted as a matter of course. The big debate now revolves around increased federal assistance and accompanying federal controls. A case may be made for increased central control over education in the name of effectiveness and efficiency, but most Americans experience a feeling of uneasiness at the prospect of supervision over education moving further and further from the local community.

NATIONAL RESPONSIBILITY

Although a federal Department of Education was not created until 1979, national support for education is no recent development. The central government began making land grants for educational purposes even before the national Constitution was adopted. Millions of acres were granted to the states without imposing controls on education policies. Although not related to primary and secondary education, federal controls emerged with the Morrill Act of 1862, and they were strengthened by later acts of Congress, particularly the Smith-Lever Act of 1914. Federal controls over public education at the primary and secondary levels, specifically in regard to vocational training, were inaugurated by the Smith-Hughes Act in 1917.

For the past half-century or so, bills have been introduced regularly into Congress to provide federal aid for schools in general, not merely for special aspects of education. Interest in such proposals has been noticeably sharpened in recent times. Launching of the Russian Sputnik in 1957 spurred nationwide interest in education. Partially as a result of this event, Congress in 1958 enacted the National Defense Education Act. This act was designed to advance the cause of education at both the higher and lower levels. Federal loans were made available to college

---

3. Complete centralization of the administration of schools is found only in Hawaii, but it has been approached in Delaware, where a minimum school program is financed by state funds.

students on liberal terms, and money was appropriated to help public schools strengthen their offerings in science, mathematics, and modern foreign languages and to improve their guidance, testing, and counseling programs.

Proposals to inaugurate a large federal program to provide aid to general education as contrasted with specialized training have stirred great controversy. Many arguments pro and con have been advanced by educators, legislators, pressure groups, and many others. The major claims in behalf of federal assistance may be summarized under eight points. (1) Because states differ so greatly in wealth, income, taxpaying ability, and other pertinent factors, federal aid is needed to equalize educational opportunities. (2) Judged on the basis of the proportion of tax revenues spent on education, poorer states generally exert greater efforts to provide their facilities than do richer states. This unfair situation can be remedied only by federal action. (3) Since citizens of the respective states are also citizens of the United States, the national government has a responsibility to see that they are provided with adequate educational opportunities. Mobility of the population stresses the national significance of the consequences of poor education. (4) Wealth should be taxed where found and services provided where needed. (5) Numerous precedents already exist to testify to the value and wisdom of federal aid. Vocational training and agricultural extension programs are generally cited as examples. (6) Functions of the national government are expanding in other areas, and its responsibilities in education should keep pace. This argument is among the weakest. (7) Increasing national taxes leave other governmental units with inadequate revenue sources. (8) Federal aid will not necessarily involve federal control.

Opponents of increased federal aid to education present a number of arguments in support of their position in addition to denying the validity and significance of the claims of the proponents. (1) Responsibility for education is reserved to the states, and this reservation should not be impaired. (2) Control of education by state and local authorities guarantees that it will be better suited to local needs than if supervised from Washington. (3) National dictation of educational practices opens the door to national regimentation of the nation's youth. (4) Federal aid will tend to weaken and destroy local initiative. (5) Increased national expenditures for education will further unbalance the national budget. (6) The states are able to do an adequate job without federal help. (7) Local school authorities might be less careful in the expenditure of money obtained from the federal government than from local taxes. (8) There exists no widespread popular demand for federal action, which has been urged upon Congress primarily by representatives of pressure groups like the National Education Association and the AFL-CIO.

The Study Committee on Federal Responsibility in the Field of Education of the Commission on Intergovernmental Relations presented a number of interesting observations and conclusions. A majority of the Committee recognized the importance of initiative and responsibility at the state and local level and then observed, "If there is a disturbing tendency of the Federal government to assume disproportionate powers, we feel there is an equally dangerous tendency of the States and communities to neglect, and even abandon, their proper roles."[4] The Committee felt that this situation was particularly regrettable because it could not find a state that was economically unable to support an adequate school system, although it recognized the existence of differences in fiscal ability among the states.

HIGHER EDUCATION

"Higher education is the formally organized process whereby our society conserves, transmits, and advances its intellectual resources. Our concept of civilization, the wellsprings of our culture, the foundation of much of our physical and material well-being, the search for truth, and the worship of God—all of these are in one way or another in some measure dependent upon higher education."[5] All levels of government have shared in organizing and supporting institutions of higher education in the United States, but primary responsibility has rested with the states.

America's first college, Harvard, was established partly as the result of an appropriation in 1636 by the Massachusetts Colonial Assembly. Nine of the nation's 2400-odd institutions of higher learning were founded during the colonial period, and their names are illustrious. In addition to Harvard, they are William and Mary, Yale, Princeton, Brown, Rutgers, Dartmouth, King's College (later Columbia), and the University of Pennsylvania. All of these institutions, excepting the University of Pennsylvania, were sectarian when established. Although each was controlled by a religious group, they all admitted students without religious restrictions. Following the Revolution, the states began to organize colleges. The curricula of these early institutions stressed classical learning in philosophy, theology, mathematics, Greek, and Latin.

Changes occurred gradually in the pattern of higher education during the nineteenth century, and developments of revolutionary proportions began to appear about the time of the Civil War. Animated by a "dual vision," the universities fastened their eyes on new intellectual horizons in the belief that scientific research would bring the world under control. The second part of the vision concerned emphasis on the creation of a center of learning where many varied subjects were taught. Increased stress was placed on professional training in such fields as law, medicine,

---

4. *Federal Responsibility in the Field of Education,* p. 6.
5. John D. Millett, *Financing Higher Education in the United States,* Columbia University Press, New York, 1952, p. 3.

agriculture, and engineering. A major factor in these shifts of emphasis was the Morrill Act of 1862, providing federal assistance to the states for the support of institutions "to teach such branches of learning as are related to agriculture and the mechanic arts." With the creation of land-grant colleges "began the era of modern development in American higher education." At least one land-grant college is found in each state today, and in all but four states they are public institutions. In Massachusetts, New York, New Jersey, and Pennsylvania, arrangements have been made for private institutions to implement the Morrill Act.

Central Administration. Great variety characterizes the administrative arrangements provided by the states for the supervision and control of higher education. The earlier pattern called for the creation of a separate governing board for each institution. In recent times the practice has been to place two or more institutions under a single lay board. Most of the states now have either coordinating or consolidated governing boards.[6] Nationally, almost three-fourths of all board members are gubernatorial appointees, while the remainder are either elected or serve *ex officio*. Often members of a single board are chosen in a combination of ways. Board members usually serve rather long terms, averaging more than five years, and overlapping terms are common. Qualifications for serving on such boards are generally not high. Requirements most often relate to residence, political party affiliation, alumni status, sex, or occupation.

The authority vested in boards of higher education varies appreciably from state to state. Nevertheless, major responsibilities are normally placed in their hands. Except where legislatures make determinations by statute, the governing boards usually exercise complete control over institutional curricula, admission requirements, degrees offered and requirements therefor, and extension programs. Subject to a variety of controls by central fiscal agencies, these boards formulate budgets for institutions under their supervision and submit them to the governor and the legislature. Legislatures commonly make appropriations for higher education in such a manner that governing boards have some control over allocations. Authority to issue bonds for capital improvements, either with or without legislative approval, is generally vested in these boards. Of course, certain limits are regularly imposed on their bonding capacity.

All boards of higher education exercise control over aspects of personnel management. Some of the more important tasks pertain to setting salary and wage scales; authorization of new staff positions; determination of policies with regard to tenure, vacations, sabbaticals, and leaves; recruitment of personnel and approval of new staff members; approval of promotions; and supervision of retirement programs. These functions are

6. Only three states (Delaware, Nebraska, and Vermont) have no central planning or coordinating agency for higher education.

sometimes shared with civil service or some other state agency such as a retirement board. Also, board control over matters like approval of new staff members and promotions is purely formal in that decisions are made at the institutional level and sent to the board for approval as a matter of routine.

Junior and "Community" Colleges. Although a few junior and community colleges were established during the nineteenth century, most are products of the twentieth. The great majority of public junior and community colleges are locally controlled and supported with state assistance. These institutions "bring education to the people" in that they enable many persons to benefit from advanced education and training who otherwise would be unable to do so. They also reduce the over-all costs of higher education because the relatively expensive facilities and staff of four-year institutions are not employed to instruct many freshmen and sophomores who are either not seriously interested in advanced education or who for one reason or another are unable to pursue it for more than two years beyond high school.

Municipal Colleges and Universities. Much less numerous than other types of institutions of higher education, municipal colleges and universities are operated by cities primarily to bring senior college education to their residents. A number of small colleges have become municipal institutions when local authorities chose to take them over from private hands rather than allow them to cease operation. The first municipal college in the United States, the College of Charleston in Charleston, South Carolina, changed from private to public hands in 1837. The second such institution is also the largest today: the City University of New York. Some of the larger municipal colleges are found in Akron, Cincinnati, and Toledo, Ohio; Louisville, Kentucky; and Omaha, Nebraska.

Federal Assistance. Although chief responsibility for higher education rests with the states, considerable help has come from the national government, which has established well-known schools, particularly the U. S. Military Academy, U. S. Naval Academy, and U. S. Air Force Academy. More important from the standpoint of impact on education nationally have been different types of assistance extended to other institutions, both public and private. Attention already has been directed briefly to results stemming from the Morrill Act. Many federal programs have been inaugurated during the present century that advance higher education. By the Smith-Lever Act of 1914 Congress provided for "agricultural extension work" to be administered cooperatively by land-grant colleges and the United States Department of Agriculture. Although the basic purpose of the program was to provide agricultural information to the farmer, it has been significantly enlarged in recent years.

in education.[9] They merely held that in the field of higher education the states must provide equal or at least comparable facilities for the education of whites and blacks.

Although these cases may in a sense have "foretold" the outlawing of segregation on the basis of race in public education, they did not soften the impact of *Brown* v. *Board of Education of Topeka, Kansas,* decided in 1954.[10] In an opinion dealing with public primary and secondary schools, the Supreme Court held that "in the field of public education the doctrine of 'separate but equal' has no place. Separate educational facilities are inherently unequal." Recognizing the tremendous implications of its decision, the Court directed gradual desegregation and turned the supervision of the process over to federal district courts in the states involved.

It is impossible to express in a few words the impact of the *Brown* case on the public educational systems in the country. Integration proceeded gradually and calmly in the border states. In other places, like Little Rock, Arkansas, efforts by local school authorities to take steps toward desegregation met with violent opposition. A few states declared a firm determination to postpone integration as long as possible. In communities all across the country, local school authorities are still struggling with the problems involved in efforts to integrate their schools.

Finances. In spite of the fact that since 1970 about half of the states have enacted fundamental reforms in school financing, public education is experiencing a period of fiscal crisis, and it has been necessary to make frequent appeals to the voters for tax levies and bond issues. With growing frequency in recent years, such appeals have been turned down, with the result that educational services may be reduced even to the point of shortening the school year and making reductions in teaching staff. In an effort to alleviate the problem, the states have continued to increase their share of the costs to the point where nationally they now assume nearly 45 per cent of the bill for primary and secondary schools. Demands for the states to assume the entire cost of such schools have been voiced with increasing frequency, due in part to the great variations that now exist among the states.

The traditional arrangements for financing public schools have been brought into serious question as a consequence of recent court decisions. In August 1971 the California Supreme Court ruled that the system of financing schools in that state, which relied heavily on the property tax as in most states, was contrary to the "equal protection" clauses of the constitutions of California and the United States.[11] The court main-

---

9. *Sipuel* v. *Board of Regents,* 332 U.S. 631 (1948); *Sweatt* v. *Painter,* 339 U.S. 629 (1950).
10. 347 U.S. 483.
11. *Serrano* v. *Priest,* 487 P.2d. 1241.

tained that such reliance made the quality of education received by children dependent upon the wealth of each district. Although the decision of the court did not invalidate the property tax as a means of financing schools, it did raise a serious question as to the manner and extent to which that tax could constitutionally be relied on to finance public education. In 1973 the U. S. Supreme Court held that variations in funding among school districts in Texas were not "invidiously discriminatory" and consequently not in violation of the Fourteenth Amendment to the U. S. Constitution.[12] This 5–4 decision left to each state the determination of the legality of its arrangements for financing education.

The outlook for higher education is also bleak. In 1970 the Carnegie Commission on Higher Education sponsored a study on the financial condition of institutions of higher education, both public and private.[13] On the basis of their study of forty-one institutions of various kinds, the staff of the Carnegie Commission concluded that more than half of such institutions in the country were either in financial difficulty or headed for it. In many states the legislatures have appropriated less money per student in recent years.

Quantity and Quality.   As noted earlier, there was a great increase in the proportion of the nation's youth in school during the first half of this century. A similar growth occurred in higher education. In 1900, only about four per cent of persons between eighteen and twenty-one years of age were enrolled in institutions of higher learning. The proportion has exceeded one-third, but is now declining. At the same time, costs are increasing, pushed up largely by inflation.

Education at all levels must compete with other governmental services for the resources of the nation. Limits, both economic and political, exist. Decisions must be made as to the most important goals to be achieved. Thus in the recent past the chief goal in primary and secondary education has been to get as many as possible of the young people under a certain age into school. The first concern was for the provision of physical plants to house the multitudes. In recent years there has been growing recognition that education for the masses alone is not an adequate goal. Not only have special classes and curricula been made available for exceptional students, a "back-to-basics" movement has developed. Some three-fourths of the states have adopted policies setting specific educational standards for students. If the nation is to make the best use of its most valuable resource, the talent of its citizens, such action is imperative. The problems associated with these efforts are insignificant in comparison with the advantages to be achieved.

---

12. *San Antonio Independent School District* v. *Rodriguez*, 93 S.Ct..1278.
13. Earl F. Cheit, *The New Depression in Higher Education*, McGraw-Hill Book Co., New York, 1971.

Agriculture and Natural Resources, Business, and Labor

24

Among the most important functions of government, both state and national, is regulation of the various aspects of the economic system. Acting under its delegated powers, particularly its authority to tax and to regulate commerce among the states, the national government has enacted a broad range of laws that affect agriculture, business, and labor. Within the limitations of superior federal law the states have also imposed numerous controls, based most often upon the police power which permits regulation for the protection of the public health, safety, welfare, and morals. Local governments also impose regulations, basing their actions upon powers derived from the states.

AGRICULTURE AND NATURAL RESOURCES

The National Role

There is no doubt that national efforts over-shadow those of the states in regard to agricultural and other resources. National programs are carried on primarily under the powers to regulate commerce, raise and spend money, and administer the public domain. In some instances national activities are conducted as purely national programs; others are cooperative ventures with state and local governments. Many national programs in these areas date well back into the nineteenth century, but many, particularly in the field of conservation, represent efforts undertaken after 1900.

The scope of federal activity is extremely broad and involves many different agencies. Within the Department of Agriculture, for example, various agencies conduct programs in agricultural marketing, price stabilization, extension of agricultural credit, and conservation. Programs relating to fish and wildlife, mineral resources, water and power development, and public land management are carried on in the Department of the Interior. Credit is made available to farmers and farm groups by the various lending agencies within the Farm Credit Administration. The Tennessee Valley Authority is active in developmental programs in the southeastern part of the country. Other agencies such as the Tariff Commission, Federal Trade Commission, and Federal Power Commission also influence developmental programs. The overseeing and evaluation of activities affecting the total environment are performed by the Council on Environmental Quality. The many federal agencies and their field organizations active in developmental programs affect virtually every aspect of agriculture and resource utilization.

State and Local Organization

State organization for the administration of programs in the fields of agriculture and natural resources is typically fragmented; that is, the functions performed by a state in these areas are usually scattered among various agencies. Even in states like Alaska, Hawaii, and New Jersey, which are organized according to the principles of "good" administration, not all functions pertaining to agriculture and natural resources are grouped in a single, integrated department.

The principal state agency in the general field of resource development is the department of agriculture, an agency known by a variety of titles across the nation. It usually is headed by a single director appointed by the governor, although in some states the office is elective, and in others a board is used. The functions of departments of agriculture vary widely. Included in a usually long list of duties are enforcement of food inspection laws, control of plant and animal diseases, inspecting and grading farm produce, issuance of various licenses, conducting research programs, rendering advice, registering agricultural products, inspecting weights and measures, eradicating insect pests, conducting fairs, operating prisons and prison farms, and compiling market reports. Some of these responsibilities are performed in cooperation with the national government, but most are solely state functions.

In addition to the department of agriculture a state may have a large number of agencies that administer one or more functions that an integrated department might perform. Conservation activities, for example, are carried on by separate agencies in three-fourths of the states, and some states have separate conservation agencies for different resources. Among the states are found numerous commissions for licensing, inspecting, and grading agricultural products and natural resources—agencies such as livestock boards, plant commissions, fish commissions, and forestry boards.

Local organization in agriculture and natural resources is, for the most part, the result of state or federal programs. For example, about 3,000 local conservation districts have been formed under a cooperative federal program. County agents who act as consultants to local farmers are available as a result of federal-state-local cooperation. Counties, towns, and townships sometimes maintain fish wardens, forest fire watchers, and veterinarians. Also, special districts for the purpose of draining land, weed control, irrigation, and flood control are common.

Resource Programs

In general, the economic well-being of a nation depends upon its natural resources. Wasteful utilization of resources can lead to their depletion and thus contribute to dependency on other countries. To avoid this danger the national government and the states have inaugurated conservation programs, some of which are cooperative federal-state ventures. Through such efforts it is possible to achieve more intelligent use of nonrenewable resources such as metals, oil, and gas, and to avoid unnecessary waste of those that can be replaced.

Soil Conservation.   One of the basic resources of any country is its soil. For generations Americans paid little attention to soil conservation. The country was vast, the population relatively small, and the danger of soil depletion seemed remote. "Worn out" farms were abandoned. Erosion by wind and water took its toll. By the 1930's and the years of the "Dust Bowl" droughts, soil depletion had become a real problem. It has been estimated that 300 million acres of formerly useful land lay ruined as a result of erosion and misuse.

After detailed research and inquiries, Congress enacted the Soil Conservation Act of 1935. Under the stimulus of this law all states have enacted legislation creating conservation agencies and permitting establishment of local soil conservation districts that work with the federal Soil Conservation Service. The local districts are created as a result of application to the state agency by interested farmers and a favorable vote in a public referendum in which affected farmers and ranchers cast ballots. Each district is headed by an elective board of three to five members. Today these districts include about ninety-seven per cent of all farms and ranches in the United States. The Soil Conservation Service works with local districts, aiding and instructing them in techniques of preserving and building up soil fertility and productivity. Federal personnel work not only with district officials. but also directly with individual farmers.

Water.   The importance of water resources is obvious, for water, like soil, is necessary to the existence of life. Throughout the history of the world, civilization has flourished only in fertile, well-watered areas. Until recent years water conservation was not a problem in the United

States and still is not in some areas. However, in densely populated, heavily industrialized areas and in regions requiring irrigation, conservation of water has assumed urgent proportions.

Although the states are active in conservation of water resources, national efforts are definitely predominant. Through its power to regulate commerce among the states, the federal government exercises control over all navigable streams in the country.[1] Federal control over such streams has been implemented since 1920 largely by the Federal Power Commission. State projects involving navigable waters must, therefore, be cleared through that agency. There have been few instances of conflict over the past forty years, and the national government has followed a policy of encouraging state action.

Paramount federal control has not caused the states to abandon the problem of water conservation. On the contrary, state action is both lively and comprehensive. The Federal Power Commission cooperates by issuing licenses for power projects only after state power agencies have given their approval. Much state effort is directed at insuring adequate supplies of water through construction of watersheds, determination of water rights, and regulation of water use. Problems of flood control and pollution of rivers and bodies of water are also of major concern to the states. These water problems are usually interrelated and are frequently associated with federal projects and programs. Regional water problems requiring interstate cooperation have been increasingly dealt with in recent years by means of interstate compacts.

Forests.   Conservation of forest resources at the state level is largely a result of national efforts. In performing the significant task of preserving and developing forest resources, practically every state has established some kind of agency to further forest conservation. Some states, especially those with large forests areas, are well organized for this function, while in others small independent agencies or departmental subdivisions do little more than attempt to prevent forest fires.

Beginning in 1911 and continuing to the present, the national government has developed conservation programs in which forest owners, both public and private, may participate. Under federal grants-in-aid states are assisted in the prevention and control of forest fires, reforestation projects, extension of forestry education, controlling some plant diseases, and eradication of insect pests. Technical aid in these areas was extended in 1950 to private owners of forest lands and to processors of forest

---

1. Federal authority was held in *The Daniel Ball,* 10 Wall. 557 (1871), to include control over rivers used "or susceptible of being used, in their ordinary condition, as highways for commerce." Federal authority was expanded in *United States* v. *Appalachian Electric Power Company,* 211 U.S. 377 (1940), which held that a stream is navigable if by improvements it can be made so. Further, federal control was not limited to navigation, but was recognized as including flood control, watershed development, and development of hydroelectric facilities.

products. All but a few states cooperate with the U.S. Forest Service through which these programs are conducted.

Mineral Resources. The poorest conservation record of the states is in regard to minerals. Except for mineral deposits under lands owned or controlled by the national government, little has been done to check depletion of these nonrenewable resources.[2] Conservation of oil and natural gas has received state attention, but they are the only mineral resources about which the states have done anything of note. Metal ores and coal have been largely ignored, although tax and safety laws have had incidental effects in the promotion of conservation.

Measures to curb waste of oil and gas appeared in the states as early as the 1880's. Pennsylvania and New York, followed soon by other states, enacted laws during that period to prohibit wasteful practices such as allowing seepage of water into wells, burning of gas, and crowding of wells.[3] Today virtually all oil-producing states have laws of this sort and cooperate with each other to conserve oil and gas resources. Thirty-three states now work together for this purpose under the Interstate Oil Compact Commission organized in 1935.

In 1914 Oklahoma introduced *proration*—a policy whereby oil production quotas are assigned to producers essentially on the basis of production capacity and market demand. Other states followed Oklahoma's example during the early years of the depression,[4] and Congress strengthened them by prohibiting oil produced in excess of state quotas—"hot oil"—from interstate commerce. Proration served during the depression to improve market prices, and many states were undoubtedly attracted to proration for that reason, but whatever the motivation for its adoption proration is an effective tool of conservation.

A development of more than usual interest was the "tidelands oil" controversy in which the national government and the states disputed control of the oil under the lands of the three-mile coastal belt. In *United States v. California*,[5] decided in 1947, the Supreme Court held that paramount rights to the oil belonged to the federal government. In 1953,

---

2. The national government reaches mineral operations on state and private lands through its powers to tax and to regulate interstate commerce. These powers have been used to regulate, to some extent, the extraction, processing, and transportation of minerals and mineral products. Even so, severe criticism of federal actions have been voiced, particularly in regard to the liberal depletion allowances permitted in taxation of mineral extraction—allowances that encourage rapid exploitation of resources.

3. The power of the states to enact laws of this type was upheld by the United States Supreme Court in *Ohio Oil Company v. Indiana,* 177 U.S. 190 (1900).

4. *Champlin Refining Company v. Corporation Commission of Oklahoma,* 286 U.S. 210 (1932), was the case in which prorationing was upheld by the United States Supreme Court.

5. 332 U.S. 19 (1947). Later suits involving oil lands off the coasts of Texas and Louisiana produced similar results. *United States v. Louisiana,* 339 U.S. 232 (1950); *United States v. Texas,* 339 U.S. 707 (1950). The struggle for control of the tidelands is related in Ernest R. Bartley, *The Tidelands Oil Controversey,* University of Texas Press, Austin, 1953.

however, Congress returned jurisdiction over resources in the marginal seas to the states after two earlier attempts to do so, in 1946 and 1952, had been defeated by presidential vetoes. Today, petroleum resources in the controversial tidelands remain under state control.

Fish and Game. Of all state efforts in the conservation field probably none has been more successful than those devoted to the protection of wildlife. Fish and game laws date back to colonial days, but it was not until the last half of the nineteenth century that state agencies began to appear. New Hampshire's fish commission created during the Civil War and broadened to include game in 1878 was, in the modern sense, the first state wildlife protection agency. Other states adopted the New Hampshire approach and, stimulated by national activity from 1871 on, more than two-thirds of the states instituted active conservation agencies by the turn of the century. Fish and game agencies now exist in every state either as independent establishments or as divisions of departments. Some states maintain fish commissions and game commissions, and a few have two fish commissions, one for fresh water and another for salt water fish.

Basically the same conservation activities are followed in all states with differing emphases according to the nature of a state's resources. Variations are based, for example, on such factors as whether a state is large or small, inland or coastal, northern or southern, mountainous or level, heavily forested or barren. The principal methods used in fish and game conservation are requirements that licenses or permits be obtained by those who hunt and fish, restrictions on the length of hunting and fishing seasons, imposition of bag limits, maintenance of fish hatcheries, game farms and game refuges for wildlife propagation, destruction of predatory animals, and operation of research and public education programs. The success of these efforts over the past seventy-five years is indicated by the fact that in many states the wildlife population, or at least that of some species, is much greater than it was when active conservation programs were begun.

Environmental Concern

The resources most likely to be taken for granted, and thus exploited and ignored, are those provided by nature. Throughout most of American history the practice has been to utilize resources at the lowest possible cost with little thought for the future. There was always more land farther west, more forests beyond the next river, and more fish, or game, or gold, over the next mountain. It was not until the turn of the present century that anything like intelligent conservation of such resources as forests, soil, minerals, and water was begun.

In regard to these basic resources the accomplishments of state and national governments have been creditable, but unfortunately, as recent developments have shown, conservationists of the past half century did not and perhaps could not anticipate the character of technology and the consumption patterns of today, nor their resultant impact on the environment. In the 1960's the American citizen learned that while water had been conserved, much of it was polluted, with whole rivers and lakes literally "dead." Motor vehicles abounded and factories were well-supplied with raw materials, but part of the price was a shroud of polluted air, and lakes, rivers, and coastal areas laden with industrial wastes. Record agricultural harvests were achieved, but at the frightful cost of infecting the nation's water systems with pesticides. In other areas, the ravages of strip mining, oil spillages, and the discharge of detergents into water courses, the threat of pipeline ruptures, the interrupted migration of fish, the disappearance of primitive and open areas, the problem of solid waste disposal, and the impending extinction of various species of wildlife indicated the seriousness of the consequences of unmindful, heedless consumption of resources. It was at this stage that government efforts in conservation and development were broadened to include measures intended to check and, it is hoped, to reverse the deterioration of environmental quality.

Under legislation enacted in 1969 and 1970, Congress created the Council on Environmental Quality, and its supporting Office of Environmental Quality, both located in the Executive Office of the President. Activity at this level consists basically of analysis and policy recommendation. Later the Environmental Protection Agency was created as an independent line department with responsibility for most federal programs involving environmental protection. During these same few years several states also created agencies with names similar to their federal counterparts, but in general existing agencies were utilized by state legislatures in matters of environmental protection. It is of course much too early to forecast the degree of success these activities will achieve, for clearly only the first steps have been taken.

It would appear that the magnitude of many problems involving environmental quality is such that individual states can hardly expect to achieve total solutions. Most difficulties extend beyond state boundaries and are regional or national—and sometimes international—in character. Consequently, if environmental quality is to be improved in any significant way, there must be strong national leadership and pervasive reforms in conservation and development programs. Even so, the role of the states remains an important one, for many problems of environmental abuse are of local orgin and are capable of solution or correction by state and local action.

REGULATION OF BUSINESS

Each state has a large number of departments, boards, commissions, and offices that are responsible for enforcement of regulations pertaining to designated aspects of business. No state maintains a central department in which are collected all such functions, nor would such an arrangement be desirable. There are so many different types of businesses and such a wide variety of business practices that a single agency could not hope to do a competent job. Consequently, state authority to regulate businesses and business practices is implemented by a profusion of administrative bodies.

Government Ownership

Although there are many examples of public ownership and operation of business enterprises, the practice is not prevalent.[6] Popular resistance to government competition with private enterprise serves as an effective check on proposals for governmental business activities. Nevertheless, states and local governments conduct various types of business enterprises, sometimes in direct competition with private firms and sometimes under conditions of monopoly. There are no discernible trends in public ownership either at the state or local level. No surge of expansion is apparent; neither is there strong demand for its contraction.

State business ventures are not numerous. One-third of the states operate monopolies in the liquor business. Operation of toll roads, toll bridges, tunnels, and port facilities are common state enterprises. The best known state organization in this respect is the Port Authority of New York-New Jersey, a bi-state corporation that controls and administers docks, terminals, airports, and related facilities. Among the fifty states North Dakota is unique in terms of its commercial interests, operating a bank, a system of mills and grain elevators, a land-sales agency, and a casualty and bonding insurance business.

It is at the local level, particularly among municipalities, that public ownership is most apparent. Most cities today own and operate their water supply systems, and power utilities are public property in many municipalities. Other activities of a commercial nature that are undertaken by local governments include the operation of waste disposal facilities, airports, transit systems, wharves and docks, slaughterhouses, public markets, golf courses, auditoriums, stadiums, and swimming pools.

---

6. Some functions now considered properly governmental in character were at one time, and in some cases still are, performed by private concerns. During the early years of the Union road construction was commonly undertaken by private agencies. Postal service was rendered briefly by the famous "Pony Express." Today, garbage and waste disposal services in some municipalities are performed by private companies.

Public ownership has been subject to attack, especially by individuals and groups who must compete with government enterprises. A long list of arguments are cited, the major ones being that public ownership is destructive of the free enterprise system, it puts "politics" above good business practices, and it creates powerful pressure groups within government. Those who favor public ownership reply that it is undertaken in the public interest and ordinarily only when private enterprise fails to serve that interest. As in so many other problem areas neither viewpoint is wholly correct. It is, in fact, necessary to examine individual situations to determine the validity of claims and counterclaims.

Regulation of General Business Practices

Each state has laws that regulate practices and procedures common to all business enterprises. Some are general laws that affect business as well as other elements of society; others are designed specifically to regulate business activities as such. In the first category, for example, are the laws on ownership, sale, and transfer of property; the laws that regulate the making of contracts; tax legislation of all descriptions; zoning ordinances; regulations promoting conservation of natural resources; and the general criminal law. The most important measures regulating business practices directly are those which are designed to control entry into business, prevent monopolies and unfair trade practices, and prevent and punish dishonest and fraudulent business practices.

Entry into Business. Before a group can do business as a corporation it must obtain a *charter*. Charters conferred by states are usually issued by the secretary of state although the function is sometimes lodged in a special administrative agency.[7] The conditions under which a corporation must operate are set forth in its charter. Since charters are legally regarded as contracts that may not be impaired under the national Constitution,[8] the states are careful to see that they contain clauses permitting subsequent necessary modification. Intended as a means of controlling corporate activity, restrictions contained in charters are not as effective as they might be, and in some states they are quite lax. This is due primarily to a desire to attract new businesses and, in some states to increase the yield of taxes placed on the privilege of doing business. A half-century ago New Jersey's incorporation laws were such that numerous corporations sought charters there. Today new corporations tend to favor Delaware charters.

---

7. Congress also has authority to grant charters to corporations. National banks and government-owned corporations, for example, are incorporated by Congress.
8. Article I, Section 10. The contract nature of corporation charters was set forth in the early case of *Dartmouth College* v. *Woodward,* 4 Wheaton 518 (1819).

Regulation of Competition. Statutes and constitutional provisions designed to prevent monopolies exist in practically all states. These regulations, some of which predate federal antimonopoly legislation, may be in the form of general prohibitions of all activities that tend to curtail competition, or they may be directed at specifically designated practices. State antimonopoly legislation has not been effective for two reasons. First, there are no special enforcement agencies. Attorney generals ordinarily are given responsibility for seeing that antimonopoly laws are obeyed although suits may also be instituted by private individuals. The second and principal reason stems from the interstate character of most modern, large businesses. Since most firms that are able to create monopolies operate in more than one state, and the power to regulate interstate and foreign commerce is vested in Congress, national leadership has dominated the field.

Since the early 1930's there has been a continuing controversy involving so-called *fair trade* laws. Such laws provide that agreements may be reached between manufacturers and retailers whereby the retail prices of the manufacturer's products may be fixed. Most contain a provision that when one or more dealers enter into such agreements the prices determined are binding upon *all* dealers who handle affected products. These "nonsigner" provisions make fair trade laws effective and at the same time stimulate controversey. At one time or another fair trade laws have been in force in forty-five states.

Congress removed the possibility of conflict of state fair trade laws with national power to regulate interstate commerce by approving the Miller-Tydings Act of 1937 specifically exempting fair trade agreements from federal antimonopoly legislation. The 1937 act did not mention nonsigner provisions, however, and in 1951 the United States Supreme Court reversed the conviction of a New Orleans retailer who, as a nonsigner, had refused to be bound under Louisiana's fair trade law.[9] The following year Congress passed the McGuire Act which bound nonsigners in interstate commerce if by state law they were bound in intrastate commerce. In 1953 the Supreme Court refused to review a court of appeals decision in favor of the Act.[10]

Those who favor fair trade laws contend that they make it possible for small merchants to compete with larger ones. Opponents insist that they violate the idea of free enterprise and are, in fact, nothing more than *price-fixing* statutes. Controversy has resulted in litigation in many states. To date, about a fourth of the fair trade laws have either been declared void or the essential nonsigner provisions invalidated.

Prevention of Fraud. Most states now have laws designed to prevent

9. *Schwegmann Brothers* v. *Calvert Distillers Corporation,* 341 U.S. 384 (1951).
10. *Schwegmann Brothers* v. *Eli Lilly and Company,* 346 U.S. 856.

and punish certain unethical business practices. False or misleading advertising, for example, is commonly prohibited. Labeling laws require that representations appearing on labels must be factual. Usury legislation regulates the maximum interest rates that may be charged, and the content of sales contracts is often fixed by state specification. New stock and security offerings are policed by the states. The effect of many such laws, although they are framed in general terms, is to regulate special businesses. In some instances they complement similar federal legislation. For example, the laws enforced by the Federal Trade Commission and the Securities and Exchange Commission affect interstate advertising and investment practices.

Regulation of Special Businesses

Some business enterprises bear a more intimate relationship to the general well-being of society than do others. Obviously, the provision of electricity, operation of transportation facilities, or management of basic credit institutions are far more important to the public than the manufacture of toys or operation of a fast-food franchise. Consequently, the business ventures of fundamental importance are closely supervised and regulated.

Public Utilities. The type of business subjected to the most extensive regulation is probably the utility. Utilities provide necessary and essential services such as gas and electric power, public transportation, telephone service, water supply, and sewage disposal. They tend to be "natural monopolies," for effective competition in the utility field is uneconomical and, in most instances, physically undesirable, if not impossible. Utilities are frequently governmentally owned and operated, especially for the provision of water and electricity, but most are in private hands. The national government shares in the function of utility regulation when interstate commerce or federal facilities are involved. Federal agencies of importance in this area are the Interstate Commerce Commission, Federal Power Commission, Federal Communications Commission, and Securities and Exchange Commission.

Each state maintains an agency for utility regulation. A commission of three to seven members, usually appointed by the governor, performs this function except in Oregon and Rhode Island, where single commissioners are used. The powers of utilities commissions are broad, including the authority to decide who shall provide what services, what the standards of service shall be, when and under what conditions service may be expanded or contracted, and the rates that may be charged. Private utilities operating in local communities are subject to regulation by state utilities commissions. Government-owned local utilities must observe various restrictions imposed by state agencies, but are largely controlled by local governing bodies.

Securities Regulations. For many years the investment field was a fertile and profitable hunting ground for swindlers and confidence men. *Caveat emptor,* a common law principle meaning "let the buyer beware," was the rule of the day. The appeal of quick profits in speculative stocks made many investors unwary and resulted in the enrichment of many unscrupulous promoters. "Blue-sky" laws designed to protect investors, or at least help them make wiser decisions, have been enacted in practically all states.[11] Rhode Island in 1910 and Kansas in 1911 enacted the first securities regulation statutes. Other adoptions came slowly but were accelerated by increased losses to swindlers during the prosperous 1920's.

Blue-sky laws usually deal with three phases of security regulation. First, new issues of stocks and securities must be approved by state officers before being offered for sale. Second, dealers in securities must be registered or licensed. Third, fraud provisions prescribe penalties for various prohibited activities in the investment field. Enforcement is undertaken in some states by securities commissions, but in most the function is assigned to an agency or department performing a related function or to the secretary of state or attorney general. Results at the state level have not been impressive because of the interstate nature of many stock swindles. Since 1934 the federal Securities and Exchange Commission has enforced national securities regulation laws on an interstate basis. National and state agencies, acting cooperatively, have effectively reduced the volume of investors' losses to dishonest promoters.

Banking. Commercial banks in the United States may be chartered either by the states or national government. Regardless of charter derivation, however, banks doing business within a state are subject to the state's banking regulations. National banks, in addition, are regulated under national law as are state banks that elect to affiliate with the Federal Reserve System and the Federal Deposit Insurance Corporation. In the event of conflicting regulations, national rules prevail.

Two-thirds of the states have banking departments headed by single administrators known as commissioners, secretaries, or examiners. Arrangements in the remaining states present a variety of administrative forms, including a few regulatory boards. The functions of a typical banking department range from issuing charters to new banks to the enforcement of regulations that affect practically every aspect of banking practice. One of the most effective tools of banking regulation is the audit. Each state maintains a staff of bank examiners whose job is to inspect the accounts of banks.

Although states exercise important functions in the regulation of banks,

---

11. The term "blue sky" is attributed to a Kansas legislator who, in supporting the 1911 bill that became that state's securities regulation act, is supposed to have remarked that some brokers were so unethical that they would sell shares in "the bright blue sky."

national control has increased considerably over the last century. National banks were authorized by the National Banking Act of 1863. The Federal Reserve System, created in 1913, extended national authority. State failures with deposit insurance laws and the large number of bank failures during the early years of the Great Depression led to the establishment, in 1933 of the Federal Deposit Insurance Corporation. Since most state banks have some connection with these or other federal agencies and programs, national authority over state banks is extensive.

Insurance. Virtually every phase of the insurance business is strictly regulated by the states. In each state there is an administrative agency, usually headed by an appointive commissioner, for the enforcement of the regulatory laws. Insurance companies must obtain licenses to sell various types of insurance, and out-of-state companies must deposit large reserves with the commissioner as a guarantee that claims within the state can be met. Individual agents must also be licensed. Investment of company assets is closely controlled by the state. Rate-setting has not developed into a general practice, but state agencies can order reduction of rates considered unreasonable or discriminatory. In some instances, as in fire insurance, rates have been governmentally fixed.[12]

The national government does not participate directly in regulating the insurance business. A Supreme Court decision in 1869 held that insurance was not interstate commerce even if sales were made across state boundaries, and thus could not be regulated by Congress.[13] This attitude prevailed until 1944 when, in an antimonopoly prosecution of a group of insurance companies, the seventy-five year old doctrine was reversed.[14] Almost immediately, however, Congress enacted legislation exempting insurance firms from federal antimonopoly legislation. To date Congress has declined to authorize national regulation of the insurance business although it has the power to do so.

Small Loans. One aspect of moneylending that is attended by special problems is the small loan. Such loans involve small amounts and are usually secured by personal property such as furniture or automobiles and sometimes only by the promise of the borrower to repay. The high risks involved discourage conventional lending institutions, particularly since usury laws do not permit high enough interest charges to compensate for losses on bad loans. As a result borrowers may, in the absence of protective state laws, fall prey to "loan sharks," lenders willing to loan small amounts at exorbitant rates of interest. All but a few states now have laws which fix the maximum rates of interest that may be charged

---

12. The power to fix rates was upheld by the United States Supreme Court in *German Alliance Insurance Company* v. *Lewis,* 233 U.S. 389 (1914).
13. *Paul* v. *Virginia,* 8 Wall. 168.
14. *United States* v. *Southeastern Underwriters Association,* 322 U.S. 533.

on small loans. There is a great deal of variation among the states, but a typical law provides for a descending scale of rates as the amount of a loan increases.

Liquor. Because of the relationship of alcoholic beverages to popular concepts of morality, the liquor trade is subjected to strict regulation. Three basic systems of control are used: prohibition, government monopoly, and licensing. Prohibition outlaws the manufacture, transportation, and sale of all beverages containing more than a specified amount of alcohol. National prohibition was effected in 1920 when the Eighteenth Amendment became a part of the United States Constitution. Approval of the Twenty-first Amendment in 1933 returned to the states the freedom to decide whether to continue prohibition. State monopolies exist in eighteen states, although in Wyoming the monopoly is limited to the wholesale level.

None of these systems of control constitutes the only method of regulation within a state. Even in "dry" areas, for example, beers and wines of low alcoholic content are sold by licensed dealers. The monopoly states generally license private clubs, hotels, and restaurants to sell liquor by the glass. In most states relying on the license system, and in some monopoly states as well, "local option" laws permit local governments to decide whether to adopt prohibition within their boundaries. Other regulatory actions include assessment of taxes, forbidding sales to minors, imposing closing hours, and limiting the number and types of liquor outlets.

Regulation of Professions and Trades

In the interest of maintaining high standards of performance, many professions are subjected to more or less extensive control. There is no precise yardstick by which to determine the extent to which a given profession ought to be regulated, but the general criterion is the degree to which a profession is considered related to the general welfare. Thus medicine is virtually completely controlled with only slightly less attention paid to other aspects of the healing arts. Law, engineering, architecture, accounting, realty, and teaching are also regulated in considerable detail. Many states also exercise appreciable control over such occupations as plumbing, contracting, midwifery, funeral direction, barbering, and the like. The authority of a state to regulate professions in pursuance of its police powers is unquestioned so long as regulatory statutes are reasonable.

Regulation at the local level is confined largely to the occupations known as "trades" as distinguished from "professions." Thus plumbers, electricians, masons, mechanics, and builders are often required to obtain occupational licenses. Local regulation is secondary to state provisions and must yield in the event of conflict. The extent of local regulation varies from place to place with the greatest incidence occurring in large cities.

REGULATION OF LABOR

When America was primarily an agricultural nation there were no labor problems in the modern sense. Most industrial products were manufactured by self-employed craft workers, and when factories existed they were small, with individual workers negotiating terms of employment. With the coming of industrialization, however, the small factory gave way to large plants, mass production became the rule, hordes of laborers moved to the cities to be near the factories, and labor problems became more important. Today both nation and states have enacted many statutes in quest of solutions to the problems of labor. These laws may be divided into two basic groups. One group relates to labor organization and activity; the second pertains to standards and conditions of labor.

State administrative organization for labor regulation takes many forms. In most states agencies responsible for the enforcement of labor statutes have been gathered into a department of labor. Such departments usually are headed by a single appointive administrator although some are elected, while in a few states boards are used. Some state labor departments contain only a few agencies and possess little or no jurisdiction over others. Thus agencies administering workmen's compensation laws or unemployment compensation statutes may be independent of the department.

LABOR ORGANIZATION AND ACTIVITY

The history of organized labor in the United States goes back to the closing years of the eighteenth century. Local unions existed before 1800, but there was no appreciable growth of unionism before the Civil War. During these early years the growth of labor unions was impeded by judicial application of the common law concept that such organizations were illegal conspiracies in restraint of trade. This ancient doctrine quickly faded, however, after the Massachusetts supreme court recognized the legality of labor unions in 1842.[15] The first labor organization to achieve national importance was the Knights of Labor, an organization begun as a secret society in 1869. Membership was open to all workers and by the mid-1880's exceeded 700,000. Failure to win key strikes and inability to attract strong political support led to the demise of the Knights, and by 1900 the union had lost its effectiveness.

15. *Commonwealth* v. *Hunt,* 45 Mass. 111.

Today's American Federation of Labor and Congress of Industrial Organizations began in 1881 as the Federation of Trades and Labor Unions. The Federation bitterly opposed the Knights of Labor and in 1886 rallied other unions to form the American Federation of Labor. The AFL was a federation of *craft* unions, each of which contained members skilled in the same trade. Over the years dissatisfaction arose among leaders of the federation over the question of taking in *industrial* unions—those composed of all workers, skilled and unskilled, in a single industry. Finally, in 1938, after expulsion from the AFL, a group of labor leaders established the Congress of Industrial Organizations. Almost twenty years later, in 1955, the rupture was healed and the two unions reunited as the AFL-CIO.

Collective Bargaining

The term "collective bargaining" refers to a method of negotiation whereby representatives of labor organizations and representatives of employers work out agreements in regard to terms and conditions of employment. This process relieves the individual laborer of the task of trying to win favorable terms of employment unassisted. Collective bargaining strengthens organized labor for if a union can speak for all or at least a large number of an employer's workers, it is in a favorable bargining position.

State efforts in behalf of labor during the first thirty years of the twentieth century were sporadic. It was not until the national government enacted a series of labor laws during the 1930's that state labor legislation began to accumulate. The Norris-LaGuardia Act of 1932 prohibited the use of injunctions as a means of preventing strikes. The National Industrial Recovery Act of 1933 provided that workers "shall have the right to organize and bargain collectively," and similar language was included in the Guffey Coal Act of 1935, but both statues were struck down by the Supreme Court.[16] The Wagner Act of 1935, sometimes referred to as the "Charter of American Labor," contained not only a solid guarantee of the right of collective bargaining but also prohibited a number of "unfair labor practices" including refusal by employers to bargain with the recognized representatives of organized employees. It also created the National Labor Relations Board, an independent agency before which disputes over alleged violations of the unfair practices provisions could be heard and decided. The national Wagner Act applies only to interstate commerce, of course, but most states have either adopted "little

---

16. The N.I.R. Act was held unconstitutional in *Schechter Poultry Corporation* v. *United States,* 295 U.S. 495 (1935), and the Guffey Coal Act was set aside in *Carter* v. *Carter Coal Company,* 298 U.S. 238 (1936). An earlier federal law which guaranteed collective bargaining rights in the railroad industry, the Railway Labor Act of 1926, was upheld in *Texas and New Orleans Railway Company* v. *Brotherhood of Railway and Steamship Clerks,* 281 U.S. 548 (1930).

Wagner Acts" or enacted various provisions dealing with an assortment of "unfair labor practices."

The Right to Strike

The ultimate weapon at the disposal of organized labor is the strike. Labor's right to resort to this drastic measure is now generally recognized. However, unions are not altogether free to use the strike when, where, and however they please. Strikes may be carried out only for a legal purpose and in a lawful manner.

A strike, or threat to strike, is used most commonly to achieve higher wages, shorter hours, and improved working conditions. However, a strike called to gain these legitimate objectives may be halted if strikers indulge in threats or acts of violence, coercion, or intimidation. The strike may not be used in connection with forbidden labor practices. For example, a strike to force an employer to hire only union members is illegal in states that outlaw the "closed shop." Forcing an employer to refuse to do business with another employer, the "secondary boycott," is commonly prohibited. "Jurisdictional strikes" to compel an employer to accept a striking union as bargaining agent rather than another labor organization are frequently forbidden. In states that have imitated the "cooling off" provision of the national Taft-Hartley Act of 1947 strikes may not be called during a compulsory waiting period. Several states specifically forbid the "sit down" strike that flourished briefly during the 1930's.[17] Other areas in which strikes of any type are, or may be, generally forbidden relate to government employment and to essential industries, particularly during times of emergency.

Open, Closed, and Union Shops

Regulations pertaining to hiring practices determine whether a place of employment is an *open, closed,* or *union* shop. An open shop is one in which the employer is free to hire workers at will, regardless of prospective employees' union status. Furthermore, employers are not compelled at a later time to join a union. A closed shop exists when only union members may be hired. Jobs in a union shop are available to nonunion members who must, as a condition of employment, join a recognized union within about thirty to sixty days.

The Taft-Hartley Act outlaws the closed shop in employment subject to federal regulation. Union shops are permitted if approved by a majority of workers in a place of employment, *except in states that prohibit*

---

17. Sit-down strikes in which strikers refuse to vacate the premises on which they work were declared illegal as applied to industries subject to federal regulation in *National Labor Relations Board* v. *Fansteel Metallurgical Corporation,* 306 U.S. 240 (1939).

union shops. Today, a third of the states have statutes or provisions in their constitutions called "right to work" laws that prohibit agreements requiring union membership as a condition of employment.[18] A dozen such laws were in existence at the time the Taft-Hartley legislation was enacted.

Organized labor bitterly opposes "right to work" laws, contending that they are designed to weaken unions and that they have the effect of extending to nonunion members the benefits of collective bargaining that are made possible by union efforts. Proponents insist that "right to work" laws preserve the freedom of individual choice in regard to union membership and have the salutary effect of forcing unions to improve themselves in order to attract members.

Mediation, Conciliation, and Arbitration

Practically all states provide means to facilitate the settlement of disputes between labor and management. In most instances assistance is offered in the form of *conciliation* and *mediation* whereby a neutral third party attempts through suggestions, to help disputants to resolve their differences. No attempt is made to force a decision upon the parties in disagreement. Generally, conciliation and mediation are synonymous with the only practical difference, if indeed there is any, being that a conciliator takes a more active part in face-to-face conferences. *Arbitration,* on the other hand, is a process in which disputants agree before negotiations begin to accept as binding the decision reached by the arbitrator. Experience with these procedures has been disappointing, for only on infrequent occasions have they been employed successfully.

In 1920 Kansas enacted a statute imposing *compulsory* arbitration upon most essential industries. Two United States Supreme Court decisions within the next five years so narrowed the application of the act, however, that it was quickly repealed.[19] At present a few states have compulsory settlement laws that apply only to utilities. Doubt has been cast on their usefulness by a 1951 Supreme Court ruling that Wisconsin's statute was invalid because of conflict with national authority to regulate interstate commerce.[20] In view of the intense opposition of both organized labor and a great many employers to compulsory arbitration, it is doubtful that such laws are practicable.

---

18. Right to work laws may also forbid *agency shop* agreements. Under these agreements employees are required to pay fees, equal in amount to union dues, to a union in return for the union's services as bargaining agent. The United States Supreme Court, in *Retail Clerks International Association v. Schermerhorn,* 375 U.S. 96 (1963), ruled unanimously that the Taft-Hartley Act permits states to outlaw union security agreements of the type represented by the so-called agency shop.
19. *Wolf Packing Company* v. *Court of Industrial Relations,* 262 U.S. 522 (1923), and *ibid.,* 267 U.S. 552 (1925), held the act invalid as applied to nonutility enterprises.
20. *Amalgamated Association* v. *Wisconsin Employment Relations Board,* 340 U.S. 383.

LABOR STANDARDS

Safety and Health

All states have enacted laws designed to protect the health of workers and to reduce the likelihood of accidental injury. For example, moving parts of dangerous machinery ordinarily must be enclosed by some sort of guard. Fire escapes and exits must be provided. Inspection of buildings, mines, and machines is generally required. Occupations that involve dangerous materials such as explosives or radioactive substances are subjected to detailed safety regulations. Statutes and regulations dealing more directly with the health of workers include those excluding children from gainful occupations. Adequate ventilation, rest periods, washrooms, and lunch facilities must be provided by many employers. The danger of occupational diseases has resulted in requirements that respirators, special clothing, masks, and the like be used or be kept readily available. The pattern and extent of safety and health regulations varies among the states, of course, depending upon the character and range of occupational pursuits in each.

Hours and Wages

For many years attempts by states to limit the number of hours a job holder might be required to work were considered by state and federal courts to be in violation of the freedom of employers and employees to contract. It was not until the 1917 decision of *Bunting* v. *Oregon*[21] that the United States Supreme Court approved a state statute prescribing a maximum number of hours for industrial workers. Minimum-wage laws did not receive the blessing of the nation's highest court until 1937, when it upheld a Washington statute setting minimum wages to be paid to women and minors.[22] Today wages and hours legislation applicable to all or some workers has been enacted in each of the states.

National wage and hour legislation applicable to all employers in interstate commerce was provided by Congress in 1938 in the Fair Labor Standards Act. Upheld by the Supreme Court in 1941,[23] the federal act, as amended in 1977, provided for a minimum wage of $3.10 per hour after January 1, 1980, with an increase to $3.35 a year later. The act also limited hours of work to eight per day and forty per week, but "overtime" or work beyond these maximums is permitted if compensated at a rate of one and one-half times the hourly minimum. Similar laws are found in most states, although the limits as to hours and wages

21.   243 U.S. 426.
22.   *West Coast Hotel* v. *Parrish*, 300 U.S. 379.
23.   *United States* v. *Darby Lumber Company*, 312 U.S. 100.

as well as coverage both of workers and employers present broad extremes from state to state.

Child Labor

Until recent years it was not uncommon to see boys and girls working long hours alongside adults. Early wage and hour legislation enacted in their behalf was not particularly successful in improving their lot. Organized labor, reform groups, and enlightened employers fought for measures to curb exploitation of children in industry. Congress responded with appropriate legislation, but in 1918 and again in 1922 the Supreme Court negated the acts.[24] In 1924 Congress proposed an amendment to the Constitution which would have delegated to the national government authority to regulate child labor. However, before the necessary number of ratifications could be secured the Supreme Court reversed its previous rulings, making the amendment unnecessary. In upholding the Fair Labor Standards Act, the Court approved provisions which forbade employers in interstate commerce to hire anyone under the age of sixteen or, in hazardous occupations, anyone under eighteen.[25]

Each of the fifty states has enacted laws strictly limiting the use of child labor in intrastate commerce. The minimum age requirement for employment is, depending upon the state, fourteen, fifteen, or sixteen. Hazardous jobs may not be held by persons under sixteen or eighteen. Many exceptions are made although only under circumstances of extreme necessity are minors permitted to work during what the law designates as school hours. The principal remaining problems relating to child labor are chiefly those associated with enforcement. Many state laws could be improved, particularly by eliminating exceptions, but greater advances could be realized by compelling stricter observation of existing laws.

Workers' Compensation

Before the development of workers' compensation programs, the worker who was disabled in industrial accidents was at extreme disadvantage. A worker could bring a suit for damages in a court of law, but prevailing common law doctrines favored the employers. The *assumption of risk* doctrine forbade awards of damages if injury resulted from the ordinary risks associated with an occupation. Workers injured as a result of their own negligence could not win damages because of the doctrine of *contributory negligence*. Similarly, the *fellow-servant rule* prevented collec-

---

24. *Hammer* v. *Dagenhart*, 247 U.S. 251 (1918); and *Bailey* v. *Drexel Furniture Company*, 259 U.S. 20 (1922).
25. *United States* v. *Darby Lumber Company*, 312 U.S. 100 (1941).

tion by a worker injured in an accident resulting from the negligence of a co-worker. It was not until 1911 when California, New Jersey, Washington, and Wisconsin adopted workers' compensation laws that the position of the injured worker began to improve. In increasing numbers states enacted similar laws on the theory that the costs of industrial accidents are legitimate costs of production. Such costs are eventually passed on to consumers in the prices they pay for goods and services. Today all states have such statutes covering all or some industrial workers.

Under a typical workers' compensation program, a disabled worker is paid a percentage of his or her weekly salary, usually about two-thirds. In one-third of the states the period of weekly payments ranges from 208 to 600 weeks; in the remainder they continue throughout the entire period of disability. The costs are borne by employers who usually insure their risks with private insurance firms. A few states require employers to insure with a special state insurance fund. Most states have special boards or commissions to administer workers' compensation programs, although in some a subordinate agency of the department of labor performs this function.

Workers' compensation programs have undergone impressive development during the past half-century, but there is still room for much improvement. Not all occupations are covered by compensation laws, with agricultural workers, domestics, and casual laborers commonly excluded. Employers who hire only a few workers are usually exempt. All occupational diseases, or some of them, are commonly not compensable. In many states employers may elect not to accept coverage of the workers' compensation law. This is not as serious a flaw as it may appear, however, for employers who decline participation are liable for damages, and the common law defenses discussed earlier are specifically denied to them.

Unemployment Compensation

Unemployment is a serious and continuing problem in an industrial society. Because of temporary fluctuations in the economy, technological advances that replace workers with machines, seasonal variations, and changes in consumer preferences, a moderate amount of unemployment is considered normal. These developments force many willing workers into temporary idleness, and for many of them these periods of unemployment are weeks or months of hardship and privation. Unemployment compensation programs are designed to ease the burden.

Early state programs, attempted during the first years of the Great Depression, were unsuccessful. The primary reasons for their failure were the reluctance of states to reduce the competitive position of home industries by placing additional taxes upon them and the deterrent effect of the added tax burden upon industrial recovery. As the Depression wore on, however, and a fourth of the labor force—over 12,000,000 workers—joined the ranks of the unemployed, action was necessary. After a period of stop-gap relief measures the national government responded with the Social Security Act of 1935 that established the cooperative state-federal program in effect today.

Under the Social Security Act a federal payroll tax is assessed with the provision that ninety per cent of the levy can be offset if that amount is paid under an equivalent state program. As a result of this feature all states have adopted unemployment compensation laws. The program is federally administered, with all tax collections paid into the United States treasury, credited to state accounts, and then released to the states as needed to meet claims. The funds collected by the federal government are used to pay the costs of administering the unemployment compensation program, including cost incurred by states that adhere to certain federally imposed conditions. These requirements include application of the merit principle in state programs, adequate administrative organization, provision of means for hearing complaints of persons denied benefits, keeping a minimum amount of funds in reserve, and paying collections into the federal treasury.

Discrimination in Employment

Since World War II impressive strides have been made toward elimination of discrimination in employment. In 1945 New York was first to adopt a "fair employment practices" law, but was followed later that year by New Jersey. Today the list includes all states other than several in the southern and Gulf Coast regions. Also, for the first time in the history of the nation, a federal fair employment state was enacted—as part of the Civil Rights Act of 1964.

FEP legislation typically forbids employers to discriminate in hiring, promotion, and firing on the basis of race, creed, color, age, sex, and national origin. Similarly, labor unions may not deny membership on such grounds, and employment agencies must also refrain from discrimination. Enforcement is accomplished by a commission which is empowered to begin proceedings on its own initiative or on the basis of complaints lodged with it. After investigation, which may entail a public hearing, the commission may issue an order directing compliance with the provisions of the statute. Refusal to obey an order may lead to court action by the commission. Rarely, however, do such cases get into the courts and only infrequently are formal hearings necessary, for in most instances persuasion is adequate. As a rule employers prefer to comply rather than face the effects of the unfavorable publicity invariably associated with noncompliance.

The new federal law established an Equal Employment Opportunities Commission with powers similar to those of state FEP commissions.

Its jurisdiction, of course, is much broader in that it may reach employers and labor organizations in all parts of the country. However, small enterprises are exempt from the processes of the EEOC and it is statutorily obliged to attempt settlements by persuasion. Unlike many state agencies the federal commission has no enforcement powers of its own. It must apply to a federal court for an order directing compliance, violation of which may be punished as a contempt of court.

Opponents of FEP laws contend that they violate the rights of employers to operate their businesses as they think best, and that they stir up more antagonisms than they eliminate. Supporters maintain that discrimination, wherever found, is un-American and is an evil that government has a duty to prevent. To what degree existing laws have achieved their objectives cannot be accurately determined. Discrimination is difficult to prove, laws are easily evaded, many violations go unreported, and as a matter of record comparatively few charges have been heard in courts.

Appendix 1
Admission of the States

Order of Admission	Territorial Status	Admission to Statehood
ORIGINAL STATES [1]		
Delaware		Dec. 7, 1787
Pennsylvania		Dec. 12, 1787
New Jersey		Dec. 18, 1787
Georgia		Jan. 2, 1788
Connecticut		Jan. 9, 1788
Massachusetts		Feb. 6, 1788
Maryland		Apr. 28, 1788
South Carolina		May 23, 1788
New Hampshire		June 21, 1788
Virginia		June 25, 1788
New York		July 26, 1788
North Carolina		Nov. 21, 1789
Rhode Island		May 29, 1790
ADMITTED TO STATEHOOD		
Vermont		Feb. 18, 1791
Kentucky		June 1, 1792
Tennessee		June 1, 1796
Ohio	July 13, 1787 [2]	Mar. 1, 1803
Louisiana	Mar. 24, 1804	Apr. 30, 1812
Indiana	May 7, 1800	Dec. 11, 1816
Mississippi	Apr. 17, 1798	Dec. 10, 1817
Illinois	Feb. 3, 1809	Dec. 3, 1818
Alabama	Mar. 3, 1817	Dec. 14, 1819
Maine		Mar. 15, 1820
Missouri	June 4, 1812	Aug. 10, 1821

Order of Admission	Territorial Status	Admission to Statehood

ADMITTED TO STATEHOOD

Arkansas	Mar. 2, 1819	June 15, 1836
Michigan	Jan. 11, 1805	Jan. 26, 1837
Florida	Mar. 30, 1822	Mar. 3, 1845
Texas		Dec. 29, 1845
Iowa	June 12, 1838	Dec. 28, 1846
Wisconsin	Apr. 20, 1836	May 29, 1848
California		Sept. 9, 1850
Minnesota	Mar. 3, 1849	May 11, 1858
Oregon	Aug. 14, 1848	Feb. 14, 1859
Kansas	May 30, 1854	Jan. 29, 1861
West Virginia		June 19, 1863
Nevada	Mar. 2, 1861	Oct. 31, 1864
Nebraska	May 30, 1854	Mar. 1, 1867
Colorado	Feb. 28, 1861	Aug. 1, 1876
South Dakota	Mar. 2, 1861	Nov. 2, 1889
North Dakota	Mar. 2, 1861	Nov. 2, 1889
Montana	May 26, 1864	Nov. 8, 1889
Washington	Mar. 2, 1853	Nov. 11, 1889
Idaho	Mar. 3, 1863	July 3, 1890
Wyoming	July 25, 1868	July 10, 1890
Utah	Sept. 9, 1850	Jan. 4, 1896
Oklahoma	May 2, 1890	Nov. 16, 1907
New Mexico	Sept. 9, 1850	Jan. 6, 1912
Arizona	Feb. 24, 1863	Feb. 14, 1912
Alaska	Aug. 24, 1912	Jan. 3, 1959
Hawaii	June 14, 1900	Aug. 21, 1959

1. Ratified United States Constitution on dates indicated.
2. Date of Ordinance creating government for the Northwest Territory.

Appendix 2
The State Constitutions

State	Date Admitted	No. of Constns.	Dates Adopted	Effective Date of Present Constitution
Alabama	1819	6	1819, 1861, 1865, 1867, 1875, 1901	1901
Alaska	1959	1	1956	1959
Arizona	1912	1	1911	1912
Arkansas	1836	5	1836, 1861, 1864, 1868, 1874	1874
California	1850	2	1849, 1879	1879
Colorado	1876	1	1876	1876
Connecticut[1]	1788	2	1818, 1965	1965
Delaware	1788	4	1776, 1792, 1831, 1897	1897
Florida	1845	6	1839, 1861, 1865, 1868, 1886, 1968	1969
Georgia	1788	9	1777, 1789, 1798, 1861, 1865, 1868, 1877, 1945, 1976	1976
Hawaii[2]	1959	1	1950	1959
Idaho	1890	1	1889	1890
Illinois	1818	4	1818, 1848, 1870, 1970	1971
Indiana	1816	2	1816, 1851	1851
Iowa	1846	2	1846, 1857	1857
Kansas	1861	1	1859	1861

State	Date Admitted	No. of Constns.	Dates Adopted	Effective Date of Present Constitution
Kentucky	1792	4	1792, 1799, 1850, 1891	1891
Louisiana	1812	11	1812, 1845, 1852, 1861, 1864, 1868, 1879, 1898, 1913, 1921, 1974	1974
Maine	1820	1	1819	1820
Maryland	1788	4	1776, 1851, 1864, 1867	1867
Massachusetts	1788	1	1780	1780
Michigan	1837	4	1835, 1850, 1908, 1963	1964
Minnesota	1858	1	1857	1858
Mississippi	1817	5	1817, 1832, 1861, 1868, 1890	1890
Missouri	1821	4	1820, 1865, 1875, 1945	1945
Montana	1889	2	1889, 1972	1972
Nebraska	1867	2	1866, 1875	1875
Nevada	1864	1	1864	1864
New Hampshire	1788	2	1776, 1784	1784
New Jersey	1788	3	1776, 1844, 1947	1948
New Mexico	1912	1	1911	1912
New York[2]	1788	4	1777, 1822, 1846, 1894	1895
North Carolina	1789	5	1776, 1861, 1868, 1876, 1970	1971
North Dakota	1889	1	1889	1889
Ohio	1803	2	1802, 1851	1851
Oklahoma	1907	1	1907	1907
Oregon	1859	1	1857	1859
Pennsylvania	1788	5	1776, 1790, 1838, 1873, 1968	1968
Rhode Island[1]	1790	1	1842	1843
South Carolina	1788	7	1776, 1778, 1790, 1861, 1865, 1868, 1895	1895

State	Date Admitted	No. of Constns.	Dates Adopted	Effective Date of Present Constitution
South Dakota	1889	1	1889	1889
Tennessee	1796	3	1796, 1835, 1870	1870
Texas	1845	5	1845, 1861, 1866, 1869, 1876	1876
Utah	1896	1	1895	1896
Vermont	1791	3	1777, 1786, 1793	1793
Virginia	1788	8	1776, 1830, 1851, 1861, 1864, 1869, 1902, 1970	1971
Washington	1889	1	1889	1889
West Virginia	1863	2	1862, 1872	1872
Wisconsin	1848	1	1848	1848
Wyoming	1890	1	1889	1890

1. Colonial charters were utilized as constitutions in Connecticut and Rhode Island until 1818 and 1842, respectively.
2. Extensive revisory amendments approved in New York in 1939 and in Hawaii in 1968 provide a credible basis for the conclusion that new constitutions were, in fact, adopted.

Appendix 3
Model State Constitution[1]

PREAMBLE

We, the people of the state of ...., recognizing the rights and duties of this state as a part of the federal system of government, reaffirm our adherence to the Constitution of the United States of America; and in order to assure the state government power to act for the good order of the state and the liberty, health, safety and welfare of the people, we do ordain and establish this constitution.

ARTICLE I
Bill of Rights

Section 1.01. *Freedom of Religion, Speech, Press, Assembly and Petition.* No law shall be enacted respecting an establishment of religion, or prohibiting the free exercise thereof, or abridging the freedom of speech or of the press, or the right of the people peaceably to assemble and to petition the government for a redress of grievances.

Section 1.02. *Due Process and Equal Protection.* No person shall be deprived of life, liberty or property without due process of law, nor be denied the equal protection of the laws, nor be denied the enjoyment of his civil rights or be discriminated against in the exercise thereof because of race, national origin, religion or ancestry.

Section 1.03. *Searches and Seizures and Interceptions.*
(a) The right of the people to be secure in their persons, houses, papers

---

1. Reprinted from the *Model State Constitution,* Sixth Edition (Revised), by permission of the National Municipal League. Copyright © 1963, 1968, the National Municipal League.

and effects against unreasonable searches and seizures shall not be violated, and no warrants shall issue, but upon probable cause, supported by oath or affirmation, and particularly describing the place to be searched and the persons or things to be seized.

(b) The right of the people to be secure against unreasonable interception of telephone, telegraph and other electronic means of communication, and against unreasonable interception of oral and other communications by electric or electronic methods, shall not be violated, and no orders and warrants for such interceptions shall issue but upon probable cause supported by oath or affirmation that evidence of crime may be thus obtained, and particularly identifying the means of communication and the person or persons whose communications are to be intercepted.

(c) Evidence obtained in violation of this section shall not be admissible in any court against any person.

Section 1.04. *Self-Incrimination.* No person shall be compelled to give testimony which might tend to incriminate him.

Section 1.05. *Writ of Habeas Corpus.* The privilege of the writ of habeas corpus shall not be suspended unless when in cases of rebellion or invasion the public safety may require it.

Section 1.06. *Rights of Accused Persons.*

(a) In all criminal prosecutions the accused shall enjoy the right to a speedy and public trial, to be informed of the nature and cause of the accusation, to be confronted with the witnesses against him, to have compulsory process for obtaining witnesses in his favor, to have the assistance of counsel for his defense, and to the assignment of counsel to represent him at every stage of the proceedings unless he elects to proceed without counsel or is able to obtain counsel. In prosecutions for felony, the accused shall also enjoy the right of trial by an impartial jury of the county [or other appropriate political subdivision of the state] wherein the crime shall have been committed, or of another county, if a change of venue has been granted.

(b) All persons shall, before conviction, be bailable by sufficient sureties, but bail may be denied to persons charged with capital offenses or offenses punishable by life imprisonment, giving due weight to the evidence and to the nature and circumstances of the event. Excessive bail shall not be required, nor excessive fines imposed, nor cruel or unusual punishment inflicted.

(c) No person shall be twice put in jeopardy for the same offense.

Section 1.07. *Political Tests for Public Office.* No oath, declaration or political test shall be required for any public office or employment other than the following oath or affirmation: "I do solemnly swear [or affirm] that I will support and defend the Constitution of the United States and the constitution of the state of .... and that I will faithfully discharge the duties of the office of .... to the best of my ability."

ARTICLE II

Powers of the State

Section 2.01. *Powers of Government.* The enumeration in this constitution of specified powers and functions shall be construed neither as a grant nor as a limitation of the powers of state government but the state government shall have all of the powers not denied by this constitution or by or under the Constitution of the United States.

ARTICLE III

Suffrage and Elections

Section 3.01. *Qualifications for Voting.* Every citizen of the age of .... years and a resident of the state for three months shall have the right to vote in the election of all officers that may be elected by the people and upon all questions that may be submitted to the voters; but the legislature may by law establish: (1) Minimum periods of local residence not exceeding three months, (2) reasonable requirements to determine literacy in English or in another language predominantly used in the classrooms of any public or private school accredited by any state or territory of the United States, the District of Columbia, or the Commonwealth of Puerto Rico, and (3) disqualifications for voting for mental incompetency or conviction of felony.

Section 3.02. *Legislature to Prescribe for Exercise of Suffrage.* The legislature shall by law define residence for voting purposes, insure secrecy in voting and provide for the registration of voters, absentee voting, the administration of elections and the nomination of candidates.

ARTICLE IV

The Legislature

Section 4.01. *Legislative Power.* The legislative power of the state shall be vested in the legislature.

Section 4.02. *Composition of the Legislature.* The legislature shall be composed of a single chamber consisting of one member to represent each legislative district. The number of members shall be prescribed by law but shall not be less than _____ nor exceed _____. Each member of the legislature shall be a qualified voter of the state and shall be at least _____ years of age.

> BICAMERAL ALTERNATIVE: Section 4.02. *Composition of the Legislature.* The legislature shall be composed of a senate and an assembly. The number of members of each house of the legislature shall be prescribed by law but the number of assemblymen shall not be less than _____ nor exceed _____, and the number of senators shall not exceed one-third, as near as may be, the number of assemblymen. Each assemblyman shall represent one assembly district and each senator shall represent one senate district. Each member of the legislature shall be a qualified voter of the state and shall be at least _____ years of age.

Section 4.03. *Election and Term of Members.* The members of the legislature shall be elected by the qualified voters of the state for a term of two years.

> BICAMERAL ALTERNATIVE: Section 4.03. *Election and Terms of Members.* Assemblymen shall be elected by the qualified voters of the state for a term of two years and senators for a term of six years. One-third of the senators shall be elected every two years.

Section 4.04. *Legislative Districts.*

(a) For the purpose of electing members of the legislature, the state shall be divided into as many districts as there shall be members of the legislature. Each district shall consist of compact and contiguous territory. All districts shall be so nearly equal in population that the population of the largest district shall not exceed that of the smallest district by more than _____ per cent. In determining the population of each district, inmates of such public or private institutions as prisons or other places of correction, hospitals for the insane or other institutions housing persons who are disqualified from voting by law shall not be counted.

(b) Immediately following each decennial census, the governor shall appoint a board of _____ qualified voters to make recommendations within ninety days of their appointment concerning the redistricting of the state. The governor shall publish the recommendations of the board when received. The governor shall promulgate a redistricting plan within ninety to one hundred and twenty days after appointment of the board, whether or not it has made its recommendations. The governor shall accompany his plan with a message explaining his reasons for any changes from the recommendations of the board. The governor's redistricting plan shall be published in the manner provided for acts of the legislature and shall have the force of law upon such publication. Upon the application of any qualified voter, the supreme court, in the exercise of original, exclusive and final jurisdiction, shall review the governor's redistricting plan and shall have jurisdiction to make orders to amend the plan to comply with the requirements of this constitution or, if the governor has failed to promulgate a redistricting plan within the time provided, to make one or more orders establishing such a plan.

BICAMERAL ALTERNATIVE: Section 4.04.   *Legislative Districts.*

(a) For the purpose of electing members of the assembly, the state shall be divided into as many districts as there shall be members of the assembly. Each district shall consist of compact and contiguous territory. All districts shall be so nearly equal in population that the district with the greatest population shall not exceed the district with the least population by more than .... per cent. In determining the population of each district, inmates of such public or private institutions as prisons or other places of correction, hospitals for the insane or other institutions housing persons who are disqualified from voting by law shall not be counted.

(b) For the purpose of electing members of the senate, the state shall be divided into as many districts as there shall be members of the senate. Each senate district shall consist of a compact and contiguous territory. All districts shall be so nearly equal in population that the district with the greatest population shall not exceed the district with the least population by more than .... per cent. In determining the population of each district, inmates of such public or private institutions as prisons or other places of correction, hospitals for the insane or other institutions housing persons who are disqualified from voting by law shall not be counted.

(c) Immediately following each decennial census, the governor shall appoint a board of .... qualified voters to make recommendations within ninety days of their appointment concerning the redistricting of the state. The governor shall publish the recommendations of the board when received. The governor shall promulgate a redistricting plan within ninety to one hundred and twenty days after appointment of the board, whether or not it has made its recommendations. The governor shall accompany his plan with a message explaining his reasons for any changes from the recommendations of the board. The governor's redistricting plan shall be published in the manner provided for acts of the legislature and shall have the force of law upon such publication. Upon the application of any qualified voter, the supreme court, in the exercise of original, exclusive and final jurisdiction, shall review the governor's redistricting plan and shall have jurisdiction to make orders to amend the plan to comply with the requirements of this constitution or, if the governor has failed to promulgate a redistricting plan within the time provided, to make one or more orders establishing such a plan.

Section 4.05. *Time of Election.* Members of the legislature shall be elected at the regular election in each odd-numbered year.

Section 4.06. *Vacancies.* When a vacancy occurs in the legislature it shall be filled as provided by law.

Section 4.07. *Compensation of Members.* The members of the legislature shall receive an annual salary and such allowances as may be prescribed by law but any increase or decrease in the amount thereof shall not apply to the legislature which enacted the same.

Section 4.08. *Sessions.* The legislature shall be a continuous body during the term for which its members are elected. It shall meet in regular sessions annually as provided by law. It may be convened at other times by the governor or, at the written request of a majority of the members, by the presiding officer of the legislature.

> BICAMERAL ALTERNATIVE: Section 4.08. *Sessions.* The legislature shall be a continuous body during the term for which members of the assembly are elected. The legislature shall meet in regular sessions annually as provided by law. It may be convened at other times by the governor or, at the written request of a majority of the members of each house, by the presiding officers of both houses.

Section 4.09. *Organization and Procedure.* The legislature shall be the final judge of the election and qualifications of its members and may by law vest in the courts the trial and determination of contested elections of members. It shall choose its presiding officer from among its members and it shall employ a secretary to serve for an indefinite term. It shall determine its rules of procedure; it may compel the attendance of absent members, discipline its members and, with the concurrence of two-thirds of all the members, expel a member, and it shall have power to compel the attendance and testimony of witnesses and the production of books and papers either before the legislature as a whole or before any committee thereof. The secretary of the legislature shall be its chief fiscal, administrative and personnel officer and shall perform such duties as the legislature may prescribe.

> BICAMERAL ALTERNATIVE: Section 4.09. *Organization and Procedure.* Each house of the legislature shall be the final judge of the election and qualifications of its members and the legislature may by law vest in the courts the trial and determination of contested elections of members. Each house of the legislature shall choose its presiding officer from among its members and it shall employ a secretary

to serve for an indefinite term, and each house shall determine its rules of procedure; it may compel the attendance of absent members, discipline its members and, with the concurrence of two-thirds of all the members, expel a member, and it shall have power to compel the attendance and testimony of witnesses and the production of books and papers either before such house of the legislature as a whole or before any committee thereof. The secretary of each house of the legislature shall be its chief fiscal, administrative and personnel officer and shall perform such duties as each such house of the legislature may prescribe.

Section 4.10. *Legislative Immunity.* For any speech or debate in the legislature, the members shall not be questioned in any other place.

Section 4.11. *Special Legislation.* The legislature shall pass no special or local act when a general act is or can be made applicable, and whether a general act is or can be made applicable shall be a matter for judicial determination.

Section 4.12. *Transaction of Business.* A majority of all the members of the legislature shall constitute a quorum to do business but a smaller number may adjourn from day to day and compel the attendance of absent members. The legislature shall keep a journal of its proceedings which shall be published from day to day. The legislature shall prescribe the methods of voting on legislative matters but a record vote, with the yeas and nays entered in the journal, shall be taken on any question on the demand of one-fifth of the members present.

BICAMERAL ALTERNATIVE: Section 4.12. *Transaction of Business.* Refer to "each house of the legislature" instead of "the legislature" wherever appropriate.

Section 4.13. *Committees.* The legislature may establish such committees as it may deem necessary for the conduct of its business. When a committee to which a bill has been assigned has not reported on it, one-third of all the members of the legislature shall have power to relieve it of further consideration. Adequate public notice of all committee hearings, with a clear statement of all subjects to be considered at each hearing, shall be published in advance.

BICAMERAL ALTERNATIVE: Section 4.13. *Committees.* Refer to "each house of the legislature" instead of "the legislature" wherever appropriate.

Section 4.14. *Bills; Single Subject.* The legislature shall enact no law except by bill and every bill except bills for appropriations and bills for the codification, revision or rearrangement of existing laws shall be confined to one subject. All appropriation bills shall be limited to the subject of appropriations. Legislative compliance with the requirements of this section is a constitutional responsibility not subject to judicial review.

Section 4.15. *Passage of Bills.* No bill shall become a law unless it has been printed and upon the desks of the members in final form at least three days prior to final passage and the majority of all the members has assented to it. The yeas and nays on final passage shall be entered in the journal. The legislature shall provide for the publication of all acts and no act shall become effective until published as provided by law.

> BICAMERAL ALTERNATIVE: Section 4.15. *Passage of Bills.* Refer to "each house of the legislature" instead of "the legislature" wherever appropriate.

Section 4.16. *Action by the Governor.*
(a) When a bill has passed the legislature, it shall be presented to the governor and, if the legislature is in session, it shall become law if the governor either signs or fails to veto it within fifteen days of presentation. If the legislature is in recess or, if the session of the legislature has expired during such fifteen-day period, it shall become law if he signs it within thirty days after such adjournment or expiration. If the governor does not approve a bill, he shall veto it and return it to the legislature either within fifteen days of presentation if the legislature is in session or upon the reconvening of the legislature from its recess. Any bill so returned by the governor shall be reconsidered by the legislature and, if upon reconsideration two-thirds of all the members shall agree to pass the bill, it shall become law.

(b) The governor may strike out or reduce items in appropriation bills passed by the legislature and the procedure in such cases shall be the same as in case of the disapproval of an entire bill by the governor.

> BICAMERAL ALTERNATIVE: Section 4.16. *Action by the Governor.* Refer to "each house of the legislature" instead of "the legislature" wherever appropriate.

Section 4.17. *Post-Audit.* The legislature shall appoint an auditor to serve at its pleasure. The auditor shall conduct post-audits as prescribed by law and shall report to the legislature and to the governor.

> BICAMERAL ALTERNATIVE: Section 4.17. *Post-Audit.* The legislature shall, by joint resolution, appoint. . . .

Section 4.18. *Impeachment.* The legislature may impeach the governor, the heads of principal departments, judicial officers and such other officers of the state as may be made subject to impeachment by law, by a two-thirds vote of all the members, and shall provide by law procedures for the trial and removal from office, after conviction, of officers so impeached. No officer shall be convicted on impeachment by a vote of less than two-thirds of the members of the tribunal hearing the charges.

BICAMERAL ALTERNATIVE: Section 4.18. *Impeachment.* Refer to "by a two-thirds vote of all the members of each house."

ARTICLE V

The Executive

Section 5.01. *Executive Power.* The executive power of the state shall be vested in a governor.

Section 5.02. *Election and Qualifications of Governor.* The governor shall be elected, at the regular election every other odd-numbered year, by the direct vote of the people, for a term of four years beginning on the first day of [December] [January] next following his election. Any qualified voter of the state who is at least .... years of age shall be eligible to the office of governor.

Section 5.03. *Governor's Messages to the Legislature.* The governor shall, at the beginning of each session, and may, at other times, give to the legislature information as to the affairs of the state and recommend measures he considers necessary or desirable.

Section 5.04. *Executive and Administrative Powers.*

(a) The governor shall be responsible for the faithful execution of the laws. He may, by appropriate action or proceeding brought in the name of the state, enforce compliance with any constitutional or legislative mandate, or restrain violation of any constitutional or legislative power, duty or right by an officer, department or agency of the state or any of its civil divisions. This authority shall not authorize any action or proceeding against the legislature.

(b) The governor shall commission all officers of the state. He may at any time require information, in writing or otherwise, from the officers of any administrative department, office or agency upon any subject relating to the respective offices. He shall be commander-in-chief of the armed forces of the state, except when they shall be called into the service of the United States, and may call them out to execute the laws, to preserve order, to suppress insurrection or to repel invasion.

Section 5.05. *Executive Clemency.* The governor shall have power to grant reprieves, commutations and pardons, after conviction, for all offenses and may delegate such powers, subject to such procedures as may be prescribed by law.

Section 5.06. *Administrative Departments.* All executive and administrative offices, agencies and instrumentalities of the state government, and their respective functions, powers and duties, shall be allocated by law among and within not more than twenty principal departments so as to group them as far as practicable according to major purposes. Regulatory, quasi-judicial and temporary agencies established by law may, but need not, be allocated within a principal department. The legislature shall by law prescribe the functions, powers and duties of the principal departments and of all other agencies of the state and may from time to time reallocate offices, agencies and instrumentalities among the principal departments, may increase, modify, diminish or change their functions, powers and duties and may assign new functions, powers and duties to them; but the governor may make such changes in the allocation of offices, agencies and instrumentalities, and in the allocation of such functions, powers and duties, as he considers necessary for efficient administration. If such changes affect existing law, they shall be set forth in executive orders, which shall be submitted to the legislature while it is in session, and shall become effective, and shall have the force of law, sixty days after submission, or at the close of the session, whichever is sooner, unless specifically modified or disapproved by a resolution concurred in by a majority of all the members.

BICAMERAL ALTERNATIVE: Section 5.06. *Administrative Departments.* Change the last phrase to read "majority of all the members of each house."

Section 5.07. *Executive Officers; Appointment.* The governor shall appoint and may remove the heads of all administrative departments. All others officers in the administrative service of the state shall be appointed and may be removed as provided by law.

Section 5.08. *Succession to Governorship.*
(a) If the governor-elect fails to assume office for any reason, the presiding officer of the legislature shall serve as acting governor until the governor-elect qualifies and assumes office or, if the governor-elect does not assume office within six months, until the unexpired term has been filled by special election and the newly elected governor has qualified. If, at the time the presiding officer of the legislature is to assume the acting governorship, the legislature has not yet organized and elected a presiding officer, the outgoing governor shall hold over until the presiding officer of the legislature is elected.
(b) When the governor is unable to discharge the duties of his office by reason of impeachment or other disability, including but not limited to physical or mental disability, or when the duties of the office are not being discharged by reason of his continuous absence, the presiding officer of the legislature shall serve as acting governor until the governor's disability or absence terminates. If the governor's disability or absence

does not terminate within six months, the office of the governor shall be vacant.

(c) When, for any reason, a vacancy occurs in the office of the governor, the unexpired term shall be filled by special election except when such unexpired term is less than one year, in which event the presiding officer of the legislature shall succeed to the office for the remainder of the term. When a vacancy in the office of the governor is filled by special election, the presiding officer of the legislature shall serve as acting governor from the occurrence of the vacancy until the newly elected governor has qualified. When the presiding officer of the legislature succeeds to the office of governor, he shall have the title, powers, duties and emoluments of that office and, when he serves as acting governor, he shall have the powers and duties thereof and shall receive such compensation as the legislature shall provide by law.

(d) The legislature shall provide by law for special elections to fill vacancies in the office of the governor.

(e) The supreme court shall have original, exclusive and final jurisdiction to determine absence and disability of the governor or governor-elect and to determine the existence of a vacancy in the office of governor and all questions concerning succession to the office or to its powers and duties.

BICAMERAL ALTERNATIVE: Section 5.08. *Succession to Governorship.* For "presiding officer of the legislature" substitute "presiding officer of the senate."

ARTICLE VI

The Judiciary

Section 6.01. *Judicial Power.* The judicial power of the state shall be vested in a unified judicial system, which shall include a supreme court, an appellate court and a general court, and which shall also include such inferior courts of limited jurisdiction as may from time to time be established by law. All courts except the supreme court may be divided into geographical departments or districts as provided by law and into functional divisions and subdivisions as provided by law or by judicial rules not inconsistent with law.

Section 6.02. *Supreme Court.* The supreme court shall be the highest court of the state and shall consist of a chief judge and _____ associate judges.

Section 6.03. *Jurisdiction of Courts.* The supreme court shall have appellate jurisdiction in all cases arising under this constitution and the

Constitution of the United States and in all other cases as provided by law. It shall also have original jurisdiction in cases arising under subsections 4.04(b) and 5.08(e) of this constitution and in all other cases as provided by law. All other courts of the state shall have original and appellate jurisdiction as provided by law, which jurisdiction shall be uniform in all geographical departments or districts of the same court. The jurisdiction of functional divisions and subdivisions shall be as provided by law or by judicial rules not inconsistent with law.

Section 6.04.   *Appointment of Judges; Qualifications; Tenure; Retirement; Removal.*

(a) The governor, with the advice and consent of the legislature, shall appoint the chief judges and associate judges of the supreme, appellate and general courts. The governor shall give ten days' public notice before sending a judicial nomination to the legislature or before making an interim appointment when the legislature is not in session.

> ALTERNATIVE: Subsection 6.04(a). *Nomination by Nominating Commission.* The governor shall fill a vacancy in the offices of the chief judges and associate judges of the supreme, appellate and general courts from a list of nominees presented to him by the appropriate judicial nominating commission. If the governor fails to make an appointment within sixty days from the day the list is presented, the appointment shall be made by the chief judge or by the acting chief judge from the same list. There shall be a judicial nominating commission for the supreme court and one commission for the nomination of judges for the court sitting in each geographical department or district of the appellate court. Each judicial nominating commission shall consist of seven members, one of whom shall be the chief judge of the supreme court, who shall act as chairman. The members of the bar of the state in the geographical area for which the court or the department or district of the court sits shall elect three of their number to be members of such a commission, and the governor shall appoint three citizens, not members of the bar, from among the residents of the same geographical area. The terms of office and the compensation for members of a judicial nominating commission shall be as provided by law. No member of a judicial nominating commission except the chief judge shall hold any other public office or office in any political party or organization, and no member of such a commission shall be eligible for appointment to a state judicial office so long as he is a member of such a commission and for [five] [three] [two] years thereafter.

(b) No person shall be eligible for judicial office in the supreme court, appellate court and general court unless he has been admitted to practice law before the supreme court for at least .... years. No person who holds judicial office in the supreme court, appellate court or general court shall hold any other paid office, position of profit or employment under the state, its civil divisions or the United States. Any judge of the supreme court, appellate court or general court who becomes a candidate for an elective office shall thereby forfeit his judicial office.

(c) The judges of the supreme court, appellate court and general court shall hold their offices for initial terms of seven years and upon reappointment shall hold their offices during good behavior. They shall be retired upon attaining the age of seventy years and may be pensioned as may be provided by law. The chief judge of the supreme court may from time to time appoint retired judges to such special assignments as may be provided by the rules of the supreme court.

(d) The judges of the supreme court, appellate court and general court shall be subject to impeachment and any such judge impeached shall not exercise his office until acquitted. The supreme court may also remove judges of the appellate and general courts for such cause and in such manner as may be provided by law.

(e) The legislature shall provide by law for the appointment of judges of the inferior courts and for their qualifications, tenure, retirement and removal.

(f) The judges of the courts of this state shall receive such salaries as may be provided by law, which shall not be diminished during their term of office.

Section 6.05. *Administration.* The chief judge of the supreme court shall be the administrative head of the unified judicial system. He may assign judges from one geographical department or functional division of a court to another department or division of that court and he may assign judges for temporary service from one court to another. The chief judge shall, with the approval of the supreme court, appoint an administrative director to serve at his pleasure and to supervise the administrative operation of the judicial system.

Section 6.06. *Financing.* The chief judge shall submit an annual consolidated budget for the entire unified judicial system and the total cost of the system shall be paid by the state. The legislature may provide by law for the reimbursement to the state of appropriate portions of such cost by political subdivisions.

Section 6.07. *Rule-making Power.* The supreme court shall make and promulgate rules governing the administration of all courts. It shall make and promulgate rules governing practice and procedure in civil and criminal cases in all courts. These rules may be changed by the legislature by a two-thirds vote of all the members.

Article VII

Finance

Section 7.01. *State Debt.* No debt shall be contracted by or in behalf of this state unless such debt shall be authorized by law for projects or objects distinctly specified therein.

Section 7.02. *The Budget.* The governor shall submit to the legislature, at a time fixed by law, a budget estimate for the next fiscal year setting forth all proposed expenditures and anticipated income of all departments and agencies of the state, as well as a general appropriation bill to authorize the proposed expenditures and a bill or bills covering recommendations in the budget for new or additional revenues.

Section 7.03. *Expenditure of Money.*

(a) No money shall be withdrawn from the treasury except in accordance with appropriations made by law, nor shall any obligation for the payment of money be incurred except as authorized by law. The appropriation for each department, office or agency of the state, for which appropriation is made, shall be for a specific sum of money and no appropriation shall allocate to any object the proceeds of any particular tax or fund or a part or percentage thereof, except when required by the federal government for participation in federal programs.

(b) All state and local expenditures, including salaries paid by the legislative, executive and judicial branches of government, shall be matters of public record.

Article VIII

Local Government

Section 8.01. *Organization of Local Government.* The legislature shall provide by general law for the government of counties, cities and other civil divisions and for methods and procedures of incorporating, merging, consolidating and dissolving such civil divisions and of altering their boundaries, including provisions:

(1) For such classification of civil divisions as may be necessary, on the basis of population or on any other reasonable basis related to the purpose of the classification;

(2) For optional plans of municipal organization and government so as to enable a county, city or other civil division to adopt or abandon an authorized optional charter by a majority vote of the qualified voters voting thereon;

(3) For the adoption or amendment of charters by any county or city for its own government, by a majority vote of the qualified voters of the

city or county voting thereon, for methods and procedures for the selection of charter commissions, and for framing, publishing, disseminating and adopting such charters or charter amendments and for meeting the expenses connected therewith.

ALTERNATIVE PARAGRAPH: Section 8.01(3). *Self-Executing Home Rule Powers.* For the adoption or amendment of charters by any county or city, in accordance with the provisions of section 8.02 concerning home rule for local units.

Section 8.02. *Powers of Counties and Cities.* A county or city may exercise any legislative power or perform any function which is not denied to it by its charter, is not denied to counties or cities generally, or to counties or cities of its class, and is within such limitations as the legislature may establish by general law. This grant of home rule powers shall not include the power to enact private or civil law governing civil relationships except as incident to an exercise of an independent county or city power, nor shall it include power to define and provide for the punishment of a felony.

ALTERNATIVE PROVISIONS FOR SELF-EXECUTING HOME RULE POWERS: Section 8.02. *Home Rule for Local Units.*

(a) Any county or city may adopt or amend a charter for its own government, subject to such regulations as are provided in this constitution and may be provided by general law. The legislature shall provide one or more optional procedures for nonpartisan election of five, seven or nine charter commissioners and for framing, publishing and adopting a charter or charter amendments.

(b) Upon resolution approved by a majority of the members of the legislative authority of the county or city or upon petition of ten per cent of the qualified voters, the officer or agency responsible for certifying public questions shall submit to the people at the next regular election not less than sixty days thereafter, or at a special election if authorized by law, the question "Shall a commission be chosen to frame a charter or charter amendments for the county [or city] of ....?" An affirmative vote of a majority of the qualified voters voting on the question shall authorize the creation of the commission.

(c) A petition to have a charter commission may include the names of five, seven or nine commissioners, to be listed at the end of the question when it is voted on, so that an affirmative vote on the question is a vote to elect the persons named in the petition. Otherwise, the petition or resolution shall designate an optional election procedure provided by law.

(d) Any proposed charter or charter amendments shall be published by the commission, distributed to the qualified voters and submitted to them at the next regular or special election not less than thirty days after publication. The procedure for publication and submission shall be as provided by law or by resolution of the charter commission not inconsistent with law. The legislative authority of the county or city shall, on request of the charter commission, appropriate money to provide for the reasonable expenses of the commission and for the publication, distribution and submission of its proposals.

(e) A charter or charter amendments shall become effective if approved by a majority vote of the qualified voters voting thereon. A charter may provide for direct submission of future charter revisions or amendments by petition or by resolution of the local legislature authority.

Section 8.03. *Powers of Local Units.* Counties shall have such powers as shall be provided by general or optional law. Any city or other civil division may, by agreement, subject to a local referendum and the approval of a majority of the qualified voters voting on any such question, transfer to the county in which it is located any of its functions or powers and may revoke the transfer of any such function or power, under regulations provided by general law; and any county may, in like manner, transfer to another county or to a city within its boundaries or adjacent thereto any of its functions or powers and may revoke the transfer of any such function or power.

Section 8.04. *County Government.* Any county charter shall provide the form of government of the county and shall determine which of its officers shall be elected and the manner of their election. It shall provide for the exercise of all powers vested in, and the performance of all duties imposed upon, counties and county officers by law. Such charter may provide for the concurrent or exclusive exercise by the county, in all or in part of its area, of all or of any designated powers vested by the constitution or laws of this state in cities and other civil divisions; it may provide for the succession by the county to the rights, properties and obligations of cities and other civil divisions therein incident to the powers so vested in the county, and for the division of the county into districts for purposes of administration or of taxation or of both. No provision of any charter or amendment vesting in the county any powers of a city or other civil division shall become effective unless it shall have been approved by a majority of those voting thereon (1) in the county, (2) in any city containing more than twenty-five per cent of the total population of the county, and (3) in the county outside of such city or cities.

Section 8.05. *City Government.* Except as provided in sections 8.03 and 8.04, each city is hereby granted full power and authority to pass laws and ordinances relating to its local affairs, property and government; and no enumeration of powers in this constitution shall be deemed to limit or restrict the general grant of authority hereby conferred; but this grant of authority shall not be deemed to limit or restrict the power of the legislature to enact laws of statewide concern uniformly applicable to every city.

FURTHER ALTERNATIVE: A further alternative is possible by combining parts of the basic text of this article and parts of the foregoing alternative. If the self-executing alternative section 8.02 is preferred but not the formulation of home rule powers in alternative sections 8.03, 8.04 and 8.05, the following combination of sections will combine the self-executing feature and the power formulation included in the basic text:

Section 8.01. *Organization of Local Government,* with alternative paragraph (3).
Alternative Section 8.02. *Home Rule for Local Units.*
Section 8.02, renumbered 8.03. *Powers of Counties and Cities.*

Article IX

Public Education

Section 9.01. *Free Public Schools; Support of Higher Education.* The legislature shall provide for the maintenance and support of a system of free public schools open to all children in the state and shall establish, organize and support such other public educational institutions, including public institutions of higher learning, as may be desirable.

Article X

Civil Service

Section 10.01. *Merit System.* The legislature shall provide for the establishment and administration of a system of personnel administration in the civil service of the state and its civil divisions. Appointments and promotions shall be based on merit and fitness, demonstrated by examination or by other evidence of competence.

Article XI

Intergovernmental Relations

Section 11.01. *Intergovernmental Cooperation.* Nothing in this constitution shall be construed: (1) To prohibit the cooperation of the government of this state with other governments, or (2) the cooperation of the government of any county, city or other civil division with any one or more other governments in the administration of their functions and powers, or (3) the consolidation of existing civil divisions of the state. Any county, city or other civil division may agree, except as limited by general law, to share the costs and responsibilities of functions and services with any one or more other governments.

Article XII

Constitutional Revision

Section 12.01.   *Amending Procedure; Proposals.*

(a) Amendments to this constitution may be proposed by the legislature or by the initiative.

(b) An amendment proposed by the legislature shall be agreed to by record vote of a majority of all of the members, which shall be entered on the journal.

(c) An amendment proposed by the initiative shall be incorporated by its sponsors in an initiative petition which shall contain the full text of the amendment proposed and which shall be signed by qualified voters equal in number to at least .... per cent of the total votes cast for governor in the last preceding gubernatorial election. Initiative petitions shall be filed with the secretary of the legislature.

(d) An amendment proposed by the initiative shall be presented to the legislature if it is in session and, if it is not in session, when it convenes or reconvenes. If the proposal is agreed to by a majority vote of all the members, such vote shall be entered on the journal and the proposed amendment shall be submitted for adoption in the same manner as amendments proposed by the legislature.

(e) The legislature may provide by law for a procedure for the withdrawal by its sponsors of an initiative petition at any time prior to its submission to the voters.

Section 12.02.   *Amendment Procedure; Adoption.*

(a) The question of the adoption of a constitutional amendment shall be submitted to the voters at the first regular or special statewide election held no less than two months after it has been agreed to by the vote of the legislature and, in the case of amendments proposed by the initiative which have failed to receive such legislative approval, not less than two months after the end of the legislative session.

(b) Each proposed constitutional amendment shall be submitted to the voters by a ballot title which shall be descriptive but not argumentative or prejudicial, and which shall be prepared by the legal department of the state, subject to review by the courts. Any amendment submitted to the voters shall become a part of the constitution only when approved by a majority of the votes cast thereon. Each amendment so approved shall take effect thirty days after the date of the vote thereon, unless the amendment itself otherwise provides.

Section 12.03. *Constitutional Conventions.*

(a) The legislature, by an affirmative record vote of a majority of all the members, may at any time submit the question "Shall there be a convention to amend or revise the constitution?" to the qualified voters of the state. If the question of holding a convention is not otherwise submitted to the people at some time during any period of fifteen years, it shall be submitted at the general election in the fifteenth year following the last submission.

(b) The legislature, prior to a popular vote on the holding of a convention, shall provide for a preparatory commission to assemble information on constitutional questions to assist the voters and, if a convention is authorized, the commission shall be continued for the assistance of the delegates. If a majority of the qualified voters voting on the question of holding a convention approves it, delegates shall be chosen at the next regular election not less than three months thereafter unless the legislature shall by law have provided for election of the delegates at the same time that the question is voted on or at a special election.

(c) Any qualified voter of the state shall be eligible to membership in the convention and one delegate shall be elected from each existing legislative district. The convention shall convene not later than one month after the date of the election of delegates and may recess from time to time.

(d) No proposal shall be submitted by the convention to the voters unless it has been printed and upon the desks of the delegates in final form at least three days on which the convention was in session prior to final passage therein, and has received the assent of a majority of all the delegates. The yeas and nays on any question shall, upon request of one-tenth of the delegates present, be entered in the journal. Proposals of the convention shall be submitted to the qualified voters at the first regular or special statewide election not less than two months after final action thereon by the convention, either as a whole or in such parts and with such alternatives as the convention may determine. Any constitutional revision submitted to the voters in accordance with this section shall require the approval of a majority of the qualified voters voting thereon, and shall take effect thirty days after the date of the vote thereon, unless the revision itself otherwise provides.

Section 12.04. *Conflicting Amendments or Revisions.* If conflicting constitutional amendments or revisions submitted to the voters at the same election are approved, the amendment or revision receiving the highest number of affirmative votes shall prevail to the extent of such conflict.

BICAMERAL ALTERNATIVE: Appropriate changes to reflect passage by two houses must be made throughout this article.

ARTICLE XIII
Schedule

Section 13.01. *Effective Date.* This constitution shall be in force from and including the first day of ...., 19 ...., except as herein otherwise provided.

Section 13.02. *Existing Laws, Rights and Proceedings.* All laws not inconsistent with this constitution shall continue in force until they expire by their own limitation or are amended or repealed, and all existing writs, actions, suits, proceedings, civil or criminal liabilities, prosecutions, judgments, sentences, orders, decrees, appeals, causes of action, contracts, claims, demands, titles and rights shall continue unaffected except as modified in accordance with the provisions of this constitution.

Section 13.03. *Officers.* All officers filling any office by election or appointment shall continue to exercise the duties thereof, according to their respective commissions or appointments, until their offices shall have been abolished or their successors selected and qualified in accordance with this constitution or the laws enacted pursuant thereto.

Section 13.04. *Choice of Officers.* The first election of governor under this constitution shall be in 19 .... The first election of members of the legislature under this constitution shall be in 19 ....

Section 13.05. *Establishment of the Legislature.* Until otherwise provided by law, members of the legislature shall be elected from the following districts: The first district shall consist of [the description of all the districts from which the first legislature will be elected should be inserted here].

BICAMERAL ALTERNATIVE: Section 13.05. *Establishment of the Legislature.* Refer to "assembly districts" and "senate districts."

Section 13.06. *Administrative Reorganization.* The governor shall submit to the legislature orders embodying a plan for reorganization of administrative departments in accordance with section 5.06 of this constitution prior to [date]. These orders shall become effective as originally issued or as they may be modified by law on [a date three months later] unless any of them are made effective at earlier dates by law.

Section 13.07. *Establishment of the Judiciary.*

(a) The unified judicial system shall be inaugurated on September 15, 19 .... Prior to that date the judges and principal ministerial agents of the judicial system shall be designated or selected and any other act needed to prepare for the operation of the system shall be done in accordance with this constitution.

(b) The judicial power vested in any court in the state shall be transferred to the unified judicial system and the justices and judges of the [here name all the courts of the state except justice of the peace courts] holding office on September 15, 19 ...., shall become judges of the unified judicial system and shall continue to serve as such for the remainder of their respective terms and until their successors shall have qualified. The justices of the [here name the highest court of the state] shall become judges of the supreme court and the judges of the other courts shall be assigned by the chief judge to appropriate service in the other departments of the judicial system, due regard being had to their positions in the existing judicial structure and to the districts in which they had been serving.

Appendix 4
Organization of Traditional State Government

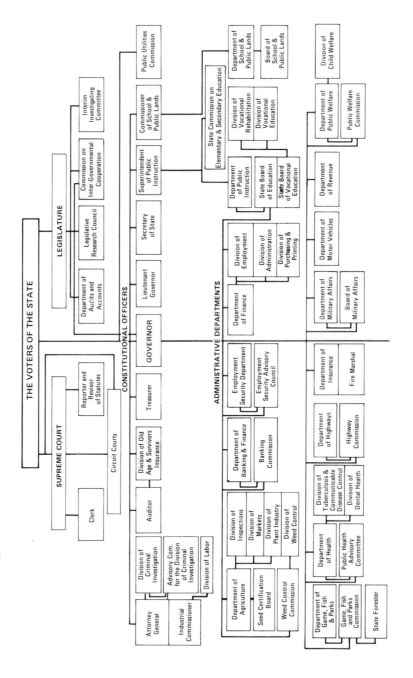

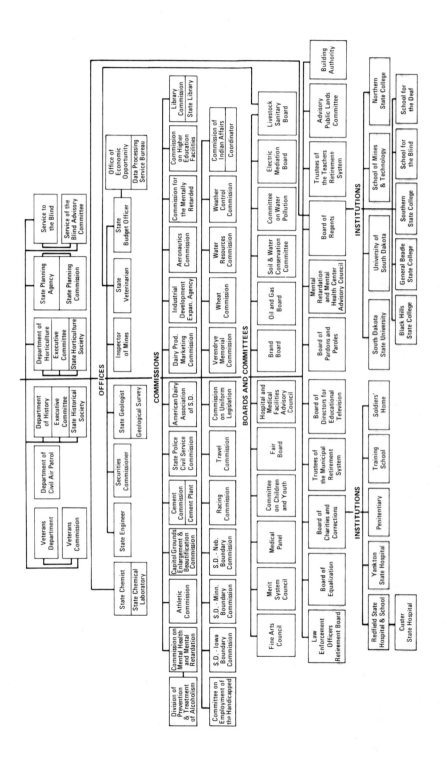

OFFICES

Veterans Department
Veterans Commission

Department of Civil Air Patrol

Department of History
Executive Committee
State Historical Society

Department of Horticulture
Executive Committee
State Horticulture Society

State Planning Agency
State Planning Commission

Service to the Blind
Service of the Blind Advisory Committee

COMMISSIONS

State Chemist
State Chemical Laboratory

Athletic Commission

Capitol Grounds Enlargement & Beautification Commission

State Engineer

Securities Commissioner

State Geologist
Geological Survey

Inspector of Mines

State Veterinarian

State Budget Officer

Office of Economic Opportunity
Data Processing Service Bureau

Commission on Mental Health and Mental Retardation

Division of Prevention & Treatment of Alcoholism

Committee on Employment of the Handicapped

S.D. - Iowa Boundary Commission

S.D. - Minn. Boundary Commission

S.D. - Neb. Boundary Commission

Cement Commission
Cement Plant

State Police Civil Service Commission

American Dairy Association of S.D.

Commission on Uniform Legislation

Dairy Prod. Marketing Commission

Industrial Development Expan. Agency

Aeronautics Commission

Commission for the Mentally Retarded

Commission on Higher Education Facilities

Library Commission
State Library

BOARDS AND COMMITTEES

Fine Arts Council

Merit System Council

Medical Panel

Committee on Children and Youth

Fair Board

Hospital and Medical Facilities Advisory Council

Verendrye Memorial Commission

Wheat Commission

Water Resources Commission

Weather Control Commission

Commission of Indian Affairs Coordinator

Racing Commission

Travel Commission

Brand Board

Oil and Gas Board

Soil & Water Conservation Committee

Committee on Water Pollution

Electric Mediation Board

Livestock Sanitary Board

Law Enforcement Officers Retirement Board

Board of Equalization

Board of Charities and Corrections

Trustees of the Municipal Retirement System

Board of Directors for Educational Television

Board of Pardons and Paroles

Mental Retardation and Mental Health Center Advisory Council

Board of Regents

Trustees of the Teachers Retirement System

Advisory Public Lands Committee

Building Authority

INSTITUTIONS

Custer State Hospital

Redfield State Hospital & School

Yankton State Hospital

Penitentiary

Training School

Soldiers' Home

INSTITUTIONS

Black Hills State College

South Dakota State University

University of South Dakota

General Beadle State College

Southern State College

School of Mines & Technology

School for the Blind

Northern State College

School for the Deaf

443

Index